THE TRENDS OF PHILOSOPHICAL THOUGHT
IN
THE MAHĀBHĀRATA

THE TRENDS OF PHILOSOPHICAL THOUGHT IN THE MAHĀBHĀRATA

Smt. Sunanda Sharad Joshi

BKP

BHARATIYA KALA PRAKASHAN
DELHI (INDIA)

First Edition : 2011

ISBN : 978-81-8090-274-1

Published by : **C.P. GAUTAM**
for BHARATIYA KALA PRAKASHAN
3421-A, IInd Floor, Narang Colony,
Tri Nagar, Delhi-110035.
Phone : (O) 32967505 Telefax : 27393083
E-mail : bkp3421@yahoo.co.in
web. : www.bkpbooks.com

Laser Typesetting by : Twinkle Graphics, Delhi-110088.

Printed by : G.S. Offset Printers, Delhi-110032.

CONTENTS

FOREWORD

The Mahābhārata is a rich mine of philosophical speculations and the source of many inchoate systems of philosophy. As an encyclopaedia of Indian culture, it has accommodated the important thought ferments of that period. If philosophy is a reflection upon varieties of human experience, or rational, methodological and systematic consideration of these topics which are of great concern to man, the great epic, the *Mahābhārata* is really a book of philosophy. Its vast canvas encompasses all aspects of human life in the early age of Indian culture which were later on crystallized into various *darśanas* of Indian philosophy. They were mainly six and practically incorporated the Indian thinking of those days. The *Mahābhārata* has given respectable place to almost all of them and consequently has become encyclopaedic in nature. Dr. Mrs. Joshi has taken an excellent survey of all those thoughts in her book entitled "*The Trends of Philosophical Thought in the Mahābhārata.*"

In her work Dr. Mrs. Joshi has appropriately explained the word 'philosophy'. As Vedānta, Sāṁkhya and Yoga constituted three important branches of Indian Philosophy, she has devoted one chapter to each one of the above mentioned systems. As Vedānta views are mostly propounded in the Upaniṣads Dr. Sunanda Joshi has copiously drawn from the Upaniṣads while explaining the basic doctrines about the Ultimate Reality (Brahman), Individual Self (Ātman), the relation of the body with the soul, the doctrine of sheaths, the sojourn of the soul after death, the characteristics of emancipated man or a Yogin, the metaphor of chariots etc. She has appropriately substantiated her mode of analysis with the views of Lokamanya Tilak, S.N. Dasgupta and R.D. Ranade.

While dealing with the topic of Sāṁkhya philosophy, Dr. Mrs. Joshi has presented brief information about twenty four categories and has extensively discussed the concepts of Puruṣa and Prakṛti in relation to different passages in the Bhagvadgītā with a comparative perspective. Her exposition of Yoga which is believed to be a communion with the Highest Reality leading to the acquisition of knowledge and resulting into emancipation of beings is also based on comparative analysis. It exhaustively covers the views of Radhakrishnan, Zimmer, Kane, Hiriyanna and others with appropriate comments upon them. She has dealt with the concepts of detachment and meditation in the *Mahābhārata* and explained their importance.

Dr. Mrs. Joshi has appropriately dealt with the references to even other systems of philosophy including the Buddhist, Jaina and Cārvāka schools. She has elucidated the concepts of *Karman* doctrine or the doctrine of transmigration of the Soul. Her addition of an interesting sub-chapter on the characters in the *Mahābhārata* and their special traits which border on philosophy of life and an appendix of the list of technical terms like *avidyā*, *niṣprapañca*, *pnāṇāyāma* and the like with the page numbers deserve special mention.

She has collected information painstakingly and presented it systematically.

In my opinion, philosophy behind political lucubrations in the *Mahābhārata* can also be studied. I hope that Dr. Mrs. Joshi will take up that study soon and present a comprehensive account of their discussions in the *Mahābhārata*.

Dr. P.G. Lalye
Ex-Professor and Head
Deptt. of Sanskrit,
Oosamania University,
Hyderabad (A.P.)

PREFACE

As I started attending the lectures of M.A. course in Sanskrit with Vedānta as my Special śāstra, I developed more and more interest in the philosophical thoughts reflected in Sanskrit Texts. While studying *Brahmasūtraśāṅkarabhāṣya* II. 2, I became an admirer of Śaṅkarācārya who ably refuted the views of the propounders of Saṁkhya, Vaiṣeśika and Yoga philosophies as also Buddhism and Jainism. I was induced to study the details of these philosophical systems as well. In the course of time, while reading the *Mahābhārata*, I came to know that a number of philosophical trends are reflected therein. I thought of undertaking an attempt to know the reasons as to why such philosophical ideas have been incorporated in the *Mahābhārata*. I wanted to know whether these ideas were in existence in the form of various systems before the *Mahābhārata* was being composed or whether they were just different trends of philosophical thought, which later on were merely transformed into different philosophical systems.

In this attempt many have helped me. I shall be failing in my duty if I do not express my feeling of gratitude towards them, but for whose assistance and guidance it would have been simply impossible for me to complete this work. I consider it my first and foremost duty to thank my guide Dr. (Smt.) A.B. Bakre, Ex-R.G. Bhandarkar, Professor and Head, Department of Sanskrit, University of Mumbai who has been always kind in sparing her valuable time in solving all my difficulties. She has given the manuscript a detailed and perceptive reading and made a number of valuable suggestions.

The work was submitted in the form of a thesis to the University of Mumbai for which I was awarded Ph.D. degree.

I am very much thankful to the authorities of Mumbai University for granting me permission to publish this thesis in the form of a book.

My sincere thanks are due to the teaching staff of Department of Sanskrit, University of Mumbai and the non-teaching staff members of the Department for their timely assistance. It is not possible to carry out Ph.D. thesis work successfully without the availability of the necessary books. In this respect, I was lucky in getting books from both the units of Mumbai University Library, *i.e.* Jawaharlal Nehru Library, Vidyanagari, Mumbai-400098 and Fort Library, Fort, Mumbai-400032, as also from the Asiatic Society of Bombay, Town Hall, Mumbai-400001. I am extremely thankful to the library staff of all the libraries for being kind and co-operative and rendering timely and valuable assistance to me.

I am grateful to Brahman Vidyarthi Sahayyak Mandal, Thane, 400601 for awaıding me A.P. Joshi scholarship for doing research based on Sanskrit Texts, during the academic year 1998-1999. I also acknowledge with thanks the concerned authorities of the Department of Sanskrit, University of Mumbai for awarding me the scholarship during the year 1999-2000.

I owe a considerable gratitude to all my family members who have been patiently helping and encouraging me till the completion of my work. My special thanks are due to my daughter-in-law Dr. Smt. Bhawisha Joshi and her friend Dr. Smt. Priti Girish for their valuable assistance.

I am extremely thankful to Dr. P.G. Lalye, Ex-Professor and Head, Department of Sanskrit, Oosmania University, Hyderabad (A.P.), for being extremely kind in sparing his valuable time in going through the present work and for whole-hearted appraisal of the same in his foreword.

I must express my sincere thanks to Sh. C.P. Gautam, Publisher, Bharatiya Kala Prakash, Delhi, who eagerly undertook this work for publication.

25th Sept. 2010 **Dr. Smt. Sunanda Sharad Joshi**
Mumbai

LIST OF ABBRIVIATIONS

Ādi. P.	:	*Ādi Parva*
Ait. Up.	:	*Aitareya Upaniṣad*
Ait. Br.	:	*Aitareya Brāhmaṇa*
Anu. P.	:	*Anuśāsana Parva*
Āran. P.	:	*Āraṇyaka Parva*
Āśram. P.	:	*Āśramvāsika Parva*
Āśva. P.	:	*Āśvamedhika Parva*
Bh. G.	:	*Bhagavadgītā*
Bh. P.	:	*Bhīṣma Parva*
Br. Up.	:	*Bṛhadāraṇyaka Upaniṣad*
Ca. Sa. Śa.	:	*Carakasaṁhitā, Katidhāpuruṣiya Śarīrādhyāya (Śārirasthanam)*
Ch. Up.	:	*Chāndogya Upaniṣad*
Droṇ. P.	:	*Droṇa Parva*
G.R.	:	*Gītārahasya*
Gauḍ K.	:	*Gauḍapādakārikā.*
Īśa Up.	:	*Īśavāsya Upaniṣad*
Karṇ P.	:	*Karṇa Parva*
Kath Up.	:	*Kaṭha Upaniṣad*
Kaus. Up.	:	*Kauṣītaki Upaniṣad*
Ken. Up.	:	*Kena Upaniṣad*
Mahāpra.	:	*Mahāprasthānika Parva*

Mait. Up.	:	*Maitrī Upaniṣad*
Maus. P.	:	*Mausala Parva*
Mbh.	:	*Mahābhārata*
Muṇḍ Up.	:	*Muṇḍaka Upaniṣad*
Māṇḍ Up.	:	*Māṇḍūkya Upaniṣad*
N.S.	:	*Nyāyasātra-s*
P.	:	*Parva*
Praś. Up.	:	*Praśna Upaniṣad*
Ṛv	:	*Ṛgveda*
Sā.K.	:	*Sāṁkhya Kārikā of Īśvarakṛṣṇa*
Sabhā P.	:	*Sabhā Parva*
Śānti P	:	*Śānti Parva*
Saup. P.	:	*Sauptika Parva*
Strī. P.	:	*Strī Parva*
Svarga. P.	:	*Svargārohaṇa Parva*
Śvet. Up.	:	*Śvetāśvatara Upaniṣad*
Tait. Br.	:	*Taittirīya Brāhmaṇa*
Tait. Up.	:	*Taittirīya Upaniṣad*
Udyog P.	:	*Udyoga Parva*
Vai. Sā.	:	*Vaiśeṣikasūtra*-s
Virāt. P.	:	*Virāṭa Parva*
Y.S.	:	*Yogasūtra*
Y.Y.	:	*Yogayājñavalkya*

CHAPTER I

INTRODUCTION

Philosophy is a subject which covers all the facets of human life. From time immemorial the human mind, awed by regular cycle of all the happenings in nature, sometimes constrained by its incapacity, helplessness to face the vagaries of nature, began to ponder over these phenomena. Man endeavoured to find out and understand the forces behind those phenomena as also the intelligence which creates and guides them. During that search, it also occurred to him, as to what is the goal of this human life? What is the relation of human being to that intelligence which guides this universe, the very substratum of all things. His speculations over these basic questions, the search for the ultimate cause of the cosmos, lead man towards philosophy.

Various Definitions of Philosophy

The scope of philosophy is so wide that the attempts to define it precisely have been proved to be unsuccessful.

According to *Encyclopedia of Philosophy*, the Greek word 'Sophia' is ordinarily translated in English as wisdom and the compound philosophia from which philosophy derives, is translated as the love of wisdom.[1] *The Chambers's Encyclopaedia* which agrees with this definition, however, states that 'Sophia' had a wider range of application than the modern English, 'wisdom'. It explains that wherever intelligence can be exercised there is room for Sophia. In constrast to this, modern English draws a sharp distinction between the search for wisdom and the attempt to satisfy intellectual curiosity.[2]

Platonic Concept of Philosophy

Plato in his *Apology* (22) states different characteristics of philosophical wisdom. Firstly, it can face the test of critical discussion.

Secondly, philosophy makes use of a method peculiar to it which he calls "dialectic" which may be explained as philosophy proceeds by criticizing received opinions.

Thirdly, philosophy is the highest form of enquiry because it does not involve presuppositions as it has direct access to "true Reality" as distinct from the ordinary world of ever changing things. Philosophy concerns itself with the relationship between eternal and unchanging entities – the only entities about which it is possible to have knowledge as distinct from mere belief or opinion. Thus, the philosopher seeks wisdom of a very special kind – the certainty about the true nature of reality that is to know what everything is for.

Fourthly, to apprehend the true nature of reality is to know what everything is for. For example, to know the true nature of man is to know towards what ideal it is man's nature to strive.

Fifthly, on account of his knowledge of ideals, the philosopher knows how men ought to live. According to Plato, the art of making immediate gains is not a form of knowledge as the Sophist professed to teach their pupils. It would help to gain worldly success. But to understand the general nature of man, and in consequence of human society, men must turn to philosophy.[3]

Philosophy as the Knowledge of the Ultimate

Devaraja N.K. in his 'Notes Towards a Definition of Philosophy' states, "for a long time, when the sciences had not yet come into prominence as respectable intellectual disciplines, philosophy was described as an inquiry into the nature of reality or ultimate reality."[4]

Banerji, Suresh Chandra's views correspond to the above definition when he defines philosophy as "search for wisdom or knowledge especially that which deals with the ultimate reality or with most general causes and principles of things and ideas and human perception and knowledge of them."[5]

The Shorter Oxford Dictionary defines philosophy on the same lines as "that department of knowledge which deals with the ultimate reality or with the most general causes and principles of things."[6]

All the above definitions substantially follow Plato's views. Plato's definition and that of Devaraja's definition are based on "the presumption that science inheriting the cosmological tradition does not offer a knowledge of 'ultimate reality'. Only philosophy can do this 'In reality, however, it is scientists who tell us what 'the ultimate reality' of the things around us consists in. Plato and the philosophers in his tradition assert that the 'general causes and principles' of the philosophers are 'higher' and 'more ultimate' than the causes and principles that science reveals to us."[7] Over the period from Plato till now his distinction between philosophy and the pursuit of worldly success has been generally accepted but as we proceed a step further to the ultimate, Plato's statement becomes intuitive.

In his earlier dialogues (*Ion, Apology*) he had repeatedly suggested that true wisdom, as distinct from inspired guesses of the poet sage, must be clear and communicable. But in the *Republic* (509) while describing the supreme end of philosophical inquiry ("the form of the good") he speaks in the manner of a sage rather than that of a philosopher. Thus, any Platonic type of metaphysics is forced to conclude that at the culminating point of philosophical enquiry the philosopher has to abandon critical discussion and fall back on direct intuition like a sage as Plato speaks the form of good lies "beyond all knowledge and being."

Thus, about the 'ultimate' any Platonic–type of metaphysics concludes that no further question can be raised.[8]

The much recent definitions of philosophy are also in tune with Plato's views. *The New Book of Knowledge* defines philosophy as thus, in the popular sense any set of deeply held belief about man, nature, society and god is called philosophy. Whereas in the technical sense philosophy means highly disciplined and reasonable method of criticizing fundamental beliefs to make them more clear and reliable.[9]

The New Encyclopaedia Britanica defines it as a reflection upon varieties of human experience or rational, methodical and systematic consideration of those topics that are of greatest concern to man.[10]

Durant Will states that philosophy is the systematic interpretation of the whole or interpretation of a part in terms of its place and value for the whole and summarizes that it is a study of experience as a whole, or a portion of experience in relation to the whole.[11]

All the above definitions and global views combined together with Plato's concept of philosophy and his views that at the culminating point of philosophical enquiry, the philosopher has to abandon critical discussion and fall back upon intuition, show resemblance to the concepts of Indian philosophy as shown below.

Philosophy in India – Definition

In India philosophy is called *Tattvajñāna.* Śivāditya in his *Saptapadārthī* defines *tattva* as *tattvam anāropitaṁ rūpam* that is *tattva* means a form not imposed upon, the real form.[12]

Thus, *tattvajñāna* is knowledge about real form of nature that is the knowledge about the ultimate reality.

Philosophy is also called *Darśana.* The word derives from the root √*dṛś* to see. *Darśana,* therefore, means viewing things in their true perspective which is meant as perceptual observation, conceptual knowledge and intuitive experience or rather to realize objects in the sense of becoming one with it.

S. Radhakrishnan's Views about Indian Philosophy

Indian philosophy according to Radhakrishnan S., is a master science guiding other sciences without which they become empty and foolish. *Muṇḍaka Upaniṣad* speaks of *Brahma - Vidyā* or the science of all eternal as the basis of all sciences, *Sarva vidyā pratiṣṭhā*. "Philosophy" says Kauṭilya, is the lamp of all sciences, the means of performing all works and the support of all the duties.

Radhakrishnan S. further adds that since philosophy is a human effort to comprehend the problems of the universe, it is subject to the influence of race and culture. Each nation has its characteristic mentality, its particular human bent. Philosophy in India is essentially spiritual. However, though the Indian philosopher makes extensive use of reason, it is by intuitional method the ultimate is to be known. It is not just to know the truth but to realise it, is the aim of the philosophy in India.[13] Hence philosophy is called *darśana*. To see is to have direct intuitive experience of the object or to realise it, to become one with it.

Exposition of Erich Frauwllner

He states that the innermost unit and the ultimate ground (cause) of the world forms the theme of the oldest Indian speculation and this has originated with religion in the closest connection with it and has unfolded itself out of its connection with the Absolute. He further adds that Indian speculation has never departed from the soil or field of religion, it nourishes itself continually and directly out of the forces of its soil unlike Greek philosophy, which has related to religion dialectically, has developed out of contrast to religion, in the form of that other religion of thought, purified through reason, formed in the form of the concept which had brought forth the philosophical God-idea, independent of religion in the idea of the good (Plato) and of the unmoved mover (Aristotle).[14]

Heinrich Zimmer's Observations

Zimmer perceives that the chief aim of Indian thought is to

unveil and integrate into consciousness what has been thus resisted and hidden by the forces of life, not to explore and describe the visible world. The supreme and characteristic achievement of the Brāhmaṇa mind was its discovery of the Self (the Ātman) as an independent, imperishable entity, underlying the conscious personality and bodily frame. Everything that we normally express about ourselves belong to sphere of change, the sphere of time and space, but the Self (the Ātman) is forever changeless, beyond time, beyond space and the veiling net of causality, beyond measure and beyond the dominion of the eye. The effort of the Indian philosophy has been to know this adamantine Self and make the knowledge effective in human life.[15]

R. Puligandla's Interpretations of Philosophy

Puligandla has compared occidental and oriental philosophical thoughts and has appropriately summarized the characteristics of Indian philosophy. He observes that the philosophy of any people is the cream of its culture, it is a product of its environment and its specific modes of cognitive, intellectual, aesthetic, moral and religious experience. He observes that the Indian and European traditions though culturally different, the basic philosophical problems and most of the solutions to them are surprisingly similar. European and Indian philosophers alike speculate on problems like monism and pluralism, change and permanence, appearance and reality, materialism, atomism, idealism, realism etc. Indian thinkers like philosophers of other traditions pondered over the fundamental questions such as the nature of reality, real nature of man, whether world is created or is it eternal. If created what is the relation of the creator to man, ultimate constituents of the world, whether man is free. If he is not free at present whether freedom can be attained by him, what is good life and how to attain it so on so forth. Even more surprising is the fact that answers to these questions in respect, are similar in both the traditions. However, there is a difference between the application of methods between the Indian and Western philosophical inquiry. Indian philosophers unlike their western counterparts do not treat metaphysics, epistemology, psychology, ethics etc. separately, but discuss each problem from all these points of view.'

He, therefore, opines that due to this practical angle, Indian philosophies are pragmatic. Indian philosophers, therefore, strongly believe that philosophy should make a difference in the style and quality of life of people. It should not be merely theoretical, it should enable man to free himself and lead a life of enlightenment.

He gives the characteristics that are common to all systems of Indian philosophy, with the single exception of materialism as follows :

1. All the schools insist that the reality should be based on reason and experience. Reason includes inductive inquiry and experience would be consisting of commonsensical and scientific experience and extraordinary state of consciousness.
2. They maintain that philosophy should aid man in realising the chief ends of human life (*puruṣārtha*-s) and they are expected to transform man's life from ignorance, darkness and bondage to that of knowledge, wisdom and freedom.
3. All the schools acknowledge man's essential spirituality and treat freedom as his highest and final goal and philosophy should facilitate him to attain the freedom.
4. All the systems proface that state of ignorance and suffering of the man is not due to original sin but due to original ignorance.
5. Hence man can achieve freedom and liberation by conquering ignorance through knowledge.
6. All the schools think that since the secret of all existence is within himself he has capacity to be infinitely perfect.

This is evident from the Upaniṣadic statement that man's innermost self (the Ātman) is Brahman and that according to the teaching of Buddhism, every man is Buddha, only he should have that awareness.

7. The systems acknowledge that absolute freedom (*mokṣa, nirvāṇa*) is to be attained here and now in the bodily existence.
8. Yoga has been accepted as the excellent spiritual discipline to attain freedom, by all the systems.
9. They admit that the empirical world is controlled through the doctrine of *karman* and rebirth, which is an impersonal universal moral order.
10. No school accepts the idea that man is nothing but a material entity.
11. They believe that the ultimate reality can be experienced only by direct intuitive mystical insight.
12. According to Indian philosophers, man's present state of ignorance, suffering, misery and bondage appear to be pessimistic. However, in the ultimate analysis, they are optimistic. They emphatically affirm that it is within man's power to attain knowledge, wisdom, peace and freedom.

Puligandla R., therefore, concludes that Indian philosophical schools categorically reject nihilism as well as philosophy of the Absurd, Angst and Nothingness and equivocally proclaim the ultimate triumph of the human spirit.[16]

Thus, philosophy in India can be defined as the highest form of enquiry to understand the real form of nature. It is a systematic interpretation of the Ultimate Reality through direct intuitive experience, perceptual observation, with spiritual inclination and application of reasoning. The Ultimate Truth is to be realised and lived with, the Indian philosophy, therefore, aims at imparting this knowledge to man guiding him on the unlit path, to free him from the state of ignorance and suffering by creating a discerning insight in him to differentiate as to what is pleasant (*preyas*) and what is really conducive to happiness (*śreyas*), enabling him to liberate himself from the bonds of life.

Six Systems of Indian Philosophy

The Indian philosophy is based on tradition. It accepts the authority of predecessors and accordingly they have been classified as orthodox and unorthodox. The orthodox system is classified as *āstika, i.e.* theistic and unorthodox as *nāstika* atheistic. The first division covers Vedic philosophy, the systems that acknowledge infallibility of Veda-s. They are called *ṣaḍdarśana*-s or six systems of philosophy and include *Nyāya-Vaiśeṣika, Sāṁkhya – Yoga, Pūrva Mīmāṁsā* and *Uttara Mīmāṁsā* or *Vedānta.*

The atheistic (*nāstika*) system includes Cārvāka, Jain and Bauddha philosophy. However, if the meaning of theistic (*āstika*) is conceived as "there is no end of life after the death", only Cārvāka can be classified as *nāstika* as Jain and Bauddha philosophy believe in life after death.

Period of Different Systems of Indian Philosophy and the Mahābhārata

Indian philosophy has extremely long and complex development. However, perhaps due to deeply philosophical nature of the ancient Indians, very little is known about the philosopher though much more is known about the philosophy. Hence it becomes difficult to place them historically. According to Radhakrishnan S. and Moore C.A., Vedic period is placed between 2500 to 600 B.C. The period of epics which includes rise and early development of Buddhism, Jainism, Śaivism and Vaiṣṇavism is approximately dated from 500 or 600 B.C. to 200 A.D. The third period dated approximately from the early centuries of the Christian era is called as *Sūtra* period. The six Hindu systems though prevalent before this period were presented in orderly and systematic way during this period.[17]

Zimmer Heinrich places Vedic period in C. 1500 – 800 B.C., Upaniṣdic period from 800 B.C. onwards, Mahāvīra, the 24th Jain Tīrthaṅkara D.C. 526, Sūtra-s between 500 B.C. and 500 A.C., Buddha c. 563 – 483 B.C. Period of Kapila, Sāṁkhya philosopher though not given precisely, it is placed between 23rd Jain Tīrthaṅkara Pārśva and Mahāvīra., *i.e.* between 772 B.C. to 526 D.C. and that of Patañjali of Yogaśāstra between Buddha 483 B.C. and Cāṇakya 32 A.D. The present form of the *Mahābhārata* and the *Bhagavadgītā* has been placed between 400 B.C. to 400 A.D.[18]

According to Macdonell A.A., Vedic period is assumed to be between 1300 B.C. and 1000 B.C. and the date of the death of Buddha was 480 B.C. The period of Brāhmaṇa-s is placed between Circa 800 to 500 B.C. and Upaniṣad-s have been stated as generally forming the part of the Brāhmaṇa-s, being continuation of this speculative side (*jñānakāṇḍa*). Kapila, the founder of Sāṁkhya system, according to Buddhist legends was pre-Buddhistic and his period is placed before the middle of the sixth century B.C. Period of Pañcaśikha, the second leading authority of Sāṁkhya has been assumed as the beginning of our era. The period of Patañjali, the expounder of Yoga philosophy has been fixed as second century B.C. The period of the founder of Vaiśeṣ ika and Nyāya systems, namely, Kaṇāda and Gautama, however, has not been stated. According to this author, original form of epic came into being about the fifth century B.C. and extension of the original work must have taken place after 300 B.C. and by the beginning of this era.[19]

After taking into consideration approximte dates given by Radhakrishnan, S. and Moore, C.A., Zimmer Heinrich and Macdonell, A.A., it can be concluded that the Sūtra period that is the period in which the six systems were presented in orderly and systematic way and the epic period coincide approximately and the doctrines propounded in the six systems were in vogue if not popular. Consequently, they seem to have been reflected in the *Mahābhārata*.

The Tradition of Philosophical Literature in India

Indian tradition has developed a system of four goals of life, *puruṣārtha*-s, namely wealth (*artha*), worldly enjoyment (*kāma*), righteousness (*dharma*) and the spiritual freedom (*mokṣa*). The first three known as *trivarga,* group of three are the pursuits of the world, the fourth one, however, is not an external materialistic aim like achieving wealth, power etc. It is a state of mind where an individual knows the truth and realises it. It is a supreme spiritual theme of liberation from ignorance as aptly described by Radhakrishnan, S.[20] However, according to Indian philosophers the realisation of the truth is not enough, the truth must be lived. An individual has to cultivate a spirituality which will help him to lead a life of purity. He, therefore, has to develop a discriminative thinking which would enable him to discern the difference between what is apparently pleasant (*preyas*) and what is really conducive to happiness (*śreyas*) and grasp the *śreyas.* To transmit this thought to the society as a whole, the Indian thinkers tried to bring about socio-spiritual reform through the medium of literature. The Indian thinkers tried to translate every principle into strong conviction so that no philosophical doctrine remained a mere tenet of the school. The philosophical literature, therefore, took the form of philosophical treatises such as Sāṁkhyakārikā as well as non-technical form such as mythological, popular literature as demanded by circumstances. Thus, hard task of popularising philosophical, metaphysical thoughts was undertaken and carried out successfully by Indian thinkers through the literature like Upaniṣad-s and *Bh.G.* These books are not only great literature of the country but are great systems of thought.

The Mahābhārata – The Great Epic of India

The Epic period is the period of the *Rāmāyaṇa* and the *Mahābhārata.* The *Rāmāyaṇa* portrays the struggle of the Āryans with the then existing natives of India and the spread of the Āryan culture. The *Mbh.* deals with the strife among the cousins of an ancient princely family claiming the throne. This conflict which turned into disastrous war affected vast majority of people. The culture of the period is reflected in the epic. It was a transitional period. According to Campbell Joseph, the epic period between 400 B.C. to 400 A.D. was a bridge between two Golden Ages. The first was the period of Indo-Āryan political and spiritual conquest of the Indus, Jamunā and Gangetic plain marked by Veda-s, Brāhmaṇa-s and Upaniṣad-s and the culminating period of Buddha. The second was the age of the Gupta dynasty (320-647 A.D.) which represents India's classic statement of her synthesized Hindu-Buddhist civilization and is the highest of an impressive series of summits of medieval creativity.[21] In this period new ideas were emerged and the older non-Āryan religious beliefs were absorbed into the developing tradition. According to Campbell Joseph, the consensus of scholarly opinion places the epic battle described in the *Mbh.* in the early years of Āryan conquest of India c. 1100 B.C.[22] Thus, the *Mbh.* is not an imaginary story but a history too. It has been regarded as the fifth Veda '*Bhārataḥ Pañchamo Vedaḥ*'. The epic besides history contains discourses on religious, philosophical texts, polity, didactic work, legends, the myths of the gods etc. In fact, the introductory stanza of the epic appropriately praises itself describing its gigantic scope when it says, "*Dharme cārthe ca kāme ca mokṣe ca Bharatarṣ abha yadihāsti tadanyatra yannehāsti na tatkvacit.*" Oh!, the best of Bhārata race, whatever is written here about the four goals of life namely righeousness, earthly wealth, pleasure and liberation would be found everywhere else and you would not find anywhere else which does not exist in this book.

Traditionally, it is viewed that the author of the work is Kṛṣṇadvaipāyana Vyāsa, however, as accepted by oriental as well as occidental scholars like Hopkins,[23] Lassen, Sörensen, Ludwig,[24] it is not the work of one author but the composite collection of literature of different period held together. *Mbh.* also supports it (*Ādi. P.* 1.8) that the work has been authored by Vyāsa, Vaiśampāyana and Sauti.

Hopkins considers that by fourth century A.D. the epic was recognised as a poem of one hundred thousand verses which implies the existence of the Harivaṁśa at that time. Northern created version contains 84, 126 verses and with 16, 375 (526) verses of Harivaṁśa make 100, 501 (651) verses. Southern recension has twelve thousand more verses than Northern recension and without Harivaṁśa contains 96, 578 verses. Thus, on the whole approximately it may be said that number of verses is rounded up to one lakh as generally Indians have a tendency to round up the numbers.[25]

Hopkins presents a table of dates from 400 B.C. to 400 A.D. giving the different stages of compilation of *Mbh.* namely Bhārata days, *Mbh.* tale with Pāṇḍu heroes, presenting Kṛṣṇa as a demigod, remaking of the epic with inclusion of didactic matter, separation of *Anuśāsana Parvan* from *Śānti P.* and occasional application. Sukthankar V.S., rejects these dates outright as hypothetical and arbitrary. He, however, agrees with Bühler who had proved from epigraphic evidence that since the epic was known as early as the fifth century A.D. as a work consisting of 1,00,000 stanzas composed by the great Ṛṣi Vyāsa, it must have been extant in the shape as at today, several centuries prior to 400 A.D.

As regards the assumption made by modern critics that the epic is definitely not the work of any one poet since no one can write unaided a poem of 1,00,000 stanzas hence the poem is a compilation, embodying the work of many writers of varying abilities, Sukthankar asserts that if the poem is analysed carefully it is obviously clear that the epic in its present form at least, has a radical defects as it consists of two mutually, incompatible elements that of 'epic nucleus' and an extensive and undigested mass of didactic episodical matter bound together. He, however, agrees with the impression of Held that this massive monument of Indian antiquity may undoubtedly lay claim to being more or less flawless from the constructional view-point and withal perfectly balanced. This view of Held has been supported by

Ludwig, when he confesses his inability to explain how, in spite of the extreme complicacies of mechanism, it operated in a manner so precise that no crass contradictions were discernible in this prodigious work as there are very vague traces of such contradictions. Sukthankar concludes his chapter, the 'Mahābhārata and Its Critics' admitting that as the poem is analysed back towards its source, it proves to have not one source but many.[26]

Thus, it can be concluded that extant version of the *Mbh.* consists of 1,00,000 stanzas and it is a work of more than one composer.

The epic is divided into eighteen major sections known as *Parvans*. Each *Parvan* is subdivided into chapters made up of verses in various metres, usually in the *śloka* form, but also in *triṣ ṭubha* and other less common metres. Thus, the sequence followed is major Section (*parvan*), chapters (*adhyāya*-s) and the verses (*śloka*-s).

The Main Theme of the Epic

The main theme of the epic is the conflict between cousins Pāṇḍava-s and Kaurava-s. The Pāṇḍava-s were treacherously defeated in the game of dice by the Kaurava-s and were exiled. After the completion of exile Pāṇḍava-s claimed their right to the throne but Duryodhana the leader of the rival party refused to part with it. To avoid any conflict, the Pāṇḍava-s were even ready to accept small portion of the kingdom. However, the adamant stance adopted by Duryodhana forced them to fight this injustice and regain their lost kingdom. The saner elements on both the sides were aware of the looming danger and tried to avoid the war but with no avail. When Kṛṣṇa's final effort to âbort the war failed, war preparations commenced in both the camps. On the first day when both the armies come face to face on the battlefield, Arjuna, the Pāṇḍava, one of the heroes of the epic who had hitherto no conflict in his mind regarding the war and did not mind slaying elders in the war, at the crucial moment develops crisis of conscience. At the sight of the elders and relatives with whom he had to fight, he loses determination to fight. He freezes and drops his weapens. To bring him out of this intellectual paralysis, Kṛṣṇa takes the command of the situation as a true charioteer, a divine charioteer and there emerges the *Bhagavadgītā* a philosophical poem to remove his hesitation to advance and fight against his kins. He convinces Arjuna that this is the war of existence and there is no alternative but to fight the war.

The second moment of crisis comes after the completion of the war. Yudhiṣṭhira the eldest Pāṇḍava is dejected due to killing of the kiths and kins at their hands and the disastrous effects of the war and is ready to abandon the kingdom and lead the life of ascetic as he feels life is not worth living. It was a negative feeling towards life. It was a time of reconstruction of the empire and this act of Yudhiṣṭhira would have greatly affected it. There was dire necessity to have a statesman, an administrator of Yudhiṣṭhira's stature to handle the reins of the state. Kṛṣṇa and Vyāsa, therefore, console him and try to dissuade him from his resolve and lead him to Bhīṣma who was lying wounded on the battlefield. Bhīṣma instructs Yudhiṣṭhira on statecraft, religion, ethics and philosophy, which cover *Śānti Parvan* and *Anuśāsana Parvan*.

This Mahābhārata war had affected the large population of Northen India. The very backbone of the society was threatened due to a decimation of the productive members of the population. The entire social structure was in danger. The composer of the *Mbh.* was well aware that at such time, society requires a philosophy of life which would enable it to come out of the crisis. He was also aware that the mankind is forever faced with a dilemma such as faced by the epic heroes at the crucial moments. There is an eternal conflict in the human mind as to what I ought to do or ought not to do. Like Arjuna, human mind with its intellect obscured by ego, to attain its higher self, has to battle with its enemies in the form of attachments such as desires, passions, envy, hate, greed etc. though they are dear to him. Like the epic heroes who feel whether the life is worth living, after killing their kiths and kins, the human mind ponders over the myriad questions as to whether the life is worth living, what is the meaning of life. The epic poets, the great philosophers take the conflict faced by the epic heroes on cosmic level. They universalize their predicaments and present solutions by application of philosophical doctrines.

In this connection the observation made by Sukthankar V.S. on the epic story from the metaphysical angle, corroborates the above view. According to him the epic poets have developed the philosophy of the Self which he regards as an attempt at the synthesis of life. To achieve this they have staged a war between the Higher Self and the lower self of man symbolized by the two families of cousins who are fighting for the sovereignty over the kingdom of the body and in this battle superman (Arjuna) under the guidance of the Super Self (Śrīkṛṣṇa) acquires insight into the nature and character of his own self and realizes the fundamental identity between the Individual Self and the Super Self destroying his own ignorance with the help of the sword of knowledge.[27]

The authors of the *Mbh.* through the medium of Arjuna and Kṛṣṇa explained this Upaniṣadic thought and taught how the state of self awareness can be achieved by attaining equanimity of mind with the help of practical Yogic philosophy. Thus, by generalizing the problems of the heroes of the *Mbh.* by relating them to the problems of mankind as such and portraying them in the light of different philosophical trends which constitute the integral part of Indian culture, the composers of the epic have lifted the conflict of the epic to altogether different level, to the transcendental plane and spared no efforts to popularise this bold Upaniṣadic theory by applying it to the problems of everyday life.

Definitions of Words – Trend and Thought

The definition of philosophy, the contents of the Mahābhārata in brief and its major theme having already explained, the meaning of the two remaining words in the title of this thesis, namely, trend and thought is as follows :

The word trend has been explained by "*Roget's Thesaurus of Synonyms and Antonyms in Dictionary Form*" as direction, course, tendency, inclination, drift, tide.[28] Whereas "*Little Oxford Dictionary*" gives its meaning as bend or turn away in specific direction, show a certain tendency, general direction, tendency or drift.[29]

The meaning of 'trend' for the purpose of this thesis is adopted as the course. That is the course of various Indian philosophical thoughts in the *Mbh.*

The meaning of the word thought has been given in the *Oxford Dictionary* as the action or process of thinking, mental action or activity in general especially that of intellect, exercise of the mental faculty, formation and of the thinkers of a particular class, time, or place, what is or has been thought by the philosophers or learned men of some specified country etc.[30]

The American Dictionary of the English Language explains it as an act or operation of the mind when attending to a particular subject or thing or it is the idea consequent on that operation, idea, conception, reflection, opinion, judgment, meditation, serious consideration, design, purpose, silent contemplation, solicitude, inward reasoning, the working of the conscious.[31] The meaning of thought adopted here is conception or what is thought by the philosophers, thinkers of this country.

This thesis, therefore, would attempt to find out the course of various Indian philosophical thoughts, conceptions propagated in different philosophical systems especially in six philosophical systems, (*ṣaḍdarśana*-s), as appearing in the *Mbh.* The thesis will endeavour to search whether the philosophical principles appearing in the contemporary philosophical systems have been presented in the *Mbh.* as fully developed systems, that is, whether these principles are generalized to form the systems as such, whether the systems appear to be in the process of development. An attempt will be undertaken to know whether these systems have strong hold on the Epic, to scrutinize the causal factors as to why these philosophical portions appear in the epic, whether there are direct references to show that these philosophical portions formed the vital constituent part of the main nucleus or whether the propounders of different systems incorporated their thoughts to propogate their own theory.

Finally, the thesis would also strive to analyse as to what is the outlook of the composers of the *Mbh.* towards life. Since the nucleus of the epic is the great *Mbh.* war, whether it was a negative outlook just portraying sufferings and futility of life or whether authors of the *Mbh.* look at life positively to show man that there is a hope. Whether the epic incorporates positive factors, present in the Indian philosophical literature which reflect inspiration to lead life happily inspite of difficulties coming across. Do they profess that the life is worth living and there is an aim for the life, *i.e.* to attain final beatitude, which can be achieved through knowledge by destroying ignorance?

Moreover, philosophy is a very wide concept. It covers even an outlook of various human beings towards life. Hence, an attempt will also be undertaken to have a glimpse into the outlooks of various characters in the *Mbh.* towards their lives.

The observations in this thesis are based on the edition of the *Mbh.* published by the Bhandarkar Oriental Research Institute, Pune, 1971.

REFERENCES

1. Article by Passmore John 'Philosophy', *The Encyclopedia of Philosophy*, Vol. 5 and 6, Ed. by Edwards Paul, 1967, p. 216.
2. Article by Farquhar J.N., 'Hinduism', *Chambers's Encyclopaedia,* Vol. II. Ed. by Heinrich Der Ghickenzaere, 1973, p. 678.
3. Article by Passmore John, *op. cit.,* pp. 216-217.
4. Devaraja N.K., *Indian Philosophy Today*, Delhi, 1975, p. 130.
5. Banerji, Suresh Chandra, *A Companion to Indian Philosophy,* Delhi, 1922, p. 1.

6. Article by Passmore John, *op. cit.*, Vol. 5 and 6, p. 217.
7. *Ibid.*, p. 217.
8. Article by Passmore John, *op. cit.*, Vol., 5 and 6, p. 217.
9. Article by Abelson Raziel A., *The New Book of Knowledge*, 'P'. Vol. 15, New York, 1972, p. 191.
10. *The New Encyclopaedia Britanica*, Vol. 14, Chicago, Landon etc., 1943-1973, p. 248.
11. Durant Will, *Pleasure of Philosophy*, Simon and Schuster, New York, 1953, p. 2.
12. Śivādityācāryasūtritā *Saptapadārthī*, for more details refer Dixit S.H., *Bhāratīya Tattvajñāna*, (Marathi), Kolhapur, 1963, p. 2
13. Radhakrishnan, S., *Indian Philosophy*, Vol. I, London, 1923, p. 23.
14. Frauwllner Erich, *History of Indian Philosophy*, Vol. I, Delhi, 1973, pp. xii-xiii.
15. Zimmer Heinrich, *Philosophies of India*, Edited by Joseph Campbell, Bollingen Series XXVI, Princeton, New Jersey, 1974, p. 3.
16. Puligandla R., *Fundamentals of Indian Philosophy*, New Delhi, 1993, pp. 2-10.
17. Radhakrishnan, S. and Moore C.A., *Source Book in Indian Philosophy*, Princeton, New Jersey, 1957, pp. xvi-xvii.
18. Zimmer Heinrich, *op. cit.*, p. 3 also Buitenen J.A.B. van, The Mahābhārata, Book I, Chicago and London, 1973, p. xxv.
19. Macdonell, Arthur A. – *A History of Sanskrit Literature*, Delhi, 1957, pp. 11, 12, 202, 218, 285-286, 343, 390, 403-405.
20. Radhakrishnan, S. and Moore, C.A., *op. cit.*, p. 576.
21. Zimmer, Heinrich, *op. cit.*, pp. 67-68.
22. Campbell, Joseph - Editor. *Ibid.*, p. 69.
23. Hopkins q. by Sutton Nicholas, *Religious Doctrines in the Mahābhārata*, Delhi, 2000, p. 1.
24. Lassen, Sörensen, Ludwig q. by Sukthankar V.S., *On the Meaning of the Mahābhārata*, Delhi, Bombay, 1957. pp. 5-7. also refer Buitenen A.B. van, *op. cit.*, p. xxiii.

25. Hopkins, E.W., *Epic Mythology,* Delhi, First published in Strassburg 1915, Reprinted in Delhi, 1974, p. 2.
26. Sukthankar, V.S., *op. cit.,* pp. 9-30. Delhi, Bombay, 1957.
27. *Ibid.*, p. 121.
28. *Roget's Thesaurus of Synonyms and Antonyms in Dictionary Form,* by Roget Peter Mark, enlarged by Roget John Lewis, Delhi, 7, 1988, p. 582.
29. *Little Oxford Dictionary* – First edited by George Ostler, Revised Seventh Edition by Maurice Waite, Delhi 1998, p. 707.
30. *The Oxford English Dictionary* – II edition, Vol. XVII – (Su – Thrivingly), prepared by J.A. Simpson and E.S.C. Weiner, First edited by James Murray and others, Oxford, New York, 1989, p. 989.
31. *The American Dictionary of the English Language.* Revised Edition by Noah Webster, New Haven, 1847, p. 1148.

CHAPTER II

THE VEDĀNTA PHILOSOPHY IN THE MAHĀBHĀRATA

The Upaniṣad-s hold an unique place in the Indian philosophy. The roots of all the later Indian philosophical systems exist in them. Ranade, R.D. opines that "There are traces of Buddhist and Jain philosophy, Sāṁkhya, Yoga, Mīmāṁsā, Śaivism, theistic-mystic philosophy of *Bh.G.*, Dvaita, Viśiṣṭādvaita as well as the Advaita system. Thus, the Upaniṣad-s have advocated various doctrines. Various streams of thoughts have sprung from the Upaniṣad-s, which gradually became more and more systematized into architectonic systems of later Indian Philosophy."[1]

Period of the Upaniṣad-s and the *Mbh.*

The Upaniṣad-s have been classified as the old and the new Upaniṣad-s on the basis of ideological developments such as presence of doctrines of transmigration, inter quotations etc. The thirteen principal Upaniṣad-s namely *Bṛhadāraṇyaka, Chāndogya, Īśa, Kena, Aitareya, Taittirīya, Kauṣītaki, Kaṭha, Muṇḍaka, Śvetāśvatara, Praśṇa, Maitrī* and *Māṇḍūkya* have been regarded as old or earlier Upaniṣad-s and the remaining ones are classified as the new or later ones.[2]

Ranade, R.D. considers the period of earlier Upaniṣad-s between 1200 and 600 B.C. and that of later ones as contemporaneous to the period of development of Buddhism, systematization of Sāṁkhya, Yoga and the composition of the *Bh.G.*[3] Radhakrishnan, S. states, "The six Hindu systems of philosophy were prevalent before 500 or 600 B.C. to 200 A.D., *i.e.* before the development of Buddhism, Jainism, Śaivism etc. However, they were systematized thereafter."[4] Macdonell, A.A. assumes circa 800 to 500 B.C. as the Upaniṣadic period[5] and Lewis, H.D. opines that the Upaniṣad-s were committed to writing at about 800 B.C.,[6] whereas Zimmer Heinrich states it as 800 B.C. onwards.[7] According to *Marathi Vishvakosh,* the principal, *i.e.* earlier Upaniṣad-s were in process of composition from about 800 B.C. to 400 B.C.[8] *Encyclopedia of Philosophy* assumes it as 800 B.C.[9] After taking into consideration the views of the different scholars, the period of earlier Upaniṣad-s would be assigned to 1200 B.C. to 600 B.C.

As regards the later Upaniṣad-s, though Desai, S.G. ascribes 200 A.D. to 1400 A.D. as their period[10], according to Hiriyanna M., there is a considerable doubt regarding the date of many of the later Upaniṣad-s.[11] Whereas Vaidya, C.V. is averse to the idea of treating them as the Upaniṣad-s. Regarding the use of the term Upaniṣad-s for the new, later literature, he states that "Their authors have abused the high name of Upaniṣad-s and have wrongly used the sacred authority of the Vedic word to preach their worthless doctrines. We would call them Purānic or Tāntric, Winternitz calls them non-Vedic properly."[12]

There is a difference of opinion among the scholars as regards the period of the *Mbh.* too. Belvalkar and Ranade regard it as post Buddhist, *i.e.* 400 B.C. and later,[13] Radhakrishnan, S. considers it as 600 to 200 B.C.[14] Kane, P.V. opines that all the parts of the *Mbh.* were earlier than the Vedāntasūtra-s.[15] According to Hopkins, E.W.[16] and Zimmer, Heinrich, it is 400 B.C. to 400 A.D.,[17] whereas Macdonell considers it to be from 500 B.C. to the beginning of Christian Era[18] and Sutton Nicholas treats it as 400 B.C. to 200 A.D.[19] Considering these diverse views, the period of the *Mbh.* has been reckoned as 600 B.C. to 400 A.D. and since the period of the earlier Upaniṣad-s precedes that of the *Mbh.,* the earlier Upaniṣad-s have been taken into account for the purpose of this thesis. As regards the later Upaniṣad-s, as there is an uncertainty about their period as well as a doubt regarding their authenticity as the Upaniṣadic work, they have not been considered here.

The Vedānta Philosophy

The Indian philosophical tradition begins with the Vedic literature in general and the Ṛgveda in particular, which comprises of the hymns to the personified forces of nature, the texts describing the efficacy of the hymns for the practical life of the sacrificer (Brāhmaṇa-s), the aphoristic rules (*sūtra*-s) and the Upaniṣad-s. The Upaniṣad-s are linked to the Brāhmaṇa-s by means of Āraṇyaka-s. The Āraṇyaka-s or "forest books" explained rituals and allegorical speculations in the Brāhmaṇa-s. Since actual sacrificial observations were no longer practical in the forests, they were substituted by these speculations in the Āraṇyaka-s. Thus, they formed a natural transition to the Upaniṣadic speculations. The Vedic instructions used to commence with the Saṁhitā-s followed by the Brāhmaṇa-s, then by the Āraṇyaka-s revealing the mysterious meanings of the ceremonies and the instructions would conclude with the exposition of the Upaniṣad. The Upaniṣad-s are, therefore, called as the Vedānta.

Different Meanings of the Word Upaniṣad

There are different interpretations of the word Upaniṣad. The *Ch. Up.* defines it as *guhyādeśaḥ,*[20] The *Kaṭh.* and *Śvet. Up.* as *paramaam guhyam.*[21] The *Śvet.* and *Mait. Up.* as *vedaguhyo-panisatsu gūḍham*[22] and *guhyatamaam*[23] respectively. The word is derived from the root, √*sad* (to sit) and preposition *upa* (near by) means sitting nearby. According to Deussen, therefore, the word implies confidential, secret sitting near somebody. On the basis of all these interpretations, Deussen gives three distinct meanings of the term Upaniṣad as a (1) secret word (2) secret text (3) secret import and accepts the third one, since the Upaniṣad-s give secret allegorical interpretations of the ritualistic practice. He quotes a passage from the *Ch. Up.*[24] which explains it as "for that which is executed with knowledge, with faith, with the Upaniṣad (knowledge of the secret meaning of Udgītha as Oṁ), that is more effective.[25]

According to Hiriyanna, the *mahāvākya-s* such as *"Tat tvam asi", "Ahaṁ Brahmāsmi"* etc., uttered by different seers, originally formed the Upaniṣads. Later on, the discussions held on them alongwith those sentences were compiled together and added to Brāhmaṇa literature, which formed the ending portion of the Vedic literature. Hence, they were called the Vedānta.[26]

Dange, S.A. contends that to know the meaning of the term Upaniṣad, it is pertinent to see the context in which this word appears in the Upaniṣad-s. He quotes a parable from the *Ken. Up.*, which relates to the greatness of the Brahman due to which it is called *Brāhmī* Upaniṣad.[27] The meaning of the term Upaniṣad, here, is explained as "the secret principle embodied in the concept of the Brahman." In the *Tait. Up.* "*Eṣa upadeśaḥ, Eṣā Vedopaniṣad, Etadanuśāsanam*", the word Upaniṣad means the ultimate principle,[28] whereas the *Śvet. Up.* clearly implies that *paraṁ brahma* alone is the Upaniṣad, when it states *'Brahmopaniṣad param'*.[29] It is evident from all these examples that the meaning of the word Upaniṣad is 'existing in secret place.'

Dange S.A. further points out that in the *Ṛv.,* the word *upa* + √*sad* connotes praise "*Emaṁ me agne samiḍham emām upasadaṁ vaneḥ.*"[30] Here, the word *upa* + √*sad* implies a praise that resides near the god. Elsewhere in the *Ṛv.*, "*Abhisvarā niṣadā*"[31] means loud prayer and "*arāḍhi hotā niṣadā*"[32] is meant as worship with the help of *niṣadā*. Thus, *upa* + √*sad* and *ni* + √*sad* both these words clearly connote praise. Hence, the concept of word Upaniṣad might have come from these two words. He, therefore, opines, "In that case, *"upa-ni-√sad*" would mean 'subtle praise' or ultimate principle." He feels that the meaning of the term Upaniṣad is to be taken as "the final goal of a man, the reflection on the principle of the Brahman, and not a performance of sacrificial rites."[33]

Thus, the Upaniṣad-s reflect a quest for the substratum underlying the phenomenal forces of nature. The Upaniṣadic thoughts have two fundamental conceptions. Besides the Brahman, there is a concept of the Ātman. The Brahman is the unknown, the first principle, that is to be explained and the Ātman is the known, the inner Self, through which the other unknown finds its explanation. The greatness of the Upaniṣadic thinkers lies in the discovery of the individual Self, inmost Ātman as the Universal Self, the inmost being of Universal nature, the Brahman.

This idea of the Brahman, the first principle as the Ātman, the inner Self is the culminating point of Indian philosophical thought. There is no original introspective thought process in the Indian philosophical tradition thereafter. There were only commentators. This is also one of the reasons due to which the Upaniṣad-s are otherwise known as the Vedānta.

The Concept of the Brahman

The most important conception of the Vedānta is the philosophy of the Brahman. In fact, the Vedānta is the source of knowledge of the Brahman. In the *Ṛv.*, it connotes extraordinary power. The Upaniṣad-s describe it as the original cause of the universe, ultimate reality, indestructible principle at the origin of the universe. Radhakrishnan, S., therefore, opines that the word has been derived from the root √*bṛḥ* (to grow) and means "that which goes on expanding, growing."[34] Deussen, too, considers its derivation from the same root and says that it would mean the praise that leads the man to the divine principle.[35] Mullick Bahadur, R.P.N. states that the word originally meant "praise" and also denoted "sacrifice" and "greatness".[36] Garg, R.K. points out that in the *Ṛv.* the Brahman is a *mantra* or prayer and gradually it acquired the sense of power or potency. He also notes that the words Brahmaṇaspati and Bṛhaspati connote the Lord of prayers.[37] Mullick Bahadur states that in the later stage of Āryan thought, it was given a new meaning as the Supreme being, who is the creator of the universe.[38]

Belvalkar and Ranade observed that in the Brāhmaṇa-s, the Brahman meant the Veda-s, being the store-house of prayers[39] and since the Veda-s are called infinite,[40] the priest, as observed in the *Tait. Brāhmaṇa,* desired to confer the highest power and poetry upon any specific formula or ritualistic detail. He designated it as the very Brahman.[41] The description of the Brahman as the Veda-s has been presented in the *Mbh.* Here Kapila says, "There are two Brahman-s namely Śabdabrahma, *i.e.* the Veda-s and the Supreme Self."[42] According Max Müller, it originally stood for what breaks forth or shines forth, that is, the word of speech.[43] Hertel derived the word from the root √*bhrāj,* to shine, to glitter and hence, Brahman. Hertel also says that the Brahman is the effulgent being (*jyotirūpa* Puruṣa).[44] The *Mbh.* also has described the Brahman as effulgent (*deva*)[45] or *jyotiḥ.*[46] A parable in the *Ken. Up.* illustrates the Brahman as an unmanifest power, which lies at the back of the manifest power of Nature and mind, which is the Primary Reality.[47] The *Mbh* also describes the Brahman as unmanifest.[48] However, according to Dange, S.A., we should not solely rely upon the Upaniṣad-s for the derivation of the word Brahman. When the concept of increased deed, expanded/extended performance (*parivṛḍhaṁ karma*) in the Veda-s is taken into consideration, it would be observed that it comes from the root √*bṛḥ* or √*vṛḥ* - √*vṛdh*, which would mean the power of manifestation. The definitions given by the etymologist Yāska and the commentator Sāyaṇa support this view. In fact, Dange, S.A. has opined, that it is not only expanded deed but the manifestation of hymns and deeds (*mantrakarmātmakam āviṣkāra*).

Thus, it is the great principle of manifestation.[49] Later on, when the Brahman was invested with concrete individuality and sacrifice was regarded as a cosmological force, the Brahman was assigned with the role of creative agency and thereafter, the idea culminated into the role of *Prajāpati* or *Svayaṁbhū.* This description of the Brahman is consistent with the *Mbh.,* when Vasiṣṭha states that the Supreme Self, which is unmanifest creates Brahmā, who is also called *Hiraṇyagarbha.* Brahmā is the first born. This entire world is the manifestation of him. Brahmā is also described as effulgent and the one who pervades this entire world.[50] The description of the Brahman given by Kapila corresponds with the various definitions given above. Kapila states that the Brahman is the order (of the world), truth or existence, the known, to be known, the Soul of all movables, immovables, excellent, benevolent, unmanifest, immutable, effulgent.[51] Kapila also describes it as unattached like the sky, eternal and permanent.

Thus, the Brahman was ultimately regarded as the support of everything. But it does not represent just a single phenomenon. It is not just present in any single object or a few objects.

The Concept of the Ātman

The word Ātman has been derived variously by various scholars. Bothlingh – Roth says that it is to be derived from *'an'* (to breathe), which came to be meant as the Soul.[52] Dange, S.A., has stated that some derive it from the root *'at'* (to wander), presuming it to be wandering of the Souls, whereas according to some others, the word *tman* in the *Ṛv.* was related to German 'atmen' (to breathe). However, Dange, S.A. maintains that the word *tman* in the *Ṛv.* appears to be one's own Self. It does not connote the principle of the substratum of cosmical life. He, therefore, feels that it can be derived from the root *an+man*, which would mean wanderer in different wombs (*yoni*-s). He further reflects that it can be derived from Indo-European root *atma*, which appears in German as 'atmen' and from *tman* in Sanskrit relating to individual breathing element, which later on culminated into the Ātman and related to creative breathing power on the cosmic level.[53]

The perception of the unity, which underlies all the phenomena of nature was already evident from the hymns of the *Ṛv.*[54] However, the eternal unity, which underlies all the phenomena of nature, remained undefined. The process began in the *Ch. up.*[55] with the question "Who is the Ātman? what is the Brahman?" Yājñavalkya, too, touches the topic when in the *Bṛ.*

Up.,[56] he says to Maitreyī that after death, where everything has become one's own self, how can one smell, see, hear, address, understand or know anyone at all, which suggests that there is no duality. This view of oneness of the ultimate entity Brahman with that of the Ātman for the first time clearly appeared in the *Tait. Up.,* where the incorporation of the Ātman in the material world and the human body as the Self dependent on the nourishment is narrated.[57] This expression corresponds to the description in the *Bh.G.* where living beings are linked to the Brahman through food, rain, sacrifice, *karman*.[58] It is, thus, further emphasised in the *Br. Up.,* "While creating this universe, the Brahman enters into it, as being expressible, self dependent consciousness, Reality, while it is in harmony with its own nature. It persists as the inexpressible, opposite, independent, unconsciousness, unreality.[59] In this section itself, Yājñavalkya first draws a picture of the individual Soul as it dwells in the heart encompassed and nourished by veins etc. and suddenly withdraws this entire individual Soul to reveal one omnipresent Supreme Soul surrounding us.

Thus, the terms 'the Brahman' and 'the Ātman' have been used in the Upaniṣad-s as synonyms. However, due to the ambiguity of the word regarding the conception of the Ātman, like that of the Brahman, there were several misunderstandings as could be observed from the fact that beyond the cosmic meaning of the Ātman as the first principle of the universe, there was also discerned its psychical meaning, the embodiment of this principle in the Self was also discernible.

The *Mbh.* categorically emphasises the oneness of the Ātman with the Brahman stating that some scriptures have described the embodied Self and the Supreme Self as different from each other. Nevertheless, one should not pay any attention to these differences. One should just continue to concentrate on the eternal Brahman.[60] The *Bh.G.* also states that this entire universe is pervaded by him through his unmanifested form (Kṛṣṇa here poses himself as the Brahman) and further asserts that all the beings abide in him, but he does not abide in them.[61] Here, he means to say that the

Supreme is the source of all the phenomena but still it is untouched by them. Though the Supreme Self creates them, he transcends them to such a degree that one cannot even say that he dwells in them. Thus, they are one yet separate. The *Bh.G.* states that the Brahman is without and within all beings. He is unmoving as well as moving. He is too subtle to be known. He is far away and yet near.[62] Vyāsa, too, describes the presence of the Brahman in all beings alongwith its opposite characters.[63] Brahmā expresses similar views when he describes the Ātman as existing in all beings and still maintains its supremacy as the creator, sustainer etc.[64]

Different Positions of the Ātman (Kṣetra Kṣētrajña-Vicāra)

The Ātman is the designation of cosmic level of the Soul, the first principle of the universe. Besides this cosmic aspect of the Soul, there are physiological and psychical aspects of the Soul. Thus, from this angle, the Ātman has three positions :

1. The corporeal/material Self, Matter.
2. The individual Soul free from the body, which as knowing subject, is contrasted with and distinct from the object, the spirit.
3. The Supreme Soul in which the subject and the object are no longer distinguished from one another.[65]

They are called as cosmos, spirit and the ultimate Soul in metaphysics.

These three different positions have been aptly described in the *Ch. Up.*, when Prajāpati explains to Indra that this body is subject to death but at the same time, the vesture of an immortal Soul. It is only when the Soul is encased in the body that it is cognisant of pleasure and pain. There is neither pleasure nor pain for the Soul, once it is relieved of its body. Just as the wind and the cloud, the lightning and the thunder are without body and arise from the heavenly space and appear in their own form, so does this serene being, namely, the Self, arise from this mortal body, reaches the highest light and then appears in his own form. This serene being, who appears in his own form, is the highest Person.[66]

This idea of the Self within the body, free from body and the Supreme Soul has been beautifully brought out by Vyāsa in the *Śānti. P.* First, he shows the position of the Self in the body, which is enveloped by sixteen qualities, namely five organs, five objects of sense, nature, movement, mind, breath, respiration (*apāna*) and the individual Soul. The seventeenth one is the Ultimate Soul. The undecaying, unchanging life element, though imperceptible, is perceived by the seers within the body. It is imperceptible in the material body, which is perishable. This Supreme Spirit pervades the entire universe. It is within all the beings.[67]

The question of the relation between the body and the Soul was raised in the *Mait. Up.,* where the sages Vālakhilya-s asked Prajāpati Kratu, "Who was the driver of the chariot of the body?" Prajāpati answered, "The mover of the body-chariot was the Soul, the pure, tranquil, imperishable, unborn entity, who stands independently in his own greatness."[68]

The *Kauṣ. Up.* tells us that the Soul must be regarded as the master of all bodily faculties, the Lord of all sense functions "As a razor is placed in a razor-case (*kṣuraḥ kṣuradhāne hitaḥ*) or fire in the fire hearth (*viśvambharo vā viśvamabharakulāye*), similarly, does this conscious Self pervade the body upto the very hair and nails."[69] It further adds, "The senses depend upon the Soul as the relatives upon the wealthy man and as the wealthy man has food with his relatives and relatives sustain themselves with his help, in the same fashion this conscious Self has food with the senses and the senses have food with the Self."[70]

Both these passages throw light on the fact that various body - senses are dependent on the Self and the Soul pervades the body.

This relation of the body with the Ātman has been discussed in the *Mbh.* as Kṣetrakṣetrajña thought. The *Mbh., Bh. P.* 35.1 states that this body is the Field (*kṣetra*). Tilak, B.G. explains the word *kṣetra* as the gross body made up of five primordial elements, the five organs of action, the five organs of perception, the five objects of these five organs of perception, namely sound, touch, colour, taste and smell, the mind, the conceiver of ideas (*saṁkalpavikalpa*) and the pure reason (*vyavasāyātmikā buddhiḥ*). Tilak, B.G. further adds that the movement, activity or the vital motion of the life forces in the gross body and the power of consciousness (*ciccaktiḥ*) by means of which movement or activity is created even in gross Matter is called *caitanya.* The *Bh.G.* includes the fundamental elements in the shape of Matter (*Prakṛti*) from which the five primordial elements have sprung in the body. The resultant product from the combination of these things is called an activated body (*savikāra śarīra*) or *kṣetra, i.e.* human body[71] or *piṇḍa.*

Thus, according to Tilak, B.G., the collection of mental and bodily elements or qualities in the shape of (*prāṇaḥ*) life force, which has specific activities (*viśiṣṭa-cetanā*), is known as *kṣetra.*[72]

Śaṅkarācārya suggests that since the fruits of action are reaped in it as in a field, it is called *kṣetra.*[73] However, according to Tilak, B.G., though *kṣetra* originally means field, here the term is used as an activated body or human body (*savikāra śarīra* or *kṣetra*).[74]

Now, the question arises – Who is the owner of this body? The bodily and mental functions of man are carried out by internal organs such as *buddhi* and organs of perception, organs of action. Here, the mind and the reason (*buddhi*) are the most supreme. However, since they too are the manifestations (*vikārāḥ*) of Matter (*Prakṛti*),[75] there is a limitation to their functioning. There is somebody who gives directions to the Mind *(manas)* and the Intellect *(buddhi)*, the element that organises their functions. The *Kaṭh. Up.* provides us the answer. It declares that the objects are higher than senses, mind is higher than the objects, intellect is higher than mind, *mahat* is higher than intellect, Avyakta is higher than *mahat* and ultimately Puruṣa is higher than Avyakta. There is nothing else higher than and outside him (Puruṣa).[76] In the *Mbh.,* Vyāsa quotes this almost verbatim. The only difference is that Puruṣa in the *Kaṭh. Up.* is replaced by *amṛtam* in the *Mbh.*[77] In the very next verse, he proclaims that it is the Paramātman hidden in the hollow of the hearts of all the beings who is not visible to the senses.[78]

The *Bh.G.* explains it with a slight difference when it states that beyond the senses is mind, beyond the mind is reason and that beyond the reason is the Puruṣa, thus, dropping out *mahat* and Avyakta, the aspects connoting the objective world.[79]

Thus, "It is the Ātman who knows the body", declares Brahmā in the *Āśvamedhika P.* It is, therefore, called the knower of the body, Kṣetrajña.[80] It is the one who controls the body, hence is called Adhiṣṭhātṛ. It stays within the body and hence is called Puruṣa. It is the twenty-fifth one, the Kṣetrajña, the knower of the body.[81] The *Bh.G.* says that it dwells in the hearts of all.[82] The *Bh.G.* has also described that the Kṣetrajña, the Lord of the field, as one who illumines this entire field (*kṣetra*) as the sun illumines this entire world.[83]

The *Śānti P.* also explains Kṣetrajña as the self illuminating element, which resides in the hearts of all the beings.[84]

In the *Āśva. P.,* a wife of a Brāhmin asks him, "How is it possible that the Soul *(jīvātman)* within the body, who is called Kṣetrajña, is said to be the form of the Brahman? Since the Soul is under the control of the Brahman, how can it be called as the form of the Brahman?" The Brāhmin then explains to her that though the individual Soul is within a body, it is devoid of any relation with the body. Hence, there is no reason why it should have any form or quality (*guṇa*). To understand it, there is only one way, that is, to abandon the efforts to perceive it, as the Kṣetrajña is imperceptible.[85]

The third aspect of the Ātman is its supremacy. This is the Soul, which is not confined to any part of the body, but it is the one which is infinite, pervading the entire space. It is present in all the beings and objects of the cosmos. It has been described variously by the different Upaniṣad-s.

The *Bṛ.Up.* expresses it as, "There is nothing besides It and outside It."[86] The *Māṇḍ. Up.* states that the Absolute is neither inwardly cognisant, nor outwardly cognition, nor on both the sides together. It is not cognition. It is neither a knower nor a non-knower. It is unseen, unpracticable, ungraspable, undefinable, unthinkable, unpointable. It is the essence of the experience of self-identity. In it all this universe ceases. It is tranquil, blessed and without a second.[87] It is described in negative terms, since it is not possible to speak of the Absolute in positive terms.

The *Mbh.* states that this great Soul is not perceptible to eyes or any other senses. It can be perceived, illuminated only by the lamp of pure mind, in the intellect. Though it is beyond the senses and devoid of touch, form, smell etc., still it stays within the body and when the Soul perceives it in all the beings and objects of the world and experiences identity with all the objects in the world, he attains that immutable element.[88] In the same *Parvan* elsewhere, it is stated that the great Soul is incognisable by senses since it is very minute (*sūkṣma*), but just because it is not visible, it cannot be said that there is no Soul. The Ātman being omniscient and all perceiver (*sākṣin*), he recognizes the senses but senses cannot recognize the Self, though it is the one which gives movement (*cetanā*) to all the senses.

The Supreme Soul is alike throughout its structure. Hence, the knowledge of any part of it is the knowledge of the whole. The *Ch. Up.* states "Just as by the knowledge of a lump of earth, everything that is made of earth can be known, the ultimate substratum of it being the earth."[90] Thus, the ultimate substratum of all is the Brahman, which is self-identical, self-sufficient and self-known. The *Bṛ.Up.* remarks that "Just as by sounding of the drums, the conch-horn or the lyre, all the notes of these instruments are coincidentally sounded.[91] In the same way, by the knowledge of the Ātman, the entire universe is known."[92] The *Muṇḍ. Up.* expresses similar views[93] The *Bṛ. Up.* declares, "In truth, he who has seen, heard, comprehended and known the Ātman, by him is this entire universe known."[94] All these passages show the Brahman to be all existing things and beings. The *Muṇḍ. Up.* described it as "eternal, all pervading, omnipresent, subtle and imperishable Soul, who is the origin of all beings, and whom the wise alone can perceive." The *Kaṭh. Up.* stated on the same lines, "The wise man ceases to grieve when he has known this great all pervading Soul."[95]

The *Bh.G.* describes its all pervasiveness when it says, "It is everywhere, enveloping all, with its hands and feet eyes, head and faces on all sides."[96] Its imperishable characteristic due to it being the origin of all the beings is also described.[97]

Its characteristic of being the substratum of all, is narrated here, when the *Bh.G.* says, "Though It appears to have qualities of all senses, yet It is without senses. Hence though unattached, It supports all, It is free from qualities (*guṇa-s*)."[98] Again in the same section, the imperishableness, unqualitative state of the Brahman is mentioned (*Bh. P.* 35.31) in the *Bh.G.* Thus, all the existence being the Brahman has been sufficiently brought out by the *Bh. G.* In the *Āśva. P.*, Vāsudeva says it can't be smelt by the nose, can't be tasted by the tongue, can't be touched by the skin. It can be cognised only by the mind. It can't be seen by the eyes, it can't be reached by the organ of hearing. There are no signs, smell, taste, touch, form and sound.[99] Thus, the description of the Brahman in negative terms also appears in the *Mbh.*

The *Śvet. Up.* describes the Ātman as neither male nor female, nor of an intermediate sex, whichever body he is associated with, in that body he is protected.[100] The same thought is reflected in the *Śānti P.*, when Manu describes the ultimate Soul. Manu says that the element from which this entire world has emanated, its nature cannot be perceived even from the Vedic hymns. It is neither female nor male, nor it is neutral (of neuter gender). It is not being, nor a non-being. It is indestructible and hence, that imperishable Supreme Soul is called imperishable (akṣara).[101]

The indescribable nature of the Brahman has been aptly brought out in this *Parva* when Manu says this indescribable element is devoid of different flavours, smell. It is devoid of sound, touch and form, it is indistinct (*avyakta*), second to none; it cannot be perceived by mind, intellect or speech. This unmanifest is devoid of form and colour. Still, it has created a world full of form, flavour etc.,[102] This paragraph reflects the undescribable nature of the Brahman defined in the *Bṛ.Up.* as "neither gross, nor subtle, neither short and nor long, neither glowing nor shadowy, not dark, free from attachment, flavour-less, the smell-less, the eye-less, the ear-less, the speech-less, the mind-less, without *prāṇa,* the mouth-less, the un-internal, the un-external, consuming nothing, and consumed by none."[103]

The *Kaṭh. Up.* describes it as "like the celestial sun, who is the eye of all the universe and untouched by the defects of our vision, the universal self is beyond all the happiness and the misery of the world; it is untouched by defects."[104] This untainted nature of the Brahman is also described in the *Bh.G.* alongwith its imperishable, beginningless qualitiless nature.[105]

The Metaphor of Aśvattha Tree

This can be compared with a similar description presented in the *Kaṭh. Up.,* which describes the Brahman using the allegory of Aśvattha tree. It has its roots upward and branches downwards. The tree is the pure immortal Brahman, in which all these worlds are situated and beyond which there is nothing.[106] The *Bh.G.* states that "The Aśvattha tree has its roots upwards and branches downwards and upwards, which are nourished by the modes (*guṇa*-s). The sensual objects are its foliage. Yet again, its infinite roots spread downwards in the form of action in the human world. It is not possible to have a glimpse of that tree here in this fashion. It has neither an end, nor a beginning, nor any stationariness whatsoever. After having cut off this Aśvattha tree, which has strong roots, by the forceful weapon of non-attachment, we should seek after that celestial abode from which there is no return, and reach the first (*ādya*) person, from whom all existence has sprung.[107]

According to Tilak, B.G., *Bh.G.* reflects an attempt to harmonize the principles of Vedic and Sāṁkhya philosophy.[108] However, Ranade, R.D. stated that the views expressed in both the passages are antagonistic to each other. According to him, in the *Kaṭh. Up.*, the Aśvattha tree is the Brahman itself, which is immortal, imperishable. Further, it is real and identical with the Brahman and therefore, it cannot be cut off. As against this, the *Mbh.* states that the Aśvattha tree must be regarded as unreal. It is identical with the existence. It is, therefore, necessary to cut off this tree of existence by the potent weapon of non-attachment.[109]

The observations made by Tilak B.G. and Ranade, R.D. are worth taking into consideration. The *Mbh.* (*Bh.G.*) has just borrowed the Upaniṣadic concept of Aśvattha tree. However, it has further moulded it to suit its purpose. The primary aim of the author of the *Mbh.* was to enable Arjuna, who was the representative of empirical beings, to free himself from the worldly attachments and attain the equanimity of mind. In fact, it is a classic example of adapting the Upaniṣadic idea and presenting it in a new garb. He, thus, has made the new thought palatable by utilizing the Upaniṣadic metaphor.

The *Mbh.* (*Śānti P.*) has also presented a metaphor of a tree. This tree is called a tree of sensual enjoyments. Its seed is delusion. Anger and pride are its main branches. Desire is a vessel containing sprinkling water. The act of finding faults with others are the leaves. The sin performed in the previous life is its bark. Sorrow is its branch. Delusion and worry are its sprouts and the thirst, which deludes the Soul is the creeper, which encircles it. People desirous of having fruits surround them. One should cut off these bonds of desire by the weapon of non-attachment.[110]

In the *Bh.G.*, the Aśvattha tree has been described as identical with existence. Here, in the above example, the tree is not named as Aśvattha. It is neither the tree of the Brahman nor that of existence. It is the tree of sensual enjoyments. However, the bonds of a delusion in the form of a creeper are to be cut by the weapon of non-attachment. Thus, in both the examples, the importance of non-attachment is emphasized.

Different Characteristics of the Ātman and the Relation of Body (*kṣetra*) with the Soul (*kṣetrajña*)

The *Kaṭh Up.* narrates the indestructible nature of the Ātman as "neither born nor killed. He never comes from anything nor becomes anything. He is unborn, imperishable, eternal, has existed for eternity. He is not destroyed when the body is distroyed."[111] It further states that if a killer thinks of killing somebody and if one who is killed thinks that he is being killed, neither of them verily knows, for the Ātman is neither killed nor ever killed.[112]

Kṛṣṇa, while explaining to a distressed Arjuna who was expected to fight with his elders and relatives, says, "One should not grieve for the dead, as these bodies of the embodied Soul have an end but the eternal Soul is indestructible and incomprehensible."[113] The two verses following this statement have been reproduced almost word by word with a few exceptions.[114] This clearly shows that the Upaniṣadic philosophy had so much sway over the minds of people in the days of the *Mbh.* that the Śatasāhasrisaṁhitā had to incorporate those contents.

The idea that the Soul has existed for eternity and is not killed has been further elaborated in the same section, when Kṛṣṇa says, "The Soul is uncleavable; it cannot be burnt, neither wetted, nor yet dried.[115] It is eternal, all pervading, unchanging and immovable. It is the same forever." The simile of "people casting off their worn out clothes and wearing new clothes compared with the Soul casting off worn-out bodies and taking on others that are new",[116] is a very beautiful simile. It appeals to the masses since it relates to everyday experience.

The *Mbh.* (*Śānti P.*) uses a different simile to depict this idea, when it says, "The Soul enters new bodies leaving old bodies like a man entering a new house."[117] Thus, the relation of the body (*kṣetra*) with the embodied Soul (*kṣetrajña*) has been brought out beautifully by relating them to everyday experiences of people.

Relation of the Individual Soul (*kṣetrajña*) and the Supreme Soul (*paramātman*)

The Ātman imprisoned within the body is called *kṣetrajña* or *jīvātman* (a personal Self). When this Ātman is released from the body, it is known as the Absolute Self (*parmātman*). The *Muṇḍ Up.* brings it out thus, "Though the individual Soul was lying with the universal Soul on the same tree, he was infatuated and was grieving on account of his complete delusion. But when he once becomes atoned with the Highest, who is the source of all power, his grief vanishes immediately and he begins to participate in the other's infinite power."[118]

Āśva. P. says, "There are two birds sitting on the tree. Though eternal, they are insentient (*acetana*). There is one more (bird), which is higher than these two, *viz.* the Ātman, the Supreme Self. It is the Highest and is sentient. The Matter is insentient. The personal Self (*kṣetrajña*) is different from the Matter. The Supreme makes the *kṣetrajña* wise by which the *kṣetrajña* is enlightened and released.[119]

Tilak, B.G. states that the world, which is the Matter can be known, is the knowledge and then the Spirit becomes knower, but the real that is to be known, that is *jñeya,* is beyond the Matter and Spirit, That is beyond knowledge and knower and is the Absolute Self (*Paramātman*, *Paramapuruṣa*).[120] This is the *Paramapuruṣa* of the *Bh.G.*[121] The *Bh.G.* also describes the Supreme Person in this body as the spectator, the approver, the sustainer, the experiencer, the Great Lord and also the Highest Self. He, who knows the Person and Nature with the strands, is never born again.[122] Puruṣa described in this section is not the

Puruṣa of Sāṁkhya theory. He is the Absolute Soul, which pervades the entire universe and maintains it eternally. The Vedānta asserts that It is one. It is Imperceptible, It is Eternal and Immutable.

In the Sāṁkhya philosophy, terms 'immutable' (*akṣara*) and 'imperceptible' (*avyakta*) are used for referring to Prakṛti (matter) as the Sāṁkhyavādins believe that it is the most subtle cause of the cosmos. However, the Vedānta considers Parabrahman alone as indestructible (*akṣara*) and unmanifest (*avyakta*). "Paramātman or the Supreme Soul alone is the cause of the cosmos," asserts the Vedānta philosophy.

This Paramātman is not perceptible (*avyakta*) to the sense organs since he does not have visible qualities. However, he is not without quality. He possesses subtle qualities and hence, has been further divided into the one possessed of qualities or qualified (*saguṇa*) and qualityless (*nirguṇa*). These qualities are to be perceived by the mind and not by the sense organs.

The *Bh.G.* states, "Non existent (*asat*) cannot come into existence and existent (*sat*) cannot be non-existent. But the knower of truth has known its end."[123] Here, according to Śaṅkara, *asat* is anything such as heat and cold, which is conditioned by causality, whereas *sat* is uncaused, of which our consciousness never fails, that is the Self.[124] Here, '*asat*' is *deha* (body) with pain and pleasure, that is, the one touched by the world of sense (*mātrāsparśaḥ*) and *sat* is an embodied Soul.

Here the stark contrast between the body and the embodied Self is brought out. The seer knows it. He also knows that the Self is all pervading, indestructible and immutable. No one can bring about its destruction. He is uncleavable. He cannot be burnt. He can neither be wetted nor dried. He is eternal, all pervading, unchanging and immovable. He is the same forever.[125]

Thus, the *Kṣetrajña* is indestructible, incomprehensible and permanent. The *kṣetra,* the empirical body, is destructible but the Soul within this body, which is actually the Supreme Soul, which pervades all the beings, is indestructible. The *Kṣetrajña*, can realise, perceive this fact and stop grieving over the destruction of the body (*kṣetra*). This embodied Self, which is veiled by nescience or Avidyā or *māyā, as* Śaṅkara calls it, gets released by knowledge (*vidyā*) of true Self. Here, Lord Kṛṣṇa stresses the point on the mind of Arjuna that the relatives, elders for whose death he is grieving, need not be lamented, as only their bodies would be killed or destroyed. Their Souls would never meet end.

The *Mbh.* states that one, who considers the Ātman to be one who slays or one who is slain, is ignorant,[126] because tnough he appears to have taken birth in the form of body, neither is he born nor does he die. Having come into being, it cannot be that he will not be born hereafter.[127] Śaṅkara, here, explains that the Self, having once existed, does not cease to be anymore, nor does the Self come into existence (like a body).[128]

Thus, here the Lord considers both *Kṣetrajña* and the Supreme Soul (*Paramātman*) to be indestructible.

The relation of the two Souls, *Kṣetrajña* and *Paramātman* (Supreme Soul), has been depicted in the Upaniṣad-s with regular intervals. The *Kaṭh. Up.* shows that both the Souls are enjoying the fruits of their action.[129] However, the *Muṇd. Up.* depicts one of them as tasting the fruit of action while the other one as merely looking at the first one, but not eating the fruit.[130] In the *Śvet. Up.,* the idea of two Ātmans is further clarified thus– "The individual Soul enjoys Prakṛti, which has three qualities, the red, the white and the black. However, the Universal Soul leaves it off."[131] The *Muṇḍ. Up.* has in the very next verse described the condition of the individual Ātman, who was so far eating the fruits of action. It says, "Though the individual Soul was perching on the same tree all along with the Universal Soul, he was yet infatuated and was grieving on account of his ignorance, but once he has become atoned with the Highest, who is the source of all power, his grief vanishes immediately and he begins to participate in the other's infinite power."[132]

The *Mbh.* also has presented metaphors of two birds and that of a tree. Here, the body has been depicted as a tree, unmanifest is its womb, intelligence its trunk, 'I'ness its branches, sense organs its sprouts and hollows; five great elements (*pañcamahābhūta-s*) decorate and support it. Its leaves are desires, actions are its flowers and its fruits are the fruits of action. There are two birds on this tree, which though active, are without consciousness. Here, these two birds are : (1) the body, *viz.* the Matter (*prakṛti*) which is unconscious, (2) *Kṣetrajña* who knows the third one, the Supreme Soul, which is the knowledge itself. After having the knowledge of the Supreme Soul, the Soul in the individual body (*jīvātman*) goes beyond the qualities and gets release from death.[133] The *Mbh.*, however, distinguishes between the deluded ones and the Yogins and clearly says that the deluded ones enjoy the sense-objects with the sense-organs but the Yogins. (*i.e.* knowledgeable persons) can perceive within themselves.[134]

In the *Mbh.*, the Lord says, "I am lodged in the hearts of all. From Me are memory and knowledge as well as their loss. I am indeed, one who is to be known by all the Veda-s. I indeed am the author of the Vedānta and I, too, am the knower of the Veda-s. There are two persons in the world, the imperishable one and the perishable one."[135] In the *Āraṇyaka P.*, the difference between the Kṣetrajña, enjoying the pleasures, and the eternal spirit, going out of the sphere of senses aided by the mind, acting through the senses, the receptacle of all perceptions, successively perceives the things, is narrated.[136] Thus, the characteristic of the *Jīvātman* knowing the Supreme Self, through knowledge has been brought out here. The Self, residing in the hearts of beings, is self-illuminative. The *Jīvātman* is the part of the Supreme Self. However, he considers the Supreme Self to be superior to himself since the Supreme Self has created this entire world.[137]

Thus, the nearness, oneness of the two Souls and the attainment of the Supreme Soul by the embodied Soul has been brought out with dexterity.

Knowledge (Vidyā) and Ignorance (*Avidyā*)

In the *Ch. Up.*, there is a conversation between Nārada and Sanatkumāra. Nārada says that even though he learned the Veda-s, the science of manes, time, ethics, the gods and different scriptures etc., he is unhappy. He studied different *mantra*-s. However, he does not know the Self. Thus, though he has empirical knowledge, he is not blissful.[138] The goal of empirical knowledge is pleasure, which brings sorrow. Hence, to obtain real bliss, he wants to have the knowledge of the immortal.

The knowledge of the eternal ultimate principle stands for Vidyā and the knowledge of the empirical reality for Avidyā. The *Kaṭh. Up.* says that the sages never find Reality and certainty in the unrealities and uncertainties of this world.[139] It observes that people living in ignorance and thinking themselves as wise, wander like blind men following the blind in search of Reality. They would have seen it easily if they had lodged themselves in knowledge instead of ignorance[140] (*avidyā*). Avidyā, according to the *Mbh.*, is the unmanifest Nature, which is characterised by the phenomena of creation and dissolution. The principle beyond it, which is free from those phenomena, is the twenty-fifth principle. This divine unmanifest is Vidyā of all the principles in the world.[141] The *Mbh.* states that to consider the body, consisting of constituents of Nature (*guṇa-s*), as the Ātman is the false knowledge (*asamyak-darśana*).[142]

The *Ch. Up.* states that the ultimate truth is hidden by a cover of untruth, like the golden treasure which is hidden from us by the earth inside it. We consciously move to the region of Truth day after day, still we, under the power of untruth (*anṛta*), go on (struggling) since we do not know the Ātman, which is within our own hearts.[143] In the *Mbh.*, Kṛṣṇa says, "I am the Ātman dwelling in the hearts of all the created things." He further states, "The imperishable is enveloped by illusion (*kūṭastha*) and I am the Supreme Person (*Uttama Puruṣa*), who is beyond perishable and imperishable."[144] Nescience leads to the belief in the world of duality or plurality. This mistaken knowledge that the individual Self, which is embodied, is different from the Supreme Self is Avidyā. This experience generates sorrow. The Soul is not affected by the pleasures and sorrows experienced by the embodied Soul. It is the false identity of the body with the Soul, which obscures man's perspective towards the phenomenon of suffering. In fact, the embodied Soul, which is the part of the Supreme Self, is untouched by the phenomena of pleasure and suffering.[145] This thought is reflected in the *Mbh.* The embodied Self, due to its association with the elements, appears like them[146] (though it is not the element but the seer). When he discards this feeling of association with the manifest world, he becomes one with the sentient.[147] This wrong notion, that is the veil of Avidyā, can be removed by the knowledge of the immortal principle. However, when it is said, "to know the Ātman", the Ātman becomes the object of the knowledge and again the concept of duality arises. Moreover, the Ātman is the knower. It is the subject; it, therefore, cannot become the object of knowledge. This problem can be solved by the Self knowing himself. The Ātman is self consciousness, ultimate existence. It can be known only by introspection. In this respect, Ranade, R.D. states that though the Self is technically unknowable, it is not merely an object of faith, but the object of mystical realisation.[148] The *Mbh.* echoes the same thought, when it states that the Soul acquires the knowledge of the Supreme Soul through its discriminative powers and contemplates, "I am like the Supreme Soul, I have become one with It. There is a similarity between both of us. This Supreme Soul is pure and I, too, am pure like Him." Thus, foresaking its mortal characteristic, it obtains the pure immortal Self.[149]

The *Tait. Up.* states about the Brahman, "Before him the words and thoughts recoil, unable to comprehend its fullness." Since it is unknowable, indescribable, It is to be realised.[150] The *Mbh.*, too, reiterates that only through contemplation it can be realised. The *Mbh.* further explains, "When the being (aspirant) regularly contemplates on the Supreme Self, he isolates himself (from the Nature) and attains the Supreme Soul (*ṣaḍviṁśa*)."[151] In this verse and the next two verses,[152] the reference to twenty-sixth and twenty-fifth (*pañcaviṁśa*) principle shows the synthesis of the Upaniṣadic philosophy with that of Sāṁkhya and Yoga. In the *Bṛ. Up.,* Yājñavalkya, while describing the reality of the Brahman, states, "It is only when there seems to be a duality, one smells the other etc. but where there is the Ātman alone, what and whereby one may smell, etc."[153] He is concealed by the (empirical) reality.[154] He is the Reality of Reality.[155] All these sentences imply that it is the Brahman alone, which is reality. Although the world of names, forms and works, is threefold, is in fact just one. It is due to Avidyā that people are not able to comprehend the Reality. Ranade opines that all these ideas show the traces of the doctrine of Māyā in the Upaniṣad-s.[156]

There are two different views regarding the Absolute, *viz.* the Brahman. From the cosmic or empirical standpoint, the world is real. This is *saprapañca* conception. It holds immanence of the Brahman in the world. The other, acosmic or transcendental point of view, considers the Brahman to be greater than the world. This is *niṣprapañca* conception. However, the Upaniṣad-s hold that the Brahman is both immanent and transcendent. Hiriyanna M. observes that probably these two different views are due to a difference in interpreting the result of the synthesis of the conceptions of the Brahman and the Ātman.[157] According to the first conception of *Saprapañca* Brahman, the manifold things of experience emerge from and are reabsorbed into the Brahman. This concept is termed as *Brahmapariṇāmavāda* by the later Vedāntic philosophers. The second, the *niṣprapañca* conception views the Brahman to be a mere appearance of the world and it is termed as *Brahmavivartavāda.* This second conception involves the notion of *māyā*, which has its roots in the Upaniṣad-s. The word *māyā*, appears in the *Bṛ. Up.* It denotes power when it states that Indra has assumed many shapes by his *māyā.*[158] The *Śvet. Up.* describes God as *māyin,* who creates this world, treating him as powerful entity.[159] However, it does not distinguish between *māyā*, that envelops the God, and the Avidyā that envelops *Jīva*, as considered by the later Vedānta philosophers. The *Kaṭh. Up.* terms it as Avidyā, *adhruva.*[160] According to the *Ch. Up.*, it is ignorance,[161] Avidyā and according to the *Praś. Up.*, it is falsehood, illusion, *anṛta.*[162]

In the *Mbh.*, Kṛṣṇa states, "People do not recognize Me. I am eternal and unborn and am covered by *yogamāyā.*"[163] He also states that *Mahadbrahma* is my womb.[164] Jñāneśvara[165] and Tilak, B.G.[166] explain *Mahadbrahma* as *māyā.* This *Mahadbrahma* is the Prakṛti of Sāṁkhya Philosophy. The *Śvet. Up.* also describes *māyā* as the Prakṛti.[167] Kṛṣṇa says, "This divine *māyā*, consisting of three constituents, is difficult to cross over."[168] It is imperceptible to the organs. However, ignorant people consider it to be perceptible and do not cognise its superior and imperceptible form. Since the Lord is veiled by *yogamāyā*, people do not recognise him.[169] Here, the term *yogamāyā*, has been used to indicate his perceptible form. The *Mbh.* again states that due to Viṣṇu's *māyā*, the person is deprived of his knowledge and discriminative power and his intellect is enveloped by desire (*kāma*).[170] The *Mbh.* also states that the god who resides in the hearts of beings and makes them whirl by his magic power (*māyā*).[171] Both references imply that *māyā* is Avidyā which prohibits the being from the attainment of the Absolute principle. Thus, the *Mbh.* has used the term *māyā* variously. However, at all places the concepts of concealment and power are implicit therein.

The *Mbh.* has accepted both the conceptions of the Brahman. When Kṛṣṇa says, "*Mahadbrahma* is my womb", the application of emanation theory is evident and the reference to his imperceptible form being obscured by *māyā* shows transcendental conception. Both the emanation and transcendental theories explain the two sides of the same Brahman. Both the theories explain the existence of the world and its relation to the Ultimate Reality. The *Mbh.* explains it beautifully, "*Karman* has emanated from the Brahman and *yajña* from the *karman*. From *yajña* rain emanates. Food grows due to rain and from the food, the beings emanate."[172] In this connection, the comments of Tilak, B.G. are significant. He has stated that, "Here, *karman* means the process of manifestation, creation from the Brahman, which is devoid of attributes. This process is called *māyā*, characterised by name and form (*nāmarūpātmaka*). This act of creation of the universe is *māyā*. It is an unimaginable sport of the Brahman. It is not an independent phenomenon."[173] Here, *rūpa* means the nature of a thing and *nāma* is the name or word that serves as its sign. The emergence of the world from the Brahman is understood as the differentiation of names and forms. Like the Upaniṣad-s, the *Mbh.,* too does not distinguish between *māyā* as the one enveloping the God and Avidyā as enveloping the individual Ātman (*jīva*). It is evident from Kṛṣṇa's statements that *māyā* is the cause of all the beings in different forms of existence (*yoni-s*).[174] Establishing myself in my own Nature, I take birth through my *māyā*.[175] The *Śānti. P.* describes the unmanifest Nature, which is characterised by the phenomena of creation and dissolution, as Avidyā.[176]

Thus, the being realises that even though the universe of names, forms and works appears to be three fold, in reality it is but one the Ātman, or the Brahman. It is concealed by the empirical reality. It is immortal. The *Mbh.* has rightly described the Ātman as *"Kūṭastha"*,[177] or *"Guḍhātmā"*,[178] *"Avyaktātparato"*[179] "*Indriyātīta*",[180] etc. Once this veil of Avidyā, *māyā* is lifted, there rises the knowledge of the Supreme Reality[181] and the being is released (from the cycle of existence) and he becomes one with the Supreme Soul.[182] The *Īśa Up.* has rightly said that "He who knows both Vidyā and Avidyā together, overcomes death through Avidyā and experiences immortality by means of Vidyā where Vidyā, stands for the science of inner world of the Soul and Avidyā for the science of the outer world."[183]

The Doctrine of Sheaths (*Kośa*-s)

Moreover, it must be noted that it is necessary to have the knowledge of the Self to remove the veil of Avidyā. The individual Soul (*jīva*), ordinarily, considers itself to be finite and distinct from the Brahman, which is infinite. However, the Upaniṣad-s regard the individual Soul as unlimited. To establish the identity of *jīva* with the Brahman, there has been a quest for the Brahman within the Self. There has been such an exercise in the *Tait. Up.* It observes that the Brahman lies in the sublime cave of the heart.[184] It is difficult to see the Brahman hidden within the heart. Śaṅkara says, "The word *guhā* also reflects intellect as we understand things through the intellect."[185] *Guhā* has also been described as the supreme space (*parama vyoman*), where a being has the sacred experience of the Brahman, who then realises that the space within us is also the space without. Thus, the experience of duality no more exists as we realize that we are one with everything.[186]

The *Mbh.* too states that the Ātman is hidden in (the hearts of) all beings. The seers realise it through their subtle (*sūkṣma*) intellect. When their minds are purified, they realise that it is within themselves. Discarding their association with both the auspicious and inauspicious actions thereafter, they experience the eternal Bliss within their Ātman.[187] The *Bh.G.* also states that, "I have entered the hearts of all and the wise (*asaṁmūḍha*) knows me as the Supreme Self. He becomes all knowing (*sarvavid*)."[188] The *Tait.Up.* reflects an attempt at discovering this hidden Ātman by uncovering the sheaths, husks (*kośa*-s). These sheaths of the Ātman form the earthly ethereal, mental, intellectual and beatific self.[189] According to Deussen, the four sheaths *viz. annamaya, prāṇamaya, manomaya* and *vijñānamaya kośa-s* surround the fifth one, which is the kernel of the Ātman.[190] However, Dixit, S.H. states that all the five aspects are the sheaths of the Ātman. The Ātman inside all the sheaths is an observer and the Bliss is its perceptible condition (*svarūpa*). If these *kośa*-s are removed one by one, we reach the innermost essential being of the man and nature.[191] Ranade, R.D. states that, Śaṅkara recognised the *kośa-s* but he, too, recognised them as merely an ideal existence. One has to think over these five *kośa-s* with discriminative intellect and find out the true Self beyond the physical body, vital principle, mind and intellect, and even beyond the beatific consciousness.[192] According to Lokeswaranand, these sheaths arranged from gross to subtle, one within the other, really speaking, are levels of consciousness and the highest of them is the level where one enjoys the Bliss of the Brahman. The goal of life is to go beyond all the levels and to reach a state where one loses his separate identity in the Brahman.[193]

In the *Mbh.,* Kṛṣṇa explains the entire knowledge, beyond which there remains nothing to be known.[194] He declares that his qualitative form, *aṣṭadhā* Prakṛti, which includes five gross elements, *manas, buddhi* and *ahaṁkāra,* is his *aparā* Prakṛti, which holds this world. But he has one more Prakṛti of him, which is *parā* Prakṛti, which is the Soul of all the beings. All the beings have emanated from both the Prakṛti-s.[195] Though Kośa doctrine is not explicit here, it shows the journey of the Self from gross level to the subtle one. The gross elements would represent the *annamaya kośa, manas* the *manomaya kośa, buddhi* and *ahaṁkāra,* which indicate self conscious, would represent *vijñānamaya kośa* and *parā* Prakṛti is the Ultimate Entity. It, however, does not indicate *prāṇamaya* and *ānandamaya kośa-s,* which according to Hiriyanna M., represent organic and self-transcendent state of the being, respectively.[196]

Hiriyanna M. has stated that this doctrine of *kośa* is the unique experience characterising the self transcendent state. It is represented as higher than the experience of conscious (*manomaya*) and the self conscious (*vijñānamaya*) levels of life, since the conflict and confusion, which are the marks of both these levels, are overcome in it and it is described as *ānandamaya*, which indicates that its essential mark is peace.[197] Yet it is not identifiable with *mokṣa* since *ānandamaya kośa* too is a passing phase. It stands midway between common experience and *mokṣa,* where the Soul's true nature is fully revealed.[198]

Tilak, B.G. has stated that the phenomenon of five aspects of the Ātman (*pañcakośa*) is the worship of the Ātman in the rising scale. This is to understand the *nirguṇa* form of the Ātman through the qualitative forms of food, life, mind, practical knowledge and joy and finally it is the *nirguṇa* Brahman alone, which pervades this universe.[199]

Satavalekar, S.D. has explained this doctrine of sheaths through a different angle. Having focused his attention on the plural form of the word *śarīra* in the *Mbh.* (*Bh. G.*),[200] he stated that the expression "Leaving the worn out bodies"[201], shows that man has many bodies, either three or more than that. The way men wear clothes such as coat, shirt, banian etc. a body also wears different clothes. A man has gross body (*sthūla śarīra*), subtle body (*sūkṣma śarīra*) and causal body (*karaṇa śarīra*). Hence, according to him, the *sthūla deha* and *sūkṣma deha* represent *annamaya deha, prāṇa deha* represents *prāṇamaya, manodeha* represents *manomaya, buddhi* represents *vijñānamaya deha.* He has compared this concept with the gradation of elements in the *Mbh.* (*Bh. G.*). The *Mbh.* (*Bh. G.*) maintains that the sense organs are beyond the body, mind is beyond the sense organs, the intellect is beyond the mind and the self is beyond the intellect.[202] The *Śānti. P.* also shows such a gradual process when it expresses the same thought with a slight difference, *i.e.* the objects of sense are higher than the sense organs, the mind is higher than the objects of sense; intellect is higher than the mind. The individual Soul is higher than intellect; Prakṛti is higher than the individual Soul (*jīva*) and the immortal entity, the Paramātman is the Ultimate.[203] The Ultimate, *viz.* the Brahman, is hidden in all the beings. It can be seen by the seers through the subtle intellect.[204] By dissolving his mind, sense organs and sense objects in the inner Soul, a being can behold the ultimate truth through his discriminative intellect.[205]

Thus, the Upaniṣad-s have given equal importance to the body, mind, intellect, which help the being in making spiritual progress. It treats gross as well as subtle elements as the Brahman, thus, establishing the unity of the individual Soul, with the world as also with the Brahman. This oneness of material body and the spiritual entity can be discerned from the *Mbh.* when Kṛṣṇa says, "Though unborn and undecaying, Īśvara of the beings, yet establishing Myself in my own nature (Prakṛti), I take birth as an empirical being."[206] On the similar lines of the Upaniṣad-s, Blondel indicates the possible path, "Matter is that which can be vitalized; Life is that which can be spiritualised and the spirit is that which can be deified."[207]

The Concept of Release according to the Vedānta

The Upaniṣad-s preach that once we know the Ātman, we attain salvation. If, however, we do not know the Ātman, there is no freedom. Who can attain freedom? Gauḍapāda says, "No Soul ever comes under any veil. The Souls are by nature pure as well as illuminated and free from the very beginning."[208] Thus, every being is already emancipated but he is not aware of it due to ignorance, which is to be removed by knowledge. In the *Ch. Up.,* Āruṇi explained to Śvetaketu that the knowledge about the subtle element alone is truth. He said, "This Ātman is of atomic nature. This Ātman is everything. That is truth, that the Ātman is you, yourself. Oh! Śvetaketu."[209]

But why should one strive to know the Ātman? The answer to this question is that the Ultimate goal of human life is to realise the Ātman. One becomes fearless because he knows that besides his own true Self, there is no other entity which might cause fear.[210]

The Upaniṣad-s preach that the Ultimate goal of a man is the realisation of the Ātman. Thus, the *Br. Up.* States, "If a man says that there is an object of love dearer to him other than the Ātman, and if another one replies that if there be God overhead, he shall destroy his object of love, verily it shall so happen as this man says. Hence, we ought to meditate on the Ātman as the only object of desire. For him, who worships, *i.e.* knows the Ātman in this way, nothing else dear shall ever perish."[211] Thus, here there is an explicit declaration, so to say, that a man would not lose anything if he worships the Ātman, that is knows the Ātman, there is a reward awaiting for him, that is immortality. However, once liberation is attained, there is no desire. He becomes free from desire.[212]

In the *Br. Up.*, Maitreyī preferred acceptance of spiritual portion of her husband's estate to that of empirical wealth, as she was desirous of attaining immortality. She then sought the advice of her husband, Yājñavalkya, who instructed her that it is not for the sake of husband, wife, children, wealth etc., that those are dear to us but it is so they are dear to us for the sake of the Ātman. So it is not for the sake of everything that everything is dear to us, but for the sake of the Ātman. He further stated that, "This Ātman ought to be seen, ought to be heard, ought to be thought about, ought to be meditated upon. For it is only when the Ātman is seen, heard, thought about and meditated upon that all this becomes verily known."[213] Thus, he systematically explained to her how the Self can be realised.

Yājñavalkya asked the king Janaka, "Since you are now rich in attendants and goods, since you have studied the Veda-s and listened to the mystical doctrine, do you know where will you go, when will you depart from here?"[214] Though Janaka was aware of the path of Devayāna and the world of Devaloka as referred to in the Veda-s and the Upaniṣad-s, he did not know the answer. Yājñavalkya explained as to how the individual Ātman, dwells in the heart, how he is nourished etc. in gross material fashion. Thereafter, he described the Ātman on the cosmic level thus, "The eastern regions of the heavens are his anterior organs; the right hand regions of the heavens are his right-hand organs" etc., "all the regions of the heavens are all his organs and still, the Ātman is not so, not so. (*neti, neti* etc.) such as he is not inapprehensible, he is indestructible, unattached; unfettered; he stirs not; he suffers no harm etc."[215]

The implication of this discourse is that after death the Soul goes nowhere, where it has not been from the very beginning, nor does it become other than that which it has always been, the one eternal omnipresent Ātman.

Again, in the *Kaṭh. Up.* the God of Death tries to allure Naciketas to accept the life of pleasures but Naciketas declined this offer, which would ultimately fetter him into an empirical life and would lead to disillusion. He does not mix up the good (*śreyas*) with the pleasant (*preyas*) and chooses the path of the *śreyas*.[216] The wise chooses the good leaving the pleasant.

The good (*śreyas*) is the truth and the *Īśa. Up.* says that the truth is veiled in this universe by the vessel of gold.[217] Unless this temptation is overcome, the path of the good would not be seen. When a man withdraws his senses from the sense-objects, the Ātman gets illuminated in his heart.

Thus, as the Soul prefers the good (*śreyas*), he becomes liberated and merges into the Absolute "just like the rivers merge into the ocean, abandon their names and forms and lose their identity, similarly the seer after freeing himself from his name and form, enters the highest heavenly Person."[218]

It is also said that the realisation of Saccidānanda character of the Brahman is the Release. Here, the Ātman is called '*Sat*' because it contains everything in the cosmos. It is called '*Cit*' as it is sentient. When one comes to know these '*Sat*' and '*Cit*' aspects of the Brahman, one experiences Bliss. Hence, *ānanda* is one more aspect of the Brahman. The Upaniṣad-s, therefore, maintain that the experience of the '*Sat*', '*Cit*', and '*ānanda*' form of the Brahman by the Soul leads to the liberation of the Soul.

The *Mbh.* states that the people, who believe in the ceremonial acts and sacrificial rites as prescribed in the Veda-s, are delighted after receiving the merits accruing to them. In the same way, the wise, who believe in knowledge, do not like anything other than knowledge. The seers, who are very intelligent, who know both the paths of action (*karman*) and knowledge (*jñāna*), prefer the path of emancipation, as it is better than the path of action. Here, the preceptor, therefore, states that one, who wishes to be released from the bodily ties, should strive for release.

He, therefore, advises that a man desirous of getting release should perform his action without expectation.[219] In the same *Parva,* Manu declares on the same lines that salvation can be gained through renunciation of material acts.[220] Here, by material acts he means the performance of ceremonial actions, sacrifices etc. with a desire to secure the fruit (*sakāma*) as enunciated in the Vedic scriptures. The views expressed in both the sections corroborate the implications of Janaka's confusion regarding the place he would lead to after learning the Veda-s and other scriptures.

The *Mbh.* also lays stress on conquering the evil of attachment as depicted in the *Kaṭh. Up.* As Naciketas shows his preference for the good (*śreyas*), rejecting worldly pleasures, the *Mbh.* too instructs that one should control one's own desires like a tortoise contracting its limbs. Once this is done the Ātman illuminates in his heart like the sun.[221] The *Bh. G.* too, elaborates the point saying, "Those who are freed from pride and delusion, who have conquered the evil of attachment, who, with all their desires stilled, are ever devoted to the Supreme Spirit, who are liberated from the dualities of pleasure and pain and are undeluded, go to that eternal state. It assures that he would attain to that Supreme abode from which there is no return.[222]

The release of the Soul is expressed in the *Mbh.* The one who is devoted to the Supreme Spirit, knows him in essence through devotion and goes to that eternal state by his favour and attains that Supreme State,[223] from which one never returns.[224] It is the instant release. However, there is a mention of "Supreme abode from which there is no return."[225] Also there is a mention of devotee entering into him, that is absorption of the devotee into the deity.[226] It is called release (*sāyujya*). Such references have led to the later philosophical doctrines of Rāmānuja and Madhva.

The *Mbh.* states that due to the sin performed by the man, he does not get release. Once the sins are destroyed, he attains release.[227] According to the *Mbh.*, man can attain emancipation with the help of compassion, patience, calmness (of mind), non-violence, truth, straightforwardness, non-injury (to other), absence of pride, modesty, forebearance and tranquility.[228]

Characteristics of the Emancipated Men

In the *Gauḍapāda-kārikā*, there is a picturesque description of the individual waking up from the slumber of *māyā*. He states that when an individual, sleeping under the influence of the world's false show, which is beginningless, is awakened, he realises the Eternal which is beyond time, sleep and dreams.[229] There is another description presented by the author of the *Muṇḍ. Up.* When one realises the Brahman, he perceives "The Brahman as being before him and behind him, to his right and to his left, above him and even below him and exclaims that this itself is universe.[230] The state of an emancipated person becomes ecstatic as "The knots of his heart are broken, all his doubts are cleared and the effects of his actions are annihilated."[231] If he knows himself to be the same, the highest Person (the Brahman), he does not entertain any desire for the fulfillment of which he would enter into a (new) body.[232]

Thus, the knowledge of the identity of the Ātman with the Brahman culminates into the release. This is a stage when one frees oneself from all sorts of cravings, desires, fears and even pain. One does not feel any need for any action to fulfill one's own desires anymore. No actions cling to him. All his doubts are cleared. There is no rebirth.[233]

All the above experiences of the emancipated man are reflected in Janaka's discourse with Sulabhā, where he says, "Having obtained this excellent intelligence, all my desires are eliminated. Even though I am a householder, I have gone beyond the state of duality. As the seeds sown in the field, watered, get sprouted, in the same way the good and bad actions of the people lead to rebirth. However, seeds roasted do not get germinated. In the same way, because of knowledge, the seeds of desires for worldly pleasures can not germinate in the heart of a wise man. My intellect, therefore, neither gets entangled in pleasure of life nor do I get angry with my enemies. Real liberation is through knowledge.[234] Sulabha states that one who has realized the Brahman, through knowledge, knows that there is no other power higher than it.[235]

The *Mbh.* also states that when one sees creatures of infinite diversity to be all one and the same and to be but diversified, emanating from the same essence, one is said to have attained the Brahman. Those who reach that state attain to that Supreme and blissfull end. Indeed everything rests on understanding.[236] The above details are in full agreement with the Vedāntic concept of release.

The above observations show that the *Mbh.* has borrowed the Vedāntic philosophical views regarding the characteristics of the persons whose Soul is liberated. According to Mahābhāratakāra, one who perceives the Highest Lord everywhere attains release and is not reborn.[237] The *Mbh.* states that when the *jīvātman* knows the Supreme Lord abiding equally in all beings, never perishing when they perish, he verily knows, for as he sees the Lord present equally everywhere, he does not injure his true Self by the Self and then attains the Supreme goal.[238] In the *Ādi. P.*, even Yayāti has stated, "When one who has controlled his senses, discards his desires and actions, achieves supernatural powers. When one conquers this world, overcomes duality through penance, one conquers the Supreme. This state of him is called immortality (*amṛtattva*)."[239] *Śanti P.* strengthens this view when it says that a person, who can perceive the imperceptible Supreme Self who dwells in all the beings, attains the state of the Brahman and immortality after having left this world.[240]

The *Mbh.* describes a *yogin* who meditates on the Brahman at the time of death and he attains the highest that is Puruṣa. These people are devoid of desire and observe celibacy. Other beings follow the cycle of birth and death.[241] Thus, the *Mbh.*

supports the two paths, one of complete release and the other of re-birth. The *Śānti P.* further narrates different states of transmigration and states that not only the seers but the people who study scriptures and follow daily rituals go to the Sanātana, eternal regions.[242] This hints at the importance attached to the performance of ritualistic practices by the masses.

The Metaphor of Chariot

The simile of a body being a chariot and a mover of this body – a chariot being an embodied Soul has been refered to in the *Mbh.* This metaphor of the chariot also appears in the *Bṛ. Up.* The Supreme Self is the king of all the individual Souls. Just as the spokes of wheel of the chariot are held together in the navel and ring of a wheel, likewise all the beings, all the gods, all the regions are consigned to this Supreme Self.[243]

However, the metaphor of the chariot has been used differently in the *Kaṭh. Up.* It compares the body to a chariot, organs to its horses which drag the chariot. The intellect (*buddhi*) is the charioteer who has to keep watch and control the reins in the shape of the mind on the path of the enjoyment of objects of delight.[244] This simile has been used in the *Mbh.* at many places, in the *Āraṇ. P.*,[245] *Strī P.*[246] and *Āśva. P.*[247] The *Strī P.* and *Āraṇ. P.* imagine the individual Self as the charioteer. The *Āśva. P.* considers mind (*manas*) as the charioteer and intellect as the reins and the chariot, which is the body, is pervaded by the Brahman. Tilak B.G. has pointed out that this simile has been so appropriate for describing the concept of the control of organs that the same has been used by the famous Greek philosopher Plato in his book *Phoedrus* (p. 246) while describing the concept of organs.[248]

Although the *Mbh.* does not use the same metaphor verbatim while explaining the idea of control of senses by the mind, it compares “the sense organs with the horses and the mind with their controller.”[249] The *Bh.G.* does not incorporate the metaphor directly. However, it does take note of the significance of this simile.[250] While describing the state of a bewildered one (*mūḍha*), Arjuna is advised to check the senses with the mind. It is stated that "The mind of a man is governed by the wandering senses like the ship carried away by the wind on the waters. Hence, one who is steadfast in his wisdom holds the senses from the objects of the senses."[251] In the latter illustration, the onus of controlling the senses falls on the intellect. In this connection, Tilak, B.G. observes that since the function of controlling the senses has been enjoined to the reason, intellect (*vyavasāyātmikā buddhi* or *karmabuddhi* as stated in illustration quoted from *Strī P.*) should become pure. The principle that there is only one Ātman in all human beings must be deeply impressed on the mind by realising the true nature of the Parameśvara, the Supreme Self.[252]

According to the *Mbh.*, desire is a foe of a man. The senses, mind and intellect constitute its base. By these, it obscures knowledge and deludes the embodied Soul. Hence, one should check the senses first and cast off the sin that destroys both knowledge and experience. It further emphasizes that the senses are high; higher than them is the mind and the intellect is higher than the mind. But He is higher than the intellect.[253] Here, '*saḥ*', *i.e.* He is stated as *kāma* by Rāmānujācārya.[254] However, the parallel passage in the *Kaṭh. Up.* makes it clear that the word '*saḥ*' stands for the Ātman[255] Thus, the *Mbh.* (*Bh.G.*) states that knowing Him to be higher than the intellect, studying the Self by the Self, slay your enemy that changes shape at will and so hard to reach. Here, the Supreme Self has taken over the role of the charioteer, who is beyond *buddhi.* In this connection, Sukthankar, V.S. observes that the Supreme Soul is symbolized in the *Bh.G.* as the Lord Śrīkṛṣṇa and the Bhārata war is to be viewed as the war against the enemies of the self.[256] Thus, one should subjugate these senses, mind to defeat the enemy. Further, no one can undertake an evil act against his desire. The action is willed by the doer and not against the desire as assumed by Arjuna.[257] Hence, he has the opportunity to control these senses and though the mind is perplexed, it knows where the duty lies. The Self, therefore, has to commune with his own Self,[258] control mind and *buddhi* and destroy his enemy of desire. Arjuna has, therefore, been advised to control his desires and perform the duties assigned to him. Thus, according to the *Mbh. (Bh.G.)*, it is the Soul which controls the senses and steers himself on the path of knowledge.

Thus, the simile has been generally used in the *Mbh.* to describe the supremacy of the Ātman over the mind, intellect and the senses etc. It is the Ātman alone who can control the wandering senses. The Ātman, the embodied Self, when bewildered loses the control over the senses. Nevertheless, ultimately it is the Ātman himself who has to commune with himself and control the senses, which carry him away from the ultimate goal. Thus, with the help of the mind, which is the receptacle of knowledge and the intellect, which has been assigned the discriminative function, the Ātman has to undertake the act of controlling. The mind and intellect are mere tools in the hands of the Soul, the Ātman. The true knowledge lies within the Self, which is part and parcel of the Universal Self from which it draws its inspiration.

The above observations show that there is a strong impact of the Vedānta philosophy on the philosophical trends reflected in the *Mbh.* The *Mbh.* has incorporated the monistic doctrine of the Upaniṣad-s and the concept of immortality or Salvation to be achieved through the highest knowledge as the ultimate goal. Transforming a negative Upaniṣadic concept of Avidyā into a concept of *māyā,* it provided a scope for contemplation for Śaṅkarācārya to develop the doctrine of *māyā.*

REFERENCES

1. Ranade, R.D., *A Constructive Survey of Upanishadic Philosophy*, Bombay, 1986, pp. 131-132.
2. *Ibid.*, pp. 9-11.
3. *Ibid.*, p. 12.
4. Radhakrishnan, S., *op. cit.*, p. xvii.
5. Macdonell, A.A., *op. cit.*, p. 203.

6. Article by Lewis, H.D., *Encyclopedia of Philosophy*, Vol. 5-6, p. 155.
7. Zimmer Heinrich, *op. cit.*, p. 3.
8. *Marathi Vishvakosh*, Vol. 3-4, pp. 156-157.
9. *The Encyclopedia of Philosophy* Vols. 5-6, p. 165.
10. Desai, S.G., *A Critical Study of the Later Upaniṣads*, Mumbai, 1996, p. xxxiv.
11. Hiriyanna M., *Outlines of Indian Philosophy*, Delhi, 1993, p. 87.
12. Vaidya, C.V., p. 162 *Mahabharata – A Criticism*, Bombay, 1904, p. 162.
13. Belvalkar, S.K. and Ranade, R.D., *History of Indian Philosophy*, Vol. 2, Poona, 1927, p.10.
14. Radhakrishnan, S., *op. cit.*, p. xvi.
15. Kane, P.V., *History of Dharmaśātra*, Poona, 1968, p. 354.
16. E.W. Hopkins, *Encyclopedia of Religion and Ethics*, Edit. James Hastings., Vol. viii. Edinburg, 1915. p. 619.
17. Zimmer Heinrich, *op. cit.*, p. 67- 68.
18. Macdonell, A.A., *op. cit.*, pp. 285-286.
19. Sutton Nicholas, *op. cit.*, p. 15.
20. *Ch. Up.*, III. 5. 2.
21. *Kaṭh. Up.*, I iii.17; *Śvet. Up.* VI. 22.
22. *Śvet. Up.*, V. 6.
23. *Mait. Up.*, VI. 29.
24. *Ch. Up.*, I. 1. 10
    यदेव विद्यया करोति श्रद्धयोपनिषदा।
    तदेव वीर्यवत्तरं भवतीति।।
25. Deussen Paul, *The Philosophy of the Upaniṣads*, New York, 1919, pp. 10-17.
26. Hiriyanna M. *Outlines of Indian Philosophy*, p. 51, q. by Dange S.A., *Hindu Dharma āṇi Tattvajñāna, (Marathi)*, Pune, 1963, p. 342.
27. *Ken. Up.*, IV. 1-7, For details refer Dange, S.A., *Ibid.*, p. 343.

28. *Tait. Up.*, I. 11, also Dange, S.A., *Ibid.*, pp. 343-344.
29. *Śvet. Up.*, I. 16.
30. *Ṛv.*, II. 6. 1.
31. *Ibid.*, II. 21.5.
32. *Ibid.*, X. 53.2.
33. Dange, S.A., *op. cit.*, pp. 341-344.
34. Radhakrishnan, S. and Moore C.A., *A Source Book in Indian Philosophy*, 1957, pp. 55 and *Ch. Up.* 3. 14 !.
    तज्जलान् शान्त उपासीत।।
35. Deussen q. by Dange, S.A., *op. cit.*, p. 375, 1973.
36. Mullick Bahadur, R.P.N., *The Mahābhārata,* Allahabad, 1934, p. 33.
37. Garg, R.K., *Upanisadic Challenge to Science*, Delhi, 1978, pp. 94-95.
38. Mullick Bahadur, R.P.N., *op. cit.*, p. 33.
39. Belvalkar, S.K. and Ranade, R.D., *op. cit.*, Vol. 2, 1927, pp. 351-352.
40. *Tait. Brāhmaṇa,* III, 10.2,3,4.
41. *Ibid.*, II 2.1.4, also *Śatapatha Brāhmaṇa* II. 1. 4. 10.
42. *Mbh, Śānti P.*, 262.1.
    वेदाः प्रमाणं लोकानां न वेदाः पृष्ठतःकृताः।
    द्वे ब्रह्मणी वेदितव्ये शब्दब्रह्म परं च यत्।
    शब्दब्रह्मणि निष्णातः परं ब्रह्माधिगच्छति।।
43. Max Müller, *Six Systems of Indian Philosophy,* New Delhi, 1899, pp. 52-70.
44. Hertel q. by, Dange S.A., *op. cit.*, pp. 375, 376.
45. *Mbh. Śānti P.,* 233.18.
    देवो यः संश्रितस्तस्मिन्नब्बिन्दुरिव पुष्करे।
    क्षेत्रज्ञं तं विजानीयान्नित्यं त्यागजितात्मकम्।।
46. *Mbh. Adi,* p. 1.28.
    युगस्यादौ निमित्तं तन्महद्दिव्यं प्रचक्षते।
    यस्मिस्तच्छ्रूयते सत्यं ज्योतिर्ब्रह्म सनातनम्।।
47. *Ken. Up.*, III. 4. 1-6.

48. *Mbh. Śānti P.,* 262. 44[d].
ब्रह्माव्यक्तं प्रभवश्चाव्ययश्च॥
49. Dange, S.A., *op. cit.,* pp. 375-376.
50. *Mbh, Śānti P.,* 291. 15-16-17[ab].
सृजत्यनन्तकर्माणं महान्तं भूतमग्रजम्।
मूर्तिमन्तममूर्तात्मा विश्वं शंभुः स्वयंभुवः।
अणिमा लघिमा प्राप्तिरीशानं ज्योतिरव्ययम्॥
सर्वतःपाणिपादान्तं सर्वतोक्षिशिरोमुखम्।
सर्वतःश्रुतिमल्लोके सर्वमावृत्य तिष्ठति॥
हिरण्यगर्भो भगवानेष बुद्धिरिति स्मृतः।
51. *Ibid.,* 262. 44. 45
ऋतं सत्यं विदितं वेदितव्यं सर्वस्यात्मा जङ्गमं स्थावरं च।
सर्वं सुखं यच्छिवमुत्तमं च ब्रह्माव्यक्तं प्रभवश्चाव्ययश्च॥
तेजः क्षमा शान्तिरनामयं शुभं तथाविधं व्योम सनातनं ध्रुवम्।
एतैः शब्दैर्गम्यते बुद्धिनेत्रैस्तस्मै नमो ब्रह्मणे ब्राह्मणाय॥
52. Bohtling – Roth, q. by Garg, R.K., *op. cit.,* p. 84.
53. Dange, S.A., *op. cit.,* pp. 377-380.
54. Deussen Paul, *op. cit.,* p. 85 also *Ṛv.* I., 164, X.129.
55. *Ch. Up.* V.11.1
को नु आत्मा किं ब्रह्मेति॥
56. *Bṛ. Up.* II. 4. 14
यत्र वा अस्य सर्वमात्मैवाभूत्तत्केन कं जिघ्रेत्तत्केन कं विजानीयाद्येनेदँ् हलन्तरे सर्वं विजानाति तं केन विजानीयाद्विज्ञातारमरे केन विजानीयादिति॥
57. *Tait. Up.,* II 2.1
"···· सर्वं वै तेऽन्नमाप्नुवन्ति॥ येऽन्नं ब्रह्मोपासते। ह्व्ह्व अन्नँ् हि भूतानां ज्येष्ठम्। तस्मात्सर्वौषधमुच्यते॥ अनाद्भूतानि जायन्ते····"
58. *Mbh. Bh., P.* 25. 14 -15
अन्नाद्भवन्ति भूतानि पर्जन्यादन्नसंभवः।
यज्ञाद्भवति पर्जन्यो यज्ञः कर्मसमुद्भवः॥
कर्म ब्रह्मोद्भवं विद्धि ब्रह्माक्षरसमुद्भवम्।
तस्मात्सर्वगतं ब्रह्म नित्यं यज्ञे प्रतिष्ठितम्॥
59. *Br. Up.,* IV 2.4 also Raju, P.T., The *Philosophical Tradition of India*, London, 1971, pp. 49-66.

60. *Mbh. Śānti P.,* 208. 25.
पृथक्त्वात्संप्रयोगाच्च नासूयुर्वेद शाश्वतम्।
स तयोरपवर्गज्ञो वीतरागो विमुच्यते॥

61. *Ibid. Bh.,* p., 31.4 - 5
मया ततमिदं सर्वं जगदव्यक्तमूर्तिना।
मत्स्थानि सर्वभूतानि न चाहं तेष्ववस्थितः॥
न च मस्थानि भूतानि पश्य मे योगमैश्वरम्।
भूतभृन्न च भूतस्थो ममात्मा भूतभावनः॥

62. *Ibid.,* 35.15
बहिरन्तश्च भूतानामचरं चरमेव च।
सूक्ष्मत्वात्तदविज्ञेयं दूरस्थं चान्तिके च तत्॥

63. *Ibid. Śānti P.,* 231.29-30
सर्वतःपाणिपादान्तं सर्वतोक्षिशिरोमुखम्।
सर्वतः श्रुतिमल्लोके सर्वमावृत्य तिष्ठति।
तदेवाणोरणुतरं तन्महद्भ्यो महत्तरम्।
तदन्तः सर्वभूतानां ध्रुवं तिष्ठन्न दृश्यते॥

64. *Ibid. Āśva,* P., 42. 59
सर्ववित्सर्वभूतेषु वीक्षत्यात्मानमात्मनि।
एकधा बहुधा चैव विकुर्वाणस्ततस्ततः॥

65. Deussen Paul, *op. cit.,* p. 94.

66. *Ch. Up.,* VIII 11-12
"....मघवन् मर्त्यं वा इदं शरीरमात्तं मृत्युना। तदस्य अमृतस्य अशरीरस्य आत्मनोऽधिष्ठानम्। आत्तो वै सशरीरः प्रियाप्रियाभ्यां न वै सशरीरस्य सतः प्रियाप्रिययोरपहतिरस्ति। अशरीरं वाव सन्तं न प्रियाप्रिये स्पृशतः। अशरीरो वायुरभ्रं विद्युत् स्तनयित्नुः अशरीराण्येतानि तद्यथैतान्यमुष्मादाकाशात्समुत्थाय परं ज्योतिरुपसंपद्य स्वेन स्वेन रूपेणाभिनिष्पद्यन्ते एवमेवैष संप्रसादोऽस्माच्छरीरात्समुत्थाय परं ज्योतिरुपसंपद्य स्वेन रूपेणाभिनिष्पद्यते स उत्तमः पुरुषः।...."

67. *Mbh. Śānti P.,* 231. 14-22.

68. *Mait. Up.,* II. 3-4.
अथ अपहतपाप्मानस्तिग्मतेजसा ऊर्ध्वरेतसो वालखिल्या इति श्रूयन्ते। अथ क्रतुं प्रजापतिमब्रुवन्। भगवन् शकटमिवाचेतनमिदं शरीरं . . . प्रचोदयिता वा अस्य यद् भगवान् वेत्सि तदस्माकं ब्रूहीति। तान् होवाचेति। यो ह खलु वाव शुद्धः . . . . शांतः . . . . शाश्वतोऽजः स्वतंत्रः स्वे महिम्नि तिष्ठति।

69. *Kauṣī. Up.*, IV. 20.
तद्यथा क्षुरः क्षुरधाने हितः, विश्वंभरो वा विश्वंभरकुलाये एवमेवैष प्रज्ञात्मा इदं शरीर मनुप्रविष्ट आलोमभ्यः आ नखेभ्यः। तमेतमात्मानं एत आत्मानोऽन्ववस्यन्ते यथा श्रेष्ठिनं स्वाः। तद्यथा श्रेष्ठी स्वैर्भुङ्क्ते यथा वा स्वाः श्रेष्ठिनं भुंजन्ति, एवमेवैष प्रज्ञात्मा एतैरात्मभिर्भुङ्क्ते एवमेवैत आत्मान एतमात्मानं भुंजान्ति।

70. *Mbh. Bh. P.*, 35. 1
इदं शरीरं कौन्तेय क्षेत्रमित्यभिधीयते।
एतद्यो वेत्ति तं प्राहुः क्षेत्रज्ञ इति तद्विदः॥

71. (*i*) *Ibid.* 35. 1-6.
(*ii*) *Ibid. Sānti P.* 294. 35.
बहुधात्मा प्रकुर्वीत प्रकृतिं प्रसवात्मिकाम्।
तच्च क्षेत्रं महानात्मा पञ्चविंशोऽधितिष्ठति॥

72. Tilak, B.G., *Śrimad Bhagavadgītā Rahasya* or *Karma-Yoga Śāstra,* translated by B.S. Sukthankar, Poona city, 1935, p. 194.

73. Śaṅkarācārya q. by Hill W. Douglas as P, *Gītābhāṣya,* London, 1928, p. 222.

74. Tilak, B.G., *op. cit.*, p. 194.

75. *Mbh. Śānti P.,* 238. 1-2.
प्रकृतेस्तु विकारा ये क्षेत्रज्ञस्तैः परिश्रितः।
ते चैनं न प्रजानन्ति स तु जानाति तानपि॥
तैश्चैष कुरुते कार्यं मनःषष्ठैरिहेन्द्रियैः।
सुदान्तैरिव संयन्ता दृढैः परमवाजिभिः॥

76. *Kaṭh. Up.,* I. 3. 10, 11.
इंद्रियेभ्यः पराह्यर्था अर्थेभ्यश्च परं मनः।
मनसस्तु परा बुद्धिर्बुद्धेरात्मा महान्परः।
महतः परमव्यक्तमव्यक्तात्पुरुषः परः।
पुरुषान्न परं किंचित्सा काष्ठा सा परा गतिः।

77. *Mbh. Sānti P.,* 238. 1-4.
इन्द्रियेभ्यः परा ह्यर्था अर्थेभ्यः परमं मनः।
मनसस्तु परा बुद्धिर्बुद्धेरात्मा महान्परः॥
महतः परमव्यक्तमव्यक्तात्परतो ऽमृतम्।
अमृतान्न परं किंचित्सा काष्ठा सा परा गतिः।

78. *Ibid,* 238. 5.

एवं सर्वेषु भूतेषु गूढोऽऽत्मा न प्रकाशते।
दृश्यते त्वग्र्या बुद्ध्या सूक्ष्मया तत्त्वदर्शिभिः।।

79. *Ibid. Bh.*, 25.42

इन्द्रियाणि पराण्याहुरिन्द्रियेभ्यः परं मनः।
मनसस्तु परा बुद्धिर्यो बुद्धेः परतस्तु सः।।

80. *Ibid. Āśva P.*, 43. 36

पुरुषस्तद्विजानीते तस्मात्क्षेत्रज्ञ उच्यते।
गुणवृत्तं तथा कृत्स्नं क्षेत्रज्ञः परिपश्यति।।

81. (*i*) *Mbh. Śānti P.*, 294. 37 - 38

क्षेत्रं जानाति चाव्यक्तं क्षेत्रज्ञ इति चोच्यते।
अव्यक्तिके पुरे शेते पुरुषश्चेति कथ्यते।
अन्यदेव च क्षेत्रं स्यादन्यः क्षेत्रज्ञ उच्यते।
क्षेत्रमव्यक्तमित्युक्तं ज्ञाता वै पञ्चविंशकः।।

(*ii*) *Ibid.*, 246. 9-10.

(*iii*) *Ibid.* 238. 1-5 *op. cit.*

82. *Ibid. Bh. P.*, 35 . 17[cd]

ज्ञानं ज्ञेयं ज्ञानगम्यं हृदि सर्वस्य विष्ठितम्।।

83. *Ibid.*, 35. 33-34

यथा प्रकाशयत्येकः कृत्स्नं लोकमिमं रविः।
क्षेत्रं क्षेत्री तथा कृत्स्नं प्रकाशयति भारत।।

84. *Ibid.*, *Śānti P.*, 233. 18

देवो यः संश्रितस्तस्मिन्नब्बिन्दुरिव पुष्करे।
क्षेत्रज्ञं तं विजानीयान्नित्यं त्यागजितात्मकम्।।

85. *Ibid.*, *Āśva P.*, 34. 4, 5. 6[ab]

यदिदं ब्रह्मणो लिङ्गं क्षेत्रज्ञमिति संज्ञितम्।
ग्रहीतुं येन तच्छक्यं लक्षणं तस्य तत्त्व नु।।
अलिङ्गो निर्गुणश्चैव कारणं नास्य विद्यते।
उपायमेव वक्ष्यामि येन गृह्येत वा न वा।।
सम्यगप्युपदिष्टश्च भ्रमरैरिव लक्ष्यते।।

86. *Br. Up.*, IV 3. 23

न तु तद्द्वितीयमस्ति ततोऽन्यद्विभक्तं यत्पश्येत्।।

87. *Mānḍ. Up.*, 6-7

नान्तः प्रज्ञं न बहिष्प्रज्ञं नोभयतः प्रज्ञं न प्रज्ञानधनं न प्रज्ञं नाप्रज्ञम्।

अदृष्टमव्यवहार्यमग्राह्यमलक्षणमचिंत्यमव्यपदेश्यमेकात्मप्रत्ययसारं प्रपञ्चोपशमं शांतं शिवं अद्वैतं चतुर्थं मन्यन्ते स आत्मा स विज्ञेयः।।

88. *Mbh. Śānti P.*, 231. 17-23.

89. *Ibid.*, 196. 1-7.

90. *Ch. Up.* VI - 1. 2-7.

91. *Bṛ. Up.* II. 4. 7-9.

92. *Muṇḍ Up.* 1. 1. 3.

93. *Br. Up.* II. 4. 7-9.
आत्मा वा अरे द्रष्टव्यः श्रोतव्यो मन्तव्यो
निदिध्यासितव्यो मैत्रेय्यात्मनो वा अरे दर्शनेन
श्रवणेन मत्या विज्ञानेनेदँ सर्वं विदितम्।।

94. *Muṇḍ. Up.* I. 1.6
यत्तदद्रेश्यमग्राह्यमगोत्रमवर्णमचक्षुःश्रोत्रं तदपाणिपादं।
नित्यं विभुं सर्वगतं सुसूक्ष्मं तदव्ययं यद्भूतयोनिं परिपश्यन्ति धीराः।।

95. *Kaṭh. Up.* I. 2. 2
श्रेयश्च प्रेयश्च मनुष्यमेतस्तौ संपरीत्य विविनक्ति धीरः।

96. *Mbh. Bh. P.* 35. 13
सर्वतःपाणिपादं तत्सर्वतोक्षिशिरोमुखम्।
सर्वतःश्रुतिमल्लोके सर्वमावृत्य तिष्ठति।।

97. *Ibid.*, 35. 31[ab]
अनादित्वान्निर्गुणत्वात्परमात्मायमव्ययः।

98. *Ibid.*, 35. 14
सर्वेन्द्रियगुणाभासं सर्वेन्द्रियविवर्जितम्।
असक्तं सर्वभृच्चैव निर्गुणं गुणभोक्तृ च।।

99. *Ibid.*, *Āśva P.* 20. 12 - 13
घ्राणेन न तदाघ्रेयं न तदाद्यं च जिह्वया।
स्पर्शेन च न तत्स्पृश्यं मनसा त्वेव गम्यते।।
चक्षुषा न विषह्यं च यत्किंचिच्छ्रवणात्परम्।
अगन्धमरसस्पर्शमरूपाशब्दमव्ययम्।।

100. *Śvet. Up.* V. 10
नैष स्त्री न पुमानेष न चैवायं नपुंसकः।
यद्यच्छरीरमादत्ते तेन तेन स रक्ष्यते।।

101. (*i*) *Mbh. Śānti P.* 194.22-24

यतो जगत्सर्वमिदं प्रसूतं ज्ञात्वात्मवन्तो व्यतियान्ति यत्तत्।
यन्मन्त्रशब्दैरकृतप्रकाशं तदुच्यमानं शृणु मे परं यत्।।
रसैर्वियुक्तं विविधैश्च गन्धैरशब्दमस्पर्शमरूपवच्च।
अग्राह्यमव्यक्तमवर्णमेकं पञ्चप्रकारं ससृजे प्रजानाम्।।
न स्त्री पुमान्वापि नपुंसकं च न सन्न चासत्सदसच्च तन्न।
पश्यन्ति यद्ब्रह्मविदो मनुष्यास्तदक्षरं न क्षरतीति विद्धि।।

(*ii*) *Ibid.*, 242. 21-23

आत्मज्ञानमिदं गुह्यं सर्वगुह्यतमं महत्।
अब्रुवं यदहं तात आत्मसाक्षिकमञ्जसा।।
नैव स्त्री न पुमानेतन्नैव चेदं नपुंसकम्।
अदुःखमसुखं ब्रह्म भूतभव्यभवात्मकम्।।
नैतज्ज्ञात्वा पुमान्स्त्री वा पुनर्भवमवाप्नुयात्।

102. *Ibid.*, 194. 23 *op. cit.*

103. *Br. Up.* III. 8.8

स होवाचैतद्वै तदक्षरं गार्गि ब्राह्मणाः अभिवदन्त्यस्थूलम-नण्वह्रस्वमदीर्घ-मलोहितमस्नेहमयमतमो ऽ वाय्यनाकाशम-सङ्गमरसमगन्धमचक्षुष्कमश्रोत्रमवाग-मनो ऽ तेजस्कमप्राणममुख-ममात्रमनन्तरमबाह्यं न तदश्नाति किंचन न तदश्नाति कश्चन।।

104. *Kaṭh. Up.* II. 5. 11

.... एकस्तथा सर्वभूतांतरात्मा न लिप्यते लोकदुःखेन बाह्यः।।

105. *Mbh. Bh. P.* 35. 31 - 32

अनादित्वान्निर्गुणत्वात्परमात्मायमव्ययः।
शरीरस्थोऽपि कौन्तेय न करोति न लिप्यते।।
यथा सर्वगतं सौक्ष्म्यादाकाशं नोपलिप्यते।
सर्वत्रावस्थितो देहे तथात्मा नोपलिप्यते।।

106. *Kaṭh. Up.* II. iii.1

ऊर्ध्वमूलोऽवाक्शाख एषोऽश्वत्थः सनातनः।
तदेव शुक्रं तद्ब्रह्म तदेवामृतमुच्यते।।
तस्मिँल्लोकाः श्रिताः सर्वे तदु नात्येति कश्चन । एतद्वैतत्।।

107. *Mbh. Bh. P.* 37. 1-4.

108. Tilak, B.G., *op. cit.*, Vol. 2, pp. 1135-1138.

109. Ranade, R.D., *op. cit.*, pp. 147-148.

110. *Mbh. Śānti P.* 246. 1-5.

111. *Kaṭh. Up.* I. 2. 18.
न जायते म्रियते वा विपश्चिन्नायं कुतश्चिन्न बभूव कश्चित्।
अजो नित्यः शाश्वतोऽयं पुराणो न हन्यते हन्यमाने शरीरे।।

112. *Ibid.,* I. 2. 19.
हन्ता चेन्मन्यते हन्तुं हतश्चेन्मन्यते हतम्।
उभौ तौ न विजानीतो नायं हन्ति न हन्यते।।

113. *Mbh. Bh. P.* 24. 18.
अन्तवन्त इमे देहा नित्यस्योक्ताः शरीरिणः।
अनाशिनोऽप्रमेयस्य तस्माद्युध्यस्व भारत।।

114. *Ibid.,* 24. 19-20.
य एनं वेत्ति हन्तारं यश्चैनं मन्यते हतम्।
उभौ तौ न विजानीतो नायं हन्ति न हन्यते।।
न जायते म्रियते वा कदाचिन्नायं भूत्वा भविता वा न भूयः।
अजो नित्यः शाश्वतोऽयं पुराणो न हन्यते हन्यमाने शरीरे।।

115. *Ibid., P.,* 24. 23.
नैनं छिन्दन्ति शस्त्राणि नैनं दहति पावकः।
न चैनं क्लेदयन्त्यापो न शोषयति मारुतः।।

116. *Ibid.,* 22.
वासांसि जीर्णानि यथा विहाय नवानि गृह्णाति नरोऽपराणि।
तथा शरीराणि विहाय जीर्णा न्यन्यानि संयाति नवानि देहा।।

117. *Ibid., Śānti P.* 15. 57.
यथा हि पुरुषः शालां पुनः संप्रविशेन्नवाम्।
एवं जीवः शरीराणि तानि तानि प्रपद्यते।।

118. *Mund. Up.* III. 1. 2.
समाने वृक्ष्ये पुरुषो निमग्नोऽनीशया शोचति मुह्यमानः।
जुष्टं यदा पश्यत्यन्यमीशमस्य महिमानमिति वीतशोकः।।

119. *Mbh. Āśva P.* 47. 15-16.
द्रावेतौ पक्षिणौ नित्यौ सखायौ चाप्यचेतनौ।
एताभ्यां तु परो यस्य चेतनावानिति स्मृतः।।
अचेतनः सत्त्वसंघातयुक्तः सत्त्वात्परं चेतयतेऽन्तरात्मा।
स क्षेत्रज्ञः सत्त्वसंघातबुद्धिर्गुणातिगो मुच्यते मृत्युपाशात्।।

120. *Ibid.,* Tilak, B.G. *op. cit.,* p. 215.

121. *Ibid., Bh. P.* 35. 12.

ज्ञेयं यत्तत्प्रवक्ष्यामि यज्ज्ञात्वामृतमश्नुते।
अनादिमत्परं ब्रह्म न सत्तन्नासदुच्यते।।

122. *Ibid.*, 35.22-23.
उपद्रष्टानुमन्ता च भर्ता भोक्ता महेश्वरः।
परमात्मेति चाप्युक्तो देहेऽस्मिन्पुरुषः परः।।
य एवं वेत्ति पुरुषं प्रकृतिं च गुणैः सह।
सर्वथा वर्तमानोऽपि न स भूयोऽभिजायते।।

123. *Mbh. Bh. P.* 24. 16.
नासतो विद्यते भावो नाभावो विद्यते सतः।
उभयोरपि दृष्टोऽन्तस्त्वनयोस्तत्त्वदर्शिभिः।।

124. *Śrīmadbhagavadgītā-Śāṅkarabhāṣyādisaptaṭīkopetā*, ed. by Vitthal Dhundiraj, Mumbai, 1908. p. 62.
इतश्च शोकमोहावकृत्वा शीतोष्णादिसहनं युक्तं यस्मात्-नासत इति। नासतोऽविद्यमानस्य शीतोष्णादेः सकारणस्य न विद्यते नास्ति भावो भवनमस्तिता।.......... यद्विषयाबुद्धिर्न. व्यभिचरति तत्सत्।।

125. *Mbh. Bh. P.* 24. 17, 24.
अविनाशि तु तद्विद्धि येन सर्वमिदं तमम्।
विनाशमव्ययस्यास्य न कश्चित्कर्तुमर्हति।
अच्छेद्योऽयमदाह्योऽयमक्लेद्योऽशोष्य एव च।
नित्यः सर्वगतः स्थाणुरचलोऽयं सनातनः।।

126. *Mbh. Bh. P.* 24. 19.
य एनं वेत्ति हन्तारं यश्चैनं मन्यते हतम्।
उभौ तौ न विजानीतो नायं हन्ति न हन्यते।।

127. *Ibid.*, 24. 20. *op. cit.*

128. Śaṅakara q. by Hill H. W. P. *op. cit.*, p. 116.

129. *Kaṭh. Up.* I. 3. 1.
ऋतं पिबन्तौ सुकृतस्य लोके गुहां प्रविष्टौ परमे परार्धे।।

130. *Muṇḍ. Up.* III. 1.1.
द्वा सुपर्णा सयुजा सखाया समानं वृक्षं परिषस्वजाते।
तयोरन्यः पिप्पलं स्वाद्वत्त्यनश्नन्नन्यो अभिचाकशीति।।

131. *Śvet. Up.* IV. 5.
अजामेकां लोहितशुक्लकृष्णां बह्वीः प्रजाः सृजमानां सरूपाः।
अजो ह्येको जुषमाणोऽनुशेते जहात्येनां भुक्तभोगामजोऽन्यः।।

132. *Muṇḍ. Up.* III. 1. 2.
समाने वृक्षे पुरुषो निमग्नोऽनीशया शोचति मुह्यमानः।
जुष्टं यदा पश्यति अन्यमीशमस्य महिमानमिति वीतशोकः।।

133. *Mbh. Āśva P,* 47. 12-16.

134. *Mbh. Bh. P.* 37. 9-11.
श्रोत्रं चक्षुः स्पर्शनं च रसनं घ्राणमेव च।
अधिष्ठाय मनश्चायं विषयानुपसेवते।।
उत्क्रामन्तं स्थितं वापि भुञ्जानं वा गुणान्वितम्।
विमूढा नानुपश्यन्ति पश्यन्ति ज्ञानचक्षुषा।।
यतन्तो योगिनश्चैनं पश्यन्त्यात्मन्यवस्थितम्।
यतन्तोऽप्यकृतात्मानो नैनं पश्यन्त्यचेतसः।।

135. *Ibid.,* 37. 15-16-17[ab]
सर्वस्य चाहं हृदि संनिविष्टो मत्तः स्मृतिर्ज्ञानमपोहनं च।
वेदैश्च सर्वैरहमेव वेद्यो वेदान्तकृद्वेदविदेव चाहम्।।
द्वाविमौ पुरुषौ लोके क्षरश्चाक्षर एव च।
क्षरः सर्वाणि भूतानि कूटस्थोऽक्षर उच्यते।।

136. *Ibid., Ārān. P,* 178. 16-20.

137. *Ibid., Śānti P.* 233. 18, 20.
देवो यः संश्रितस्तस्मिन्नब्बिन्दुरिव पुष्करे।
क्षेत्रज्ञं तं विजानीयान्नित्यं त्यागजितात्मकम्।।
सचेतनं जीवगुणं वदन्ति स चेष्टते चेष्टयते च सर्वम्।
ततः परं क्षेत्रविदो वदन्ति प्रावर्तयद्यो भुवनानि सप्त।।

138. *Ch. Up.* VII. 1.2-3.
स होवाच ऋग्वेदं भगवोऽध्येमि यजुर्वेदं राशिं दैवं निधिं वाकोवाक्यमेकायनं देवविद्यां ब्रह्मविद्यां भूतविद्यां नक्षत्रविद्या ँ सर्पदेवजनविद्यामेतद्भगवोऽध्येमि सोऽहं भगवो मंत्रविदेवास्मि नात्मविछद्दतं ह्येव मे भगवद्दृशेभ्यस्तरति शोकमात्मविदिति सोऽहं भगवः शोचामि तं मा भगवान् शोकस्य पारं तारयत्विति।।

139. *Kaṭh. Up.* II. 4 . 2. also Deussen P. *op. cit.,* p. 74, 77.
अथ धीरा अमृतत्वं विदित्वा ध्रुवं अध्रुवेष्विह न प्रार्थयन्ते।

140. *Ibid.,* I. 2. 4-5.
दूरमेते विपरीते विषूची अविद्या या च विद्येति ज्ञाता।
अविद्यायामन्तरे वर्तमानाः स्वयं धीराः पंडितं मन्यमानाः
दंद्रम्यमाणाः परियन्ति मूढा अन्धेनैव नीयमानाः यथांधाः।

141. *Mbh. Śānti P.* 295. 2.
अविद्यामाहुरव्यक्तं सर्गप्रलयधर्मि वै।
सर्गप्रलयनिर्मुक्तं विद्यां वै पञ्चविंशकम्।

142. *Ibid.*, 212. 14.
इमं गुणसमाहारमात्मभावेन पश्यतः।
असम्यग्दर्शनैर्दुःखमनन्तं नोपशाम्यति।।

143. *Ch. Up.* VIII. 3. 1-3.
त इमे सत्या .... अनृतमपिधानम्। यो ....। .....तद्यथा हि हिरण्यनिधिं निहितं अक्षेत्रज्ञा उपर्युपरि संचरन्तो न विन्देयुः एवमेव इमाः सर्वाः प्रजाः अहरहर्गच्छन्त्यः एतं ब्रह्मलोकं न विन्दन्ति अनृतेन हि प्रत्यूढाः। स वा एष आत्मा हृदि ....।

144. *Mbh. Bh. P.* 37. 7 [ab], 15 [a], 16[d], 18.
ममैवांशो जीवलोके जीवभूतः सनातनः।
सर्वस्य चाहं हृदि संनिविष्टो .... ।
.... कूटस्थोऽक्षर उच्यते।।
यस्मात्क्षरमतीतोऽहमक्षरादपि चोत्तमः।
अतोऽस्मि लोके वेदे च प्रथितः पुरुषोत्तमः।।

145. *Ch. Up.* VIII. 12.
आत्तो वै सशरीरः प्रियाप्रियाभ्यां न वै सशरीरस्य सतः प्रियाप्रियोरपहतिरस्ति। अशरीरं वाव सन्तं न प्रियाप्रिये स्पृशतः। .... परं ज्योतिरुपसंपद्य स्वेन रूपेणाभिनिष्पद्यते स उत्तमः पुरुषः।

146. *Mbh. Śānti P.* 295. 14.

147. *Ibid.*, 295. 22.
यदा तु गुणजालं तत्प्राकृतं विजुगुप्सते।
पश्यते चापरं पश्यं तदा पश्यन्न संज्वरेत्।।

148. Ranade, R.D. *op. cit.*, p. 198.

149. *Mbh. Śānti P.* 295. 27[cd], 28, 38[cd], 39[ab]
साम्यमेकत्वमायातो यादृशस्तादृशस्त्वहम्।।
तुल्यतामिह पश्यामि सदृशोऽहमनेन वै।
अयं हि विमलो व्यक्तमहमीदृशकस्तथा।।
...एवं परमसंबोधात्पञ्चविंशोऽनुबुद्धवान्।।
अक्षरत्वं नियच्छेत त्यक्त्वा क्षरमनामयम।

150. *Tait. Up.* II. 4.
यतो वाचो निवर्तन्ते अप्राप्य मनसा सह।

151. *Mbh. Śānti P.* 306. 53.
यदा तु पश्यतेऽत्यन्तमहन्यहनि काश्यप।
तदा स केवलीभूतः षड्विंशमनुपश्यति॥

152. *Ibid.,* 54, 55.
अन्यश्च शश्वदव्यक्तस्तथान्यः पञ्चविंशकः।
तस्य द्वावनुपश्येत तमेकमिति साधवः।
तेनैतन्नाभिजानन्ति पञ्चविंशकमच्युतम्।
जन्ममृत्युभयाद्योगाः सांख्याश्च परमैषिणः॥

153. *Br. Up.* II. 4. 13-14.
यत्र हि द्वैतमिव भवति तदितर इतरं जिघ्रति....... तत्केन कं जिघ्रेत तत्केन कं पश्येत् .... येनेदं सर्वं विजानाति तं केन विजानीयात्। विज्ञातारमरे केन विजानीयादिति॥

154. *Ibid.,* I. 6. 3.
अमृतं सत्येन छन्नम्।

155. *Ibid.,* II. 1.20.
सत्यस्य सत्यम्।

156. Ranade, R.D., *op. cit.,* p. 165.

157. Hiriyanna M., *Outlines of Indian Philosophy,* Delhi, 1994, p. 62.

158. *Br. Up.* II. 5. 19.
रूपं रूपं प्रतिरूपो बभूव तदस्य रूपं प्रतिचक्षणाय।
इंद्रो मायाभिः पुरुरूप ईयते युक्ता ह्यस्य हरयः शतादश॥
also *Ṛv.* VI. 47. 18.

159. *Śvet. Up.* IV. 9
अस्मान्मायी सृजते विश्वमेतत्। तस्मिंश्चान्यो मायया संन्निरुद्धः।

160. *Kath. Up.* I. 2. 5, II. 1.2[cd].
अविद्यायामन्तरे वर्तमानाः स्वयं धीराः पंडितं मन्यमानाः।
दंद्रम्यमाणाः परियन्ति मूढा अन्धेनैव नीयमाना यथांधाः॥
अथ धीराः अमृतत्त्वं विदित्वा ध्रुवं अध्रुवेष्विह न प्रार्थयन्ते।

161. *Ch. Up.* I. 1. 10.
नाना तु विद्या अविद्या च।

162. *Praś. Up.* I . 16.
तेषां असौ विरजो ब्रह्मलोको न येषु जिह्मं अनृतं न माया चेति।

163. *Mbh. Bh. P.* 29. 25
नाहं प्रकाशः सर्वस्य योगमायासमावृतः।
मूढोऽयं नाभिजानाति लोको मामजमव्ययम्॥

164. *Ibid.*, 36. 3[a].
मम योनिर्महद्ब्रह्म।

165. Jñāneśvara, *Jñāneśvarī* (*Marathi*) 14. 68. 70.

166. Tilak, B.G., *Gītārahasya* (*Marathi*), Pune, 1998, p. 220.

167. *Śvet. Up.* IV. 10.
मायां तु प्रकृतिं विद्यात्....।

168. *Mbh. Bh. P.* 29. 14[ab].
दैवी ह्येषा गुणमयी मम माया दुरत्यया।

169. *Ibid.*, 25 *op. cit.*

170. *Ibid.*, *Śānti. P.* 206. 2-3.
विष्णुमव्यक्तसंस्थानं विशन्ते देवसत्तमम्।
तस्य मायाविदग्धाङ्गा ज्ञानभ्रष्टा निराशिषः।
मानवा ज्ञानसंमोहात्ततः कामं प्रयान्ति वै॥

171. *Ibid.*, *Bh. P.* 40. 61.
ईश्वरः सर्वभूतानां हृद्देशेऽर्जुन तिष्ठति।
भ्रामयन्सर्वभूतानि यन्त्रारूढानि मायया॥

172. *Ibid.*, *P.* 25. 14-15[a].
अन्नाद्भवन्ति भूतानि पर्जन्यादन्नसंभवः।
यज्ञाद्भवति पर्जन्यो यज्ञः कर्मसमुद्भवः॥
कर्म ब्रह्मोद्भवं विद्धि...... ।

173. Tilak, B.G., *Gītārahasya (Marathi)*, pp. 222, 223.

174. *Mbh. Bh. P.* 36. 4.
सर्वयोनिषु कौन्तेय मूर्तयः संभवन्ति याः।
तासां ब्रह्म महद्योनिरहं बीजप्रदः पिता॥

175. *Ibid.*, 26.6[cd].
प्रकृतिं स्वामधिष्ठाय संभवाम्यात्ममायया॥

176. *Ibid.*, *Śānti P.*, 295. 2, *op. cit.*

177. *Ibid.*, *Bh. P.* 37.16[d].
..... कूटस्थो ऽ क्षर उच्चते॥

178. *Ibid., Śānti P.* 238. 5.
एवं सर्वेषु भूतेषु गूढाऽत्मा न प्रकाशते।

179. *Ibid.,* 4[ab].
महतः परमव्यक्तमव्यक्तात्परतोऽमृतम्।।

180. *Ibid.,* 196. 4.
न चक्षुषा पश्यति रूपमात्मनो न पश्यति स्पर्शनमिन्द्रियेन्द्रियम्।
न श्रोत्रलिङ्गं श्रवणे निदर्शनं तथागतं पश्यति तद्विनश्यति।।

181. *Ibid., Bh P.* 37.10[cd].
विमूढा नानुपश्यन्ति पश्यन्ति ज्ञानचक्षुषः।

182. *Ibid.,* 36.2.
इदं ज्ञानमुपाश्रित्य मम साधर्म्यमागताः।
सर्गेऽपि नोपजायन्ते प्रलये न व्यथन्ति च।।

183. *Īśa Up.* 11.
विद्यां चाविद्यां च यस्तद्वेदोभयं सह।
अविद्यया मृत्युं तीर्त्वा विद्ययाऽमृतमश्नुते।।

184. *Tait. Up.* II. 1.
यो वेद निहितं गुहायां परमे व्योमन्।।

185. Śaṅkara. q. by Lokeswarananda - *Taittirīya Up.* translated and with notes based on Śaṅkara's commentary, Culcutta, 1996, p. 64.

186. *Ibid.,* 64-65.

187. *Mbh. Śānti P.* 180. 27-29.
एवं सर्वेषु भूतेषु गूढश्चरति संवृतः।
दृश्यते त्वग्र्यया बुद्ध्या सूक्ष्मया तत्त्वदर्शिभिः।।
तं पूर्वापररात्रेषु युञ्जानः सततं बुधः।
लघ्वाहारो विशुद्धात्मा पश्यत्यात्मानमात्मनि।।
चित्तस्य हि प्रसादेन हित्वा कर्म शुभाशुभम्।
प्रसन्नात्मात्मनि स्थित्वा सुखमक्षयमश्नुते।।

188. *Ibid., Bh. P.* 37. 15[a], 19[abc].
सर्वस्य चाहं हृदि संनिविष्टो।
यो मामेवमसंमूढो जानाति पुरुषोत्तमम्।
सर्वविद्भवति ....।

189. *Tait. Up.* II. 2-5.

तस्माद्वा एतस्माद्न्नरसमयात्। अन्योऽन्तर आत्मा प्राणमयः। तेनैष पूर्णः। स वा एष पुरुषविध एवा ......। ...... एतस्मात् प्राणमयात् अन्योऽन्तर आत्मा मनोमयः। .....। ..... पुरुषविध एव। ......। ..... अन्योऽन्तर आत्मा विज्ञानमयः। ...... तेनैष पूर्णः। स वा एष पुरुषविध एव। .....। ..... विज्ञानमयात्। अन्योऽन्तर आत्माऽऽनन्दमयः। तेनैष पूर्णः। स वा एष पुरुषविध एव।

190. Deussen P. *op. cit.*, p. 97.

191. Dixit, S.H., *op. cit.*, pp. 319-320.

192. Śaṅkara, q. by Ranade, R.D., *op. cit.*, p. 103.

193. Lokeswarananda, *op. cit.*, p. 5.

194. *Mbh. Bh. P.* 29. 2.
ज्ञानं तेऽहं सविज्ञानमिदं वक्ष्याम्यशेषतः।
यज्ज्ञात्वा नेह भूयोऽन्यज्ज्ञातव्यमवशिष्यते॥

195. *Ibid.*, 29-4-5.
भूमिरापोऽनलो वायुः खं मनो बुद्धिरेव च।
अहंकार इतीयं मे भिन्ना प्रकृतिरष्टधा॥
अपरेयमितस्त्वन्यां प्रकृतिं विद्धि मे पराम्।
जीवभूतां महाबाहो ययेदं धार्यते जगत्॥

196. Hiriyanna M. *op. cit.*, p. 67.

197. *Ibid.*, *op. cit.*, p. 67.

198. *Tait Up.* II. 5.1.
ब्रह्म पुच्छं प्रतिष्ठा।

also Hiriyanna M., *op. cit.*, p. 67.

199. Tilak, B.G., *op. cit. (Marathi)*, pp. 277-78.

200. Satavalekar, S.D. *Śrīmadbhagavadgītā Puruṣārthabodhinī Tīkā*. pp. 101-102.

201. *Mbh. Bh. P.* 24-22[cd].
तथा शरीराणि विहाय जीर्णान्यन्यानि संयाति नवानि देही॥

202. *Ibid.*, 25.42.
इन्द्रियाणि पराण्याहुरिन्द्रियेभ्यः परं मनः।
मनसस्तु परा बुद्धिर्यो बुद्धेः परतस्तु सः॥

203. *Ibid.*, *Śānti P.* 238. 3-4.
इन्द्रियेभ्यः परा ह्यर्था अर्थेभ्यः परमं मनः।
मनसस्तु परा बुद्धिर्बुद्धेरात्मा महान्परः॥

महतः परमव्यक्तमव्यक्तात्परतोऽमृतम्।
अमृतान्न परं किंचित्सा काष्ठा सा परा गतिः।।

204. *Ibid.*, 5.

एवं सर्वेषु भूतेषु गूढाऽऽत्मा न प्रकाशते।
दृश्यते त्वग्र्यया बुद्धया सूक्ष्मया तत्त्वदर्शिभिः।

205. *Ibid.*, 6-7.

अन्तरात्मनि संलीय मनःषष्ठानि मेधया।
इन्द्रियाणीन्द्रियार्थांश्च बहु चिन्त्यमचिन्तयम्।।
ध्यानोपरमणं कृत्वा विद्यासंपादितं मनः।
अनीश्वरः प्रशान्तात्मा ततोऽर्छत्यमृतं पदम्।।

206. *Ibid., Bh. P.,* 26. 6.

अजोऽपि सन्नव्ययात्मा भूतानामीश्वरोऽपि सन्।
प्रकृतिं स्वामधिष्ठाय संभवाम्यात्ममायया।।

207. Blondel Mourice, q. by Krisna Chaitanya, *The Mahabharata–A Literary Study*, New Delhi, 1955, p. 244.

208. *Gaud. K.* IV. 98.

अलब्धावरणाः सर्वे धर्माः प्रकृतिनिर्मलाः।
आदौ बुद्धास्तथा मुक्ता बुध्यन्त इति नायकाः।।

209. *Ch. Up.* VI. 8. 7.

स य एषोऽणिमा ऐतदात्म्यमिदं सर्वं तत्सत्यं स आत्मा तत्त्वमसि श्वेतकेतो।

210. *Br. Up.* I. 4. 2.

सोऽबिभेत् तस्मादेकाकी बिभेति हायमीक्षांचक्रे यन्मदन्यन्नास्ति तस्मान्नु बिभेमीति तत एवास्य भयं वीवाय द्वितीयाद्वै भयं भवति।

211. *Ibid.*, I. 4. 8.

..... स योऽन्यमात्मनः प्रियं ब्रुवाणं ब्रूयात् प्रियं
रोत्स्यतीतीश्वरो ह तथैव स्यादात्मानमेव प्रियमुपासीत
स य आत्मानमेव प्रियमुपास्ते न हास्य प्रियं प्रमायुकं भवति।

212. *Ibid.*, IV. 4. 6-7.

अथाकामयमानो योऽकामो निष्काम आप्तकाम आत्मकामो न तस्य प्राणा उत्क्रामंति ब्रह्मैव सन् ब्रह्माप्येति। तदेष श्लोको भवति। यदा सर्वे प्रमुच्यंते कामा येऽस्य हृदि श्रिताः। अथ मर्त्योऽमृतो भवत्यत्र ब्रह्म समश्नुत इति।

213. *Br. Up.* II. 4. 2-5.

214. *Ibid.*, IV. 2.

215. *Br. Up.* IV. 2. 4.

216. *Kaṭh. Up.* I. 2. 2.
श्रेयश्च प्रेयश्च मनुष्यमेतस्तौ संपरीत्य विविनक्ति धीरः।
श्रेयो हि धीरोऽभिप्रेयसो वृणीते प्रेयो मन्दो योगक्षेमाद् वृणीते।

217. *Īśa.Up.* 15.
हिरण्मयेन पात्रेण सत्यस्यापिहितं मुखम्।
तत्त्वं पूषन्नपावृणु सत्यधर्माय दृष्टये।।

218. *Muṇḍ. Up.* III. 2. 8.
यथा नद्यः स्यन्दमानाः समुद्रेऽस्तं गच्छन्ति नामरूपे विहाय।
तथा विद्वान्नामरूपाद्विमुक्तः परात्परं पुरुषमुपैति दिव्यम्।।

219. *Mbh. Śānti P.* 205. 1-5.

220. *Ibid.,* 194. 10-13.

221. *Ibid.,* 21. 2-5.

222. *Ibid., Bh. P.,* 37. 5-6[cd].
निर्मानमोहा जितसङ्गदोषा अध्यात्मनित्या विनिवृत्तकामाः।
द्वंद्वैर्विमुक्ताः सुखदुःखसंज्ञैर्गच्छन्त्यमूढाः पदमव्ययं तत्।।
यद्गत्वा न निवर्तन्ते तद्धाम परमं मम।।

223. *Ibid.,* 40. 55[ac], 56[cd].
भक्त्या मामभिजानाति........।
ततो मां तत्त्वतो ज्ञात्वा..........।।
मत्प्रसादादवाप्नोति शाश्वतं पदमव्ययम्।।

224. *Ibid.,* 37. 4[b].
यस्मिन्गता न निवर्तन्ति भूयः।

225. *Ibid.,* 37. 6[ab].
यद्गत्वा न निवर्तन्ते तद्धाम परमं मम।।

226. *Ibid.,* 55[d].
...... विशते तदनन्तरम्।।

227. *Ibid., Śānti P.* 197. 6-8
तर्षच्छेदो न भवति पुरूषस्येह कल्मषात्।
निवर्तते तथा तर्षः पापमन्तं गतं यथा।।
विषयेषु च संसर्गाच्छाश्वतस्य नसंश्रयात्।
मनसा चान्यदाकाङ्क्षन्परं न प्रतिपद्यते।।

ज्ञानमुत्पद्यते पुंसां क्षयात्पापस्य कर्मणः।
अथादर्शतलप्रख्ये पश्यत्यात्मानमात्मनि।।

228. *Ibid.*, 262.37-38[ab].

आनृशंस्यं क्षमा शान्तिरहिंसा सत्यमार्जवम्।
अद्रोहो नाभिमानश्च ह्रिस्तितिक्षा शमस्तथा।।
पन्थानो ब्रह्मणस्त्वेते एतैः प्राप्नोति यतपरम्।।

229. *Gauḍ. K.* 1. 16.

अनादिमायया सुप्तो यदा जीवः प्रबुध्यते।।
अजमनिद्रमस्वप्नमद्वैतं बुध्यते तदा।।

230. *Muṇḍ. Up.* II. 2. 11.

ब्रह्मैवेदममृतं पुरस्ताद् ब्रह्म पश्चाद् ब्रह्म दक्षिणतश्चोत्तरेण।
अधश्चोर्ध्वं प्रसृतं ब्रह्मैवेदं विश्वमिदं वरिष्ठम्।

231. *Muṇḍ. Up.* II. 2. 8.

भिद्यते हृदयग्रंथिश्छिद्यंते सर्वसंशयाः।
क्षीयंते चास्य कर्माणि तस्मिन्दृष्टे परावरे।।

232. *Br. Up.* IV. 4. 12.

आत्मानं नेद्विजानीयादयमस्मीति पूरुषः।
किमिच्छन् कस्य कामाय शरीरमनुसंज्वरेत्।।

233. *Muṇḍ. Up.* II. 2. 8. *op. cit.*

234. *Mbh. Śānti P.* 308. 31-39, 50-53.

235. *Ibid.*, 308. 177 [cd].

नान्यदन्यदिति ज्ञात्वा नान्यदन्यत्प्रवर्तते।।

236. *Ibid.*, 17. 19-23.

237. *Ibid.*, 242. 21-23.

238. *Ibid.*, *Bh. P.* 35. 27-28.

समं सर्वेषु भूतेषु तिष्ठन्तं परमेश्वरम्।
विनश्यत्स्वविनश्यन्तं यः पश्यति स पश्यति।।
समं पश्यन्हि सर्वत्र समवस्थितमीश्वरम्।
न हिनस्त्यात्मनात्मानं ततो याति परां गतिम्।।

239. *Ibid.*, *Ādi. P,* 86. 14 , 16, 17.

यस्तु कामान्परित्यज्य त्यक्तकर्मा जितेन्द्रियः।
आतिष्ठेत मुनिर्मौनं स लोके सिद्धिमाप्नुयात्।।

तपसा कर्शितः क्षामः क्षीणमांसास्थिशोणितः।
यदा भवति निर्द्वन्द्वो मुनिर्मौनं समास्थितः।
अथ लोकमिमं जित्वा लोकं विजयते परम्॥

आस्येन्न तु यदाहारं गोवन्मृगयते मुनिः।
अथास्य लोकः पूर्वो यः सोऽमृतत्वाय कल्पते॥

240. *Mbh. Śānti P.* 231. 18-22.

241. *Ibid., Bh. P.* 30. 10, 11, 16[ab].

प्रयाणकाले मनसाचलेन भक्त्या मुक्तो योगबलेन चैव।
भ्रुवोर्मध्ये प्राणमावेश्य सम्यक्स तं परं पुरुषमुपैति दिव्यम्॥

यदक्षरं वेदविदो वदन्ति विशन्ति यद्यतयो वीतरागाः।
यदिच्छन्तो ब्रह्मचर्यं चरन्ति तत्ते पदं संग्रहेण प्रवक्ष्ये॥
आ ब्रह्मभुवनाल्लोकाः पुनरावर्तिनोऽर्जुन।

242. *Ibid., Śānti P.* 19. 11.

तपःस्वाध्यायशीला हि दृश्यन्ते धार्मिका जनाः।
ऋषयस्तपसा युक्ता येषां लोकाः सनातनाः॥

243. *Br. Up.* II. 5-15.

स वा अयमात्मा सर्वेषां भूतानां राजा, तद्यथा रथनाभौ
च रथनेमौ च अराः सर्वे समर्पिताः
एवमेवास्मिन्नात्मनि सर्वाणि भूतानि सर्वे देवाः
सर्वे लोकाः सर्व एत आत्मानः समर्पिताः॥

244. *..ṭh. Up.* I. 3. 4-6.

इन्द्रियाणि हयानाहुर्विषयांस्तेषु गोचरन्।
आत्मेन्द्रियमनोयुक्तं भोक्तेत्याहुर्मनीषिणः॥

यस्त्वविज्ञानवान्भवत्ययुक्तेन मनसा सदा।
तस्येन्द्रियाण्यवश्यानि दुष्टाश्वा इव सारथेः॥
यस्तु विज्ञानवान्भवति युक्तेन मनसा सदा॥
तस्येन्द्रियाणि वश्यानि सदश्वा इव सारथेः॥

245. *Mbh. Āraṇ P.* 202. 21-25

246. *Ibid., Strī P.* 7. 13-15.

247. *Ibid., Āśva. P.* 50. 1-10.

248. Tilak, B.G., *op. cit.*, p. 190.

249. *Mbh. Śānti P.* 231. 9-13.

250. *Ibid., Bh. P.*, 25. 7.

यस्त्विन्द्रियाणि मनसा नियम्यारभतेऽर्जुन।
कर्मेन्द्रियैः कर्मयोगसक्तः स विशिष्यते॥

251. (*i*) *Ibid.,* 24. 67-68.

इन्द्रियाणां हि चरतां यन्मनोऽनुविधीयते
तदस्य हरति प्रज्ञां वायुर्नावमिवाम्भसि॥

तस्माद्यस्य महाबाहो निगृहीतानि सर्वशः।
इन्द्रियाणीन्द्रियार्थेभ्यस्तस्य प्रज्ञा प्रतिष्ठिता॥

(*ii*) *Ibid.,* 28. 24-26.

संकल्पप्रभवान्कामांस्त्यक्त्वा सर्वानशेषतः।
मनसैवन्द्रियग्रामं विनियम्य समन्ततः॥

शनैः शनैरूपरमेद्बुद्ध्या धृतिगृहीतया
आत्मसंस्थं मनः कृत्वा न किंचिदपि चिन्तयेत्।
यतो यतो निश्चरति मनश्चञ्चलमस्थिरम्।
ततस्ततो नियम्यैतदात्मन्येव वशं नयेत्॥

252. Tilak, B.G., *op. cit.,* p. 191.

253. *Mbh. Bh. P.* 25. 37-43.

254. Rāmānuja, q. Hill W.D.P., *op. cit.,* p. 135, Note 3.

255. *Kaṭh. Up.* I. 3. 10-10. *op. cit.*

256. Sukthankar, V.S., *op. cit.,* p. 112.

257. *Mbh. Bh. P.* 25. 36.

अथ केन प्रयुक्तोऽयं पापं चरति पूरुषः।
अनिच्छन्नपि वार्ष्णेय बलादिव नियोजितः॥

258. Sukthankar, V.S., *op. cit.,* p. 112.

CHAPTER III

SĀMKHYA PHILOSOPHY IN THE MAHĀBHĀRATA

Having discussed the nature of the elements of the Vedānta philosophy in the *Mbh.*, it will now be proper to have an in-depth study of the principles of Sāṁkhya philosophy in the same.

Chronology of the Treatises on Sāṁkhya Philosophy

The Sāṁkhya system is one of the major philosophical systems of India. According to Radhakrishnan, S. and Moore, C.A., tradition has ascribed the authorship of the Sāṁkhya system to Kapila, a legendary figure and 7th century B.C. has been assigned as his period. However, there is no evidence to show that the *Sāṁkhya Pravacana Sūtra,* which was attributed to him, was written by him. They further opine that Sāmakhyakārikā of Īśvarakṛṣṇa, the work of 3rd century A.D., is the earliest available text on the Sāṁkhya philosophy.[1] According to them, *Sāṁkhya Pravacana Sūtra*-s date back to 14 A.D. and Vṛtti of Aniruddha to 15 A.D. Tilak, B.G. considers period of Īśvarakṛṣṇa as 240 A.D.[2] Macdonell, A.A. assigns the middle of the 6th B.C. as the period of Kapila and confirms that no work of his, if ever committed to writing, has been preserved.[3] Sutton Nicholas has also opined that the extant Sāṁkhya Śāstra is the *Sāṁkhya Kārikā* attributed to Īśvarakṛṣṇa, probably composed in the 5th century A.D.[4]

Marathi Vishvakosha states that no work of Kapila, the philosopher (*darśanakāra*), is available. It is believed that *Sāṁkhya sūtra*-s, consisting of six chapters and *Tattvasamāsa*, containing twenty three *sūtra*-s, are the books of Kapila. However, they have been composed after *Sāṁkhya Kārikā* was composed. Also, the works, *viz. Kapilagītā, Kapilapañcarātra, Kapilasmṛti* etc. are ascribed to him but it is doubtful whether those are his works.[5]

Bhāratīya Saṁskṛti Kośa states that Kapila was probably born a century before Buddha's birth (600 B.C.). *Sāṁkhyasūtra*-s, *Tattvasamāsa, Vyāsaprabhākara, Kapilagītā* (regarding Vedānta) *Kapilapañcatantra, Kapilasaṁhitā, Kapilastotra* and *Kapilasmṛti* are supposed to be the works of Kapila.[6]

The details of other Sāṁkhya philosophers are also given

(*i*) **Āsurī :** His name appears in the Śatapatha Brāhmaṇa.[7]

(*ii*) **Pañcaśikha :** He obtained Kapila's *ṣaṣṭhītantra* from Āsurī and tought them to his disciples Janaka, Vasiṣṭha etc. However, no work of his is available.[8]

(*iii*) **Vindhyavāsa (3rd to 4th A.D.)** had written a treatise entitled *Hiraṇyasaptati* on the Sāṁkhya philosophy. However, this work is also not available. It is observed that some scholars believe that Vindhyavāsa is none other than Īśvarakṛṣṇa. But there is no reliable proof in support of it.[9]

(*iv*) **Vasubandhu (4th A.D.) :** He wrote *Paramārthasaptati* refuting the *Hiraṇyasaptatī* of Vindhyavāsa, the same is not extant.[10]

(*v*) **Vijñānabhikṣu (16th A.D.) :** *Sāṁkhyapravacana, Yogavārtika, Vijñānāmṛtabhāṣya, Sāṁkhyasāra, Yogasāra* are ascribed to him.[11]

(*vi*) **Īśvarakṛṣṇa :** Generally his period is considered as the 4th century A.D. However, Upadhyaya, Baldeo opines that it might be earlier than this. His *Sāṁkhya-Kārikā* was translated in Chinese in the 6th century A.D. It is called *Hiraṇyasaptati* or *Suvarṇasaptati* in Chinese language.[12]

Marathi Viśvakośa states that Dr. Takakusu has considered Īśvarakṛṣṇa's period as 450 A.D., Keith, A.B. considers it as the 4th Century; Upadhyay, Baldeo states that it is not before the first century. Some other scholars treat him as the contemporary of Vasubandhu. His *Kārikā*-s have been considered as the earliest and popular Sāṁkhya work.[13]

The Encyclopedia of Indian Philosophies gives the details of various treatises on Sāṁkhya philosophy and of the authors. Their tentative chronology is as follows :

1. "*Ṣaṣṭhītantra* – a tradition of sixty topics" that was either a format for the treatment of philosophy of Sāṁkhya or the actual name of a text, an old form of which was attributed to Kapila or Pañcaśikha (100 B.C. – 200 C.E.).[14]
2. Paurika, Pañcādhikaraṇa, Patañjali and other early philosophical *ācāryas* – 100-300 C.E.[15]
3. Vārṣagaṇya – composed a revision of *ṣaṣṭhītantra* – C.A. 100-300 C.E.[16]
4. The followers of Vārṣagaṇya including :
   - (*a*) Vindhyavāsin, C. 300-400 – who further revised the Sāṁkhya system and carried on a vigorous polemic with Buddhist.
   - (*b*) Īśvarakṛṣṇa, c. 350-450 – Composed a definitive summary of the Sāṁkhya position, the *Sāṁkhyakārikā* based on Vārṣagaṇya's *ṣaṣṭhītantra* but corrected as a result of the Buddhist debates and the works of Vindhyavāsin.[17]
5. Mādhava – "the destroyer of Sāṁkhya" who goes even further in adjusting the views of Sāṁkhya to Vaiśeṣika and Buddhist thought. C.A. 450-500.[18]
6. PataZjali's *Yogasūtra*-s and Vyāsa's *Yogasūtrabhāṣya*, which possibly preserve the older interpretation of Vārṣagaṇya, Vindhyavāsin regarding Sāmakhya in the format of Pātañjala - Sāmakhya C.A. 500-700.[19]

According to Sutton Nicholas, *Yoga-sūtra*-s of Patañjali attained its final form in the 3rd century A.D.[20]

Īśvarakṛṣṇa's *Sāmakhyakārikā* marks the beginning of technical philosophy of Sāmakhya system. Upto this time, there has been no available Sāmakhya textual tradition and the historical account has been based on the reconstruction and occasional references in the ancient literature.[21]

The Encyclopedia has assigned 100-200 C.E. as the period of Caraka, the propounder of *Carakasamahita* (*Āyurveda*).[22] *Bhāratīya Viśvakośa* treats the period of presently available *Carakasamahitā* modified by Dṛḍhabala Pāñcanada as prior to the 6th century A.D.[23]

Dasgupta S.N. considers the period of the Sāmakhyakārikā of Īśvarakṛṣṇa as about 200 A.D. As regards the system of Sāmakhya by Caraka, which he opines is an earlier school of Sāmakhya, it has been assigned a period of 78 A.D. Patañjali's *Yoga Sūtra* not earlier than 147 B.C. and Vyāsa's commentary on it by 400 A.D. *Vyāsa's bhāṣya* on *Yoga-Sūtra* commented by Vācaspati Mishra (ninth century) and *Sāmakhya- Sūtra*-s were commented upon by Vijñāna Bhikṣu (called *Pravacanabhāṣya*) in the sixteenth century.[24]

Thus, the *Sā. K*, of Īśvarakṛṣṇa, Caraka's Sāmakhya system and Seśvara Yoga system are the extant works on the Sāmakhya system which were prevalent during the period of the *Mbh.* namely between 600 B.C. and 400 A.D. This chapter takes into consideration the *Sā. K.* and Caraka's work. The third work of Yoga system has been considered separately in the chapter Yoga Philosophy.

The Upaniṣad-s and the Sāmakhya system have developed simultaneously and there might have been borrowing of ideas by both the systems from each other. However, since the Upaniṣad-s are more ancient of the two, it is probable that Kapila might have borrowed ideas from the Upaniṣad-s.[25] Since Gauḍapāda and Śanakarācārya have not taken into consideration in their works, Kapila's Sāmakhyaśāstra, many scholars have opined that it is not ancient. Instead the *Sāmakhyakārikā* of Īśvarakṛṣṇa is regarded as older.[26] Smith Vincent has fixed the date of Īśvarakṛṣṇa at about 240 A.D.[27] Since the period of the *Mbh.* has been considered as between 600 B.C. to 600 A.D., the principles of Sāmakhya system as expounded in Īśvarakṛṣṇa's *Sāmakhya-kārikā* can reflect in the *Mbh.*

Definition of Word Sāṁkhya

According to Tilak B.G., the term Sāmakhya is used in two different senses.

(*i*) Philosophy in general and including even the Vedānta philosophy.

(*ii*) Sāmakhya philosophy in particular.

Etymologically, the word Sāmakhya is to be derived from the root *Sama* + √*khyā* (to calculate) and its primary meaning is 'to count'. Since the fundamental elements according to the Kapila's philosophy are twenty five in number, the followers of that philosophy got the name of 'Sāmakhya'.[28]

Satavalekar S.D. has stated different meanings of the word Sāmakhya. The word Sāmakhya means :

1. *'Samyak khyānam'* *viz.* discussion for establishing any principle.[29]

2. Definite knowledge about the Self. Sāmakhya, therefore, would mean proving the doctrine through reasoning.[30]

3. The theory of systematic knowledge of all the elements in the world.[31]

4. According to the *Mbh.* (*Śānti. P.*), consideration of the merits and demerits of any doctrine and the discussion of the same. The theory that considers the number of merits and demerits of a theme under consideration is the Sāṁkhya system.[32]

He has finally concluded that the theory of Sāṁkhya has determined the sentient and the insentient elements in the world as also their effects.[33]

The Student's Sanskrit : *English Dictionary* states "this philosophy is so called because it 'enumerates' twenty five *tattva-s* or true principles and its chief object is to effect the final emancipation of the twenty fifth *tattva, i.e. Puruṣa* or the Soul from the bonds of worldly existence by conveying a correct knowledge of the twenty four other *tattva*-s and by properly discriminating the Soul from them."[34]

According to *Bhāratīya Saṁskṛtikośa* since this system for the first time counted the elements and has given importance to the numbers (*saṁkhyā*), it is called Sāṁkhya. Secondly, the word Sāmakhya also means discriminative knowledge. The being, due to ignorance about the Person (puruṣa) and Primordial Matter (*prakṛti*), gets trapped into the cycle of births and deaths and gets released from it on knowing that Puruṣa (*jīva*) is different and independent of Prakṛti. This system gives importance to this discriminative knowledge. Hence, it is called Sāṁkhya.[35]

Systems of the Sāṁkhya Philosophy

The Upaniṣad-s describe Brahman as the Ultimate Reality. They conceive Brahman as the infinite and regard it as the only truth from which all others derived their powers. In the course of time, the concept of Brahman reached such a supreme level that the worldly reality and the truth were ignored. The same thought finally culminated into absolute monism of Vedānta as explained by Śaṅkara. According to the Sāṁkhya system, however, the world is not unreal. Nothing new comes into existence in this world. One thing gives rise to another thing. According to this system, this world has evolved out of two categories, Puruṣa, the knowing subject and Prakṛti the known object. Also, the Primordial matter (Prakṛti) is the source of the world. It is a potentiality and with the help of three constituents (*guṇa-s*), *sattva, rajas* and *tamas*, the Matter evolves in the presence of Person (*Puruṣa*), and the world comes into the existence. The Person is a witness. However, he is indifferent or unconcerned. It is the Prakṛti that creates.

According to Dasgupta, S.N., there is one more line of Sāṁkhya thought, which forms the link between the Upaniṣad-s and the generally commented upon Sāṁkhya theory which is based on Īśvarkṛṣṇa's *Sāṁkhyakārikā.* He terms this system as the earliest form of Sāṁkhya in a systematic form and the one based on the Īśvarakṛṣṇa's *Sāṁkhyakārikā* as the orthodox Sāmakhya system.[36]

Dasgupta points out that Guṇaratna (14th A.D.), a commentator of *ṣaḍdarśana samuccaya,* mentions two other authoritative Sāṁkhya works as *Māṭharabhāṣya* and *Ātreyatantra.* Nothing is known of *Māṭharabhāṣya*, but according to Dasgupta, S.N., the latter is probably the same as Caraka's treatment of Sāṁkhya, since the sage Atri is the speaker in Caraka's work.[37]

The main features of this doctrine are as follows :

1. Puruṣa is the state of *avyakta.*[38]
2. By a fusion of this *avyakta* with its later products, a group is formed which generates the so called living beings.[39]
3. The *tanmātra-s* are not mentioned.[40] Instead *Indriyārtha*-s are considered as elements (*tattva-s*).
4. The *Rajas* and *tamas* represent bad states of the mind and the *sattva,* the good one.[41]
5. The ultimate state of emancipation is either absolute annihilation or characterless absolute existence and it is spoken of as the *Brahman* state. There is no consciousness in this state, for consciousness is due to a conglomeration of the self with its evolutes, *buddhi, ahaṁkāra* etc.[42]
6. The senses are formed of Matter (*bhautika*).[43]

This line of Sāṁkhya assumes twenty four categories as follows :

Mahat, ahaṁkāra, five *tanmātra*-s, five organs of sense, five organs of action, *manas,* five *mahābhūta-s* such as space (Ākaśa), air (Vāyu), fire (Agni), water (Jala) and the earth (Pṛthvī) and *para, i.e. Avyakta* totalling to twenty four elements. Caraka also recognises six *dhātu-s i.e.* five elements Ākaśa, Vāyu, Agni, Jala, Pṛthvī and Cetana as Puruṣa. The *dhātu* Cetana alone too is considered as Puruṣa.[44] Puruṣa is excluded from twenty four elements. Here Caraka does not mention *tanmātra*-s. The conglomeration formed of sense objects (*indriyārtha*-s) or gross matter, the ten senses, *manas*, the five subtle *bhūta*-s, Prakṛti, *mahat*, *ahaṁkāra* make up Puruṣa.

As regards the exclusion of Puruṣa from the list of the elements, Cakrapāṇi, who has commented upon *Carakasaṁhitā,* has stated that Prakṛti and Puruṣa both being unmanifest, the two together have been counted as one.[45]

The Concept of Puruṣa in Sāṁkhya Philosophy

According to Sāṁkhya philosophy, when one is oppressed by the threefold sufferings, there arises a desire to know the means to alleviate them. They, therefore, propose a superior way as compared to the means shown by the scriptures which are associated with the lack of purity, decay and gradation. This Superior path refers to discriminative knowledge of the manifest world, the unmanifest source of that world and the knower. This knowledge leads to the cessation of the man's sufferings.[46] The Sāṁkhya-s believe that the universe is made of two constituent factors, the sentient and the insentient. The insentient matter exists in two forms one is the root cause (Prakṛti), which is not manifest and not evolved from another matter. From this root cause, there is further evolution which is called the manifest world. The sentient, however, does not evolve into any other form. Also, it is not an evolute of any cause. The evolution process of nature commences in the presence of this sentient, which is the Self, Person (Puruṣa). In fact, the manifestation of the unmanifest takes place only when it is united with the Puruṣa.

Prakṛti, according to Sāṁkhya-s, undertakes the entire process of evolution for the final release, isolation of Person, the Self.[47] This Person is a witness, isolated, possesses neutrality, is a seer and inactive.[48] It is attributeless, distinguishable, uncommon, unproductive. Thus, it is a seer. It just witnesses the reation, which is the work of Prakṛti.

In the *Mbh.*, Vasiṣṭha has elaborated Sāṁkhya philosophy. He says, "this manifest world is made up of five elements. This manifestation begins with intelligence (*mahat*) and consists of twenty three elements. It is perishable. The twenty fourth element is the manifest Nature. Beyond these twenty four elements is the Lord Viṣṇu, the twenty-fifth element."[49] Since it supports elements (*tattva*-s), it is called an element (*tattva*). This twenty-fifth element is formless, conscious, eternal, all pervading, which resides in the hearts of all the beings.[50] The creation and dissolution is the nature of Matter and the Person is not related to this process. However, due to its association with Prakṛti, it appears to be related with the process of creation and dissolution.[51] Further, though it is not cognised by senses, it appears to be so. It does not possess qualities, still it appears to be possessing the qualities. Even though it is not evolved, it appears to be so. Due to its association with Nature, he thinks himself to be possessing the constituents of goodness (*sattva*), action (*rajas*) and darkness, inertia (*tamas*) and takes birth in various species (*yoni-s*). He then starts thinking as "I am such and such a person, the son of somebody." Owing to this false notion he goes on getting births in different bodies[52] and experiences the pairs of opposite such as pleasure and suffering etc.[53] *Sa. K.* substantiates this view.[54] He further goes on narrating how the Self goes on experiencing the life. In fact, it is Prakṛti which enjoys the effects of action. However, due to ignorance, the Self assumes that it is he who experiences.[55] This Self is devoid of senses, yet he feels that it possesses senses. He is imperishable and yet considers itself to be perishable. He is eternal but thinks to be perishable due to its connection with the body. Though it does not even possess subtle body it considers itself to be the possessor of the body and though it is not at all related to Prakṛti, it imagines itself to be a part of the creation. This twenty fifth element, the Self is blemishless and pure, but because of ignorance, this unfettered Ātman becomes blemished and impure like the things which he enjoys. He becomes like Nature (Prakṛti). Karālajanaka compares here the relation of the Person (Puruṣa) and Primordial Nature (Prakṛti) with that of a man and a woman. The man and the woman give birth to a child by resorting to qualities of each other.[57] Hence Karālajanaka feels it is difficult for a man to get released.[58] The implication of the statement that Prakṛti and Puruṣa resort to each others qualities is that Person gets enveloped by the grossness of the Matter and resorts to its sorrow etc. sufferings and the Matter envelops the Person's quality of happiness and takes resort to quality of consciousness of the Puruṣa.

However, *Sa. K.* explains this association of Prakṛti and Puruṣa like that of blind man and the lame man, where the Self provides the sight and the Matter helps Puruṣa for the isolation.[59] This comparison facilitates easy isolation of the two elements.

Vasiṣṭha thereafter speaks of the Self (*liṅgin*), which is neither Nature nor Person.[60] It is different from the Person and the Matter. The product of Person and the Matter, made up of the categories proceeding from intelligence onwards is an indicatory mark (*liṅga*).[61] The *liṅgin* is the Ātman, the substratum of all, which is pure consciousness, is the twenty-fifth element.[62] *Sā. K.* gives the details of the indicatory mark (*liṅga*) which is described as prior born, unattached, constant and consisting of categories from intellect to the subtle ones (*tanmātra-s*).[63] Vasiṣṭha further clarifies that the Self (Puruṣa) is eternal, unlimited, seer, it is unblemished, full of bliss.[64] However, due to its false inclination towards attributes (*guṇa*-s), it considers itself to be possessing attributes. It is only when embodied Soul realises that these attributes are the effects of Nature and abandons the feeling of 'Individuation', that he perceives the Supreme Soul.[65] He again asserts that the Sāṁkhya-s state that the twenty fifth element, which is beyond intelligence, which is the highest knowledge, the conscious, unperceivable by senses, unmanifest, qualitative Īśvara, devoid of qualities, is eternal and is the substratum of the universe.[66] About this twenty fifth principle, Vasiṣṭha says that it recognises unmanifest Matter. Hence it is called Budhyamāna. However, it does not recognise the twenty sixth element, which is unblemished, knower, eternal, enlightened (Buddha), the Brahman. This Brahman is second to none, imperceptible, but it pervades all the perceptible and imperceptible things. When the embodied soul (*jīvātman*), the twenty-fifth element, fixing its gaze on the unmanifest Brahman realises that he is distinct from the Matter, he becomes the master, the controller of the Matter.[67]

Vasiṣṭha, thus, has brought out almost all the characteristics of Person (Puruṣa). These characteristics are coherent with those described in the *Sā. K.* However, there is a deliberate effort to synthesize the Sāṁkhya concepts with that of Upaniṣadic philosophy. The reference to the Supreme Soul as Viṣṇu shows the shade of Nārāyaṇīya cult.

Brahmā in the *Āśva. P.* has explained in detail the constituents (*guṇa*-s), characteristics of elements and process of creation in the Sāṁkhya system. However, the details pertaining to Puruṣa are very few. The Ātman has been described as existing in all the beings.[68] and has been also narrated as Viṣṇu Mitra, Varuṇa, Agni, Prajāpati, the sustainer, the Supreme Lord etc.[69] He has also described it as the knower of the Self (Kṣetrajña) and that it does not have any other mark to specify itself. It is self illuminated, possesses no qualities. Mere knowledge is the indicative mark (*lakṣaṇa*) of it.[70] He adds that the Ātman recognises the unmanifest Nature which is the source of creation and resort of the beings on dessolution. It recognises the embodied Soul and hence it is called as the knower of the body, field (*kṣetrajña*). It perceives the beginning, middle and the end of all the created things as well as the work of all the constituents (*guṇa*-s). However, the constituents do not recognise the Self. In fact nobody can perceive that highest principle, which is of the nature of truth, the knower of the field. When the sins of man are eliminated, he enters that pure Supreme Soul. This knower of the field is beyond the pairs of the pleasure and pain etc.[71] In these excerpts, there are few direct references to Sāṁkhya term of Person (Puruṣa). However, the description of other Sāṁkhya elements along with the Upaniṣadic terms of *kṣ etra* and *kṣetrajña* correlates it with the Sāṁkhya concepts of the Prakṛti and the Puruṣa. In section 46 of this *Parvan*, he is described as possessing no limbs, without senses, constituents etc. second to none, pure, immovable, not an object of knowledge, desireless, certain, immortal, immovable, divine, existing among all the beings. Thus, there is a brief description of the Person and that too is synthesized with Upaniṣadic concepts.[72]

Pañcaśikha in his discourse with Janaka briefly deals with the subject after refuting the views of atheists. He explains that Ātman is perceived only by inference. It is without form and it is not an evolute of any element.[73] While answering Janaks's query as to whether there is any contact of the embodied soul (*jīvātman*) with gross elements after the death of the being, he says he would expound the theory of Sāṁkhyas. However, this system of Sāṁkhya referred to by Pañcaśikha has special reference to concept of renunciation (*saṁnyāsa*). Here, he expounded the different elements of Sāṁkhya like intelligence (*buddhi*), mind (*manas*) etc.[74] He does not directly refer to the concept of Prakṛti and the Puruṣa, but refers to them as *kṣetra* and *kṣetrajña*.[75]

The *Bhagavadgītā* too uses the word 'Puruṣa' very often. Examination of these various references, with a view to see whether they are identical with the concept of Person in Sāṁkhya, reveals the following facts :

The word Puruṣa in section 25, section 31 and section 39 is applicable to human beings,[76] whereas the word *Puruṣa* appearing in section 40 connotes strength.

In the *Mbh.,* Kṛṣṇa while explaining to Arjuna that the embodied Self is eternal, indestructible, states that the notion that some one kills and some other is being killed is erroneous. He describes Puruṣa as the one who is not born, who does not die, who having once existed, will not be non-existent in future. He is unborn, everlasting, unchangeable and very ancient. He is not killed when the body is killed.[77] All these thoughts suggest that the description is directed towards the Ātman or the Soul of the Vedāntins.

Other reference in Section 25 refers to the Supreme Self, Brahman of the Vedānta.[78] In section 30, there is a detailed narration of Matter, which is of eight types (*aṣṭadhā*). It is destructible (*kṣara*).[79] According to Satavalekar, Para Prakṛti which is indestructible (*akṣara*) is the one which Kṛṣṇa called *adhidaivata.*[79] It is the *jīva*, the Ātman, element, which is called Person here.[80] In the same section, the word 'Parama Puruṣa' occurs. It is the Supreme Divine being, who is described as an ancient seer, a ruler, more minute than the minutest atom. All these adjectives are applicable to the Brahman of the Vedānta philosophy. The same can be said about the other two references where the Puruṣa has been called as ancient seer who is to be meditated upon.[81] As regards verses quoted in section 31, Kṛṣṇa describes himself to be unconcerned, unattached to the actions of Nature and he is the one who supervises the process of creation of movable and immovable brought out by Nature.[82] Here, there is some similarity with the Person of Sāṁkhya who is an unconcerned onlooker. However, the Person of Sāṁkhyavādin-s does not participate in the creation by the Prakṛti. Here, Kṛṣṇa's identification with that Puruṣa, denotes the term the God (Īśvara), who is an overall supervisor of the world.[83]

Again, in section 32, the description of Puruṣa as eternal, unborn[84] can be made applicable to Sāṁkhya Puruṣa. However, from the context that Śrī Kṛṣṇa is being addressed by these epithets by Arjuna, it is clear that it is not the Puruṣa of Sāṁkhya. Moreover, the word *vibhu* has been explained by Satavalekar as majestic power, super-human power, Puruṣa. The meaning of the word Puruṣa has been given as "one who resides in the city of entire universe (*viṣva-rūpi puri*) that is pervading the entire universe."[85] Thus, this description applies only to Brahman. The term 'Puruṣottama' the best of being, has been directed to Kṛṣṇa in[86] this section and not to the Puruṣa of Sāṁkhyas. In Section 33, the term person has been applied to the eternal being (*sanātan* Puruṣa).[87] This description is identical with Puruṣa in tenth *maṇḍala* of Ṛgveda and this description matches with the concept of Brahman of Upaniṣad.[88] In another verse, the epithet 'primal god' (*ādidevaḥ*) can be made applicable to the description of Person of Sāṁkhya. However, this eulogy of Kṛṣṇa by Arjuna, shows Kṛṣṇa as qualitative (*saguṇa*), personified Brahman.[89]

While explaining the concept of *kṣetra* and *kṣetrajña*, the terms of Sāṁkhya system of philosophy, Person and Matter have been used throughout the chapter thirty five of the *Bh. P.*[90] Here the highest entity has been delineated as the object of knowledge, having known which, one reaches immortality. It neither has a beginning, nor an end, which cannot be said to be existent or non-existent. According to Śaṅkara, this cannot be made applicable to Brahman, since the words indicate a class, a quality, an action or a relation, hence none of these can be predicated of the Brahman.[91]

The actual description of Primordial matter and Person in Sāṁkhya terms begins here. Kṛṣṇa says 'know Prakṛti and Puruṣ a both to be without a beginning and know all modifications as the creations of Nature. Puruṣa experiences pleasures and sorrows. Residing in Prakṛti, he enjoys the constituents of Prakṛti.[92] Here, this description of Person is similar to that described in the Sāṁkhya system. The Supreme Spirit in this body is called a supervisor, adviser, supporter, enjoyer, the great Lord and even the Supreme Self. While commenting on this part of the *Mbh.*, it is noteworthy that Telang, K.T. has quoted *Nṛsiṁha tāpinī Up.*, which describes the spirit as an adviser, because, though he does not interfere, he sees and therefore, may be said to sanction the operations alluded to.[93] He is the supporter of body and limbs etc. in their workings.[94] In the next section, Kṛṣṇa states that *mahadbrahman* is his womb (*yoni*).[95] Though, it is the description of Matter made up of qualities and the embodied Soul bound by the strands (*guṇa-s*) of Nature, both of them cannot be compared with the principles of Sāṁkhya. The Matter of Sāṁkhyavādins creates on its own. The Person is just an onlooker. Hence, the Matter cannot be identified with the womb of Brahman. It is noteworthy that Dandekar, S.V. considers *Mahadbrahma* as Māyā.

Bh. P. cites primal being (*ādya* Puruṣa) from whom the primordial nature has emanated. This also cannot be identified with Person of Sāṁkhya system.[96] In this section there is a reference to two beings, one of them is destructible and the other one indestructible. The destructible stands for all the things and beings and the unconcerned one is called indestructible.[97] The third one is the highest Self, who is other than these two, the Highest Lord who pervades the three worlds and supports them.[98] Here, the destructible person is the same as the Primordial Matter (Prakṛti) and the indestructible one is Person (Puruṣa) of the Sāṁkhya system of philosophy.[99] It is to be noted that Uttama Puruṣa stands for the Brahman of the Vedānta system.

Thus, throughout the *Bh. G.*, the composer of the *Mbh.* has used the most prominent terms of the Sāṁkhya system of philosophy. However, he does not regard them to be the creators of the world. According to him, Uttama Puruṣa who is on par with Brahman of the Vedānta system is beyond Prakṛti and Puruṣa, who supervises these two and induces them to create.

It is significant to note that even though the Mahābhāratakāra has incorporated the terms Prakṛti and Puruṣa and other principles considered to be the outcomes of Prakṛti and Puruṣa by the Sāṁkhyavādins, he has not accepted Sāṁkhya thought of philosophy fully. After all, Prakṛti of Sāṁkhyavādins is insentient and Puruṣa is indifferent (*udāsīna*); hence the union of these two can never create the world. The composer of the *Mbh.*, therefore, considered the existence of Uttama Puruṣa, who presides over these two and induces them to create the world, as essential. It is obvious, that this Uttama Puruṣa is the same as the Brahman of the Vedāntins. The composer of the *Mbh.*, thus, has beautifully blended these two important systems of philosophy so as best to synthesise them.

In the *Mbh.*, Janaka questions Pañcaśikha about the state of the Self after death. Since the Self would not have any consciousness, what would be the use of knowledge or ignorance? Whether the Self has any association after the death with the gross elements which are perishable?[100] Pañcaśikha explains that the Self is imperishable and formless. The form, which is visible, is the conglomeration of the body, organs and the mind.[101] The people, who consider this conglomeration as Self, have to face inexhaustible suffering due to this improper knowledge.[102] The life element in the mind is the Kṣetrajña and the conglomeration of the three above is the *kṣetra.*[103] Pañcaśikha does not state here specifically that Kṣetrajña is Puruṣa. However, Kṣetrajña is the term utilised by the Vedāntins for the embodied soul. He further states that since Kṣetrajña is the life principle, there can neither be any eradication of this life principle nor can it have eternal association with the gross elements.[104]

Caraka, however, has presented three definitions of Puruṣa 1. Five gross elements *ākāśa* etc. and *cetana* is called Puruṣa. 2. *cetana* alone is called Puruṣa and 3. twenty four elements including the five organs of action and five organs of senses, five *indriyārtha*-s, five great elements, *manas, ahaṁkāra, mahat* etc.[105] The soul is called *avyakta,* Kṣetrajña, *śāśvata* (eternal), *vibhu, avyaya.*[106] Caraka does not consider Puruṣa as a separate element from the group of twenty four elements. The commentator Cakrapāṇi states that Prakṛti and Puruṣa being unmanifest the two together have been counted as one.[107]

Nature (Prakṛti) according to Sāṁkhya

The Sāṁkhya philosophy believes in the proposition that

whatever is produced along with its present accompaniment and qualities must have been in existence in the past, in some form or other, in its original cause. This is known as 'Satkāryavāda'. Thus, it is the theory of something being produced out of something which existed, that is, a theory of cause and effect.[108] This is reflected in the statement in the *Bh.G.* "That which does not exist will never come into existence."[109] There is a fundamental substance at the root of all the things in the world and the Sāṁkhyavādins call it Prakṛti, the original source from which arise the subsequent elements which are termed as *vikṛti* or modifications (*vikāra*-s) which are the transformations of the Primordial matter (Prakṛti). This Matter has three constituents or integral parts which are goodness (*sattva*), action or passion (*rajas*), ignorance (*tamas*). The *Sā. K.* specifically declares that these constituents of the unmanifest Matter (Pradhāna) are capable of producing, creating (the world).[110]

This Matter has been termed as *'avyakta'* since it is not perceptible in equable state of the three constituents. However, the *Sā. K.* says it is not cognised, not because of its non existence but because of its subtlety. It is cognised from its effects and this cognition begins with the intellect *(mahat)* which is similar and dissimilar to the cause.[111]

However, this Matter is *acetana*, it does not have life. If the Spirit, Person (Puruṣa) is passive and qualitiless, how can there be a creation in the absence of the third principle? To this question Sāṁkhya-s answer that just as the cow gives milk for its calf or iron acquires the quality of attraction by the proximity of a magnet, Similarly, the Matter coming into contact with Person starts disintegration of its constituents for the final release of the Self (Puruṣa)[112] and as soon as the Self realises that it is different from the Matter it gets released. Sāṁkhyas' creation begins in a successive manner. Intelligence (*mahat*) is the first element in the process of evolution then comes the self-sense (*ahaṁkāra*), and the mind (*manas*) follows.[113] The process of evolution from Nature by diffusion of its constituents *(guṇa-s),* is reflected in different

Parva-s of the *Mbh.* Prominent among them are *Bhīṣma Parva,* the *Bhagavadgītā* precisely; *Śānti Parva* and *Āśvamedhika Parva.*

Vasiṣṭha describes to Karālajanaka that the Lord Hiraṇyagarbha, who has emanated from the imperishable Supreme, is called Viśvātman, Ekākṣara in the Sāṁkhya system.[114] This is the Nature (Prakṛti), which is the manifestation of the unmanifest element. This Primordial matter emanated from the unmanifest is the creation of the nature of knowledge (*vidyā sarga*) and the creation from intellect (*mahat*) and self sense (*ahaṁkāra*), which are the evolutes of the primal Nature, is the creation of the nature of non-knowledge (*avidyāsarga*).[115] He further describes the evolution of five subtle elements from the *ahaṁkāra* as the third stage of creation and the evolution from the self-sense, with the three constituents *sattva, rajas* and *tamas,* which is called a modified creation, as the fourth stage. This modified creation includes five gross elements, namely the ether, the air, the fire, the water and the earth, the five cbjects of sense, namely sound, smell, light, taste and touch. The fifth stage of creation consists of five sense organs namely eyes, nose, ear, skin and tongue and the five organs of action speech, hands, legs, organs of excretion and of generation and the mind.[116] Thus, the bodies of the beings consist of these twenty four elements.[117] He further declares that when the primal Nature comes into contact with the Person, it creates *'mahat'* element. Then onwards from the presence of illuminated things, the presence of Nature is felt as the formless season's (*ṛtu*) presence is known by flowers and fruits.[118] He further specifies that Prakṛti by its very nature is inclined to create and dissolve. The person (Puruṣa) is not at all related to Primordial Nature.[119]

Vasiṣṭha expounds that the Sāṁkhya-s treat primordial Nature as the unmanifest (*avyakta*) and from it emanates the *mahat* element, from the *mahat* evolves the self conscious (*ahaṁkāra*), from it evolve five subtle elements (*tanmātra*-s). These are the seven primary elements out of which sixteen modified elements arise.[120] This description fully agrees with the contents of the *Sā. K.*[121]

Thus, the *Sā. K.* treats primal Nature (*mūla* Prakṛti) as unmodified Nature whereas the creation from intelligence *(mahat)* onwards is modified Nature (Prakṛti-*vikṛti*). The *Sā. K.* clarifies this distinction between unmanifest and manifest Nature.[122] The root cause, which is unmanifest (*mūla* Prakṛti), is the cause of the manifest Matter (*vyakta*). This proposition of the *Sā. K.*, tallies with Vasiṣṭha's above cited view that primordial Nature is unmanifest (*avyakta*).

Sharma, H.D. explains the sixteen modifications as five organs of sense, five organs of action, five gross elements and the sixteenth as mind (*manas*).[123] He also states that at the time of dissolution, the matter becomes homogenous and becomes manifold as the creation proceeds. It is the twenty-fifth element Paramātman, which manifolds the Matter. The Matter and its modifications (*vikāra*-s) constitute *kṣetra*.[124]

Further, it is also said that the Nature does not recognise Parabrahman, whether it is qualified (*saguṇa*) or without qualities (*nirguṇa*), as it is senseless (*jaḍa*). It is, therefore, called as unintelligent, ignorant (*apratibuddha*). Only when it is united with the twenty fifth element (Paramapuruṣa) it recognises the Parabrahman.[125]

The scrutiny of the characteristics of Nature and its modification and the successive evolution as given above display certain features. The description of evolution through intelligence (*mahat*) with the constituents (*guṇa*-s) as also the person being *adhiṣṭhata, avyakta* are on the lines of the *Sā. K.*[126] However, the statement that Nature has emanated from the 'Imperishable' that is Hiraṇyagarbha, is not a Sāmakhya concept. According to Sāṁkhya-s, primal Nature has not come out of any cause. It is the root.[127] It is the manifest world that has modifications. It has come out of unmanifest nature. Thus, this feature and also the designation of Prakṛti and its modifications as *kṣetra* show the synthesis of the Upaniṣadic philosophy with the Sāṁkhya philosophy. Thus, here the synthesis of both the systems is evident.

The Mahābhāratakāra says that the 'unmanifest' which is of the nature of creation and dissolution, is nescience (*avidyā*) and the twenty-fifth element, which is devoid of creation and dissolution is knowledge (*vidyā*).[128] The phenomenon of creation and dissolution ascribed to the unmanifest tallies with the contents of the *Sā. K.*[129]

As regards the concepts of *vidyā* and *avidyā* in the *Śānti P.*, it is stated that the creation out of *avyakta i.e.* unmanifest Prakṛti is *vidyāsarga*, whereas the creation out of *Mahat* etc. is *avidyāsarga,*[130] which seems to contradict the view expressed in the above mentioned instance of section 295.

The *Mbh.* further narrates that the twenty-fifth element, which is inactive, passive, in union with the Prakṛti thinks itself to be something other than himself. He begins to think himself–'I am this' and 'that person'. However, once he realises that he is different from Nature, he is released. He realises that the suffering is by Nature and he is not bound by the strands of Prakṛti.[131] This description agrees with the contents of the *Sā. K.*[132]

Brahmā in *Āśvamedhic P.* has stated the same facts as described by Vasiṣtha in the *Śānti P.* as regards the evolution of the world. However, he calls Prakṛti as unmanifest (*avyakta*), which is in consistence with the concept of the Nature explained in the *Sā. K.*, which is primordial Matter, the root of material forms. This is the undeveloped source (*avyakta*). From this Matter emanates intellect (*mahat*), from intellect or understanding emanates self sense or egoism (*ahaṁkāra*) and then the whole cycle of creation follows. He also mentions the stages of creation, that is, the emanation from the unmanifest Matter of the intellect, understanding, is the first stage[133] and the creation of self sense (*ahaṁkāra*) from the understanding as second stage.[134] He does not indicate the following stages of creation as described by Vasiṣ ṭha. He further states that it is the self-sense, which is responsible for the modification like gross elements.[135] This is in tune with *Sā. K.*[136] The verse six of chapter 42,[137] states "sound, touch etc.

subtle elements (*tanmātra-s*) being subtle along with the organs which hold them do not get dissolved at the time of dissolution." This statement is in consonance with the contents of the *Sā. K.*,[138] which explains that subtle body (*liṅga*) composed of intellect and the rest, down to subtle elements migrates. He also specifies that being the source of creation and dissolution of the three constituents (*guṇa*-s), the unmanifest (*avyakta*) Prakṛti is called *kṣetra* and it is he (Brahmā) who recognises her (Prakṛti) and hears her by contacting himself with her.[139] Here, he identifies himself with the Person (Puruṣa).

In the *Śanti P.* again, there is a conversation between Janaka and Pañcaśikha on Sāṁkhya system. Here, Pañcaśikha states the discerning difference in the categories mentioned by him five sense organs, five organs of action and *cetana* as eleven categories.[140] However, instead of *tanmātra*-s, he considers the objects of sense (*indriyārtha*-s) as a group of five elements. He joins the sense organs and the doer in the form of (*citta*) and forms five groups of three each with objects of sense organs, namely sound, touch, form, taste and smell and calls all these five groups as constituents (*guṇa*-s).[141] These five groups of three each added with five organs of action, mind (*manas*), intellect, *cetana* amount to twenty three elements. The conglomeration of the body, organs and *manas* is considered as a *kṣetra* and the life element in the mind (*cetana*) is called Kṣetrajña[142] Pañcaśikha also considers the elements of space, air, fire, water and the earth within the body as five properties (*dhātu*-s).[143]

Though this theory of Pañcaśikha does not totally agree with the Sāṁkhya theory expounded by Caraka, it shows some resemblance to it. Caraka assumes twenty-four categories-ten senses, five cognative elements and five conative senses; mind, five objects of senses (*indriyārtha*-s) and eight-fold Matter, which includes Matter, *mahat, ahaṁkāra* and five gross elements *ākāśa, vāyu, agni, jala and pṛthvī.*[144] He also recognises six properties (*dhātu*-s) consisting of five elements space, air etc. and *cetana* who is called *Puruṣa.*[145] He does not mention *tanmātra*-s. The conglomeration formed of sense objects, the ten senses, mind, five gross elements, matter, intelligence, self sense make up Puruṣ a.[146] The orthodox Sāṁkhya states that Prakṛti is made up of these twenty four elements. Caraka considers Prakṛti too as *avyakta* like Puruṣa.[147]

The similarities observed in Pañcaśikha's system and Caraka's system – Pañcśikha considers five gross elements in the body as properties (*dhātu*-s),[148] whereas Caraka treats five gross elements and *cetana* as six properties (*dhātu*-s).[149] Both of them do not recognise *tanmātra*-s as elements. Pañcaśikha treats *Cetana* as Kṣetrajña,[150] which is called Ātman in the Vedānta parlance, while Caraka considers it as Puruṣa.[151] Pañcaśikha states conglomeration of senses and body[152] as *kṣetra*, which Vedānta treats as body and Caraka calls conglomeration of sense objects, ten senses, mind (*manas*), five gross elements (*bhūta*-s), Prakṛti, *mahat, ahaṁkāra* as the man that is the body.[153]

In this connection, the remark of Dasgupta, S.N. that Sāṁkhya system appears to be a connecting link between the Upaniṣads and orthodox Sāṁkhya system is definitely noteworthy. This remark is valid in the case of Pañcaśikha's Sāṁkhya system as well.

At the very beginning of philosophical discourse in the *Bh. G.*, which is a part of the *Mbh.* itself, there is an indirect reference to Prakṛti. Kṛṣṇa says "Non-existent does not have existence and the existent one cannot be non-existent. The knowers of the truth have seen the essence of both of them." Here, according to Śaṅkarācārya, *'asat'* is anything such as heat and cold and their causes, which is conditioned by causality and *'sat'* is uncaused, that is the Self. *'Asat'* is body (*deha*) with pleasure and pain and *'sat'* is the embodied soul (*dehin*).[154] Here, the contrast is being shown between the self and non-self, which is Brahman veiled by *māyā*, opines Hill W.D.P.[155] However, the body which is the conglomeration of senses and elements is Nature (Prakṛti), according to Sāṁkhya terminology. There is one more reference of being and no-being in the *Bh. G.*[156] Here Śaṅkarācārya calls *'sat'* as the manifested, the effect and *'asat'* as the unmanifested, the cause.

Rāmānuja explains *'sat'* as present existence and *'asat'* as past and future existence. [157]

However, Thomson J.C. identifies *'sat'* in the *Bh. G.* with the Spirit and *'asat'* with Matter.[158] Thus, there appears to be a lot of scope for interpretation of these two terms. Here, it may be pointed out that Prakṛti before manifestation, that is, when it is in the state of equipoise, is unmanifest, hence here *'asat'*, may be taken as the nomenclature of Prakṛti.

Kṛṣṇa asserts that the three constituents goodness (*sattva*), action (*rajas*) and ignorance (*tamas*) are the strands (*guṇa*-s), which spring from Nature. They bind the embodied, immutable Soul in the body.[159] The *Sā. K.* points out this fact.

The *Bh. G.* recognises the Primordial matter (*Prakṛti*) and Person (*Puruṣa*) as beginningless and states that the changes (*vikāra*-s) and constituents (*guṇa*-s) are born of Prakṛti and Puruṣ a abiding in this Matter enjoys the constituents of Prakṛti. Due to his attachment to constituents, he becomes the cause of the creation of the world.[160] This agrees with *Sā. K.* 45.[161]

About himself, Kṛṣṇa says a part of myself, which is eternal, has become the Soul and it drags the mind and the five senses, which rest in Matter (*Prakṛti*).[162] He further adds that though unborn and immutable in essence, though the Lord of beings, of governing nature, which is mine, I take birth, having presided over Prakṛti by my delusive power (*māyā*).[163] Here, when Kṛṣṇa says, 'myself', he refers to himself as *Paramātman.* In this verse, there is a clear synthesis of Sāṁkhya thought with that of the Vedānta. Thus, he has synthesized Sāṁkhya theory with the theory of absolute monism (of Śaṅkarācārya), which considers that there is only one entity in the universe, which is unborn, immutable Brahman and this world gets manifested from it.

Speaking about the constituents, the *Bh. G.* says, "All the beings on the earth and the heaven are bound by the strands (*guṇa*-s) of the Primordial matter."[164] Kṛṣṇa also states, "Deluded by these constituents of Matter, men are attached to the activities, being performed due to constituents (of Prakṛti)."[165] Hence, "Oh Arjuna, cast off all the activities on me and fix your thought on the essential Self, hope for naught, devoid of the feeling of mineness and fight your enemies."[166] Here, according to Rāmānuja, Arjuna is made aware of the fact that the Supreme Spirit performs all the activities for the Ātman in one's own body and derives all energies for him.[167]

Rāmānuja thinks that this context seems to demand that Kṛṣ ṇa should be identifying himself with the lower Nature, which is his eightfold Prakṛti.[168] In this chapter, he has also identified himself with the higher Nature. However, the higher Nature, which upholds this universe,[169] the very life, which is termed as *jīvabhūta,* is not the Person of Sāṁkhyavādin's. Barnett L.D. translates *jīvabhūta* as 'Elemental Soul', whereas, Śaṅkarācārya calls it as Kṣetrajña and identifies it with Person,[170] as narrated in the *Bh. G.* (*Mbh. Bh. P.* 35.21).

The *Bh. G.* describes the Person and the Primordial matter. The Mahābhāratakāra has explained how embodied Puruṣa experiences the constituents (*guṇa*-s) of primordial matter and takes birth.[171] He further clarifies that all the things, moving or unmoving, are produced from the union of the 'field' and 'the Knower of the field.'[172] According to Śaṅkarācārya, this union is purely illusory.[173]

The *Sā. K.* describes their association as that of a lame man and a blind man.[174] Here, Puruṣa is the one who sees and Primordial matter is the one who moves *i.e.* implements. When they both reach the goal they separate and are isolated. Thus, they have distinct functions to carry out and are different in nature in the Sāṁkhya system. The *Mbh.* has also shown the difference between them while describing the 'field' (*kṣetra*) and 'the knower of the field' (*kṣetrajña*). The *Mbh.* states all the modifications (*vikāra*-s) and constituents are born of Prakṛti.[175] Prakṛti is the cause of action[176] and it is the Prakrti alone which acts.[177] Puruṣ a, however, is devoid of qualities, constituents.[178] He does not perform any actions.[179] He is an onlooker, who approves (*anumantra*), sustains and enjoys the qualities of Prakṛti.[180] Further, though he dwells in the body, he is not besmeared (*alipta*)[181] (by the actions of the body). These thoughts tally with the contents of the *Sā. K.,* which are as follows : The great element (*mahat*) etc. are the seven modifications (*vikṛti*-s) of the Prakṛti.[182] Prakṛti is endowed with constituents, while he (*Puruṣa*) is without constituents (*aguṇa*).[183] It states (when the constituents are in the state of equilibrium), there has to be some external stimulus, which can bring about the change, *i.e.* disequilibrium of the constituents. He (just) controls and experiences. He is the Person, who is different from constituents (*guṇa*-s of Prakṛti),[184] and the activity of (Prakṛti) takes place for the isolation of this Self.

Mbh. further states "In the production of effects from causes, Primordial nature is said to be the cause; in experiencing pleasure and pain, the Person is said to be the cause".[185] This can be compared to the following contents of *Sā. K.* "the manifest has a cause"[186] which means Prakṛti is responsible for all the creation (manifestation), while Puruṣa is responsible for experiencing pleasures and sorrows.[187] The nature of the cause which is unmanifest, is totally different from that of the effect, which is manifest, dependent and full of parts. As is rightly pointed out by Telang, K.T. regarding Prakṛti and Puruṣa, Prakṛti is said to be the origin of the capacity of working (residing) in the body and the senses.[188] However, the Person as being the cause for experiencing pleasure and pains is illusory, since he is neither an agent in activity nor the cause of activity. Moreover, since he is neutral, a witness, with no part in events, that is, the changes and movements in the world, and as such does not manifest, the question of he being a cause does not arise.[189] Thus, the difference between the Primordial matter and the Person has been shown clearly here. But again at an other place, Kṛṣṇa says that "Person is the resort of the Brahman. At the time of the destruction all the beings merge into my Nature (*Prakṛti*)[190] and at the beginning of creation, I create the beings again, resorting to my Prakṛti which is my own."[191] He further states "The Nature gives birth to all the moving as well as unmoving things presided over by me."[192] Here, again there is a shade of Sāṁkhya Person as the one who presides over Nature. However, this whole exercise of showing a difference in the Puruṣa and Prakṛti of Sāṁkhya has only one purpose, *viz.*, proving the Vedānta concept of the monism, as is evident from the statement "Nature is my own" and "it is me who is responsible for all the happenings in the universe." Kṛṣṇa, therefore, advises Arjuna, "That the being, deluded by the strands of Nature, starts thinking that he is the one who thinks, he is the one who does[193] is a wrong notion. Arjuna, you should not think in this way. If you turn to the thought 'I' and think I will not fight, it is a futile resolve. Nature will constrain you. You should, therefore, fix your thought on me, you would not perish then."[194] He further emphasizes that, "Enveloped by delusion, even if you do not desire to do that thing, you shall do it, since by nature, you are bound by your own duty, though it may be against your wish."[195]

From the description of Prakṛti in the *Mbh.*, it can be observed that Kṛṣṇa emphasises that Prakṛti is the resort of Brahman. It is Prakṛti, which is presided over by him, which creates all the beings and beings merge into him at the time of dissolution. He, therefore, advises Arjuna not to worry, with the thought that he would kill his kiths and kins and incur sin thereby.[196] He further points out that Arjuna was bound by his nature. Whether he liked it or not, he will have to carry out his duties.[197] He, therefore, advises Arjuna to think over the knowledge imparted to him and act the way he wishes.[198] Being fully convinced of the importance of this advice, Arjuna was determined to fight.[199] It must be noted that this was possible only due to the manner in which the thoughts of the Vedānta and Sāṁkhya systems were synthesized by the Mahābhāratakāra.

The Concept of Constituents (*guṇa*-s) in the Sāṁkhya Philosophy

Sāṁkhya philosophy propogates that Matter is formed of three modes. When the matter is unmanifest, these modes are in a state of equilibrium. When the creation ensues, this equilibrium gets disturbed. As pointed out by Davies John, the introduction of constituents (*guṇa*-s) of Nature (*Prakṛti*) is an important part of physical and moral teachings. These *guṇa*-s are called as qualities, strands or modes. However, they are constituents of the Matter.[200] Even Colebrooks considered, "These three qualities are not mere accidents of Nature, but are of its essence and enter into its composition." He has further stated that according to Sāṁkhya system, before the creation, these constituents are in a state of equipoise. When Nature begins to act, though unconsciously, for the welfare of the Soul, due to the influence of the constituents of action or passion (*rajas*), there is an activity, which causes an imbalance and leads to creation.[201] There are three constituents, *viz.* goodness (*sattva*) which is light or subtle and it illuminates or manifests; passion or action (*rajas*), which is stimulating and mobile; and darkness or materiality (*tamas*), which is heavy and enveloping. According to *Sā. K.* 12 and 13, they have a joyous, grievous and stupefying nature. They intend to enlighten, activate and restrain respectively. They function through mutual dependence, mutual production and mutual combination.[202]

The *Mbh.* has presented a detailed description of the nature of the constituents of Matter, their effect on the various elements in the *Bh. P., Śānti P.* and *Āśva. P.* While narrating Pañcaśikha's theory, Bhīṣma described five groups of three each, made up of the sense organs like (*i*) ears, eyes, (*ii*) the objects of senses like sound, form and (*iii*) the thinking faculty (*citta*) and termed them all as qualities (*guṇa*-s) with the help of which, a being grasps different objects of sense such as sound, touch etc. Hence, often there is a repetition of such triangular state.[203] He has further divided them into good, passion and ignorance, which in turn leads to three types of experiences. The dark (*tamas*) constituent leads to indiscrimination, delusion (*moha*), intoxication, laziness etc. and when one is happy the *sattva* element predominates. The feeling that fosters dissatisfactions or anguish is the outcome of the preponderance of passion or action.[204] Caraka, whose theory shows resemblance with that of Pañcaśikha, has stated that the association of Puruṣa with *rajas* and *tamas, i.e.* with the twenty-four elements is eternal. When the *sattva* constituent preponderates, *rajas* and *tamas* are destroyed and the Soul gets released.[205] The creation is due to the constituents of *rajas* and *tamas.*

According to the *Mbh.,* the three constituents, goodness, action and ignorance have emanated from Nature. They exist in all the beings equally and they can be identified on the basis of their functioning in beings.[206]

When one is calm, happy, one can rest assured that it is the constituent of goodness, which is at work. The experience of anguish indicates that the constituent of passion or action has settled in oneself. When the mind is overcast by delusion, when logic does not work, mind is flustered, one can know that it is due to the preponderace of the element of ignorance. It is the soul that creates the element of goodness or (other) elements. The elements do not know the soul. However, the soul always knows the element.[207]

Asita in the *Śānti. P.* has considered the three constituents as *bhāva*-s and form (*rūpa*), smell (*gandha*), taste (*rasa*) and life elements as *guṇa*-s.[208] This does not agree with the preposition of *Sā. K.* 11, which states that manifested (*vyakta*) has three constituents.[209]

It is further stated that the Supreme Soul, which is not a substance (*nirdravya*), devoid of sense organs (*nirindriya*), without cause (*abīja*) is devoid of constituents (*guṇa*-s). These elements emanate from Nature as they are its constituents.[210] When the soul realises that the elements are the constituents of Nature, it can have the knowledge of the Supreme Soul.[211] These elements get dissolved into their causes. They merge into Nature.[212] He further adds that when the Person develops aversion towards these constituents, he perceives the Supreme Soul.[213] This is the state of release of the being. Thus, this argument implies that due to the existence and proximity of these constituents with the Soul, the Soul gets entangled in the cycle of births and can get release from the world only after realising that the release contains in breaking of this mesh of constituents.

In this Parvan, Yājñavalkya states that the constituents of Nature are the ever-remaining parts of the entire world.[214] The person in whom goodness predominates attains the supreme state, whereas one possessing the elements of passion and ignorance attains the middling and the lowest states respectively.[215] When there is a preponderance of goodness, the being attains the abode of the gods. One having a combination of passion and goodness attains the world of humans and one having a combination of passion and ignorance gets born as an animal or bird etc. When there is a combination of goodness, passion and ignorance one is born as a human being. The qualities like boldness, happiness, love, progress, light, health etc. are the characteristics of the element of goodness.[216] Beauty, wealth, enjoyment, pride, talkativeness etc. are the qualities of the element of passion, whereas delusion, ignorance, insatiable thirst for material gain, dirty environment etc. are the attributes of the element of ignorance.[217] Yājñavalkya answering Gandharva Viśvāvasu's question as to what is *'Viśva'* and *'Aviśva'*, explains *viśva* is an unmanifest Nature consisting of three constituents. The one, which is different from it, is *aviśva* that is devoid of constituents.[218]

It is further stated that the group of the three constituents, *sattva, rajas* and *tamas* alongwith five *mahābhūta*-s, five *tanmātra*-s (*paramāṇu*), five *indriya*-s and *mahat* constitute a group of seventeen, which is termed as unmanifest. After adding five *indriyārtha*-s, manifest (*vyakta*) and unmanifest (*avyakta*) they amount to twenty-five elements.[219] However, treating the group of three *guṇa*-s as the constituents is not in consonance with the *Sā. K.* which treats the three *guṇa*-s as the constituents of Nature and not as separate elements (*tattva*-s).[220]

There is a narration of discourse of Vāsudeva with Nārada. The deity Vāsudeva says that "The three constituents of goodness, passion and ignorance exist and move about in the body. The embodied soul enjoys these constituents (of Nature) but the constituents do not enjoy him, since he is free from constituents (*nirguṇa*), the enjoyer of the constituents (*guṇabhuk*), the creator of the constituents and superior to them."[221] Here, the statement that the Soul is the creator of the constituents *(guṇasraṣṭṛ)* does not tally with the *Sā. K.* 11. which specifies that it is Nature which creates and Puruṣa is the reverse of that.[222] According to the *Sā. K.*, the Soul is neither the creator, nor the created, evolute (*vikṛti*).[223] This feature of creation of constituents by the Self is the same as that stated by the Vedāntins. This can be substantiated by the contents of the *Mbh.* according to which the unmanifest gets dissolved into the passive Person, which is the Supreme Person.[224] Thus, the *Mbh.* shows the tendency of synthesizing the principles of Sāṁkhya philosophy with those of the Vedānta.

The *Āśva. P.* contains detailed descriptions about the qualities, work, effect of these constituents on various beings from different angles. It is stated that when there is an equilibrium of the three constituents, the matter is not manifest. Hence, it is called unmanifest (*avyakta*). The moment there is an imbalance in these constituents, the act of manifestation commences.[225] The constituents goodness, passion and ignorance are pairs, which are dependent on each other. They follow and blend with each other.[226] All the five gross elements are made up of three elements (*guṇa*-s). The constituent goodness pairs with ignorance, the element of passion pairs with goodness and vice-a-versa. When the element of ignorance is controlled, there is a preponderance of passion and when passion is restrained, the goodness gets augmented. The element of ignorance has a form of darkness. It is also called delusion. It marks unrighteousness and is present in sinners. It remains in combination with other elements.[227] Regarding the element of passion, it is stated that this element is the form of the Matter, it is the cause of creation and it is characterised by visibility.[228]

The qualities of light, faith and absence of pride are consequences of the element of goodness.[229] The element of ignorance represents delusion, absence of the spirit of sacrifice, indecision, laziness, sinfulness, wickedness, destruction, rivalry and all that is inauspicious, bad etc.[230] The people, in whom this element predominates, are likely to insult the deities, brahmins and the Veda-s. They are not inclined to give alms.[231] All the sinners have the preponderance of the element of ignorance. They are reborn as lower things or beings such as like insects, animals, demons etc.[232] The element of passion generates anger, beauty, sorrow, heat, cold, wealth, prosperity, strength, tolerance, censure, inclination to fight, the tendency to be interested in looking after the family and helping nature, that of serving sick people with a view to secure some fruit or the other.[233] The impact of this element on the principles such as mind, intellect etc. differs from case to case.[234] The performance of periodical rites, ceremonies, sacrifice etc. with the intention of fruit, rage, disbelief etc. are also the impacts of the element of passion. Passion leads to avarice.[235] Injury, delusion, pride, theft, disgust, arrogance, enjoyment of all kinds etc. are the qualities of people characterised by the element of action or passion. These people go on worrying about the past, present and future occurrences. They follow righteousness and are after wealth and sensual pleasures.[236] They behave as they like, they are graded as the lower ones (*arvāksrotas*). These people are born and reborn again and again, enjoy life and perform rituals with the intention of some or the other gain.[237]

The third element of goodness is the characteristic of great people. It is the best of all the constituents, beneficial to all beings and the uncensured duty of good persons.[238] Happiness, pleasantness, progress, light, boldness, faith, forgiveness, non-violence, equality, truth, straight forwardness, purity, affection etc. are the characteristics of the constituents of goodness.[239] This constituent frees one from pride, hope and enables him to stabilize his intellect and perform activities without expecting any fruit.[240]

Those having the element of *sattva* predominant in them attain the highest position, those having *rajas* element predominant in them remain in the middle, whereas those having *tamas* element predominant in them go to the lower world.[241] It is also stated that there is a preponderance of the element of the goodness in the Brāhmins, that of action in the Kṣatriya-s and of ignorance in the Śūdra-s. The existence of constituents of Nature in different entities like the sun, the static elements (*sthāvara-s*) has been described as well as the working of these constituents in one and the same entity. This can be noticed from the description that the light of the sun is the constituent of goodness, its heat is the constituent of action and the sun getting eclipsed on the new moon day is considered to be the constituent of ignorance.[242] The corporeal and incorporeal things like the past, the present, the future, the way of life, the wealth, the sensual pleasure, the vital breath etc. are made up of three constituents.[243] The Matter, made up of these three constituents, is eternal.[244] Throughout this dissertation, there appears to be a constant effort on the part of Brahmā to show how all the facets of life are touched by the three constituents of the Matter.

Although the *Bh. G.*, does not give the detailed description at a stretch as given by Brahmā in *Āśva P.*, it covers in different sections all the effects of the three constituents on human behaviour. While answering Arjuna's question, as to what is the way to attain the highest good, Kṛṣṇa states that "There is a twofold path of Sāṁkhya and Yoga." Here, he states that nobody ever remains even for an instant without performing some action, since the qualities of Prakṛti constrain everybody to action, and nobody is having free will to action.[245] All kinds of work are done by the constituents of Nature. However, due to self-sense the bewildered Soul thinks, 'I am a doer', but one who knows the truth about the distinction of the Soul from the constituents of Nature, does not get attached.[246] Then in chapter 29, Kṛṣṇa says, "all the entities which are of the quality of harmonious (*sāttvika*), passionate (*rājas*) and slothful (*tāmas*), are from me."[247] He further reasons that "I am not in them but they are in Me." This statement is explained in the *Gītārahasya* as, "since there does not exist diversity in his qualityless (*nirguṇa*) form, he is not in them but they are in him."[248] Here, the duality of Sāṁkhya is negated and the concept of threefold constituents is synthesized with the Upaniṣadic concept of monism. He further resumes that the world does not recognize him, the imperishable one, as it is deluded by the threefold constituents of Nature.[249] This three constituted Nature, is his divine power (*Māyā*).[250] The *G.R.* states that this Māyā, ignorance is the inherent quality of senses in which the three constituents are embodied. It is not the quality of Ātman.[251] Thus, emphasizing the Ātman theory of the Upaniṣad-s. He further states that forms (*vikāra*-s) and modes are born of Nature and the soul joined with Nature enjoys the qualities born of Nature. The connection of the Soul with the qualities is the cause of its birth in good or evil wombs.[252] The three constituents born of Nature tie up the indestructible soul in the body. Out of these three constituents, goodness, being pure, causes illumination and health. It binds the soul by the bond of happiness and knowledge.[253] The constituent of passion, which springs from desire, has attraction as its characteristic. It fastens the being by action. The dullness (*tamas*), however, is born of ignorance. It deludes all the embodied beings and binds them up by negligence, indolence and sleep (as a result of which they are unable to achieve salvation). The constituent of goodness creates happiness, passion leads to action and dullness, veiling wisdom leads to mistakes.[254] The *Bh. G.* describes the prevalence of the constituents in different situations. It states that when the passion and ignorance (*tamas*) are suppressed, goodness stands and when the passion and goodness are restrained, ignorance prevails. Likewise, when ignorance and goodness are overpowered, passion prevails. When the light of knowledge streams forth in the entire body, that is an indication of the predominince of goodness. Greed, activity, unrest, craving and action are indicative of the prepondernce of the element of passion. Want of light, want of activity, heedlessness and delusion are produced when ignorance dominates.[255] It is obvious that these principles tally with the contents of the *Sā. K.*[256]

The *Bh. G.* also narrates the modes (*gati*-s) of the embodied Soul, when it encounters death. If goodness predominates, one attains untainted worlds, whereas when the constituent of passion is dominating, one is born as a person attached to action. On the contrary, if one dies when the constituent of ignorance preponderates, one is born as an ignorant one.[257] The above contents are in agreement with those of the *Sā. K.*[258]

The *Bh. G.* describes the nature of the fruit of action in accordance with that of three constituents. "The fruit of meritorious action is good and untainted, while that of passion is misery and the ignorance is the fruit of *tamas*."[259] The goodness produces knowledge, passion produces avarice and from *tamas* arises negligence, error, delusion and ignorance. Those who resort to goodness rise upwards, the passionate remain in the middle, while the ignorant ones sink downwards.[260] This description tallies with the contents of the *Sā. K.* 54.[261] It is further stated that the embodied Soul attains immortality only after transcending these three constituents.[262] The *Bh. G.* explains the character of the one who goes beyond the three constituents.[263] The entire discourse in this section briefly mentions the impacts of the preponderance of one of the three constituents on the embodied Self. It has stated the same five causes of completion of all the actions, which have been enumerated by the Sāmakhya system.[264] While commenting on this verse, Satvalekar, S.D., has stated that Sāṁkhya theory is called *Kṛtānta*. According to Sāṁkhya theory, a deed performed with an impartial intellect (*saṁbuddhi*) is neither obstructed by any hurdles, nor is it destroyed and it is always perfect.[265] Regarding this system, the *Bh. G.* says that the completion of work is brought about by five factors, namely the substratum (*adhiṣṭhāna*), the agent (*kartṛ*), the various sorts of organs (*karaṇa*-s), the various, distinct movements (*ceṣṭā*-s) and destiny (*daiva*) to complete all the works.[266] Thus, it is totally wrong to consider the Self to be the doer or the agent. Hence, one who is devoid of egoistic feeling, whose mind is untainted, is never fettered.[267] According to the *Mbh.*, reason (*buddhi*) is threefold. That which discriminates between action (*pravṛtti*) and inaction (*nivṛtti*), between that which is worthy of being done and not worth being done, between fear and absence of fear, between bondage and salvation is *sāttvikī*. The passionate reason (*rājasī buddhi*) is that by which one is unable to distinguish between duty or piety *(dharma)* and otherwise, between activity and otherwise. The reason through which impiety is mistaken for piety is enveloped with ignorance.[268] Similarly, courage also is threefold. That by means of which mind, life-breath and functions of senses are curbed through restraint is *sāttvikī*. The courage that adheres to lust, wealth and attachment and expects the fruit is the passionate and the courage of undiscerning man is *tāmasī*.[269] The happiness, which is felt as poison initially but is comparable to nectar in the long run, is termed as good, whereas passionate happiness is just the opposite of the happiness characterised by goodness, which appears as nectar but will be like poison in the long run. The happiness arising out of the constituent of ignorance deludes the Self.[270] According to the *Bh. G.,* the fourfold classification of society (Brāhmaṇa-s, Kṣatriya-s, Vaiśya-s and Śūdra-s) is based on the threefold division of the constituents of Prakṛti.[271]

The *Bh. P.* states that action performed without attachment and any fruit in view is *sāttvika* and the doer performing such action, who is free form egoism, is courageous, energetic and unaffected by success or failure, is a *sāttvika* type of agent. The *rājasa* type of action is performed with a desire to secure the fruit, with a sense of ego. The doer, who is characterized by the sense of attachment and the desire to have fruit, who is covetous, cruel, impure and hence affected by the pairs of opposite such as happiness and sorrow, is the passionate one. *Tāmasa* type of action needs to be performed with many efforts, without taking into consideration the consequences, loss, injury or strength and *tāmasa* type of doer is stubborn, crafty, lazy, dejected and slow.[272]

One, who is self-restrained, unattached, free from desires, obtains the highest perfection through renunciation.[273] Obviously, these thoughts are based on the discussion regarding the three constituents of Prakṛti presented in the Sāṁkhya system of philosophy.

Elements (*Tattva*-s) in the Sāṁkhya Philosophy

The Sāṁkhya system considers that this world consists of twenty-five elements. In fact, due to a systematic study of these elements based on counting, it is called as Sāṁkhya system. The Nature (Prakṛti) is the creative principle from which intellect, self-sense etc. and twenty-three elements emanate. The twentyfifth element is the person (*Puruṣa*), who is passive. However, due to its proximity to the Nature, creation takes place.[274]

The *Mbh.* has a detailed description of these elements. Vyāsa in the *Śānati P.*, while explaining to Śuka, his son, the knowledge of the self, has elaborated upon the nature, work etc. of these elements. He says there are two principal elements – the Matter and the Person. He calls the Person as Kṣetrajña, who is passive and observes the creation by the Matter.[275] He further states that there are five sense organs in the body, the sixth element is mind, the seventh is the intellect and Kṣetrajña, the embodied Self, is the eight element.[276] The self-sense (*ahaṁbhāva*) in the body is the modification of intellect.[277] The intellect, mind and self-sense have emanated-out of their own impression of earlier existence.[278] Intellect, he says, is the presiding element of all the sense organs (*indriyas*).[279] Intellect acquires the modes and gets modified and the modifications are called the sense-organs.[280] The first modification of intellect is the mind. Thereafter, mind carries out the act of creation of the world.[281] He also gives gradation of the elements. Accordingly, the objects of sense are higher than the sense organs, as the objects attract the sense-organs towards them. The mind is higher than the objects of sense, intellect is higher than the mind as the intellect keeps the mind under control. However, the highest among all the elements is the Soul (Ātman),[282] because it is the Soul which supervises the intellect.

Further, he states that the intellect acquires different forms for hearing, smelling etc. and these forms are the five organs of sense as ears and nose etc.[283] In the earlier section, he had given the description of five great elements (*pañca mahābhūta*-s) from which this entire movable and immovable world comes into existence.[284] Different qualities of the gross elements have been explained by him, such as sound, ear and all the openings of the body are the qualities of space; breath, movement and touch are the qualities of air, light or form, eyes and stomach are the forms of fire; taste, tongue and lubrications are the qualities of water and smell, nose and the body are the qualities of the earth.[285]

As has been already stated Vasiṣṭha's description is systematic. Step by step, he unfolds all the elements of the Sāṁkhya system. His description of the Nature in the section 294 reveals the unfolding of creation process. He says, "At the time of dissolution, the Nature is homogeneous and the unmanifest Nature becomes manifest after the creation."[286] It can, therefore, be known that before the creation, the Nature is unmanifest and homogeneous. It is the Supreme Self, which manifolds Nature in different forms.[287] From this Nature immerges intellect, out of it self-sense and from it, is the emanation of subtle elements and the modified evolution due to three constituents.[288] This process of emanation concurs with the *Sā. K.* 24.[289] The Nature is the cause of emanation of the world, Vasiṣṭha asserts, and this agrees with the contents of the *Sā. K.*[290] He also states that the Nature, intellect, self-sense, mind, five gross elements, five sense organs, five subtle elements, five objects of sense all these twenty-four elements are material (*jaḍa*) elements. However, the Self, the twenty-fifth element, is unlike other twenty-four elements. It is termed as *'nistattva'*.[291] Puruṣa, described in the *Sā. K.* 19,[292] is different from this twenty fifth element. The twenty-fifth element in the *Mbh.* is homogeneous at the time of dissolution like the Nature. However, at the time of creation, since it is a stimulating factor for the creation, it appears as if it is manifold. This feature of multiplicity is imposed upon it due to its proximity to the

Nature as it imagines itself as affected by modifications. It is like Brahman of the Upaniṣad-s. Brahmā in the *Āśva P.* expounds the knowledge of the Self. He states that this world consists of twenty-five elements. According to the Vedic texts, the first stage of creation consists of twenty-four elements, namely, unmanifest Nature, intellect, self-sense, ten senses, mind, five gross elements and sound etc. specific qualities. The Self is the twenty-fifth element. He further explains that in the unmanifest Nature, the three constituents are in a state of equipoise.[293] When there is an imbalance in these constituents, then the Matter manifests into the material.

The body made up of five gross elements is the city of nine ates. The soul residing in this city is drawn towards the objects f sense by the eleven sense organs including the mind.[294] The tellect is the master of the body, and the mind does the job of anifestation.[295] This thought agrees with the *Sā. K.* 37.[296] In the ght of the remark of Wilson quoted by Davis John, it must be oted that the intellect is the master of the body. The *manas,* ving received ideas from the external organs, transfers them to e intellect. The intellect, the general superintendent, takes the arge of them for the use of the sovereign Soul.[297]

In the *Śānti P.*, Yājñavalkya, says that there are eight primary ements out of which one is unmanifest and the remaining seven manifest, which include the intellect, self-sense and five gross ements, space, air etc.[298] and sixteen modifications, which are olved products consisting of five sense-organs, five subtle ements like speech, touch etc., five organs of action such as nds, legs etc. He further clarifies that five organs of action and ech etc. objects of sense are called attributes, five sense organs l intellect are treated as elements possessing qualities. He states t all these attributes exist in five gross elements.[299]

Asita in the *Śānti P.* narrates that Kāla urged by the Ātman ated this universe through five gross elements.[300] These five ss elements (*pañcamahābhūta*-s), *āpas, tejas, vāyuḥ, antarikṣa, pṛthivī* and Kāla are the six elements which are eternal, steady and firm.[301] The conglomeration of *citta*, five sense organs, *viz.* eyes, nose, ears, skin and tongue together with *manas* and *buddhi*– these eight are called the organs of sense (*jñānendriya*-s) by the philosophers.[302] The five organs of action (*karmendriya*-s) and vigour (*balam*) form a group of six elements.[303] *Sāttvika, rājasa* and *tāmasa* are the *bhāva*-s.[304] Thus, the group of eight *jñānendriya*-s, the group of six, *karmendriya*-s and *balam,* three *bhāva*-s (*sāttvika, rājasa* and *tāmasa*) form seventeen elements. With the embodied self (*dehin*)*, ekam* (probably *mahat*) and the heat (*uṣman*), the twenty elements together are called the conglomeration of five elements (*saṅghātaḥ pāñcabhautikaḥ*).[305] If five gross elements and Kāla are added to this conglomeration, the total number of elements would be twenty-six. If Kāla is excluded, being a creator, they would amount to twenty-five. However, Asita has not specifically stated it. But the treatment of the *bhāva*-s as elements, which are actually the constituents of the Nature (*guṇa*-s), does not agree with the *Sā. K.*[306]

Nārada instructs Śuka that since the world has originated from gross elements, the body is consisted of gross material. The intellect, five gross and five subtle elements, five sense organs and three *guṇa*-s as one element form group of seventeen, which is construed as unmanifest. After adding five sense objects, mind, self-sense and the Person the unmanifest and manifest, elements are regarded twenty-five.[307] Consideration of the *guṇa*-s as elements disagrees with the contents of the *Sā. K.* 11.[308] Also, the emanation of the world from five gross elements does not agree with the *Sā. K.* 22.[309] which states emanation of the world from the primordial Nature. Also the *Sā. K.* 38 considers five gross elements have proceeded from five subtle elements, which are the products of self sense.[310]

In the *Śānti P.*, again, *Pañcaśikha* while explaining to Janaka the state of the Soul after death, does not state the number of total elements in the world specifically. However, in place of subtle elements (*tanmātra*-s), he considers objects of sense (*indriyārtha*-

s) as elements. He considers a set each of sense organs, their respective sense objects and the doer (*kartṛ*) in the form of reasoning faculty (*citta*) and forms five groups of these three each. These five groups of three each enable the being to grasp the objects of sense such as sound (*śabda*), form (*rūpa*) etc.[311] The elements stated are five sense-organs, five organs of action, *manas*, five *indriyārtha*-s, five great elements (*mahābhūtā*-s) unmanifest (*avyakta*), intellect and *ahaṁkāra* these amount to twenty four.[312]

This theory has a resemblance to Caraka's Sāṁkhya system as mentioned earlier. Caraka considers the elements in the world as twenty-four. [313] Hindi Commentary on *Caraka Saṁhitā* by Shastri, Kashinath and Chaturvedi, Gorakhnath enumerates these twenty-four elements as *mahat, ahaṁkāra,* five *tanmātra*-s, which emanate from *buddhi,* five organs of sense, five organs of action, *manas,* five *mahābhūta*-s and *para* means *avyakta.* All these elements together make the Puruṣa.[314]

In the *Mbh.*, the reference to all the elements of Sāṁkhya system appear in the Chapter 35 of the *Bhīṣma P.* While explaining the Upaniṣadic concept of *kṣetra* and *kṣetrajña*, Kṛṣṇa begins his discourse declaring that he himself is Kṣetrajña[315] and directly connects him to Him, Brahman. He then describes *kṣetra* as made up of great elements, self-sense or egoism, the intellect, the unmanifest that is the Nature, ten senses and the one that is mind, five objects of sense, desire, aversion, pleasure, pain, body, consciousness, courage, *i.e.* in brief, the *kṣetra* with changes or developments.[316] Further, in the same section, he states that the Nature and the soul both are without beginning and all the developments such as body, senses etc. and qualities like pleasure and pain etc. are produced from Nature. Nature is the origin of the capacity of working in the body and the senses, and the Soul is said to be the origin of the capacity of enjoying pleasures and pains. The Soul (Puruṣa), joined with Nature, enjoys the qualities born of Nature. The cause of its birth in good or evil wombs is its connection with the qualities, constituents of Nature.[317] He then goes on to describe the Supreme Spirit in this body, who is the supervisor, enjoyer, the great lord and the Supreme Self also and declares that who thus knows the Nature and the Soul, together with the qualities is not born again. In section 32, there is a description of unmanifest nature from which all perishable things are produced on the advent of the day of Brahmā and on the advent of the night of him, they dissolve in the same principle.[318] The *Mbh.* further states that "There is another entity unmanifest and eternal and distinct from this unmanifest principle, which is not destroyed when all entities are destroyed"[319] It is the highest goal and nobody returns after attaining it. It is His Supreme abode. That Supreme Being in whom all the entities dwell permeates this universe.[320] Here, the first reference to unperceived principle is directed towards the unmanifest Nature, which produces all the perishable things and the another entity, which is unperceived and eternal, is the Supreme being, Brahman.

In the section 29 of *Bh. P.*, it is pointed out by Kṛṣṇa that five great elements (*mahābhūtā*–s), mind, understanding and egoism is his eight-fold Nature. However, it is his lower Nature and higher than that, there is another Nature of him, which upholds this universe. He is the producer and destroyer of the whole universe.

He further asserts that there is nothing else higher than himself.[321] In section 24, there comes a reference, which states that "man's mind is steady when he withdraws his senses from the objects of sense."[322] He further proclaims that the boisterous senses carry away by force the mind even of a wise man and hence, one should restrain them to enable him to attain emancipation.[323]

In the next section 25 of the *Bh. P.,* he states that it is the desire that is the foe of the being in this world.[324] The senses, the mind, and the understanding are said to be its seat.[325] The object is perceived by the senses, the mind ponders over it, the understanding determines and then the desire awakens. Hence, he advises Arjuna to restrain his senses. Thereafter, he starts with the description of the gradation of the elements. He says, "Great are the senses, greater than the senses is the mind, greater than the mind is the understanding and greater than the understanding is the Supreme being."[326] He then counsels Arjuna thus, "By knowing that highest principle and restraining yourself by yourself, destroy this unmanageable enemy in the form of desire."[327]

At the end of his discourse, Kṛṣṇa advises Arjuna that no embodied being can abandon action. However, one who abandons the fruit of action, is said to be a sacrificer (*tyāgin*).[328] He then explains the threefold division of intelligence and steadiness according to the constituents (*guṇa*–s). He says that "Intelligence, which understands, action and inaction etc., is good intelligence, and thereafter describes passionate and dark intelligence. He says that intelligence, which cannot make a proper discrimination between righteous and unrighteous, doable and not-doable, is passionate intelligence and that, which gives perverse, contrary verdict on all matters, is dark intelligence.[329] He emphasizes that man possessed of a pure understanding and "controlling his Self by courage, discarding the objects of sense etc., and abandoning egoism becomes tranquil and fit for assimilation with the Brahman."[330]

Tilak B.G., commenting on the division of intelligence, states that there can be an intelligence (*buddhi*), which has the *sāttvika* quality of choosing only the right thing. It is acquired by previous impressions, or by education, or by control of organs etc. In the absence of such factors as previous impressions etc., that same intelligence (*buddhi*) becomes passionate (*rājasa*) or dark (*tāmasa*) not only in the matter of discrimination between the doable and the not-doable but in all matters."[331] The import of the argument is that one can easily make one's intelligence *sāttvika* by controlling the organs, by not allowing the *buddhi* to become the slave of the mind and the organs and by deeply impressing upon the mind the principle that the Ātman in all the human beings is the same.

The feature of ranking the elements has been observed in the discourses of Vyāsa and Kṛṣṇa in *Mbh.*[332] The ranking is for obvious reasons as can be observed from the functioning of senses, organs of action, mind and intellect. The mind presents various particulars, ideas about certain things. Intellect has the discerning capacity. It decides whether an object or an action is good or bad. The mind, then, gets the work done through the organs of action. Hence, the intellect has been considered as superior to the mind and the organs. Moreover, knowledge of anything cannot be acquired unless it is identified by the intellect. Further, unless we acquire the knowledge of that object, we do not conceive the intention or the desire for obtaining the object and the fruit to be derived from it. Thus, the superiority of intellect is evident. The simile of body as chariot, organs as horses, *buddhi* as charioteer and mind as reins appearing in the (*Mbh. Van. P.*[333], *Strī P.*[334], *Ā,,va. P.*[335], and *Bh. P.*[336]) presents the same idea.

The Consideration of Mutable and Immutable-Kṣarākṣara Vicāra

To know the true nature of the Soul, one has to take into consideration not only the body and the Soul, but their relation to the cosmos, the external world (Brahmāṇḍa). In the Vedānta philosophy, the individual Soul is designated as the Brahman or the Ātman on cosmic level, whereas on physiological level, it is related to the material Self. The Vedāntin-s consider that this Soul is the subject and the material body is the object. Nevertheless, this distinction of the subject and object does not exist in the Supreme Self as it is the root cause, *i.e.* the source from which both the subject and object come into existence, the object being body and the material world. Both of them are mutable, whereas the Supreme Soul is immutable.

The relation of the cosmos with the soul has also been examined by the Sāṁkhya philosophy synthetically. It is called as the consideration of the mutable and immutable or of the perceptible and imperceptible. The Sāṁkhya system believes in the Satkāryavāda, that is, the theory, which propounds that the things are produced out of something, which was already in existence.[337] Accordingly, Sāṁkhyavādin-s state that the original fundamental substance at the root of all the things in the cosmos is Prakṛti and the subsequent emanation from Prakṛti is called transformation (*vikṛti* or *vikāra*).[338] This is a modification of the fundamental substance. In view of Satkāryavāda, if the fundamental element had only one constituent quality, the things emanating from it would not have possessed a variety of qualities. For things to have diverse qualities, the fundamental substance also should have different qualities in it. The Sāṁkhya philosophy had, therefore, made a provision of three classes of constituents inherent in the Matter (*Prakṛti*) *viz. sattva, rajas* and *tamas.*[339] These qualities are present in the Matter from the very beginning. However, before the creation and after the dissolution of the world, they are in the state of equilibrium. When Prakṛti comes into contact with Puruṣa, this equilibrium is disturbed and Prakṛti begins to unfold itself before the Soul (*Puruṣa*) and manifestation, creation takes place.[340] There is a variance in the intensity of these constituents, which results in the creation. Due to a diversity in these constituents, the Matter, which was originally homogeneous, assumes different forms such as the earth, water, sky, different animals, metals, human beings etc. As per the preponderance of one of these constituents, the things are described as *sāttvika, rājasa* and *tāmasa.*

The *Mbh.* represents these views when Kṛṣṇa states "All entities possessing qualities of *sāttvika, rājasa* and *tāmasa* constituents are from me."[341] The *Mbh.* also states that the moment there is an imbalance in the constituents the act of manifestation commences.[342]

When the Matter is unmanifest and the constituents are in the state of equilibrium, it is called imperceptible (*avyakta*) to the senses. The things, which have come into existence due to the movement of the constituents of *sattva, rajas* and *tamas,* are called perceptible (*vyakta*). These perceptible objects are gross (*sthūla*) or subtle (*sūkṣma*). At every dissolution, the perceptible objects become imperceptible and perceptible at the time of creation. The imperceptible unmanifest Prakṛti is also called immutable (*akṣara*) and the perceptible things, which have come into existence from it, are called mutable (*kṣara*). The term *kṣara* does not indicate that these things are completely destroyed. It suggests that they become imperceptible, it is in the sense of imperceptibility since they merge into Prakṛti.

According to the *Mbh.*, there are two kinds of Puruṣa – the perishable one and the imperishable one. All the beings are perishable and the Soul within is said to be imperishable.[343] The *Mbh.* also states that both Prakṛti and Puruṣa are perishable (*kṣara*) and imperishable (*akṣara*). The unmanifest Prakṛti is called imperishable (*akṣara*) due to its nature of creation and dissolution. When Prakṛti manifests, it gets modified repeatedly. Hence, it is considered as perishable (*kṣara*). The elements like *mahat, ahaṁkāra* are produced by the union of Prakṛti and Puruṣa. Hence, they become the substratum of each other. Puruṣa, therefore, is called *kṣetra,*[344] which is perishable (*kṣara*). When the being with discriminative knowledge recognizes its real form, he discards the mutable Prakṛti and attains pure imperishable state. Hence, Puruṣa is considered to be imperishable (*akṣara*).[345] The same thought appears again. It states that the world is mutable. Hence it is called *kṣara* and the immortal soul is immutable (*akṣara*). Both of these elements exist in each being (being material constituent of the world and the Soul). Along with them, there is the Supreme Soul.[346] When the being recognizes the manifest Prakṛti and perceives the sentient element in all the beings,[347] he is released from all the earlier impressions and attains that tranquil, immovable eternal immutable Supreme Soul.[348]

Thus, the *Mbh.* has synthesized this Sāṁkhya concept of mutable and immutable with that of the Vedānta. It designated the Brahman as Paramātman and stated that from the Supreme Soul, the unmanifest Nature (Pradhāna, Prakṛti) has evolved. From Pradhāna, the manifest world has come into existence.[349] It also states that the Supreme Soul, which is eternal, creates Brahmā. Brahmā is looked upon as the element *mahat* by the Sāṁkhya-vādin-s.[350] The intellect (*mahat*) originates from the unmanifest Prakṛti according to the Sāṁkhya philosophy.

Thus, the Sāṁkhya philosophy classifies the world under two categories-the mutable one and the immutable one. Prakṛti is immutable. The elements which come under the category of mutable are the transformations of Prakṛti. Accordingly, the mind, intellect, self-sense (*ahaṁkāra*) are the qualities of gross matter. The gross matter consists of the five great elements (*mahābhūta*-s). All the remaining elements are the modifications of these elements. However, the twenty-fifth element, consciousness, which is the knower, which experiences the objective world is altogether different from the Matter.[351] This element, which perceives the unmanifest Matter and gross manifest Matter, is the Soul (Puruṣa). Unlike Prakṛti, he is devoid of qualities. Hence, he is beyond the three constituents of Prakṛti. This Puruṣa does not get transformed. Hence, he is immutable. He is a mere onlooker and inactive, too.[352] He does not interfere into the creative activities of the Matter. He is eternal, independent and self-created like the Matter (Prakṛti).

The *Mbh.* accepts these views and states that Prakṛti and Puruṣa both are without a beginning and eternal. It further describes that both of them are immutable and both together are called Īśvara. It also states that the functions of a body (and the world too) are carried out by the Prakṛti[353] and Puruṣa is the experiencer of the pleasure and pain.[354] Though the *Mbh.* subscribes the idea of Prakṛti and Puruṣa to be eternal, it does not accept the view that both of them are independent and self-created entities. According to the *Mbh.*, it is Parabrahman which is the creator of all. The Matter is its part[355] and creation takes place under its supervision.[356]

Thus, here also the *Mbh.* has synthesized Sāṁkhya and Vedānta philosophy and assigned the task of creation to Brahman.

Prakṛti of the Sāṁkhyavādins is not vitalized, is insentient (*acetana*) and hence, logically it cannot create on its own. Whereas, Puruṣa is without qualities and it is not possible for Puruṣa to create the qualitative world. Moreover, Puruṣa is passive, uninterested. Hence, he would not undertake the task of creation. Under these circumstances, creation by them would not be feasible. The *Mbh.* has, therefore, considered the Supreme Self (Paramātman) to be one who presided over these two and impelled them to create the world. These two elements, *viz.* Prakṛti and Puruṣa, originated from the Supreme Self.[357] Under his supervision, the creation of the world was brought about.[358] Here, the *Mbh.* has modified the Sāṁkhya doctrine of creation by bringing the two entities under the Supreme Self to make the creation of the world rationally possible. Tilak, B.G. has, rightly opined that, the *Bh. G.* has gone one step further from the Sāṁkhya philosophy.[359]

The Concept of Deliverance According to the Sāṁkhya Philosophy

According to the Sāṁkhya system (orthodox), the empirical Self is composed of free Spirit and Matter, where the Spirit (*Puruṣa*) forgets its true nature and is deluded into a belief that it thinks, feels and acts. Intelligence (*buddhi*), by means of the reflection of the Self (Puruṣa), which is adjacent to it, becomes its form and experiences objects. In Sāṁkhya system, salvation is phenomenal. In reality, nobody (Spirit) is bound or liberated. It is the primal Nature that is bound and liberated and transmigrated. Thus, bondage is the activity of primordial Matter (*Prakṛti*), which ties down one who lacks the power of discrimination. Prakṛti remains inactive towards one who is endowed with discriminating ability and consequently, he gets release. The discriminative knowledge can be obtained by the practice of virtue and Yoga.

Zimmer Heinrich aptly describes the manner in which the process of release takes place in the Sāṁkhya system. He says, "When the contemplative power (*sattva*) of the thinking substance (*buddhi*) is freed from the defilement of the active power (*rajas*) and the force of inertia (*tamas*), and has no further task of removing difference between itself (*sattva*) and the Soul (Puruṣa), and when the interior seeds of hindrance (*kleśa*) have all been burned, then contemplative power (*sattva*) enters into the state of purity, which is equal to that of the Soul. The Soul (*jīvātman*), which aspires for salvation, is to purge the intelligence (*buddhi*) of *rajas* and *tamas* so that only *sattva* remains. Thus, it becomes clear and unagitated and reflects the Puruṣa without distinction. When the Puruṣa is so reflected, the aspirant has just to recognize that the reflection is not Puruṣa. Thus, there is a cessation of the false attributes of experience to the individual Soul (*jīvātman*). Once this awareness dawns upon the Soul (*jīvātman*), he is released."[360]

According to Caraka's Sāṁkhya thought, all pleasures and pains are felt by the conglomeration of elements and not by the Ātman presiding over it. From the enjoyment and suffering comes desire (*tṛṣṇā*), consisting of wish and antipathy and from desire again comes pleasure and pain. *Mokṣa* means complete cessation of pleasure and pain arising through the association of the Self, the mind (*manas*), the senses and the sense objects.[361]

Sāṁkhya philosophy of the *Mbh.* is mostly based on orthodox Sāmakhya concept. In the *Mbh.*, Bhīṣma begins his discourse with Yudhiṣṭhira stating that the Supreme Soul exists in the embodied Self with all the placid, active and dark constituents alongwith the intelligence, mind, gross elements etc.[362] When the embodied Self (*jīvātman*) transgresses Matter and the sense organs, he attains the Supreme Soul (*Paramātman*) who is eternal, without duality. This Supreme Self is of the form of *Nārāyaṇa.*[363] Thus, here, the Ultimate release is merging into the Supreme Self. The Soul, free from sins and merits, once merged into the Supreme Self does not return to this world.[364] However, if due to fate his body remains even after the realization, his mind and sense etc. organs continue to exist and in due course, after death, he attains ultimate peace.[365] The *Mbh.* has synthesized the principles of the

Sāṁkhya philosophy with those of the Vedānta when it states that the highest principle of the Sāṁkhya philosophy is certainly eternal, indestructible, unmanifest Brahman. Further, though the Mahābhāratakāra holds the view that the Sāṁkhya philosophy itself is the manifestation of that Ultimate Supreme Self and whatever knowledge that exists in this world accepts the Sāṁkhya thought,[366] the impact of the Vedānta philosophy and Nārāyaṇīya religion is visible in this discourse. The very fact that the Ultimate Reality according to Bhīṣma is Brahman, who is termed as Nārāyaṇa, the Sāṁkhya concepts have been used as a mere tool to express his views.[367]

The Mahābhāratakāra states that the qualities exist in the qualitative element. However, the Soul is without qualities. Hence, the scients maintain that when the soul realizes that the qualities, *i.e.* modes, are the constituents of Matter and discards the sense of individuation with those qualities of Matter, he perceives the Ultimate Entity (*Paramātman*).[368] The *Mbh.* has explained this thought in the next section, wherein it is stated that when the twenty-fifth element perceives itself as different from Nature and realizes that it is eternal and consists of pure intelligence (*cinmaya*), it then attains liberation (*kevala* state).[269] Here, the embodied Soul is called Buddhyamāna, one which is of the nature of knowledge, which is distinct from Nature. It is declared that the Soul of such a being does not return to this world; he attains the ultimate, immutable state.[370] It is further maintained that due to its contact with the elements of Matter, the Soul wrongly considers himself to be the doer and only on acquiring pure and supreme intellect, he perceives the unmanifest Brahman, the Supreme Soul and merges into It.[371] It is further stated that the individual Soul, on the strength of discriminating power, can have the perception that he is the twenty sixth element and thereafter he attains the state of the Supreme Spirit.[372] However, if the embodied Soul does not have the knowledge of the Supreme Soul, it remains ignorant. Once the Soul knows that it is not the gross body and severs its ties with it, he establishes his identity with the Supreme Soul.[373]

Having realized this, the individual Soul (*jīvātman*) becomes one with the Supreme Soul.[374] From the above narration, it is clear that even here, the monistic Vedānta philosophy is synthesized with that of the Sāṁkhya philosophy.

Here, in this discourse, there is a description of the ignorant (*apratibuddha*), the immutable (*akṣara*) and the Supreme Soul, which is enlightened. The *Mbh.* has emphasized the eternal nature of the Soul, and its identity with the Supreme Soul. By this, human beings become hopeful that release (*mokṣa*) does not annihilate the Soul. Individual Soul becomes identical with the Supreme Soul.[375]

Yājñavalkya in his discussion with Janaka has glorified the place realized by *sāttvika* type of person as the highest place.[376] The embodied Soul, who constantly reflects on the Supreme Soul, frees himself from the Primordial Matter and attains the identity with It.[377] It is further clarified that the ignorant people think that the twenty-fifth element, the individual Soul, and the Supreme Soul (*Paramātman*) are different from each other. However, the scients treat it as only one. The Sāṁkhyavādins and Yogins treat them as one and the same.[378] Thus, there is a synthesis of Sāṁkhya, Vedānta and Yoga Philosophy.

The *Mbh.* contains an episode of Sulabhā, a scholarly female ascetic, who entered the body of the king Janaka in order to know whether he has really attained the final beatitude during life-time (*jīvanmukta* stage). To her query whether he was released, Janaka stated that knowledge leads to detachment, which in turn enables one to achieve salvation.[379] The being is emancipated by knowledge alone.

His nescience has been removed, he has discarded his association with all worldly things and hence, even though he is a householder, he does not perceive duality anymore.[380] According to him, there are three paths leading to salvation, one is of knowledge (*jñānaniṣṭhā*), the other one of renunciation (*saṁnyāsa*) and desireless work (*karmaniṣṭhā*) is the third one. His preceptor, however, taught him the third *niṣṭhā*, which is different from just knowledge and just work.[381] By this path even a householder can achieve salvation. When a man discards desire, hatred and an interest in acquisition etc., even in a state of being a householder, he can achieve liberation. He is able to cut off the bonds of attachment by the weapon sharpened on the stone of deliverance of the Soul (*mokṣa*). The weapon is of non-attachment and indifference towards world's affairs.[382] This is exactly in consonance with Karma-yoga taught in the *Bh. G.*

The *Mbh.* describes the characteristics of the ascetics, who are released and who perceive the Supreme Brahman. Renunciation is the best penance (*tapas*) and the knowledge is the form of Supreme Brahman.[383] When one discards the constituent of action, follows the path of renunciation and knows the Brahman with the help of penance, he obtains the Supreme deity.[384] A person, who knows the Matter and its qualities and frees himself from the feeling of 'I'ness, attains salvation. One who does not entertain any desire, one who is free from affection and pride, attains emancipation even in this world.[385] The ascetic, who discontinues all the auspicious as well as inauspicious works on account of three constituents (of Matter) along with the truth and untruth, attains release.[386] This concept of total renunciation is unlike that of Janaka. He does not believe in discarding everything, every work like an ascetic. Janaka believes that a householder, who follows the duties assigned to him can attain release by performing his welfare activities.[387]

Vyādha describes the qualities of three constituents of *sattva, rajas* and *tamas.*[388] When there is a preponderance of the constituent of the goodness, a being realizes the full significance of the world. He then hates it and thereafter develops indifference towards worldly affairs. His arrogance declines and humbleness predominates. His conflicting moral sentiments (*sarvadvandvāni*) get reconciled and then self-restraint becomes unnecessary.[389]

He then narrates the path of Yoga and states that a man after cleansing his mind by asceticism obtains pure knowledge and then the Self is perceived only through subtle intellect.[390] The being ultimately attains the Brahman by discarding the pairs of pleasure and pain etc.[391] Thus, once again, there is a synthesis of the Vedānta, Sāṁkhya and Yoga Philosophy.

The *Bh. G.* states that it is the Prakṛti that acts. However, Puruṣa, overwhelmed by the dance of primordial Matter, has false notion that he is the doer and thinks himself to be an agent of the activity of Nature.[392] However, when the Self realizes that it is distinct from the Matter, it attains Brahman.[393] Kṛṣṇa says, "A being established in goodness (*sattva*) rises upwards.[394] The embodied Soul, the seer, perceives that there is no agent other than the constituents of Nature.[395] He neither abhors illumination, activity and delusion, when they arise and does not long for them, when they cease to remain. Unconcerned, unperturbed by the Matter, he stands apart without wavering, but knowing that it is the work of constituents and recognizes one who is beyond constituents.[396] Such a Soul rises above the three constituents and is free from birth and death, old age and pain and attains eternal life."[397]

There is a beautiful simile describing the state of the released soul. Here, the Matter is compared to a mirror. It portrays the Soul in it.[398] According to the *G.R.*, when intelligence becomes contemplative *(sāttvika),* the Spirit realizes its identity and knows itself to be different from the Matter and the Matter having been seen by the Self stops dancing and retires.[399] *Sā. K.* 59 presents this simile.[400] While commenting on this phenomenon, Davis John states, it is in fact Prakṛti which gets released from the Self (*Puruṣa*).[401]

Thus, there are innumerable Souls and when in an individual Self, the Matter takes a placid (*sāttvika*) form, there arises a contemplative knowledge[402] and such a Self is released. The beings possessing the constituent of action and ignorance remain in the middle and lower regions respectively.[403] Thus, it is the release of an individual Self; the other Souls (*Ātman*-s) continue their worldly life. According to Sāṁkhyavādin-s, when the Spirit attains the state of isolation (*kaivalya*), it does not mean that the Self liberates from the bonds of Nature by leaving the body and the organs which are the manifestation of Matter. The Soul continues to remain connected with the Matter till the body perishes.

The *Sā. K.* describes it thus "By the attainment of complete knowledge, the bondages in the form of virtue and other factors become incapable (of producing bondages). However, the being continues to remain with a body on account of the residues, like the whirling of the wheel."[404] Kunhan Raja C. explains this as "The intellect (*buddhi*) has eight forms, four forms of placid (*sāttvika*) and four of ignorance (*tāmasa*) type. The placid forms are righteousness (*dharma*), realization (*jñāna*), asceticism (*virāga*), power (*aiśvarya*), and that of *tamas* are unrighteousness (*adharma*), ignorance (*ajñāna*), attachment (*rāga*) and the absence of power (*anaiśvaryam* or *āsakti*). When the knowledge, realization (*jñāna*) shines forth, the others cease to be the cause for any such production of activities and stages. The body, however, does not immediately fall down at the time of real knowledge. The gross body and the life phenomena of such an individual, who has attained perfect knowledge, still continues till the close of the natural life and this stage is called *jīvanmukti*, final and absolute release even during life."[405] The *Sā. K.* 68 further states that it is only when the soul is dissociated from the body, it goes away from Primordial Matter, that is, he obtains isolation of both the kinds invariable and absolute.[406] It is at this time that ultimate knowledge is secured and the subtle body does not exist. In the absence of this body, even gross body cannot exist. Individual soul cannot have its existence without this body. There will be no gross body. According to Kunhan Raja, what is called *Kaivalya* is not a state of freedom from all limitations and bondages for the individual. It is the termination of any further state.[407]

As is rightly pointed out by Kunhan Raja C., when *Sā. K.* 68 is examined in the light of *Sā. K.* 67, it reveals that even after obtaining complete knowledge, the body remains like a wheel of a potter, which continues to whirl even after serving the purpose. Likewise, persons who have obtained knowledge become *jīvanmukta*-s. They are released. Yet they continue to live with their bodies like Kapila, Sanaka, Vedavyāsa and Śaṅkarācārya. After attaining the highest knowledge, they need not wait till their bodies fall. They continue performing their assigned duties.[408] Obviously, they are *karmayogin*-s.

The *Mbh.* describes the person who is beyond the three constituents of Nature. Kṛṣṇa describes such a person as indifferent (*udāsīna*),[409] who is beyond happiness and sorrow, treats all the things on par, does not get flattered or discouraged by praise or censure, accepts whatever comes in his stride and still remains composed. He does not discriminate between friends and foes. He, in fact, is beyond the three constituents of Prakṛti.[410] Kṛṣṇa says a person who worships him, goes beyond the three constituents of Matter and attains Brahman, which is imperishable, eternal and place of ultimate happiness. "The person, who attains the state of eternity (*avyayapada*), is devoid of pride, is discerning, wise, the seeker of spiritual knowledge, impassionate, beyond the pairs of opposites like happiness and sorrow etc. He attains imperishable supreme stage.[411] The beings, who have acquired perfection to attain Brahman, are beyond pride, power, passion, anger, arrogance and possessiveness. They are calm and unattached and are always happy. They do not grieve and treat all the creatures equally. They become one with the Supreme Reality and acquire the highest devotion and attain the eternal indestructible place due to my favour."[412]

According to Pañcaśikha, when one relinquishes all the actions in the imperishable (*avyaya*), which is the highest and the essence of (all) knowledge, he realizes that the manifest (world) is *anātman*. He becomes unattached and free from sorrow.[413] Hence, when an individual is freed from worldly bonds and progeny etc., he does not experience pleasure or pain. He goes beyond the *liṅga śarīra* and attains the ultimate state. He merges (his identity) like the rivers merging their identity and name into the ocean. This is the final release (*sattvasaṅkṣaya*).[414] This thought is identical with that expressed in the *Mūṇḍ up.*[415] It also states that such a seer transgresses sorrow and sin. Such similarities substantiate Dasgupta's opinion that the theory of Caraka, which is reflected in Pañcaśikha's thought, forms a link between the Vedānta and the orthodox Sāṁkhya system.[416] According to Caraka too, *mokṣa* is a complete cessation of pleasure and pain arising on account of the Self's association with *manas,* the sense organs and the sense objects. If *manas* is settled in the Self, there is neither pleasure nor pain.[417] At this time, *rajas* and *tamas* do not exist in the *manas,* strong actions get dissolved and the being is separated from the bonds of action. Thereafter, the being is not reborn. It, thus, is the final release (*mokṣa*).[418] He also states that when the constituents of *rajas* and *tamas* are absent and there is a preponderance of *sattva*, the being is released.

Thus, according to both Pañcaśikha and Caraka, when the being experiences neither pleasure nor pain, he is free from all the worldly bonds, that is, he is unattached and his actions are completely destroyed. His actions are not fructified and the being is released.

Taking into consideration the contents of various Sāṁkhya-kārikā-s, the concept of final release according to Sāṁkhya system could, thus, be explained. According to Sāṁkhya philosophy, it is the Prakṛti that endeavours for the liberation of Puruṣa.[419] It is also stated that Puruṣa is a witness, an isolated, neutral onlooker.[420] He is neither bound nor liberated, nor does he migrate. In fact, it is the Prakṛti abiding in manifold forms that migrates or is bound or liberated.[421] Prakṛti binds herself by means of seven forms. She causes deliverance for the benefit of the subject through the eighth form.[422] The seven forms are virtue (*dharma*), non-attachment, power, vice, ignorance, attachment and absence of power.[423] By practising the principles, that is, by the repeated study of the truth, the Puruṣa knows that 'I do not exist', 'This is not my body', 'My body is different from me.' Having known this, there is nothing that is yet to be known. All doubts are dispelled. Hence, this knowledge is pure, complete, absolute.[424] Puruṣa, the spectator, then perceives Prakṛti, which has ceased to be productive, and hence has reverted back to seven forms[425] and Puruṣa, who is different, spectator in the play thinks that I have known her. Consequently, he loses his interest in everything. Prakṛti (too) thinks that Puruṣa has known (seen) me. She, therefore, stops functioning.[426] The righteousness (*dharma*) etc. cease to function. Thereafter, even though they are united, there is no further motive to evolve as producers. Puruṣa is associated with the body due to past impressions, even though he attains perfect knowledge.[427] Finally, when Puruṣa is separated from the body, as the purpose of Prakṛti is served, she ceases to act and Puruṣa attains eternal and absolute isolation.[428]

According to Zimmer H., when one acquires perfect knowledge of Puruṣa and when the forces of the work already bearing fruit are exhausted, death overtakes him and there is no return. The gross body dissolves, the subtle body too gets dissolved, inner organs dissolve, the *guṇa*-s are released from their agitation in their vertex and the individual is no longer disturbed. But the life monad continues to exist as an individual entity for and by itself. Without the apparatus of the gross body and the subtle body, Puruṣa is completely out of contact with the sphere of *guṇa*-s. He is not to be reached by anybody. He is unattainable, absolutely isolated. This is real isolation. This is in contrast with the Vedānta philosophy.[429] In this respect, the views expressed by Macdonell, A.A. and Hiriyanna, M. are noteworthy. Macdonell A. stated that, when the salvation of Sāṁkhyavādin, the absolute cessation of pain, is obtained, the internal body is dissolved into its material elements and the Soul, becoming finally isolated, continues to exist individually, but in absolute unconsciousness.[430] Hiriyanna M. maintains that there are three levels of life, the first in which *rajas* and *tamas* is the chief governing factor, the second in which *sattva* predominates and the third which transcends the element of *sattva*. When a person has reached this third stage and his lease of life runs out, he attains *Kaivalya* once for all and there is no return from there. This is called *videhamukti.*[431]

Both the Sāṁkhyavādin-s and the Upaniṣadic authors believed that it is the knowledge, which is the key to attain *Mokṣa.* However, their views differed in respect of the nature of knowledge. The Sāṁkhyavādin-s believed in dualistic theory and stated that aloofness of Puruṣa would lead to release. In this state, Puruṣa escapes from the experience of sufferings.[432] He obtains freedom from the bondage of *guṇa*-s. Thus, the release of Sāṁkhyavādin-s is a negative concept. The Upaniṣad-s on the other hand have a positive concept of release. They associated it with Bliss (*ānanda*). According to the Upaniṣad-s, realization of 'Saccidānanda' character of Brahman is release. Here *'sat'* means everything in the cosmos, *'cit'* means sentient element and when a being knows *'sat'* and *'cit'* aspects of Brahman, he experiences *ānanda.* Thus, experience of *'sat' 'cit'* and *'ānanda'* forms of Brahman is the deliverance, according to them. Moreover, the Upaniṣadic doctrine of Brahman is based on monism, which believes in the non-duality of the individual and the Supreme Souls.[433] The paramount concept of the Upaniṣad-s is that all the things in the cosmos are the same, 'Everything is Brahman alone.'[434] and the knower of Brahman merging into Brahman becomes Brahman which is the ultimate state of the being.[435]

According to Radhakrishnan, S., the psychology and the order of creation of the Sāṁkhya are accepted by the *Bh. G.,* though the metaphysical implications are rejected.[436] When the doctrines of Sāṁkhya philosophy and the Upaniṣadic philosophy are examined vis-à-vis philosophical excerpts of the *Mbh.,* this observation of Radhakrishnan, S. appears true in the case of the *Mbh.* too. The *Mbh.* has accepted the Sāṁkhya concept of *guṇa*-s consisting the triple string of bondage and the concept of the realization of the Self as being separate from Prakṛti, which would release the Self from the bondage of *guṇa*-s. However, actual release according to the *Mbh.* is due to the merging of the Self into the Brahman or a deity, which is equivalent to Brahman.

Thus, dualism of Sāṁkhyavādin-s reflected in the idea of aloofness of Puruṣa from Prakṛti does not find acceptance in the *Mbh.* Instead the identity of the embodied Soul with the Supreme Soul, the Ultimate Entity, forms the core of the *Mbh.*'s concept of release. This displays the impact of the Upaniṣadic doctrine of monism on the philosophy of the *Mbh.*

In the *Mbh.*, Kṛṣṇa states that the beings, who realize the separateness of Puruṣa from Prakṛti *i.e.* the Soul from Nature, attain Ultimate Reality.[437] Thus, he considers a person who has realized the Supreme Self (*Paramātman*) which is beyond both Matter and Spirit, to be a released one.[438] Similarly, the final release according to Bhīṣma is the attainment of thorough knowledge of the Highest Reality, which is eternal without duality.[439] However, Brahman as described by Bhīṣma, is the supreme deity Nārāyaṇa. Vasiṣṭha's enumeration appears to be an answer to the philosophical queries of Janaka. Although Vasiṣṭha accepts the Sāṁkhya concept according to which the Soul has the wrong notion of being the doer due to his association with the Matter, Vasiṣṭha too, reverts back to the Upaniṣadic concept of Brahman and professes that on acquiring supreme intellect, the being attains the unmanifest Brahman.[440] Thus, it is not the *kevala* state of Puruṣa as delineated in the Sāṁkhya system. The discourse of Yājñavalkya is also purely for clarifying the doubts raised by Janaka about certain philosophical concepts such as what is unmanifest, what is the form of the Brahman, what are creation and dissolution etc.[441] Yājñavalkya considers the identity of the individual Soul with the Supreme Soul, which is the twenty sixth principle, as the final release.[442] In the *Śānti P.* again, Janaka has described a man, who has attained deliverance and who still continues to live.[443] The deliverance attained by Janaka here is on the lines of Sāṁkhya philosophy. He is *jīvanmukta*. There are germs of Karmayoga in Janaka's discourse, which have been elaborated in the *Bh. G.* However, Janaka here does not describe the final state of release as to whether it would be *kaivalya* on the lines of the Sāṁkhya system or the identity with the Supreme Self based on the Upaniṣadic doctrine of monism.

According to Brahmā, one, who abandons all planned actions and controls the Self within the Self, knows Brahman and is not reborn.[444] In the *Āraṇ P.*, the hunter too regards the ultimate release as the same as the attainment of Brahman.[445]

However, he, too, synthesizes it with the Sāṁkhya philosophy while enumerating his thoughts.[446] Thus, as has been already explained, throughout the *Mbh.*, the principles of Sāṁkhya philosophy have been synthesized with those of the Vedānta philosophy mainly to propound the monism of Upaniṣad-s, according to which the Brahman being the one and only one entity in this world.

Thus, the principles of Prakṛti and Puruṣa and the concept of the creation of the world evolving out of Prakṛti and the concept of *traiguṇya* were acceptable to the *Mbh.* However, the *Mbh.* did not accept dualism.

REFERENCES

1. Radhakrishnan, S., Moore, C.A., *op. cit.* pp. 425.
2. Tilak, B.G. *op. cit.*, p. 208.
3. Macdonell, A.A., *op. cit.*, p. 393.
4. Sutton, Nicholas, *op. cit.*, p. 25.
5. *Marathi Vishvakośa* Vol. 3, Editor - Joshi Laxman, p. 287.
6. *Bhāratīya Sanskriti Kośa* (Marathi) Vol. 2, Editior - Joshi. Mahadeo, Hodarkar Padmaja, Pune, 1976. p. 75.
7. *Ibid.*, Vol. 1, p. 525.
8. *Ibid.*, Vol. 5, p. 294.
9. *Ibid.*, Vol. 8, p. 649.
10. *Ibid.*, p. 529.
11. *Ibid.*, p. 6.
12. *Ibid.*, Vol. 1, p. 576.
13. *Marathi Vishvakośa,* Vol. 2, p. 702.
14. *Encyclopedia of Indian Philosophies*, Vol. 4, Editors - Larson, G.J., Bhattacharya, R.S., Delhi, p. 13.

15. *Ibid.*, p. 13.
16. *Ibid.*, p. 13.
17. *Ibid.*, p. 13.
18. *Ibid.*, p. 13.
19. *Ibid.*, p. 13.
20. Sutton, Nicholas, *op. cit.*, p. 24.
21. *Encyclopedia of Indian Philosophies*, *op. cit.*, p. 14.
22. *Ibid.*, p. 15.
23. *Bhāratīya Sanskriti Kośa*, *op. cit.*, Vol. 3, p. 334.
24. Dasgupta, S.N. *op. cit.*, p. 212.
25. Tilak, B.G., *op. cit.*, p. 201.
26. *Ibid.*, p. 207.
27. Smith Vincent, *Early History of India,* 3rd Edition, p. 328, q. by Tilak, B.G., *ibid.*, p. 208.
28. *Ibid.*, p. 207.
29. *Amarakośa* चर्चा संख्या विचारणा।
30. *Hemakośa* संख्यैकादौ विचारे च।
31. Madhusūdana Sarasvatī Commentary on *Gi.* 3/3/5/4 संख्या सम्यगात्मबुद्धिः।

    Śabdenduśekhara. 145 सम्यक्ख्यानं संख्याक्रमवैशिष्ट्येन ज्ञानम्।

    Madhusūdana, Tilak on *Gitā.* 18-13.

    पदार्थाः संख्यायन्ते व्युत्पाद्यन्ते अस्मिन् इति सांख्यम्।
32. *Mbh, Śānti P.,* 308.82. 294. 26^{cd}, 41^{ab}

    दोषाणां च गुणानां च प्रमाणं प्रविभागशः।
    कंचिदर्थमभिप्रेत्य सा संख्येत्युपधार्यताम्।।
    सांख्यज्ञानं प्रवक्ष्यामि परिसंख्यानिदर्शनम्।
    सांख्यदर्शनमेतावत्परिसंख्यानदर्शनम्।।
33. Satavalekar, S.D., *Śrīmadbhagavadgītā Puruṣārtha Bodhinī Tīkā* (Marāthi) III edition, V. S. Satavalekar Swādhyaya Mandal, Pardi (Dis. Surat), 1952. p. 80.
34. *The Student's Sanskrit English Dictionary* by Apte V. S., Motilal Banarsidass Publishers Pvt. Ltd., Delhi, 1890, p. 596.

35. *The Bhāratīya Sanskriti Kośa, op. cit.,* Vol. 9, 1976, (Vihar to Sindhi Lok,) p. 702.
36. Dasgupta, S.N., *Philosophical Essays*, University of Calcutta, Calcutta, 1941, pp. 217, 218.
37. *Ibid.,* p. 216.
38. *Carakasamhitā, Katidhāpuruṣīyaśārīrādhyāya I. Śārirasthānam.* 61[ab]

    अव्यक्तमात्मा क्षेत्रज्ञः शाश्वतो विभुरव्ययः।
39. *Ibid.*, 66, 67[ab]

    जायते बुद्धिरव्यक्ताद् बुद्ध्याऽहमिति मन्यते।
    परं खादीन्यहङ्कारादुत्पद्यन्ते यथाक्रमम्॥
    ततः संपूर्णसर्वाङ्गो जातोऽभ्युदित उच्यते।
40. *Ibid.*, 17, 31[cd]

    पुनश्च धातुभेदेन चतुर्विंशतिकः स्मृतः।
    मनो दशेन्द्रियाण्यर्थाः प्रकृतिश्चाष्टधातुकी॥
    अर्थाः शब्दादयो ज्ञेया गोचरा विषया गुणाः॥
41. *Ibid.*, 68[cd], 69

    रजस्तमोभ्यामाविष्टश्चक्रवत् परिवर्तते।
    येषां द्वन्द्वे परा सक्तिरहङ्कारपराश्च ये।
    उदयप्रलयौ तेषां न तेषां ये त्वतोऽन्यथा॥
42. *Ibid.*, 155

    अतः परं ब्रह्मभूतो भूतात्मा नोपलभ्यते।
    निःसृतः सर्वभावेभ्यश्चिह्नं यस्य न विद्यते॥
43. *Ibid.*, 24

    एकैकाधिकयुक्तानि खादीनामिन्द्रियाणि तु।
    पञ्च कर्मानुमेयानि येभ्यो बुद्धिः प्रवर्तते॥
44. *Ibid.*, 16, 17, 35

    खादयश्चेतनाषष्ठा धातवः पुरुषः स्मृतः।
    चेतनाधातुरप्येकः स्मृतः पुरुषसंज्ञकः॥
    पुनश्च धातुभेदेन चतुर्विंशतिकः स्मृतः।
    मनो दशेन्द्रियाण्यर्थाः प्रकृतिश्चाष्टधातुकी॥

    बुद्धीन्द्रियमनोऽर्थानां विद्याद्योगधरं परम्।
    चतुर्विंशतिको ह्येष राशिः पुरुषसंज्ञकः।

45. Cakrapāṇi – q. by Dasgupta, S.N. p. 213.
प्रकृतिव्यतिरिक्तश्चोदासीनं पुरुषमव्यक्तत्वसाधर्म्यात्।
अव्यक्तायां प्रकृतावेव प्रक्षिप्य अव्यक्तशब्देनैव गृह्णाति।।
Caraka, Śārīra, Harināth Viśārada's edition p. 4.

46. *Īśvarakṛṣṇa Sā. K.* 1-2
दुःख-त्रयाऽभिघाताज्जिज्ञासा तदभिघातके हेतौ।
दृष्टे साऽपार्था चेन्नैकान्ताऽत्यन्ततोऽभावात्।।
दृष्टवदानुश्रविकः स ह्यविशुद्धिक्षयातिशययुक्तः।
तद्विपरीतः श्रेयान् व्यक्ताऽव्यक्तज्ञविज्ञानात्।।

47. *Ibid.*, 58.
औत्सुक्य-निवृत्त्यर्थं यथा क्रियासु प्रवर्तते लोकः।
पुरुषस्य विमोक्षार्थं प्रवर्तते तद्वदव्यक्तम्।।

48. *Ibid., K.* 19.
तस्माच्च विपर्यासात् सिद्धं साक्षित्वमस्य पुरुषस्य।
कैवल्यं माध्यस्थ्यं द्रष्टृत्वमकर्तृभावश्च।।

49. *Mbh. Śānti P.* 291. 37-38
पञ्चविंशतिमो विष्णुर्निस्तत्त्वस्तत्त्वसंज्ञकः।
तत्त्वसंश्रयणादेतत्तत्त्वमाहुर्मनीषिणः।।
यदमूर्त्यसृजद्व्यक्तं तत्तन्मूर्त्यधितिष्ठति।
चतुर्विंशतिमो व्यक्तो ह्यमूर्तः पञ्चविंशकः।।

50. *Ibid.*, 291.39
स एव हृदि सर्वासु मूर्तिष्वातिष्ठतेऽऽत्मवान्।
चेतयंश्चेतनो नित्यः सर्वमूर्तिरमूर्तिमान्।।

51. *Ibid.*, 291.40
सर्गप्रलयधर्मिण्या असर्गप्रलयात्मकः।
गोचरे वर्तते नित्यं निर्गुणो गुणसंज्ञकः।।

52. *Ibid.*, 292.1
एवमप्रतिबुद्धत्वादबुद्धमनुवर्तते।
देहाद्देहसहस्राणि तथा समभिपद्यते।।

53. *Ibid.*, 292. 5
द्वंद्वमेति च निर्द्वंद्वस्तासु तास्विह योनिषु।
शीर्षरोगेऽक्षिरोगे च दन्तशूले गलग्रहे।।

54. *Sā. K.* 55

तत्र जरा-मरण-कृतं दुःखं प्राप्नोति चेतनः पुरुषः।
लिङ्गस्याविनिवृत्तेस्तस्माद् दुःखं स्वभावेन॥

55. *Mbh. Śānti P.* 292.40

प्रकृतिः कुरुते कर्म शुभाशुभफलात्मकम्।
प्रकृतिश्च तदश्नाति त्रिषु लोकेषु कामगा॥

56. *Ibid.*, 293.9-10

पञ्चविंशस्तथैवात्मा तस्यैवा प्रतिबोधनात्।
विमलस्य विशुद्धस्य शुद्धानिलनिषेवणात्॥
अशुद्ध एव शुद्धात्मा तादृग्भवति पार्थिव।
अबुद्धसेवनाच्चापि बुद्धोऽप्यबुधतां व्रजेत्॥

57. *Ibid.*, 293.14

अन्योन्यस्याभिसंबन्धादन्योन्यगुणसंश्रयात्।
रूपं निर्वर्तयत्येतदेवं सर्वासु योनिषु॥

58. *Ibid.*, 293.19

एवमेवाभिसंबद्धौ नित्यं प्रकृतिपूरुषौ।
पश्यामि भगवंस्तस्मान्मोक्षधर्मो न विद्यते॥

59. *Sā. K.* 21

पुरुषस्य दर्शनार्थं कैवल्यार्थं तथा प्रधानस्य।
पङ्ग्वन्धवदुभयोरपि संयोगस्तत्कृतः सर्गः॥

60. *Mbh. Śānti P.* 293. 36.

पुमांश्चैवापुमांश्चैव त्रैलिङ्ग्यं प्राकृतं स्मृतम्।
नैव पुमान्पुमांश्चैव स लिङ्गीत्यभिधीयते॥

61. *Ibid.*, 293.37[ab]

अलिङ्गा प्रकृतिर्लिङ्गैरुपलभ्यति सात्मजैः।

62. *Ibid.*, 293.38

एवमप्यनुमानेन ह्यलिङ्गमुपलभ्यते।
पञ्चविंशतिमस्तात लिङ्गेष्वनियतात्मकः॥

63. *Sā. K..* 40

पूर्वोत्पन्नमसक्तं नियतं महदादिसूक्ष्मपर्यन्तम्।
संसरति निरुपभोगं भावैरधिवासितं लिङ्गम्॥

64. *Mbh. Śānti P.* 293.39[ab]

अनादिनिधनोऽनन्तः सर्वदर्शी निरामयः।

65. *Ibid.*, 41

यदा त्वेष गुणान्सर्वान्प्राकृतानभिमन्यते।
तदा स गुणवानेव परमेणानुपश्यति।।

66. *Ibid.*, 42-43

यत्तद्बुद्धेः परं प्राहुः सांख्या योगाश्च सर्वशः।
बुध्यमानं महाप्राज्ञमबुद्धपरिवर्जनात्।।

अप्रबुद्धमथाव्यक्तं सगुणं प्राहुरीश्वरम्।
निर्गुणं चेश्वरं नित्यमधिष्ठातारमेव च।।

67. *Ibid.*, 296. 6-10

68. *Ibid.*, *Āśva. P.* 42.59

सर्ववित्सर्वभूतेषु वीक्षत्यात्मानमात्मनि।
एकधा बहुधा चैव विकुर्वाणस्ततस्ततः।।

69. *Ibid.*, 42.60[cd], 61[ab]

स वै विष्णुश्च मित्रश्च वरुणोऽग्निः प्रजापतिः।
स हि धाता विधाता च स प्रभुः सर्वतोमुखः।।

70. *Ibid.*, 43.34

अलिङ्गग्रहणो नित्यः क्षेत्रज्ञो निर्गुणात्मकः।
तस्मादलिङ्गः क्षेत्रज्ञः केवलं ज्ञानलक्षणः।।

71. *Ibid.*, 43.36.40

72. *Ibid.*, 46. 45-47

अपाणिपादपृष्ठं तमशिरस्कमनूदरम्।
प्रहीणगुणकर्माणं केवलं विमलं स्थिरम्।।

अगन्धरसमस्पर्शमरूपाशब्दमेव च।
अत्वगस्थ्यथ वामज्जममांसमपि चैव ह।।

निश्चिन्तमव्ययं नित्यं हृदिस्थमपि नित्यदा।
सर्वभूतस्थमात्मानं ये पश्यन्ति न ते मृताः।।

73. *Ibid.*, *Śānti P.* 211. 25

अस्ति नास्तीति चाप्येतत्तस्मिन्नसति लक्षणे।
किमधिष्ठाय मद्ब्रूयाल्लोकयात्राविनिश्चयम्।।

74. *Ibid.*, 212.34

स्वकर्मयुगपद्भावो दशस्वेतेषु तिष्ठति।
चित्तमेकादशं विद्धि बुद्धिर्द्वादशमी भवेत्।।

75. *Ibid.*, 40

एवमाहुः समाहारं क्षेत्रमध्यात्मचिन्तकाः।
स्थितो मनसि यो भावः स वै क्षेत्रज्ञ उच्यते।।

76. *Ibid.*, *Bh. P.* 25. 4. 31. 3, 39. 3

न कर्मणामनारम्भानैष्कर्म्यं पुरुषोऽश्नुते।
न च संन्यसनादेव सिद्धिं समधिगच्छति।।

अश्रद्धधानाः पुरुषा धर्मस्यास्य परंतप।
अप्राप्य मां निवर्तन्ते मृत्युसंसारवर्त्मनि।।

सत्त्वानुरूपा सर्वस्य श्रद्धा भवति भारत।
श्रद्धामयोऽयं पुरुषो यो यच्छ्रद्धः स एव सः।।

77. *Ibid.*, 24.20-21

न जायते म्रियते वा कदाचिन्नायं भूत्वा भविता वा न भूयः।
अजो नित्यः शाश्वतोऽयं पुराणो न हन्यते हन्यमाने शरीरे।।

वेदाविनाशिनं नित्यं य एनमजमव्ययम्।
कथं स पुरुषः पार्थ कं घातयति हन्ति कम्।।

78. *Ibid.*, 25.19

तस्मादसक्तः सततं कार्यं कर्म समाचार।
असक्तो ह्याचरन्कर्म परमाप्नोति पूरुषः।।

79. *Ibid.*, 30.4

अधिभूतं क्षरो भावः पुरुषश्चाधिदैवतम्।
अधियज्ञोऽहमेवात्र देहे देहभृतां वर।।

80. Satavalekar, S.D., *op. cit.*, pp. 528-529

81. *Mbh. Bh. P.* 30. 10^{cd}, 9^{ab} 22^{ab}.

भ्रुवोर्मध्ये प्राणमावेश्य सम्यक्स तं परं पुरुषमुपैति दिव्यम्।
कविं पुराणमनुशासितारमणोरणीयांसमनुस्मरेद्यः।
पुरुषः स परः पार्थ भक्त्या लभ्यस्त्वनन्यया।

82. *Ibid.*, 31.9-10^{ab}

न च मां तानि कर्माणि निबध्नन्ति धनंजय।
उदासीनवदासीनमसक्तं तेषु कर्मसु।।
मयाध्यक्षेण प्रकृतिः सूयते सचराचरम्।

83. Satavalekar, S.D., *op. cit.*, p. 575.

84. *Mbh. Bh. P.* 32.12.

परं ब्रह्म परं धाम पवित्रं परमं भवान्।
पुरुषं शाश्वतं दिव्यमादिदेवमजं विभुम्।।

85. Satavalekar, S.D., *op. cit.*, p. 628.

86. *Mbh. Bh. P.* 32. 15[ab]
स्वयमेवात्मनात्मानं वेत्थ त्वं पुरुषोत्तम।

87. *Ibid.*, 33-18[d]-20
सनातनस्त्वं पुरुषो मतो मे।।
अनादिमध्यान्तमनन्तवीर्यमनन्तबाहुं शशिसूर्यनेत्रम्।
पश्यामि त्वां दीप्तहुताशवक्त्रं स्वतेजसा विश्वमिदं तपन्तम्।।
द्यावापृथिव्योरिदमन्तरं हि व्याप्तं त्वयैकेन दिशश्च सर्वाः।
दृष्ट्वाद्भुतं रूपमिदं तवोग्रं लोकत्रयं प्रव्यथितं महात्मन्।।

88. *Ṛv.* X. 90. 1, 2[ab], 12.
सहस्रशीर्षा पुरुषः सहस्राक्षः सहस्रपात्।
स भूमिं विश्वतो वृत्वात्यतिष्ठद्दशाङ्गुलम्।।
पुरुष एवेदं सर्वं यद्भूतं यच्च भव्यम्।।
ब्राह्मणोऽस्य मुखमासीद्बाहू राजन्यः कृतः।
ऊरू तदस्य यद्वैश्यः पद्भ्यां शूद्रो अजायत।।

89. *Mbh. Bh. P.* 33. 38[a]
त्वमादिदेवः पुरुषः पुराणः।

90. *Ibid.*, 35.19[ab], 20[cd], 21[ab]
प्रकृतिं पुरुषं चैव विद्ध्यनादी उभावपि।
पुरुषः सुखदुःखानां भोक्तृत्वे हेतुरुच्यते।।२०।।
पुरुषः प्रकृतिस्थो हि भुङ्क्ते प्रकृतिजान्गुणान्।

91. Telang, K.T., *op. cit.*, p. 103, Note No. 7.

92. *Mbh. Bh. P.* 35-19-21

93. Telang, K.T., *op. cit.*, p. 105.

94. *Nṛsimaha tāpinī Up.* q. by Telang, K.T., *op. cit.*, p. 224.

95. *Mbh. Bh. P.* 36.3[ab],
मम योनिर्महद्ब्रह्म तस्मिन्गर्भं दधाम्यहम्।
also Dandekar, S.V. Sārtha Jñāneshvarī (critical edition) (Marathi), Svanand Prakashan, Pune, p. 507.

96. *Mbh. Ibid.*, 37.4
तमेव चाद्यं पुरुषं प्रपद्ये यतः प्रवृत्तिः प्रसृता पुराणी।

97. *Ibid.*, 37. 16.
द्वाविमौ पुरुषौ लोके क्षरश्चाक्षर एव च।
क्षरः सर्वाणि भूतानि कूटस्थोऽक्षर उच्यते।।
98. *Ibid.*, 37. 17.
उत्तमः पुरुषस्त्वन्यः परमात्मेत्युदाहृतः।
यो लोकत्रयमाविश्य बिभर्त्यव्यय ईश्वरः।।
99. Satvalekar, S.D., *op. cit.*, p. 836.
100. *Śanti P.* 212. 1-4.
101. *Ibid.*, 6[abcd].
उच्छेदनिष्ठा नेहास्ति भावनिष्ठा न विद्यते।
अयं ह्यपि समाहारः शरीरेन्द्रियचेतसाम्।
102. *Ibid.*, 14
इमं गुणसमाहारमात्मभावेन पश्यतः।
असम्यग्दर्शनैर्दुःखमनन्तं नोपशाम्यति।।
103. *Ibid.*, 40
एवमाहुः समाहारं क्षेत्रमध्यात्मचिन्तकाः।
स्थितो मनसि यो भावः स वै क्षेत्रज्ञ उच्यते।।
104. *Ibid.*, 41
एवं सति क उच्छेदः शाश्वतो वा कथं भवेत्।
स्वभावाद्वर्तमानेषु सर्वभूतेषु हेतुतः।।
105. *Ca. Sa. Śa.* I. 16, 17, 35 *op. cit.*
106. *Ibid.*, 61
अव्यक्तमात्मा क्षेत्रज्ञः शाश्वतो विभुरव्ययः।
तस्माद्यदन्यत्तद्व्यक्तं वक्ष्यते चापरं द्व्यम्।।
107. Cakrapāṇi *q.*, by Dasgupta, S.N., *op. cit.* p.213.
108. *Sā. K.* 9
असदकरणादुपादानग्रहणात् सर्वसंभवाभावात्।
शक्तस्य शक्यकरणात् कारणभावाच्च सत्कार्यम्।।
109. *Mbh. Bh. P.* 24. 16[ab]
नासतो विद्यते भावो नाभावो विद्यते सतः।
110. *Sā. K.* 11
त्रिगुणमविवेकि विषयः सामान्यमचेतनं प्रसवधर्मि।
व्यक्तं तथा प्रधानं तद्विपरीतस्तथा च पुमान्।।

111. *Ibid., K.* 8

सौक्ष्म्यात् तदनुपलब्धिर्नाभावात् कार्यस्तदुपलब्धेः।
महदादि तच्च कार्यं प्रकृतिविरूपं सरूपं च॥

112. *Ibid.*, 57

वत्सविवृद्धिनिमित्तं क्षीरस्य यथा प्रवृत्तिरज्ञस्य।
पुरुषविमोक्षनिमित्तं तथा प्रवृत्तिः प्रधानस्य॥

113. *Ibid.*, 22.

प्रकृतेर्महांस्ततोऽङ्कारस्तस्मात्त्गणश्च षोडशकः।
तस्मादपि षोडशकात् पञ्चभ्यः पञ्च भूतानि॥

114. *Mbh. Śānti P.* 291. 17-19.

हिरण्यगर्भो भगवानेष बुद्धिरिति स्मृतः।
महानिति च योगेषु विरिञ्च इति चाप्युत॥

सांख्ये च पठयते शास्त्रे नामभिर्बहुधात्मकः।
विचित्ररूपो विश्वात्मा एकाक्षर इति स्मृतः॥

वृत्तं नैकात्मकं येन कृत्स्नं त्रैलोक्यमात्मना।
तथैव बहुरूपत्वाद्विश्वरूप इति स्मृतः॥

115. *Ibid.*, 20-21.

एष वै विक्रियापन्नः सृजत्यात्मानमात्मना।
अहंकारं महातेजाः प्रजापतिमहंकृतम्॥

अव्यक्ताद्व्यक्तमुत्पन्नं विद्यासर्गं वदन्ति तम्।
महान्तं चाप्यहंकारमविद्यासर्गमेव च॥

116. *Ibid.*, 291.22-27

117. *Ibid.*, 291-28[ab]

एषा तत्त्वचतुर्विंशा सर्वाकृतिषु वर्तते।

118. *Ibid.*, 293.37

अलिङ्गा प्रकृतिर्लिङ्गैरुपलभ्यति सात्मजैः।
यथा पुष्पफलैर्नित्यमृतवो मूर्तयस्यथा॥

119. *Ibid.*, 291.40[ab]

सर्गप्रलयधर्मिण्या असर्गप्रलयात्मकः।

120. *Ibid.*, 294.27-29

121. *Sā. K.* 3.

मूल प्रकृतिरविकृतिर्महदाद्याः प्रकृतिविकृतयः सप्त।
षोडशकस्तु विकारो न प्रकृतिर्न विकृतिः पुरुषः॥

122. *Ibid.*, 10.

हेतुमदनित्यमव्यापि सक्रियमनेकमाश्रितं लिङ्गम्।
सावयवं परतन्त्रं व्यक्तं विपरीतमव्यक्तम्।।

123. Sharma, Har Dutt, *The Sāṁkhya-Kārikā-Śrīmadīśvar-kṛṣṇapraṇitāḥ Sagaudapādabhāṣyāḥ,* Oriental Book Agency, Poona, 1933, p. 5.

124. *Mbh. Śānti P.* 294. 34-35.

एकत्वं च बहुत्वं च प्रकृतेरनु तत्त्ववान्।
एकत्वं प्रलये चास्य बहुत्वं च प्रवर्तनात्।।

बहुधात्मा प्रकुर्वीत प्रकृतिं प्रसवात्मिकाम्।
तच्च क्षेत्रं महानात्मा पञ्चविंशोऽधितिष्ठति।।

125. *Ibid., P.* 296. 4-5

न त्वेव बुध्यतेऽव्यक्तं सगुणं वाथ निर्गुणम्।
कदाचित्त्वेव खल्वेतदाहुरप्रतिबुद्धकम्।।

बुध्यते यदि वाव्यक्तमेतद्वै पञ्चविंशकम्।
बुध्यमानो भवत्येष सङ्गात्मक इति श्रुतिः।।

126. *Op. cit., Sā. K.* 17

सङ्घातपरार्थत्वात् त्रिगुणादिविपर्ययादधिष्ठानात्।
पुरुषोऽस्ति भोक्तृभावात् कैवल्यार्थं प्रवृत्तेश्च।।

127. *Ibid.*, 3.

128. *Mbh. Śānti P.* 295.2

अविद्यामाहुरव्यक्तं सर्गप्रलयधर्मि वै।
सर्गप्रलयनिर्मुक्तं विद्यां वै पञ्चविंशकम्।।

129. *Sā. K.* 11

त्रिगुणमविवेकि विषयः सामान्यमचेतनं प्रसवधर्मि।
व्यक्तं तथा प्रधानं तद्विपरीतस्तथा च पुमान्।।

130. *Mbh. Śānti P.* 291. 21.

अव्यक्ताद्व्यक्तमुत्पन्नं विद्यासर्गं वदन्ति तम्।
महान्तं चाप्यहंकारमविद्यासर्गमेव च।।

131. *Ibid.*, 293. 41.

यदा त्वेष गुणान्सर्वान्प्राकृतानभिमन्यते।
तदा स गुणवानेव परमेणानुपश्यति।।

132. *Sā. K.* 62.

तस्मान्न बध्यतेऽसौ न मुच्यते नाऽपि संसरति कश्चित्।
संसरति बध्यते मुच्यते च नानाश्रया प्रकृतिः॥

133. *Mbh. Āśva. P.* 40. 1.

अव्यक्तात्पूर्वमुत्पन्नो महानात्मा महामतिः।
आदिर्गुणानां सर्वेषां प्रथमः सर्ग उच्यते॥

134. *Ibid.*, 41. 1.

य उत्पन्नो महान्पूर्वमहंकारः स उच्यते।
अहमित्येव संभूतो द्वितीयः सर्ग उच्यते॥

135. *Ibid.*, *P.* 42.1-2

अहंकारात्प्रसूतानि महाभूतानि पञ्च वै।
पृथिवी वायुराकाशमापो ज्योतिश्च पञ्चमम्॥

तेषु भूतानि मुह्यन्ते महाभूतेषु पञ्चसु।
शब्दस्पर्शनरूपेषु रसगन्धक्रियासु च॥

136. *Sā. K.* 24.

अभिमानोऽहङ्कारस्तस्माद् द्विविधः प्रवर्तते सर्गः।
एकादशकश्च गणस्तन्मात्रः पञ्चकश्चैव॥

137. *Mbh. Āśva.* 42. 6.

शब्दः स्पर्शस्तथा रूपं रसो गन्धश्च पञ्चमः।
क्रियाकारणयुक्ताः स्युरनित्या मोहसंज्ञिताः॥

138. *Sā. K.* 40

पूर्वोत्पन्नमसक्तं नियतं महदादि सूक्ष्मपर्यन्तम्।
संसरति निरुपभोगं भावैरधिवासितं लिङ्गम्॥

139. *Mbh. Āśva. P.* 43.35

अव्यक्तं क्षेत्रमुद्दिष्टं गुणानां प्रभवाप्ययम्।
सदा पश्याम्यहं लीनं विजानामि शृणोमि च॥

140. *Ibid.*, *Śānti P.* 212. 20-21.

पञ्च ज्ञानेन्द्रियाण्युक्त्वा मनःषष्ठानि चेतसि।
मनःषष्ठानि वक्ष्यामि पञ्च कर्मेन्द्रियाणि तु॥

हस्तौ कर्मेन्द्रियं ज्ञेयमथ पादौ गतीन्द्रियम्।
प्रजनानन्दयोः शेफो विसर्गे पायुरिन्द्रियम्॥

141. *Ibid.*, 212. 22-24.

वाक्तु शब्दविशेषार्थं गतिं पञ्चान्वितां विदुः।
एवमेकादशैतानि बुद्ध्या त्ववसृजन्मनः॥

कर्णौ शब्दश्च चित्तं च त्रयः श्रवणसंग्रहे।
तथा स्पर्शे तथा रूपे तथैव रसगन्धयोः॥
एवं पञ्चत्रिका ह्येते गुणास्तदुपलब्धये।
येन यस्त्रिविधो भावः पर्यायात्समुपस्थितः॥

142. *Ibid.*, 212.6[cd], 40
अयं ह्यपि समाहारः शरीरेन्द्रियचेतसाम्।
एवमाहुः समाहारं क्षेत्रमध्यात्मचिन्तकाः।
स्थितो मनसि यो भावः स वै क्षेत्रज्ञ उच्यते॥

143. *Ibid.*, 212.7
धातवः पञ्चशाखोऽयं खं वायुर्ज्योतिरम्बु भूः।
ते स्वभावेन तिष्ठन्ति वियुज्यन्ते स्वभावतः॥

144. *Ca. Sa. Śā.* 1. 17.
पुनश्च धातुभेदेन चतुर्विंशतिकः स्मृतः।
मनो दशेन्द्रियाण्यर्थाः प्रकृतिश्चाष्टधातुकी॥

145. *Ibid.*, 16[ab]
खादयश्चेतनाषष्ठा धातवः पुरुषः स्मृतः।

146. *Ibid.*, 35

147. *Ibid.*, 61[cd]
तस्माद्यदन्यत्तद्व्यक्तं वक्ष्यते चापरं द्व्यम्।

148. *Mbh. Śānti P.* 212. 7[ab]

149. *Ca. Sa. Śā.* 1 .16[ab]

150. *Mbh. Śānti P.* 212. 40[cd]
स्थितो मनसि यो भावः स वै क्षेत्रज्ञ उच्यते।

151. *Ca. Sa. Śā.* 1. 16[cd]
चेतनाधातुरप्येकः स्मृतः पुरुषसंज्ञकः।

152. *Mbh. Śānti P.* 212. 40[ab]
एवमाहुः समाहारं क्षेत्रमध्यात्मचिन्तकाः।

153. *Ca. Sa. Śā.* 17.

154. *Mbh. Bh. P.* 24. 16.
नासतो विद्यते भावो नाभावो विद्यते सतः।
उभयोरपि दृष्टोऽन्तस्त्वनयोस्तत्त्वदर्शिभिः॥
also *Śāṅkarābhāṣya*

इतश्च शोकमोहावकृत्वा शीतोष्णादिसहनं युक्तं यस्मात्-नासत इति। नासतोऽविद्यमानस्य शीतोष्णादेः सकारणस्य न विद्यते नास्ति भावो भावनमस्तिता। न हि शीतोष्णादि सकारणं प्रमाणैनिरूप्यमाणं वस्तु सम्भवति।

155. *Bhagavadgītā* translated and commented upon by Hill W. Douglas P., London, 1928, p. 114.

156. *Mbh. Bh. P.* 31. 19[cd]

अमृतं चैव मृत्युश्च सदसच्चाहमर्जुन।।

157. Śaṅkaracārya and Rāmānujācārya q. by Hill W.D.P., *op. cit.*, p. 185.

158. *Thomson, J.C.* q. by Hill W.D.P., *op. cit.,* p. 185.

159. *Mbh. Bh. P.* 36. 5.

सत्त्वं रजस्तम इति गुणाः प्रकृतिसंभवाः।
निबध्नन्ति महाबाहो देहे देहिनमव्ययम्।।

160. *Ibid. P.* 35. 19, 21.

प्रकृतिं पुरुषं चैव विद्ध्यनादी उभावपि।
विकारांश्च गुणांश्चैव विद्धि प्रकृतिसंभवान्।।
पुरुषः प्रकृतिस्थो हि भुङ्क्ते प्रकृतिजान्गुणान्।
कारणं गुणसङ्गोऽस्य सदसद्योनिजन्मसु।।

161. *Sā. K.* 45[b]

संसारो भवति राजसाद्रागात्।

162. *Mbh. Bh. P.* 37. 7

ममैवांशो जीवलोके जीवभूतः सनातनः।
मनःषष्ठानीन्द्रियाणि प्रकृतिस्थानि कर्षति।।

163. *Ibid.*, 26. 6

अजोऽपि सन्नव्ययात्मा भूतानामीश्वरोऽपि सन्।
प्रकृतिं स्वामधिष्ठाय संभवाम्यात्ममायया।।

164. *Ibid.*, 40.40

न तदस्ति पृथिव्यां वा दिवि देवेषु वा पुनः।
सत्त्वं प्रकृतिजैर्मुक्तं यदेभिः स्यात्त्रिभिर्गुणैः।।

165. *Ibid.*, 25.29[ab]

प्रकृतेर्गुणसंमूढाः सज्जन्ते गुणकर्मसु।

166. *Ibid., P.* 25. 30

मयि सर्वाणि कर्माणि संन्यस्याध्यात्मचेतसा।
निराशीर्निर्ममो भूत्वा युध्यस्व विगतज्वरः।।

167. Rāmānuja q. by Hill W.D.P., *op. cit.*, p. 133.
168. *Mbh. Bh. P. Ibid.*, 29. 4.
भूमिरापोऽनलो वायुः खं मनो बुद्धिरेव च।
अहंकार इतीयं मे भिन्ना प्रकृतिरष्टधा।।
169. *Ibid.*, 29. 5.
अपरेयमितस्त्वन्यां प्रकृतिं विद्धि मे पराम्।
जीवभूतां महाबाहो ययेदं धार्यते जगत्।।
170. Barnett, L.D. and Śaṅkarācārya q. by Hill W.D.P., *op. cit.*, p. 166.
171. *Mbh. Bh. P.* 35. 19-21.
172. *Ibid.*, *P.* 35.26
यावत्संजायते किंचित्सत्त्वं स्थावरजङ्गमम्।
क्षेत्रक्षेत्रज्ञसंयोगात्तद्विद्धि भरतर्षभ।।
173. Śaṅkarācārya q. by Hill W.D.P., *op. cit.*, p. 228.
174. *Sā. K.* 21.
175. *Mbh Bh. P.* 35. 19[cd]
विकारांश्च गुणांश्चैव विद्धि प्रकृतिसंभवान्।।
176. *Ibid.*, 20[ab]
कार्यकारणकर्तृत्वे हेतुः प्रकृतिरुच्यते।
177. *Ibid.*, 29[ab]
प्रकृत्यैव च कर्माणि क्रियमाणानि सर्वशः।
178. *Ibid.*, 31[ab]
अनादित्वान्निर्गुणत्वात्परमात्मायमव्ययः।
179. *Ibid.*, 29[cd]
यः पश्यति तथात्मानमकर्तारं स पश्यति।।
180. *Ibid.*, 22[ab]
उपद्रष्टानुमन्ता च भर्ता भोक्ता महेश्वरः।
181. *Ibid.*, 31[cd]
शरीरस्थोऽपि कौन्तेय न करोति न लिप्यते।
182. *Sā. K.* 3[b]
महदाद्याः प्रकृति-विकृतयः सप्त।

183. *Ibid.*, 60[cd]
गुणवत्यगुणस्य सतस्तस्मात्कार्यमपार्थकं चरति।।

184. *Ibid.* 17.
सङ्घातपरार्थत्वात् त्रिगुणादिविपर्ययादधिष्ठानात्।
पुरुषोऽस्ति भोक्तृभावात् कैवल्यार्थं प्रवृत्तेश्च।।

185. *Mbh. Bh. P.* 35. 20.
कार्यकारणकर्तृत्वे हेतुः प्रकृतिरुच्यते।
पुरुषः सुखदुःखानां भोक्तृत्वे हेतरुच्यते।।

186. *Sā. K.* 10
हेतुमदनित्यमव्यापि सक्रियमनेकमाश्रितं लिङ्गम्।
सावयवं परतन्त्रं व्यक्तं विपरीतमव्यक्तम्।।

187. *Ibid.*, 17[c]
पुरुषोऽस्ति भोक्तृभावात्।।

188. *Mbh. Bh. P.* 35. 29[ab]
प्रकृत्यैव च कर्माणि क्रियमाणानि सर्वशः।।

189. Telang, K.T., *op. cit.*, p.55, Note 1

190. *Mbh. Bh. P.* 31. 7.
सर्वभूतानि कौन्तेय प्रकृतिं यान्ति मामिकाम्।
कल्पक्षये पुनस्तानि कल्पादौ विसृजाम्यहम्।।

191. *Ibid.*, 8
प्रकृतिं स्वामवष्टभ्य विसृजामि पुनः पुनः।
भूतग्राममिमं कृत्स्नमवशं प्रकृतेर्वशात्।।

192. *Ibid.*, 10
मयाध्यक्षेण प्रकृतिः सूयते सचराचरम्।
हेतुनानेन कौन्तेय जगद्विपरिवर्तते।।

193. *Ibid.*, 25.27
प्रकृतेः क्रियमाणानि गुणैः कर्माणि सर्वशः।
अहंकारविमूढात्मा कर्ताहमिति मन्यते।।

194. *Ibid.*, 40.57-59
चेतसा सर्वकर्माणि मयि संन्यस्य मत्परः।
बुद्धियोगमुपाश्रित्य मच्चित्तः सततं भव।।

मच्चित्तः सर्वदुर्गाणि मत्प्रसादात्तरिष्यसि।
अथ चेत्त्वमहंकारान्न श्रोष्यसि विनङ्क्ष्यसि।।

यदहंकारमाश्रित्य न योत्स्य इति मन्यसे।
मिथ्यैष व्यवसायस्ते प्रकृतिस्त्वां नियोक्ष्यति।।

195. *Ibid.*, 40.60

स्वभावजेन कौन्तेय निबध्दः स्वेन कर्मणा।
कर्तुं नेच्छसि यन्मोहात्करिष्यस्यवशोऽपि तत्।।

196. *Ibid.*, 33. 33^{cd}-34^{cd}

मयैवैते निहताः पूर्वमेव निमित्तमात्रं भव सव्यसाचिन्।
मया हतांस्त्वं जहि मा व्यथिष्ठा युध्यस्व जेतासि रणे सपत्नान्।।

197. *Ibid.*, 40. 60. *op. cit.*
198. *Ibid.*, 63

इति ते ज्ञानमाख्यातं गुह्याद्गुह्यतरं मया।
विमृश्यैतदशेषेण यथेच्छसि तथा कुरु।।

199. *Ibid.*, 73

नष्टो मोहः स्मृतिर्लब्धा त्वत्प्रसादान्मयाच्युत।
स्थितोऽस्मि गतसंदेहः करिष्ये वचनं तव।।

200. Davies John, *The Sāṅkhya Kārikā of Īśvara Kṛṣṇā,* translated and commented, Calcutta, 1928, p. 23.
201. Colebrooks q. by Davis, John, *op. cit.*, p. 23.
202. *Sā. K.* 12-13
203. *Mbh. Śānti P.* 212. 23-24.

कर्णौ शब्दश्च चित्तं च त्रयः श्रवणसंग्रहे।
तथा स्पर्शे तथा रूपे तथैव रसगन्धयोः।।
एवं पञ्चत्रिका ह्येते गणास्तदुपलब्धये।
येन यस्त्रिविधो भावः पर्यायात्समुपस्थितः।।

204. *Ibid.*, 212. 25-28.
205. *Ca. Sa. Śā.* I. 36.

रजस्तमोभ्यां युक्तस्य संयोगोऽयमनन्तवान्।
ताभ्यां निराकृताभ्यां तु सत्त्ववृद्ध्या निवर्तते।।

206. *Mbh. Śānti P.* 239. 16.

रजस्तमश्च सत्त्वं च त्रय एते स्वयोनिजाः।
समाः सर्वेषु भूतेषु तद्गुणेषूपलक्षयेत्।।

207. *Ibid., P.* 240. 18.

सत्त्वमात्मा प्रसवति गुणान्वापि कदा च न।
न गुणा विदुरात्मानं गुणान्वेद स सर्वदा।।

208. *Ibid.*, 267. 15, 25[ab], 28.

रूपं गन्धं रसं स्पर्शं शब्दं चेतांस्तु तद्गुणान्।
इन्द्रियाणि न बुध्यन्ते क्षेत्रज्ञस्तैस्तु बुध्यते॥

सात्त्विकाश्चैव ये भावास्तथा राजसतामसः।
इन्द्रियाणि च भावाश्च गुणोः सप्तदश स्मृताः॥

तेषामष्टादशो देही यः शरीरे स शाश्वतः।

209. *Sā. K.* 11, *op. cit.*

210. *Mbh. Śānti.* 293-33. 34.

निरिन्द्रियस्याबीजस्य निर्द्रव्यस्यास्य देहिनः।
कथं गुणा भविष्यन्ति निर्गुणत्वान्महात्मनः॥

गुणा गुणेषु जायन्ते तत्रैव निविशन्ति च।
एवं गुणाः प्रकृतितो जायन्ते च न सन्ति च॥

211. *Ibid.*, 293-41.

यदा त्वेष गुणान्सर्वान्प्राकृतानभिमन्यते।
तदा स गुणवानेव परमेणानुपश्यति॥

212. *Ibid.*, 295.16

गुणा गुणेषु लीयन्ते तदैका प्रकृतिर्भवेत्।
क्षेत्रज्ञोऽपि यदा तात तत्क्षेत्रे संप्रलीयते॥

213. *Ibid.*, 295.22

यदा तु गुणजालं तत्प्राकृतं विजुगुप्सते।
पश्यते चापरं पश्यन् तदा पश्यन्न संज्वरेत्॥

214. *Ibid.*, 302.1

एते प्रधानस्य गुणास्त्रयः पुरुषसत्तम।
कृत्स्नस्य चैव जगतस्तिष्ठन्त्यनपगाः सदा॥

215. *Ibid.*, 302.3

सात्त्विकस्योत्तमं स्थानं राजसस्येह मध्यमम्।
तामसस्याधमं स्थानं प्राहुरध्यात्मचिन्तकाः॥

216. *Ibid.*, 302. 7-8.

अव्यक्तसत्त्वसंयुक्तो देवलोकमवाप्नुयात्।
रजःसत्त्वसमायुक्तो मनुष्येषूपपद्यते॥

रजस्तमोभ्यां संयुक्तस्तिर्यग्योनिषु जायते।
रजस्तामससत्त्वैश्च युक्तो मानुष्यमाप्नुयात्॥

217. *Ibid.*, 301. 17-27

218. *Ibid.*, 306. 36-37

विश्वाविश्वेति यदिदं गन्धर्वेन्द्रानुपृच्छसि।
विश्वाव्यक्तं परं विद्याद्भूतभव्यभयंकरम्।।

त्रिगुणं गुणकर्तृत्वादविश्वो निष्कलस्तथा।
अश्वस्तथैव मिथुनमेवमेवानुदृश्यते।।

219. *Ibid., P.* 316. 44-46.

इदं विश्वं जगत्सर्वमजगच्चापि यद्भवेत्।
महाभूतात्मकं सर्वं महद्यत्परमाणु यत्।।

इन्द्रियाणि च पञ्चैव तमः सत्त्वं रजस्तथा।
इत्येष सप्तदशको राशिरव्यक्तसंज्ञकः।।

सर्वैरिहेन्द्रियार्थैश्च व्यक्ताव्यक्तैर्हि संहितः।
पञ्चविंशक इत्येष व्यक्ताव्यक्तमयो गुणः।।

220. *Sā. K.*11, *op. cit.*

221. *Mbh.Śanti P.* 326.26.27

सत्त्वं रजस्तमश्चैव गुणानेतान्प्रचक्षते।
एते सर्वशरीरेषु तिष्ठन्ति विचरन्ति च।।

एतान्गुणांस्तु क्षेत्रजो भुङ्क्ते नैभिः स भुज्यते।
निर्गुणो गुणभुक्चैव गुणस्रष्टा गुणाधिकः।।

222. *Sā. K.* 11.

223. *Ibid.*, 3.

224. *Mbh.Śanti P.* 326. 30.

अव्यक्तं पुरुषे ब्रह्मन्निष्क्रिये संप्रलीयते।
नास्ति तस्मात्परतरं पुरुषाद्वै सनातनात्।।

225. *Aśva P..* 36.1-2

तदव्यक्तमनुद्रिक्तं सर्वव्यापि ध्रुवं स्थिरम्।
नवद्वारं पुरं विद्यात्त्रिगुणं पञ्चधातुकम्।।

एकादशपरिक्षेपं मनो व्याकरणात्मकम्।
बुद्धिस्वामिकमित्येतत्परमेकादशं भवेत्।।

226. *Ibid.*, 4-5

तमो रजस्तथा सत्त्वं गुणानेतान्प्रचक्षते।
अन्योन्यमिथुनाः सर्वे तथान्योन्यानुजीविनः।।

अन्योन्यापाश्रयाश्चैव तथान्योन्यानुवर्तिनः।
अन्योन्यव्यतिषक्ताश्च त्रिगुणाः पञ्च धातवः॥

227. *Ibid.*, 6-8

तमसो मिथुनं सत्त्वं सत्त्वस्य मिथुनं रजः।
रजसश्चापि सत्त्वं स्यात्सत्त्वस्य मिथुनं तमः॥

नियम्यते तमो यत्र रजस्तत्र प्रवर्तते।
नियम्यते रजो यत्र सत्त्वं तत्र प्रवर्तते॥

नैशात्मकं तमो विद्यात्त्रिगुणं मोहसंज्ञितम्।
अधर्मलक्षणं चैव नियतं पापकर्मसु॥

228. *Ibid.*, 9

प्रवृत्त्यात्मकमेवाहू रजः पर्यायकारकम्।
प्रवृत्तं सर्वभूतेषु दृश्यतोत्पत्तिलक्षणम्॥

229. *Ibid.*, 10

प्रकाशं सर्वभूतेषु लाघवं श्रद्दधानता।
सात्त्विकं रूपमेवं तु लाघवं साधुसंमितम्॥

230. *Ibid.*, 11-16.

231. *Ibid.*, 17-21.

232. *Ibid.*, 22-25.

233. *Ibid.*, 37.1-7.

234. *Ibid.*, 8.

संस्कारा ये च लोकेऽस्मिन्प्रवर्तन्ते पृथक्पृथक्।
नृषु नारीषु भूतेषु द्रव्येषु शरणेषु च॥

235. *Ibid.*, 9-10.

236. *Ibid.*, 14.

भूतभव्यभविष्याणां भावानां भुवि भावनाः।
त्रिवर्गनिरता नित्यं धर्मोऽर्थः कामः इत्यपि॥

237. *Ibid.*, 15-16

कामवृत्ताः प्रमोदन्ते सर्वकामसमृद्धिभिः।
अर्वाक्स्रोतस् इत्येते तैजसा रजसावृताः॥

अस्मिँल्लोके प्रमोदन्ते जायमानाः पुनः पुनः।
प्रेत्यभाविकमीहन्त इह लौकिकमेव च।
ददति प्रतिगृह्णान्ति जपन्त्यथ च जुह्वति॥

238. *Ibid.*, 38.1
अतः परं प्रवक्ष्यामि तृतीयं गुणमुत्तमम्।
सर्वभूतहितं लोके सतां धर्ममनिन्दितम्॥

239. *Ibid.*, 2-4.

240. *Ibid.*, 5.
निर्ममो निरहंकारो निराशीः सर्वतः समः।
अकामहत इत्येष सतां धर्मः सनातनः॥

241. *Ibid.*, 39. 10.
ऊर्ध्वं गच्छन्ति सत्त्वस्था मध्ये तिष्ठन्ति राजसाः।
जघन्यगुणसंयुक्ता यान्त्यधस्तामसा जनाः॥

242. *Ibid.*, 15
प्राकाश्यं सत्त्वमादित्ये संतापो राजसो गुणः।
उपप्लवस्तु विज्ञेयस्तामसस्तस्य पर्वसु॥

243. *Ibid.* 20
भूतं भव्यं भविष्यश्च धर्मोऽर्थः काम इत्यपि।
प्राणापानावुदानश्चाप्येत एव त्रयो गुणाः॥

244. *Ibid.*, 21[cdef]
त्रयो गुणाः प्रवर्तन्ते अव्यक्ता नित्यमेव तु।
सत्त्वं रजस्तमश्चैव गुणसर्गः सनातनः॥

245. *Ibid.*, *Bh. P.* 25. 5.
न हि कश्चित्क्षणमपि जातु तिष्ठत्यकर्मकृत्।
कार्यते ह्यवशः कर्म सर्वः प्रकृतिजैर्गुणैः॥

246. *Ibid.*, 25.27-28
प्रकृतेः क्रियमाणानि गुणैः कर्माणि सर्वशः।
अहंकारविमूढात्मा कर्ताहमिति मन्यते॥
तत्त्ववित्तु महाबाहो गुणकर्मविभागयोः।
गुणा गुणेषु वर्तन्त इति मत्वा न सज्जते॥

247. *Ibid.*, 29.12
ये चैव सात्त्विका भावा राजसास्तामसाश्च ये।
मत्त एवेति तान्विद्धि न त्वहं तेषु ते मयि॥

248. Tilak, B.G., *op. cit.*, p. 1117.

249. *Mbh. Bh. P.* 29. 13
त्रिभिर्गुणमयैर्भावैरेभिः सर्वमिदं जगत्।
मोहितं नाभिजानाति मामेभ्यः परमव्ययम्॥

250. *Ibid.*, 29.14

दैवी ह्येषा गुणमयी मम माया दुरत्यया।
मामेव ये प्रपद्यन्ते मायामेतां तरन्ति ते।।

251. Tilak, B.G., *op. cit.*, p. 1018.

252. *Mbh. Bh. P.* 35. 19-21.

प्रकृतिं पुरुषं चैव विद्ध्यनादी उभावपि।
विकारांश्च गुणांश्चैव विद्धि प्रकृतिसंभवान्।।

कार्यकारणकर्तृत्वे हेतुः प्रकृतिरुच्यते।
पुरुषः सुखदुःखानां भोक्तृत्वे हेतुरुच्यते।।

पुरुषः प्रकृतिस्थो हि भुङ्क्ते प्रकृतिजान्गुणान्।
कारणं गुणसङ्गोऽस्य सदसद्योनिजन्मसु।।

253. *Ibid.*, 36.5-6

सत्त्वं रजस्तम इति गुणाः प्रकृतिसंभवाः।
निबन्धन्ति महाबाहो देहे देहिनमव्ययम्।।

तत्र सत्त्वं निर्मलत्वात्प्रकाशकमनामयम्।
सुखसङ्गेन बध्नाति ज्ञानसङ्गेन चानघ।।

254. *Ibid.*, 36.7-9

रजो रागात्मकं विद्धि तृष्णासङ्गसमुद्भवम्।
तन्निबध्नाति कौन्तेय कर्मसङ्गेन देहिनम्।।

तमस्त्वज्ञानजं विद्धि मोहनं सर्वदेहिनाम्।
प्रमादालस्यनिद्राभिस्तन्निबध्नाति भारत।।

सत्त्वं सुखे सञ्जयति रजः कर्मणि भारत।
ज्ञानमावृत्य तु तमः प्रमादे सञ्जयत्युत।।

255. *Ibid.*, 36.10-13

रजस्तमश्चाभिभूय सत्त्वं भवति भारत।
रजः सत्त्वं तमश्चैव तमः सत्त्वं रजस्तथा।।

सर्वद्वारेषु देहेऽस्मिन्प्रकाश उपजायते।
ज्ञानं यदा तदा विद्याद्विवृद्धं सत्त्वमित्युत।।

लोभः प्रवृत्तिरारम्भः कर्मणामशमः स्पृहा।
रजस्येतानि जायन्ते विवृद्धे भरतर्षभे।।

अप्रकाशोऽप्रवृत्तिश्च प्रमादो मोह एव च।
तमस्येतानि जायन्ते विवृद्धे कुरुनन्दन।।

256. *Sā. K.*13
सत्त्वं लघु प्रकाशकमिष्टमुपष्टम्भकं चलं च रजः।
गुरु वरणकमेव तमः प्रदीपवच्चाऽर्थतो वृत्तिः।।

257. *Mbh. Bh. P.* 36.14-15
यदा सत्त्वे प्रवृद्धे तु प्रलयं याति देहभृत्।
तदोत्तमविदां लोकानमलान्प्रतिपद्यते।।
रजसि प्रलयं गत्वा कर्मसङ्गिषु जायते।
तथा प्रलीनस्तमसि मूढयोनिषु जायते।।

258. *Sā. K.*44[ab]-45[ab]
धर्मेण गमनमूर्ध्वं गमनमधस्ताद्भवत्यधर्मेण।
वैराग्यात् प्रकृतिलयः संसारो भवति राजसाद्रागात्।।

259. *Mbh. Bh. P.* 36. 16
कर्मणः सुकृतस्याहुः सात्त्विकं निर्मलं फलम्।
रजसस्तु फलं दुःखमज्ञानं तमसः फलम्।।

260. *Ibid.*, 36. 17-18
सत्त्वात्संजायते ज्ञानं रजसो लोभ एव च।
प्रमादमोहौ तमसो भवतोऽज्ञानमेव च।।
ऊर्ध्वं गच्छन्ति सत्त्वस्था मध्ये तिष्ठन्ति राजसाः।
जघन्यगुणवृत्तस्था अधो गच्छन्ति तामसाः।।

261. *Sā. K.* 54
ऊर्ध्वं सत्त्व-विशालस्तमो-विशालश्च मूलतः सर्गः।
मध्ये रजोविशालो ब्रह्मादिस्तम्बपर्यन्तः।।

262. *Mbh. Bh. P.* 36. 20
गुणानेतानतीत्य त्रीन्देही देहसमुद्भवान्।
जन्ममृत्युजरादुःखैर्विमुक्तोऽमृतमश्नुते।।

263. *Ibid.*, 22-23.
प्रकाशं च प्रवृत्तिं च मोहमेव च पाण्डव।
न द्वेष्टि संप्रवृत्तानि न निवृत्तानि काङ्क्षति।।
उदासीनवदासीनो गुणैर्यो न विचाल्यते।
गुणा वर्तन्त इत्येव योऽवतिष्ठति नेङ्गते।।

264. *Ibid.*, 40. 13.
पञ्चैतानि महाबाहो कारणानि निबोध मे।
सांख्ये कृतान्ते प्रोक्तानि सिद्धये सर्वकर्मणाम्।।

265. Satvalekar, S.D., *op. cit.,* p. 900.

266. *Mbh. Bh. P.* 40. 14.

अधिष्ठानं तथा कर्ता करणं च पृथग्विधम्।
विविधाश्च पृथक्चेष्टा दैवं चैवात्र पञ्चमम्।।

267. *Bh. P.* 40.17[ab]

यस्य नाहंकृतो भावो बुद्धिर्यस्य न लिप्यते।

268. *Ibid., P.* 40. 30-32

प्रवृत्तिं च निवृत्तिं च कार्याकार्ये भयाभये।
बन्धं मोक्षं च या वेत्ति बुद्धिः सा पार्थ सात्त्विकी।।

यया धर्ममधर्मं च कार्यं चाकार्यमेव च।
अयथावत्प्रजानाति बुद्धिः सा पार्थ राजसी।।

अधर्मं धर्ममिति या मन्यते तमसावृता।
सर्वार्थान्विपरीतांश्च बुद्धिः सा पार्थ तामसी।।

269. *Ibid., P.* 40. 33-35

धृत्या यया धारयते मनःप्राणेन्द्रियक्रियाः।
योगेनाव्यभिचारिण्या धृतिः सा पार्थ सात्त्विकी।।

यया तु धर्मकामार्थान्धृत्या धारयतेऽर्जुन।
प्रसङ्गेन फलाकाङ्क्षी धृतिः सा पार्थ राजसी।।

यया स्वप्नं भयं शोकं विषादं मदमेव च।
न विमुञ्चति दुर्मेधा धृतिः सा पार्थ तामसी।।

270. *Ibid.,* 36-39.

सुखं त्विदानीं त्रिविधं शृणु मे भरतर्षभ।
अभ्यासाद्रमते यत्र दुःखान्तं च निगच्छति।।।

यत्तदग्रे विषमिव परिणामेऽमृतोपमम्।
तत्सुखं सात्त्विकं प्रोक्तमात्मबुद्धिप्रसादजम्।।

विषयेन्द्रियसंयोगाद्यत्तदग्रेऽमृतोपमम्।
परिणामे विषमिव तत्सुखं राजसं स्मृतम्।।

यदग्रे चानुबन्धे च सुखं मोहनमात्मनः।
निद्रालस्यप्रमादोत्थं तत्तामसमुदाहृतम्।।

271. *Ibid.,* 41

ब्राह्मणक्षत्रियविशां शूद्राणां च परंतप।
कर्माणि प्रविभक्तानि स्वभावप्रभवैर्गुणैः।।

272. *Ibid.*, 20-28.

273. *Ibid.*, 40. 49.

असक्तबुद्धिः सर्वत्र जितात्मा विगतस्पृहः।
नैष्कर्म्यसिद्धिं परमां संन्यासेनाधिगच्छति॥

274. *Sa K.* 3, 22.

मूलप्रकृतिरविकृतिर्महदाद्याः प्रकृतिविकृतयः सप्त।
षोडशकस्तु विकारो न प्रकृतिर्न विकृतिः पुरुषः॥
प्रकृतेर्महान् ततोऽहङ्कारः तस्मात्तणश्च षोडशकः।
तस्मादषि षोडशकात् पञ्चभ्यः पञ्च भूतानि॥

275. *Mbh. Śanti P.* 241. 1

सृजते तु गुणान्सत्त्वं क्षेत्रज्ञस्त्वनुतिष्ठति।
गुणान्विक्रियतः सर्वानुदासीनवदीश्वरः॥

276. *Ibid.*, 239. 14

इन्द्रियाणि नरे पञ्च षष्ठं तु मन उच्यते।
सप्तमीं बुद्धिमेवाहुः क्षेत्रज्ञं पुनरष्टमम्॥

277. *Ibid.*, 239. 18

यदूर्ध्वं पादतलयोरवाङ्मूर्ध्नश्च पश्यति।
एतस्मिन्नेव कृत्ये वै वर्तते बुद्धिरुत्तमा॥

278. *Ibid.*, 239. 13

मनो बुद्धिश्च भावश्च त्रय एतेऽत्मयोनिजाः।
न गुणानतिवर्तन्ते गुणेभ्यः परमा मताः॥

279. *Ibid.*, 240. 3

बुद्धिरात्मा मनुष्यस्य बुद्धिरेवात्मनोऽऽत्मिका।
यदा विकुरुते भावं तदा भवति सा मनः॥

280. *Ibid.*, 6

इन्द्रियाणीति तान्याहुस्तेष्वदृश्याधितिष्ठति।
तिष्ठती पुरुषे बुद्धिस्त्रिषु भावेषु वर्तते॥

281. *Ibid.*, 1

मनः प्रसृजते भावं बुद्धिरध्यवसायिनि।
हृदयं प्रियाप्रिये वेद त्रिविधा कर्मचोदना॥

282. *Ibid.*, *P.* 240. 2

इन्द्रियेभ्यः परा ह्यर्थाः अर्थेभ्यः परमं मनः।
मनसस्तु परा बुद्धिर्बुद्धेरात्मा परो मतः॥

283. *Ibid.*, 240. 4

इन्द्रियाणां पृथग्भावाद्बुद्धिर्विक्रियते ह्यणु।
शृण्वती भवति श्रोत्रं स्पृशती स्पर्श उच्यते॥

284. *Ibid.*, 239. 3

भूमिरापस्तथा ज्योतिर्वायुराकाशमेव च।
महाभूतानि भूतानां सागरस्योर्मयो यथा॥

285. *Ibid.*, 239. 9-12.

शब्दः श्रोत्रं तथा खानि त्रयमाकाशसंभवम्।
प्राणश्चेष्टा तथा स्पर्श एते वायुगुणास्त्रयः॥

रूपं चक्षुर्विपाकश्च त्रिधा ज्योतिर्विधीयते।
रसोऽथ रसनं स्नेहो गुणास्त्वेते त्रयोऽम्भसाम्॥

घ्रेयं घ्राणं शरीरं च भूमरैते गुणास्त्रयः।
एतावानिन्द्रियग्रामो व्याख्यातः पाञ्चभौतिकः॥

वायोः स्पर्शो रसोऽद्भ्यश्च ज्योतिषो रूपमुच्यते।
आकाशप्रभवः शब्दो गन्धो भूमिगुणः स्मृतः॥

286. *Op. cit.*, 294. 34

287. *Ibid.*, 294. 35

बहुधात्मा प्रकुर्वीत प्रकृतिं प्रसवात्मिकाम्।
तच्च क्षेत्रं महानात्मा पञ्चविंशोऽधितिष्ठति॥

288. *Ibid.*, 294. 27-28

अव्यक्तमाहुः प्रकृतिं परां प्रकृतिवादिनः।
तस्मान्महत्समुत्पन्नं द्वितीयं राजसत्तम॥

अहंकारस्तु महतस्तृतीयमितिः नः श्रुतम्।
पञ्च भूतान्यहंकारादाहुः सांख्यानुदर्शिनः॥

289. *Sā. K.* 24.

अभिमानोऽहङ्कारस्तस्माद् द्विविधः प्रवर्तते सर्गः।
एकादशकश्च गणस्तन्मात्रः पञ्चकश्चैव॥

290. *Sā. K.* 22, 26

प्रकृतेर्महांस्ततोऽहङ्कारस्तस्माद् गणश्च षोडशकः।
तस्मादपि षोडकशकात् पञ्चभ्यः पञ्च भूतानि॥

बुद्धीन्द्रियाणि चक्षुः - श्रोत्र - घ्राण - रसन - त्वगाख्यानि।
वाक् - पाणि - पाद - पायूपस्थान् कर्मेन्द्रियाण्याहुः॥

291. *Mbh. Śanti P.* 293. 50
निस्तत्त्वं पञ्चविंशस्य परमाहुर्निदर्शनम्।
वर्गस्य वर्गमाचारं तत्त्वं तत्त्वात्सनातनात्।।

292. *Sā. K.* 19.
तस्माच्च विपर्यासात् सिद्धं साक्षित्वमस्य पुरुषस्य।
कैवल्यं माध्यस्थ्यं द्रष्टृत्वमकर्तृभावश्च।।

293. *Mbh. Āsva. P.* 35. 37-38.
महानात्मा तथाव्यक्तमहंकारस्तथैव च।
इन्द्रियाणि दशैकं च महाभूतानि पञ्च च।।
विशेषाः पञ्चभूतानामित्येषा वैदिकी श्रुतिः।
चतुर्विंशतिरेषा वस्तत्त्वानां संप्रकीर्तिता।।

294. *Ibid.* 36. 1
तदव्यक्तमनुद्रिक्तं सर्वव्यापि ध्रुवं स्थिरम्।
नवद्वारं पुरं विद्यात्त्रिगुणं पञ्चधातुकम्।।

295. *Ibid.*, 36. 2
एकादशपरिक्षेपं मनो व्याकरणात्मकम्।
बुद्धिस्वामिकमित्येतत्परमेकादशं भवेत्।।

296. *Sā. K.* 37.
सर्वं प्रत्युपभोगं यस्मात् पुरुषस्य साधयति बुद्धिः।
सैव च विशिनष्टि पुनः प्रधान - पुरुषान्तरं सूक्ष्मम्।।

297. Wilson q. by Davis John, *The Sāṅkhya Kārikā of Īśvara Kṛṣṇa*, p. 51.

298. *Mbh. Śanti P.* 298. 10.
अष्टौ प्रकृतयः प्रोक्ता विकाराश्चापि षोडश।
अथ सप्त तु व्यक्तानि प्राहुरध्यात्मचिन्तकाः।।

299. *Ibid.*, 12 - 14.

300. *Ibid.*, 267. 4-5[ab]
येभ्यः सृजति भूतानि कालो भावप्रचोदितः।
महाभूतानि पञ्चेति तान्याहुर्भूतचिन्तकाः।।
तेभ्यः सृजति भूतानि काल आत्मप्रचोदितः।

301. *Ibid.*, 6 - 7
विद्धि नारद पञ्चेताञ्शाश्वतानचलान्ध्रुवान्।
महतस्तेजसो राशीन्कालषष्ठान्स्वभावतः।।

आपश्चैवान्तरिक्षं च पृथिवी वायुपावकौ।
असिद्धिः परमेतेभ्यो भूतेभ्यो मुक्तसंशयम्।

302. *Ibid.*, 12[abc] - 18

चक्षुषी नासिकाकर्णौ त्वग्जिह्वेति च पञ्चमी।
इन्द्रियाणीन्द्रियार्थानां...........
चित्तमिन्द्रियसंघातं मनो बुद्धिं तथाष्टमीम्।
अष्टौ ज्ञानेन्द्रियाण्याहुरेतान्यध्यात्मचिन्तकाः।।

303. *Ibid.*, 21-22[ab]

पायूपस्थौ विसर्गार्थमिन्द्रिये तुल्यकर्मणी।
विसर्गे च पुरीषस्य विसर्गे चाभिकामिके।।
बलं षष्ठं षडेतानि वाचा सम्यग्यथागमम्।

304. *Ibid.*, 25[ab]

सात्त्विकाश्चैव ये भावास्तथा राजसतामसाः।

305. *Ibid.*, 30

एकश्च दश चाष्टौ च गुणाः सह शरीरिणाम्।
ऊष्मणा सह विंशो वा संघातः पाञ्चभौतिकः।।

306. *Sā. K.* 11.

त्रिगुणमविवेकि विषयः सामान्यमचेतनं प्रसवधर्मि।
व्यक्तं तथा प्रधानं तद्विपरीतस्तथा च पुमान्।।

307. *Mbh. Śanti P.* 316. 44 - 46.

इदं विश्वं जगत्सर्वमजगच्चापि यद्भवेत्।
महाभूतात्मकं सर्वं महद्यत्परमाणु यत्।।

इन्द्रियाणि च पञ्चैव तमः सत्त्वं रजस्तथा।
इत्येष सप्तदशको राशिरव्यक्तसंज्ञकः।।

सर्वैरिहन्द्रियार्थैश्च व्यक्ताव्यक्तैर्हि संहितः।
पञ्चविंशक इत्येष व्यक्ताव्यक्तमयो गुणः।।

308. *Sā. K.* 11.

309. *Ibid.*, *K.* 22.

310. *Ibid.*, 38.

तन्मात्राण्यविशेषास्तेभ्यो भूतानि पञ्च पञ्चभ्यः।
एते स्मृता विशेषाः शान्ता घोराश्च मूढाश्च।।

311. *Mbh. Śanti P.* 212. 20-24.

312. *Ibid.*, 7[ab], 9[ab], 20, 40[ab]

धातवः पञ्चशाखोऽयं खं वायुर्ज्योतिरम्बु भूः।
इन्द्रियाणीन्द्रियार्थाश्च स्वभावश्चेतना मनः।।

पञ्च ज्ञानेन्द्रियाण्युक्त्वा मनःषष्ठानि चेतसि।
मनःषष्ठानि वक्ष्यामि पञ्च कर्मेन्द्रियाणि तु।।
एवमाहुः समाहारं क्षेत्रमध्यात्मचिन्तकाः।

313. *Ca. Sa. Śā.* 1. 35.

बुद्धीन्द्रियमनोऽर्थानां विद्याद्योगधरं परम्।
चतुर्विंशतिको ह्येष राशिः पुरुषसंज्ञकः।।

314. Shastri, Kashinath and Chaturvedi Gorakhnath *Carakasmhitā Savimarśa-Vidyotinī Hindi Vyakhyopetā* (Hindi commentary) p. 810.

315. *Bh. P.* 35. 2

क्षेत्रज्ञं चापि मां विद्धि सर्वक्षेत्रेषु भारत।
क्षेत्रक्षेत्रज्ञयोर्ज्ञानं यत्तज्ज्ञानं मतं मम।।

316. *Ibid.*, 5. 6

महाभूतान्यहंकारो बुद्धिरव्यक्तमेव च।
इन्द्रियाणि दशैकं च पञ्च चेन्द्रियगोचराः।।

इच्छा द्वेषः सुखं दुःखं संघातश्चेतना धृतिः।
एतत्क्षेत्रं समासेन सविकारमुदाहृतम्।।

317. *Ibid.*, 19-21 *op.cit.*

318. *Ibid.*, 30. 18-19

अव्यक्ताद्व्यक्तयः सर्वाः प्रभवन्त्यहरागमे।
रात्र्यागमे प्रलीयन्ते तत्रैवाव्यक्तसंज्ञके।।

भूतग्रामः स एवायं भूत्वा भूत्वा प्रलीयते।
रात्र्यागमेऽवशः पार्थ प्रभवत्यहरागमे।।

319. *Ibid.*, 20

परस्तस्मात्तु भावोऽन्योऽव्यक्तोऽव्यक्तात्सनातनः।
यः स सर्वेषु भूतेषु नश्यत्सु न विनश्यति।।

320. *Ibid.*, 30. 21, 22[cd]

अव्यक्तोऽक्षर इत्युक्तस्तमाहुः परमां गतिम्।
यं प्राप्य न निवर्तन्ते तद्धाम परमं मम।।
यस्यान्तःस्थानि भूतानि येन सर्वमिदं ततम्।।

321. *Ibid.*, 29. 4-5 *op.cit.*

322. *Ibid.*, 24. 58-59

यदा संहरते चायं कूर्मोऽङ्गानीव सर्वशः।
इन्द्रियाणीन्द्रियार्थेभ्यस्तस्य प्रज्ञा प्रतिष्ठिता।।

विषया विनिवर्तन्ते निराहारस्य देहितः।
रसवर्जं रसोऽप्यस्य परं दृष्ट्वा निवर्तते।।

323. *Ibid.*, 60-61

यततो ह्यपि कौन्तेय पुरुषस्य विपश्चितः।
इन्द्रियाणि प्रमाथीनि हरन्ति प्रसभं मनः।।

तानि सर्वाणि संयम्य युक्त आसीत मत्परः।
वशे हि यस्येन्द्रियाणि तस्य प्रज्ञा प्रतिष्ठिता।।

324. *Ibid., Bh. P.* 25. 37.

काम एष क्रोध एष रजोगुणसमुद्भवः।
महाशनो महापाप्मा विद्ध्येनमिह वैरिणम्।।

325. *Ibid.*, 40.

इन्द्रियाणि मनो बुद्धिरस्याधिष्ठानमुच्यते।
एतैर्विमोहयत्येष ज्ञानमावृत्य देहिनम्।।

326. *Ibid.*, 42.

इन्द्रियाणि पराण्याहुरिन्द्रियेभ्यः परं मनः।
मनसस्तु परा बुद्धिर्यो बुद्धेः परतस्तु सः।।

327. *Ibid.*, 43.

एवं बुद्धेः परं बुद्ध्वा संस्तभ्यात्मानमात्मना।
जहि शत्रुं महाबाहो कामरूपं दुरासदम्।।

328. *Ibid.*, 40. 11.

न हि देहभृता शक्यं त्यक्तुं कर्माण्यशेषतः।
यस्तु कर्मफलत्यागी स त्यागीत्यभिधीयते।।

329. *Ibid.*, 29-32.

330. *Ibid.*, 51, 53.

बुद्ध्या विशुद्धया युक्तो धृत्यात्मानं नियम्य च।
शब्दादीन्विषयांस्त्यक्त्वा रागद्वेषौ व्युदस्य च।।

अहंकारं बलं दर्पं कामं क्रोधं परिग्रहम्।
विमुच्य निर्ममः शान्तो ब्रह्मभूयाय कल्पते।।

331. Tilak, B.G., *op. cit.*, pp. 189-191.
332. *Mbh. Śānti P.* 240. 2; *Bh. P.* 25. 42.
333. *Ibid., Van. P.* 202. 21-25.
334. *Ibid., Strī. P.* 7. 13-15.
335. *Ibid., Āsva. P.* 50. 1-10.
336. *Ibid., Bh. P.* 24. 67-68, 28. 24-26.
337. *Sā. K.* 9.
338. *Ibid.*, 3.
339. *Ibid.*, 11.
340. *Ibid.*, 57.
341. *Mbh. Bh. P.*25. 27-28.
342. *Ibid., Āśva. P.* 36. 1-2.
343. *Ibid., Āśva. P.* 37-16.
344. *Ibid., Śānti. P.* 295. 11[ab] 13-14.

   उभावेतौ क्षरावुक्तावुभावेतौ च नश्वरौ।
   सर्गप्रलयधर्मित्वादव्यक्तं प्राहुरक्षरम्।
   तदेतद्गुणसर्गाय विकुर्वाणं पुनः पुनः।।

   गुणानां महदादीनामुत्पद्यति परस्परम्।
   अधिष्ठानात्क्षेत्रमाहुरेतत्पञ्चविंशकम्।।

345. *Ibid.*, 38[cd], 39[ab]

   एवं परमसंबोधात्पञ्चविंशोऽनुबुद्धवान्।
   अक्षरत्वं नियच्छेत त्यक्त्वा क्षरमनामयम्।

346. *Ibid., Āsva. P.* 18. 26,

   इह तत्क्षरमित्युक्तं परं त्वमृतमक्षरम्।
   त्रयाणां मिथुनं सर्वमेकैकस्य पृथक्पृथक्।।

347. *Ibid.*, 32.

   जातीमरणरोगैश्च समाविष्टः प्रधानवित्।
   चेतनावत्सु चैतन्यं समं भूतेषु पश्यति।।

348. *Ibid.*, 19. 13.

   विमुक्तः सर्वसंस्कारैस्ततो ब्रह्म सनातनम्।
   परमाप्नोति संशान्तमचलं दिव्यमक्षरम्।।

349. *Ibid., Śānti. P.* 327. 24[ab], 25.
परमात्मेति यं प्राहुः सांख्ययोगविदो जनाः।
तस्मात्प्रसूतमव्यक्तं प्रधानं तद्विदुर्बुधाः।
अव्यक्ताद्व्यक्तमुत्पन्नं लोकसृष्ट्यर्थमीश्वरात्।।

350. *Ibid.*, 291. 15[ab], 17.
सृजत्यनन्तकर्माणं महान्तं भूतमग्रजम्।
हिरण्यगर्भो भगवानेष बुद्धिरिति स्मृतः।
महानिति च योगेषु विरिञ्च इति चाप्युत।।

351. *Sā. K.* 17.

352. *Ibid.*, 19.

353. *Mbh. Śānti. P.* 295. 14.

354. *Ibid., Bh. P.* 35. 20.
कार्यकारणकर्तृत्वे हेतुः प्रकृतिरुच्यते।
पुरुषः प्रकृतिस्थो हि भुङ्क्ते प्रकृतिजान्गुणान्।

355. *Ibid., Śānti. P.* 327. 24[ab]-25
also *Ibid., Bh. P.* 37. 7[ab]
ममैवांशो जीवलोके जीवभूतः सनातनः।

356. *Ibid., Śānti. P.* 293. 43[cd]

357. *Ibid.*, 327. 25

358. *Ibid., Bh. P.* 31. 10[ab]

359. Tilak, B.G., *op. cit.*, p. 220.

360. Zimmer, Henrich, *op. cit.*, p. 293

361. Dasgupta, S.N., *op. cit.* p. 215

362. *Mbh. Śānti P.* 290. 87-89.
सत्त्वस्य च गुणान्कृत्स्नान्रजसश्च गुणान्पुनः।
गुणांश्च तमसः सर्वान्गुणान्बुद्धेश्च भारत।।
गुणांश्च मनसस्तद्वन्नभसश्च गुणांस्तथा।
गुणान्वायोश्च धर्मात्मंस्तेजसश्च गुणान्पुनः।।
अपां गुणांस्तथा पार्थ पार्थिवांश्च गुणानपि।
सर्वात्मना गुणैर्व्याप्य क्षेत्रज्ञः स युधिष्ठिर।।

363. *Ibid.*, 91.
प्रकृतिं चाप्यतिक्रम्य गच्छत्यात्मानमव्ययम्।
परं नारायणात्मानं निर्द्वंद्वं प्रकृतेः परम्।।

364. *Ibid.*, 92.

विमुक्तः पुण्यपापेभ्यः प्रविष्टस्तमनामयम्।
परमात्मानमगुणं न निवर्तति भारत॥

365. *Ibid.*, 93-94.

शिष्टं त्वत्र मनस्तात इन्द्रियाणि च भारत।
आगच्छन्ति यथाकालं गुरोः संदेशकारिणः॥

शक्यं चाल्पेन कालेन शान्तिं प्राप्तुं गुणार्थिना।
एवं युक्तेन कौन्तेय युक्तज्ञानेन मोक्षिणा॥

366. *Ibid.*, 95-96.

सांख्या राजन्महाप्राज्ञा गच्छन्ति परमां गतिम्।
ज्ञानेनानेन कौन्तेय तुल्यं ज्ञानं न विद्यते॥

अत्र ते संशयो मा भूज्ज्ञानं सांख्यं परं मतम्।
अक्षरं ध्रुवमव्यक्तं पूर्वं ब्रह्म सनातनम्॥

367. *Ibid.*, 109-110.

सांख्यं विशालं परमं पुराणं महार्णवं विमलमुदारकान्तम्।
कृत्स्नं च सांख्यं नृपते महात्मा नारायणो धारयतेऽप्रमेयम्॥

एतन्मयोक्तं नरदेव तत्त्वं नारायणो विश्वमिदं पुराणम्।
स सर्गकाले च करोति सर्गं संहारकाले च तदत्ति भूयः॥

368. *Ibid.*, 293. 40-41.

गुणा गुणवतः सन्ति निर्गुणस्य कुतो गुणाः।
तस्मादेवं विजानन्ति ये जना गुणदर्शिनः॥

यदा त्वेष गुणान्सर्वान्प्राकृतानभिमन्यते।
तदा स गुणवानेव परमेणानुपश्यति॥

369. *Ibid.*, 294. 43.

पञ्चविंशोऽप्रबुद्धात्मा बुध्यमान इति स्मृतः।
यदा तु बुध्यतेऽऽत्मानं तदा भवति केवलः॥

370. *Ibid.*, 294. 46.

न त्वेवं वर्तमानानामावृत्तिर्विद्यते पुनः।
विद्यतेऽक्षरभावत्वादमरस्परमव्ययम्॥

371. *Ibid.*, 296. 11-13.

बुध्यते च परां बुद्धिं विशुद्धाममलां यदा।
षड्विंशो राजशार्दूल तदा बुद्धत्वमाव्रजेत्॥

ततः केवलधर्मासौ भवत्यव्यक्तदर्शनात्।
केवलेन समागम्य विमुक्तोऽऽत्मानमाप्नुयात्॥

372. *Ibid.*, 16.

षड्विंशोऽहमिति प्राज्ञो गृह्यमाणोऽजरामरः।
केवलेन बलेनैव समतां यात्यसंशयम्॥

373. *Ibid.*, 18.

चेतनेन समेतस्य पञ्चविंशतिकस्य च।
एकत्वं वै भवत्यस्य यदा बुद्ध्या न बुध्यते॥

374. *Ibid., P.* 296. 11.

375. *Ibid., P.* 296. 13.

376. *Ibid.*, 302. 3[a].

सात्त्विकस्योत्तमं स्थानं।

377. *Ibid.*, 306. 53.

यदा तु पश्यतेऽत्यन्तमहन्यहनि काश्यप।
तदा स केवलीभूतः षड्विंशमनुपश्यति॥

378. *Ibid.*, 306. 54-55.

अन्यश्च शश्वदव्यक्तस्तथान्यः पञ्चविंशकः।
तस्य द्वावनुपश्येत तमेकमिति साधवः।
तेनैतन्नाभिजानन्ति पञ्चविंशकमच्युतम्।
जन्ममृत्युभयाद्योगाः सांख्याश्च परमैषिणः॥

379. *Ibid.*, 308. 29.

वैराग्यं पुनरेतस्य मोक्षस्य परमो विधिः।
ज्ञानादेव च वैराग्यं जायते येन मुच्यते॥

380. *Ibid.*, 308. 30-31.

ज्ञानेन कुरुते यत्नं यत्नेन प्राप्यते महत्।
महत्द्वंद्वप्रमोक्षाय सा सिद्धिर्या वयोतिगा।
सेयं परमिका बुद्धिः प्राप्ता निर्द्वंद्वता मया।
इहैव गतमोहेन चरता मुक्तसङ्गिना॥

381. *Ibid.*, 308. 38-40.

मोक्षे च त्रिविधा निष्ठा दृष्टा पूर्वैर्महर्षिभिः।
ज्ञानं लोकोत्तरं यच्च सर्वत्यागश्च कर्मणाम्॥

ज्ञाननिष्ठां वदन्त्येके मोक्षशास्त्रविदो जनाः।
कर्मनिष्ठां तथैवान्ये यतयः सूक्ष्मदर्शिनः॥

प्रहायोभयमप्येतज्ज्ञानं कर्म च केवलम्।
तृतीयेयं समाख्याता निष्ठा तेन महात्मना॥

382. *Ibid.*, 41-52.

383. *Ibid.*, *Āsva. P.* 47. 1.

संन्यासं तप इत्याहुर्वृद्धा निश्चितदर्शिनः।
ब्राह्मणा ब्रह्मयोनिस्था ज्ञानं ब्रह्म परं विदुः।।

384. *Ibid.*, 3-4.

ज्ञानेन तपसा चैव धीराः पश्यन्ति तत्पदम्।
निर्णिक्ततमसः पूता व्युत्क्रान्तरजसोऽमलाः।।

तपसा क्षेममध्वानं गच्छन्ति परमैषिणः।
संन्यासनिरता नित्यं ये ब्रह्मविदुषो जनाः।।

385. *Ibid.*, 8-9.

यो न कामयते किंचिन्न किंचिदवमन्यते।
इहलोकस्थ एवैष ब्रह्मभूयाय कल्पते।।

प्रधानगुणतत्त्वज्ञः सर्वभूतविधानवित्।
निर्ममो निरहंकारो मुच्यते नात्र संशयः।।

386. *Ibid.*, 11.

हित्वा गुणमयं सर्वं कर्म जन्तुः शुभाशुभम्।
उभे सत्यानृते हित्वा मुच्यते नात्र संशयः।।

387. *Ibid.*, *Śanti P.* 308. 30-31.

388. *Ibid.*, *Āran. P.* 203-4.

मोहात्मकं तमस्तेषां रज एषां प्रवर्तकम्।
प्रकाशबहुलत्वाच्च सत्त्वं ज्याय इहोच्यते।।

389. *Ibid. Āsva. P.* 203. 7-10.

प्रकाशबहुलो धीरो निर्विवित्सोऽनसूयकः।
अक्रोधनो नरो धीमान्दान्तश्चैव स सात्त्विकः।।

सात्त्विकस्त्वथ संबुद्धो लोकवृत्तेन क्लिश्यते।
यदा बुध्यति बोद्धव्यं लोकवृत्तं जुगुप्सते।।

वैराग्यस्य हि रूपं तु पूर्वमेव प्रवर्तते।
मृदुर्भवत्यहंकारः प्रसीदत्यार्जवं च यत्।।

ततोऽस्य सर्वद्वंद्वानि प्रशाम्यन्ति परस्परम्।
न चास्य संयमो नाम क्वचिद्भवति कश्चन।।

390. *Ibid.*, 15-34.

391. *Ibid.*, 50.

परित्यजति यो दुःखं सुखं चाप्युभयं नरः।
ब्रह्म प्राप्नोति सोऽत्यन्तमसङ्गेन च गच्छति।।

392. *Ibid., Bh. P.* 25. 27.

393. *Ibid.,* 35. 29-30.

प्रकृत्यैव च कर्माणि क्रियमाणानि सर्वशः।
यः पश्यति तथात्मानमकर्तारं स पश्यति॥

यदा भूतपृथग्भावमेकस्थमनुपश्यति।
तत एव च विस्तारं ब्रह्म संपद्यते तदा॥

394. *Ibid.,* 36. 18.[a]

ऊर्ध्वं गच्छन्ति सत्त्वस्था.............।

395. *Ibid.,* 19.

नान्यं गुणेभ्यः कर्तारं यदा द्रष्टानुपश्यति।
गुणेभ्यश्च परं वेत्ति मद्भावं सोऽधिगच्छति॥

396. *Ibid.,* 22-23.

प्रकाशं च प्रवृत्तिं च मोहमेव च पाण्डव।
न द्वेष्टि संप्रवृत्तानि न निवृत्तानि काङ्क्षति॥

उदासीनवदासीनो गुणैर्यो न विचाल्यते।
गुणा वर्तन्त इत्येव योऽवतिष्ठति नेङ्गते॥

397. *Ibid.,* 20.

गुणानेतानतीत्य त्रीन्देही देहसमुद्भवान्।
जन्ममृत्युजरादुःखैर्विमुक्तो ऽ मृतमश्नुते॥

398. *Ibid., Śānti P.* 197. 8.

ज्ञानमुत्पद्यते पुंसां क्षयात्पापस्य कर्मणः।
अथादर्शतलप्रख्ये पश्यत्यात्मानमात्मनि॥

399. Tilak, B.G., *op. cit.,* p. 233.

400. *Sā. K.* 59

रङ्गस्य दर्शयित्वा निवर्तते नर्तकी यथा नृत्यात्।
पुरुषस्य तथाऽत्मानं प्रकाश्य विनिवर्तते प्रकृतिः॥

401. Davis, John, *Sāmakya kārikā of Īśvarakṛṣṇa* (translation with commentary) *op. cit.,* p. 67.

402. *Mbh. Bh. P.* 36. 17[a].

सत्त्वात्संजायते ज्ञानं ....।

403. *Ibid.,* 36. 18[bcd].

.... मध्ये तिष्ठन्ति राजसाः।
जघन्यगुणवृत्तस्था अधो गच्छन्ति तामसाः॥

404. *Sā. K.* 67.
सम्यग्ज्ञानाऽधिगमाद्धर्माऽऽदीनामकारणप्राप्तौ।
तिष्ठति संस्कारवशाच्चक्रभ्रमवद्धृतशरीरः॥

405. Kunhan Raja C., *The Sāṁkhya Kārikā of Īśvarakṛṣṇa*, Hoshiarpur, 1963, p. 165.

406. *Op. cit., Sā. K.* 68.
प्राप्ते शरीरभेदे चरितार्थत्वात् प्रधानविनिवृत्तेः।
ऐकान्तिकमात्यन्तिकमुभयं कैवल्यमाप्नोति॥

407. Kunhan Raja, *op. cit.,* p. 167.

408. *Ibid.,* pp. 168, 169.

409. *Mbh. Bh. P.* 36. 23[a], 24-25.
उदासीनवदासीनो.......।
समदुःखसुखः स्वस्थः समलोष्टाश्मकाञ्चनः।
तुल्यप्रियाप्रियो धीरस्तुल्यनिन्दात्मसंस्तुतिः॥
मानावमानयोस्तुल्यस्तुल्यो मित्रारिपक्षयोः।
सर्वारम्भपरित्यागी गुणातीतः स उच्यते॥

410. *Ibid.,* 26-27.
मां च योऽव्यभिचारेण भक्तियोगेन सेवते।
स गुणान्समतीत्यैतान्ब्रह्मभूयाय कल्पते॥
ब्रह्मणो हि प्रतिष्ठाहममृतस्याव्ययस्य च।
शाश्वतस्य च धर्मस्य सुखस्यैकान्तिकस्य च॥

411. *Ibid.,* 37. 5.
निर्मानमोहा जितसङ्गदोषा अध्यात्मनित्या विनिवृत्तकामाः।
द्वन्द्वैर्विमुक्ताः सुखदुःखसंज्ञैर्गच्छन्त्यमूढाः पदमव्ययं तत्॥

412. *Ibid.,* 40. 53, 54, 56.
अहंकारं बलं दर्पं कामं कोधं परिग्रहम्।
विमुच्य निर्ममः शान्तो ब्रह्मभूयाय कल्पते॥
ब्रह्मभूतः प्रसन्नात्मा न शोचति न काङ्क्षति।
समः सर्वेषु भूतेषु मद्भक्तिं लभते पराम्॥
सर्वकर्माण्यपि सदा कुर्वाणो मद्व्यपाश्रयः।
मत्प्रसादादवाप्नोति शाश्वतं पदमव्ययम्॥

413. *Śānti P.* 212. 13, 15.
तेषु कर्मनिसर्गश्च सर्वतत्त्वार्थनिश्चयः।
तमाहुः परमं शुक्रं बुद्धिरित्यव्ययं महत्॥

अनात्मेति च यद्दृष्टं न ममेत्यपि।
वर्तते किमधिष्ठाना प्रसक्ता दुःखसंततिः॥

414. *Ibid.*, 42, 43, 45.

यथार्णवगता नद्यो व्यक्तीर्जहति नाम च।
न च स्वतां नियच्छन्ति तादृशः सत्त्वसंक्षयः।
एवं सति कुतः संज्ञा प्रेत्यभावे पुनर्भवेत्।
प्रतिसंमिश्रिते जीवे गृह्यमाणे च मध्यतः।
दृढैश्च पाशैर्बहुभिर्विमुक्तः प्रजानिमित्तैरपि दैवतैश्च।
यदा ह्यसौ सुखदुःखे जहाति मुक्तस्तदाग्र्यां गतिमेत्यलिङ्गः॥

415. *Mund. Up.* III. 2. 8.

यथा नद्यः स्यदमानाः समुद्रे अस्तं गच्छन्ति नामरूपे विहाय।
तथा विद्वान् नामरूपाद्विमुक्तः परात्परं पुरुषमुपैति दिव्यम्॥

416. Dasgupta, S.N., *op. cit.*, p. 218.

417. *Ca. Sa. Śā.* I. 138.

आत्मेन्द्रियमनोऽर्थानां सन्निकर्षात् प्रवर्तते।
सुखदुःखमनारम्भादात्मस्थे मनसि स्थिरे॥

418. *Ibid.*, 142.

मोक्षो रजस्तमोऽभावात् बलवत्कर्मसंक्षयाद्।
वियोगः सर्वसंयोगैरपुनर्भव उच्यते॥

419. *Sā. K.* 56.

इत्येष प्रकृतिकृतो महदादिविशेषभूतपर्यन्तः।
प्रतिपुरुषविमोक्षार्थं स्वार्थ इव परार्थ आरम्भः॥

420. *Ibid.*, 19.

421. *Ibid.*, 62.

422. *Ibid.*, 63.

रूपैः सप्तभिरेव तु बध्नात्यात्मानमात्मना प्रकृतिः।
सैव च पुरुषार्थं प्रति विमोचयत्येकरूपेण॥

423. Sharma, H.D., *op. cit., Sāṁkhya Kārikā* with commentary, p. 75.

424. *Sā. K.* 64.

एवं तत्त्वाऽभ्यासान्नास्मि न मे नाहमित्यपरिशेषम्।
अविपर्ययाद्विशुद्धं केवलमुत्पद्यते ज्ञानम्॥

425. *Ibid.*, 65.

तेन निवृत्तप्रसवामर्थवशात् सप्तरूपविनिवृत्ताम्।
प्रकृतिं पश्यति पुरुषः प्रेक्षकवदवस्थितः स्वस्थः॥

426. *Ibid.*, 66.
दृष्टा मयेत्युपेक्षक एको दृष्टाहमित्युपरमत्येका।
सति संयोगेऽपि तयोः प्रयोजनं नास्ति सर्गस्य।।

427. *Ibid.*, 67[abc].
सम्यग्ज्ञानाऽधिगमाद्धर्माऽऽदीनामकारणप्राप्तौ।
तिष्ठति संस्कारवशात् ....।।

428. *Ibid.*, 68.
प्राप्ते शरीरभेदे चरितार्थत्वात् प्रधानविनिवृत्तौ।
ऐकान्तिकमात्यन्तिकमुभयं कैवल्यमाप्नोति।।

429. For more details see Zimmer H. *Op. cit.*, p. 329.

430. Macdonell, A.A. *Op. cit.*, p. 392.

431. Hiriyanna, M., *Op. cit.*, p. 296 - 297.

432. *Sā. K.* 55.
तत्र जरामरणकृतं दुःखं प्राप्नोति चेतनः पुरुषः।
लिङ्गस्याविनिवृत्तेः ....

433. (*i*) *Br. Up.* I. 4. 10.
अहं ब्रह्मास्मि।
(*ii*) *Chānd. Up.* VI. 8. 7.
तत्त्वमसि।

434. *Ibid.*, III. 14. 1.
सर्वं खल्विदं ब्रह्म।

435. ब्रह्मविद् ब्रह्मैव भवति।

436. Radhakrishnan, S., *Indian Philosophy, op. cit.*, p. 528.

437. *Mbh.Bh. P.* 35. 34.
क्षेत्रक्षेत्रज्ञयोरेवमन्तरं ज्ञानचक्षुषा।
भूतप्रकृतिमोक्षं च ये विदुर्यान्ति ते परम्।।

438. *Ibid.*, 35. 30.
यदा भूतपृथग्भावमेकस्थमनुपश्यति।
तत एव च विस्तारं ब्रह्म संपद्यते तदा।।

439. *Ibid.*, *Śanti P.* 290. 91.

440. *Ibid.*, 296. 16[cd].
केवलेन बलेनैव समतां यात्यसंशयम्।।

441. *Ibid.*, 298. 5-6.

कतीन्द्रियाणि विप्रर्षे कति प्रकृतयः स्मृताः।
किमव्यक्तं परं ब्रह्म तस्माच्च परतस्तु किम्।।

प्रभवं चाप्ययं चैव कालसंख्यां तथैव च।
वक्तुमर्हसि विप्रेन्द्र त्वदनुग्रहकाङ्क्षिणः।।

442. *Ibid.*, 306. 53.

443. *Ibid.*, 308. 51-53[ab]

तस्माद्धर्मार्थकामेषु तथा राज्यपरिग्रहे।
बन्धनायतनेष्वेषु विद्ध्यबन्धे पदे स्थितम्।।

राज्यैश्वर्यमयः पाशः स्नेहायतनबन्धनः।
मोक्षाश्मनिशितेनेह छिन्नस्त्यागासिना मया।।
सोऽहमेवंगतो मुक्तो जातास्थस्त्वयि भिक्षुकि।

444. *Ibid.*, *Āśva. P.* 50. 34[cdef]

अपोह्य सर्वसंकल्पान्संयम्यात्मानमात्मनि।
स तद्ब्रह्म शुभं वेत्ति यस्माद्भूयो न विद्यते।।

445. *Ibid.*, *Āraṇ. P.* 203. 50.

446. *Ibid.*, 4.

CHAPTER IV

YOGA PHILOSOPHY AS REFLECTED IN THE MAHĀBHĀRATA

The elements of Sāṁkhya and Vedānta philosophy in the *Mbh.* were dealt with in the earlier chapters. In this chapter light will be thrown on the reflections of Yoga philosophy in the *Mbh.* The classification of the Indian philosophy into theistic (*āstika*) and atheistic (*nāstika*) is based on the criterion of the belief in the existence of God. Accordingly, the materialistic system of Sāṁkhya is to be considered as atheistic. This individualistic theory of Sāṁkhya which analysed the material world on the basis of reasoning appealed to the masses which gave impetus to the individualistic system of Cārvāka which carried materialistic theory to absurdity. It also gave rise to the nihilistic theories of Buddhism and Jainism. According to Chakravarti, S.C., the idealistic systems of monistic and theistic believers found that persisting in the course of analysis originated by the Sāṁkhya system, so many gaps were brought to light. Consequently, it became increasingly difficult to bridge them over and solve the problem of existence since the progress in the field of science was feeble during these days. During this period of stagnation, materialism would have marched. But the intelligentsia developed a new kind of philosophy known as Yoga system.[1] It concentrated on the Self, the Ego for solving the problem of existence. It helped the individual to win the battle of idealism. The inward turned (spiritual) experiences practised by Yoga interpreted the traditional beliefs afresh, corrected and reinforced them. *Mokṣa* or release being the ultimate aim of all the Indian philosophical systems excluding that of Cārvāka, the Yoga philosophy, which disciplines the mind and body of man by controlling his passions (*vāsanā-s*) his reactions, lead him to reach the transcendental plane, by enabling him to attain self-realisation. It made him the master of his destiny by unfolding the path of eightfold accessories of Yoga.

Tradition, however, has grouped Yoga with the Sāṁkhya system, since they have chosen the basis of Sāṁkhya. They recognise twenty five elements of Sāṁkhya philosophy which are instrumental in the creation of the world. They rank Īśvara with these principles purely on external grounds as the twenty sixth principle.

Definition of Yoga

The word Yoga, is to be derived from the root √*yuj* to join, to unite, to yoke. Patañjali defines Yoga as the restraint of mental modifications,[2] that is the control of the activities of the mind. *Tattva Vaiśāradi* explains it as that particular state of mind in which the manifestation of real cognition etc. has been restrained in the state of Yoga.[3] Here *citta* is *manas* which obtains various experiences through the five organs of sense namely eyes, ears etc. Thus, mind (*manas*) goes out through these organs. However, when it does not wander, it turns inward, this turning inside of the *manas* is called restraint (*nirodha*). The *manas* can reach the Ātman only if it has an inward movement. Thus, the union of *manas* with Ātman, is Yoga.[4] *Yogayājñavalkya* defines Yoga as the union (*saṁyoga*) of the individual Soul with the Supreme Soul.[5] However, according to Mitra R., Yoga is not union but disunion. He states that Weber in his *History of Indian Literature* has entirely mispresented Pātañjal philosophy. Weber says "One very peculiar side of the Yoga doctrine is that *yoga* practice, that is, the outer means, such as penance, mortification and the like whereby this absorption into the Supreme Godhead is sought to be attained." Mitra R. refutes this observation and says "The idea of absorption into the Supreme Godhead forms no part of the Yoga theory. Patañjali rests satisfied with the isolation of the Soul and does not pry into how and where the soul abides after separation."[6] Max Müller F., therefore, opines that Yoga in the philosophy of Patañjali and Kapila, did not mean union with God or anything but an effort (*Udyoga* not *Saṁyoga*) of pulling onself together, exertion, concentration. Yoga might mean union but the proper term would have been *saṁyoga.* Max Müller further quotes Bhojadeva's commentary on the *Y.S.* which states, "With the true *Yogin,* joining or union (Yoga), really means *viyoga*, separation or *viveka*, discrimination between Puruṣa and Prakṛti, subject and object, Self and Nature, as taught in the Sāṁkhya system "*Puṁprakṛtyoḥviyogopi yoga ityudito yayā*" Hence (in the teaching of Patañjali), *Yoga* (union) is said to be *viyoga,* separation of Prakrti from Puruṣa."[7]

The *Mait. Up.* defines the word *yoga* as "It is so said since, one joins in this way the breath, Oṁ and all in its manifold forms or they join with him. Hence, it is called *yoga*. The union of breath and mind, of the organs and relinquishment of all existence is called *yoga.*"[8] Max Müller's statement that it is the effort of pulling oneself together, exertion etc. sounds similar to the first part of this definition regarding the union of breath, Oṁ etc. with hirn. The latter portion regarding the relinquishment of all existence resembles the statement in Bhojadeva's commentary that Yoga means the knowledge of separation of Puruṣa from Prakṛti.

Pandit, S.G. states, Pāṇini derives the word *yoga* from *yuj-samādhau, i.e.* in the sense of concentration.[9] Yoga system emphasises on the concentration of mind, by controlling the senses, aims at attaining equanimity and behold the Self by the Self. Thus, Yoga would be communion with the higher Self. The *Bh.G.* explains the word 'Yoga' in three different ways – 1. *Samatvaṁ yoga ucyate.*[10] Satavalekar, S.D explains it as follows – A man suffers from duality of feelings hot and cold etc. By nature the mind is fickle, it runs after various objects of senses and in that case it cannot work properly. Hence, one is supposed to restrain the mental modifications, so that the control remains within, it no more comes under the control of things outside and this is called Yoga. Its nomenclature is equanimity, where there is no sense of duality. The *Bh. G.* also defines it as, "*Yogaḥ karmasu kauśalam,*"[11] the skill in performing actions with the state of equanimity which enables one to remain indifferent in achievements and non-achievements, work zealously in the interest of mankind and finally reach the highest. The third definition is *Duḥkhasaṁyoga-viyoga*,[12] that is, dissociation with the contact of pain which is possible only through the state of equanimity with reference to sense of duality.[13]

Chronology of the Yoga Philosophy

The period of Patajñali, according to Radhakrisnan and Moore, is after Buddha 563-483 B.C.[14] Zimmer considers it as second century B.C.[15] According to Kane, P.V., it is 150 B.C.[16] and in the opinion of Macdonell it is 200 B.C.[17] *The Encyclopedia of Indian Philosophies* considers it as 400-500 A.D.[18] and Sutton, N. as 300 A.D.[19] Hiriyanna, M., however, states it as 500 A.D. [20] According to the *Encyclopedia of Philosophy*, the period of *sūtra*-s falls between 400 B.C. to 600 A.D. [21] Since a majority of scholars consider the period of Patajñali's *Yoga-sūtra*-s around 2nd century B.C., *Yoga-sūtra*-s have been taken into account for the purpose of this thesis.

Elements According to Yoga Philosophy

The Yoga philosophy considers, the three constituents (*guṇa-s*) namely *sattva, rajas* and *tamas* have qualities of effulgence, action and inaction. Due to mutual help of these *guṇa-s* the manifestation (*dṛśya*) takes place. The *dṛśya* (Prakṛti) has the quality of light (*prākāśya*), action (*kriyā*) and inaction (*sthiti*) due to these three *guṇa-s* respecively.[22] The *guṇa*-s have four stages which are specified (*viśeṣa*), the unspecified (*aviśeṣa*), the undifferentiated phenomenal (*liṅgamātra*) and noumenal (*liṅga*).[23] The undifferentiated phenomenal stage is the state of three *guṇa*-s before creation. The state of change, action in these three *guṇa*-s means *buddhi* (*mahat*). When there is only pulsation (*spandana*) of the *guṇa*-s in Mahat it is called *liṅgamātra*. This *mahāttatva* is the modification (*vikṛti*) of unmanifest (*Prakṛti, Dṛśya*). It is the Prakṛti of further creation. From this *mahat,* self sense that is *asmitā,* or *ahaṁkāra* appears. The reflection of the conscious in this *asmitā,* is the being (*jīva*) which has the preponderance of *sattva.* This *jīva* is made up of five gross elements. From this *asmitā* due to constituent of *tamas,* five *tanmātra*-s emanate. The group of *ahaṁkāra* and these five subtle elements (*tanmātra-s*) is called *aviśeṣa.* From the constituent of *sattva* existing in five *tanmātra*-s, five sense organs and mind emanate. From *rajas* five organs of action and from the constituent of *tamas* five gross elements are born. All these sixteen elements constitute the specified state (*viśeṣa*). Thus, the knower (*draṣṭṛ*), Puraṣa, manifestation (*dṛśya*) that is Prakṛti, Mahat, Ahaṁkāra, five *tanmātra*-s, five sense organs, five organs of actions, *manas* and five gross elements, form the twenty five elements. These twenty five elements as considered by the Sāṁkhya system have been adopted by the Yoga system. However, in addition to these twenty five elements, Yoga philosophy also includes Īśvara to these elements, as the twenty sixth element. The concept of Īśvara has been discussed separately is this chapter.

Draṣṭṛ, the seer is consciousness only. However, even through He is pure, he cognises ideas by ignorance.[24] In fact, he is not touched by the qualities, He is nothing other than the power of becoming conscious, still he recognises intellect (*buddhi*) by reflex action. He is neither similar nor dissimilar to *buddhi.* Due to ignorance, he, as if, becomes one with *buddhi* and cognises ideas as *buddhi* and gets transformed into them. He then appears, as it were, the very self of the *buddhi* although in reality he is not so. The purpose of knowable *dṛśya,* is for the knower.[25] The conjunction of *Draṣṭṛ* and *dṛśya* is brought about by Avidyā. The *Draṣṭṛ* is conjoined with *dṛśya* for the purpose of knowing. Once there is knowledge of the nature of the knower, the being is emancipated. Thus, this conjunction ends when it has caused knowledge. Knowledge is the cause of separation of the knower and the knowable.

Here, the emphasis of the Yoga on acquisition of knowledge for the emancipation of the being, shows the optimistic outlook of this system. The aspirant having known the purpose of the creation of the world and getting assured that the phenomenon of creation takes place for the release of a man, is motivated by the almighty to attain release. The Yoga system provides the practical aid for achieving the same. The Yoga system adopts the concept of elements on the lines of Sāṁkhya system.˙ Hence, the *Mbh.* also does not describe the elements of Yoga philosophy separately. Accordingly, the *Mbh.* considers twenty five elements inclusive of Puruṣa and Prakṛti. The emphasis of the *Mbh.* is on the practical aspect of Yoga, that, is *yama, niyama, āsana, prāṇāyāma, pratyāhāra, dhāraṇā, dhyāna* and *samādhi* which enable the aspirant to steady his body and mind and make them fit, *i.e.* conducive to achieve the final goal of human life.

Thus, the *Mbh.* mentions twenty five elements of Sāṁkhya system. It states *avyakta* Prakṛti as the twenty fourth and the Mahān Ātman which recognises, Prakṛti, as the twenty fifth element.[26] The principle which is pure, unblemished, knower, boundless (*aprameya*), eternal as the twenty-sixth element.[27] This unmanifest is without a second (*kevala*), who knows both the manifest and the unmanifest and whom the *jīvātman* recongnises by his discriminative power (*balam*).[28] This twenty-sixth element is the knower himself, knowledge and the undecaying immortal principle.[29]

This description is similar to that of the *draṣṭṛ* and the Īśvara of the *Y.S.* and the Brahman of the Vedānta philosophy too. However, the further description of *jīva* recognising the twenty sixth element and merging himself in the Ātman,[30] clarifies that it is Brahman of Vedānta. Nevertheless, the distinction and similarities are so much blurred that they can be applied to any of them. Thus, all these concepts are synthesized by the *Mbh.*

Again, in the *Mbh.* the distinctions and similarities between Brahman and Īśvara are mixed up and are applied to Kṛṣṇa who has the qualities of Īśvara and Brahman. The adjectives *viz.* omniscient (*kavi*), ancient (*purāṇa*), the ruler (*anuśāsitṛ*) and the supporter of the world (*dhātṛ*)[31] are equally applicable to Īśvara and Brahman. The description of effulgent (*divya*) Puruṣa,[32] principal sacrifice (*adhiyajña*) in the bodies of the being,[33] Supreme Self (*Parama Puruṣa*)[34] and "I am the one who has pervaded this entire world",[35] shows resemblance to Brahman and is applicable to Kṛṣṇa too. The references where Kṛṣṇa says, "The *yogin* who recites the syllable Oṁ, which is a symbol of Brahman and recollects me at the time of death, he attains the Supreme State,[36] the *yogin* who constantly recollects me by steadying his mind, attains to me easily,[37] or the creation takes place under my supervision.[38] However, people do not recognize me who is Īśvara of the beings, since I am dwelling in human body,[39] show the synthesis of Yoga concepts with those of the Vedānta. This description of Kṛṣṇa is similar to Īśvara, Prakṛtilaya-s and Puruṣa of the Yoga doctrine.

The Concept of Vidyā and Avidyā according to Yoga Philosophy

Avidyā is a nescience. This nescience is to consider that Ātman and Anātman are one, not to understand the difference between eternal and non-eternal and indiscrimination between desirable (*preyas*) and benificial (*śreyas*). Nescience, egoism (*asmitā*), attachment (*rāga*), aversion (*dveṣa*), and love of life (*abhiniveśa*) are the five types of affliction (*kleśa*), which trouble the being (*jīvātman*) according to Yoga philosophy.[40] Avidyā is the field, the breeding ground (*kṣetra*) for the other five *kleśa*-s. There are four states of afflictions, *viz.* dormant (*prasupta*) tenuous (*tanu* or *kṣīṇa*), alternated (*vichinna*) and fully operative (*udāra*).[41] These *kleśa*-s or *vāsana*-s are said to be dormant when they exist in the mind in a germinal state. When this dormant power is awake it turns towards its objects. However, in case of a person possessing discriminative knowledge (*viveka*) these germs disappear.

When the desires oppose these *kleśa*-s they become tenuous and disappear. When the *kleśa*-s are in alternate stage they appear and disappear and if the aspirant does not try to fulfill them they disappear. The fourth state is the fully operative one, which finds manifestation in the objects. It is the *udāra* state. All these do not pass beyond the sphere of affliction. In the fourth state (*udāra*), if the desires are pure they impel the aspirant to perform benevolent actions. The *kleśa*-s appear only in the form which is put upon an object by Avidyā. They exist simultaneously with the cognition of the unreal and disappear when nescience disappears.[42] Thus, according to Patañjali, Avidyā is to consider the non-eternal (*anitya*) as eternal, the impure (*aśuci*) as pure, the painful (*duḥkha*) as pleasurable and the non-self (*anātman*) as Ātman, Self. Egoism (*asmitā*) is the appearance of identity in the natures of the subjective power of consciousness (*draṣṭr*) and the instrumental power of seeing (*darśana*).[43] Here the instrument of seeing etc. means different sense organs, organs of action, *manas*, *buddhi* etc. all the organs, which facilitate the being to have experience of the world. The Ātman is the subjective power of consciousness (*draṣṭr*) and the instrumental power of seeing (*darśana*) etc. is Prakṛti. To recognise the Ātman and Prakṛti as one is *asmitā, ahaṁkāra* according to Yoga philosophy. *Rāga* is the attachment towards pleasure[44] and *dveṣa* is the aversion towards pain.[45] The wise (and the unwise both) believe that the body is myself and do not like to die. This affliction is called love of life (*abhiniveśa*).[46] All these *kleśa*-s when their germinating ability is destroyed, can disappear.[47] Along with this, *yogin's* mind, having fulfilled the purpose of its existence, becomes latent. The modifications of these *kleśa*-s are destroyed by meditation.[48] If one desires to avoid pain in future, he has to destroy *avidyā*, the cause of conjunction of the knower and knowable.[49] The conjunction is brought about by the purpose of existence. This is the cause of an avoidable pain. This conjunction brings about the recognition of the nature of the power of owning (*svāmiśaktiḥ*) and the capacity of being owned (*sva*). The Puruṣa is the owner, the knower.[50] The knowable is whatever is owned. The former is cognized with the latter for the purpose of knowing.[51] The object of the 'knowable' (*Prakṛti*), is for the fulfilment of object of the Puruṣa and for the experience and emancipation of Puruṣa.[52] This conjunction takes place due to *avidyā*, it is the effective cause of this conjuction.[53] Once the ignorance is destroyed this conjunction breaks and this is the state of *kaivalya.*[54]

The knowledge of the nature of the knower is emancipation. This conjunction of the knower and the knowable ceases when it has caused knowledge. Knowledge is, therefore, called the cause of separation. Knowledge is contradictory to ignorance. This ignorance can be removed by the practice of discrimination.[55]

The *Mbh.* considers unmanifest, which is characterised by creation and dissolution, as *avidyā.*[56] Thus, it is Prakṛti, which is made up of twenty four elements. Puruṣa, who is beyond these twenty four elements, *i.e.* the twenty fifth element, is Vidyā. It is the highest knowledge. However, it also describes Prakṛti as knowledge of *buddhi* etc. all the elements. It is the ultimate means (*vidhi*) for acquiring knowledge. The twenty fifth element about which the explanation is being given here, is itself called as the ultimate knowledge of unmanifest Nature. It is the knowable (*jñeya*) of all the knowledge.[57] Thus, the knowledge of the elements is called *avyakta* and the knowable (*jñeya*) is called Supreme Self (Parama Puruṣa). The same thought is expressed in the earlier section.[58] In reality *kṣetra* and *kṣetrajña* are different from each other *kṣetra* is *avyakta* and *kṣetrajña* the knower of *kṣ etra* is the Ātman, the twenty fifth element. Knowledge and knowable are different. Knowledge is *avyakta* and knowable is Ātman. The *yogin* with the help of Yoga dissolves the other element in the *avyakta* Prakṛti and alongwith this the twenty fifth element too is dissolved in the Ātman. When the Prakṛti composed of three constituents gets dissolved[59], Puruṣa who is not touched by the three constituents of Prakṛti (*guṇa*-s), goes beyond them. This way the wise (*yogin*) realises that he is different from Prakṛti; he becomes pure.[60]

Though Kṛṣṇa does not use the term Avidyā anywhere, there is a reference to attachment desire, anger, loss of memory etc. hurdles in the path of *yogin* to attain *samādhi.* He states that if the person constantly thinks about the objects of senses, there arises desire towards them. From desire, there appears anger, from anger bewilderment, then there is a loss of memory, destruction of intelligence and then the being perishes.[61] These obstructions, which delude the intelligence of the being, are similar to the obstructions stated in *Y.S.*, which describe the sins that cause injury to others, etc., are preceded by desire, anger, ignorance, which are slight, middling and intense. They result in an infinity of pain and loss of wisdom.[62] The being, therefore, must develop the tendencies which would counter such hindrances.

The *Bh. G.* has also described the afflictions which are similar to those narrated in *Y.S.*[63] It states that casting aside self sense (*ahaṁkāra*), force (*bala*), arrogance (*darpa*), desire (*kāma*), anger (*krodha*), possession (*parigraha*) the *yogin* should become egoless, tranquil in mind, only then he would become worthy of becoming Brahman.[64] Also when ignorance (*ajñāna*) is destroyed by wisdom (*jñāna*), wisdom lights up the Supreme Self, like the sun and the aspirant then reaches the state from where there is no return.[65] Kṛṣṇa further declares that there is nothing on the earth which is equal in purity to wisdom. He who has become prefect by Yoga realises this and finds himself in his own self (Ātman) during the course of time.[66] There is also a description of the ascetic whose Soul is satisfied with wisdom (*jñāna*) and knowledge (*vijñāna*), who is the master of his senses, he excels in Yoga.[67] This thought is in consonance with the *Y.S.* which states, once the ignorance is destroyed the being attains the state of *kaivalya* and this can be achieved by the constant practice of discrimination.[68] Here, the discriminative knowledge is said to be undisturbed (*aviplava*), this is the Supreme state. The knowledge is undisturbed when he attains *kaivalya,* hence, there is no return from this state.

The *Mbh.*, thus, considers the unmanifest *avyakta* Prakrti as Avidyā, which has the nature of creation and dissolution and the twenty fifth principle, *viz.* Puruṣa as Vidyā.[69] The *Mbh.* terms this (Avidyā) as ignorance which is to be removed by wisdom. The *yogin* by the practice of *Yoga* can dissolve the other elements in Prakṛti and at that moment, Prakṛti and Puruṣa, everything becomes one and Kṣetrajña, the embodied soul also dissolves. The Puruṣ a becomes devoid of constituents (*guṇa*-s).[70]

Control of Senses – *Pratyāhāra*

A being derives pleasure or pain from his virtuous or vicious actions.[71] However, a discriminating person (*vivekin*) experiences pain even from the pleasures derived from good actions. These pains are due to change, anxiety, habituation and the activities of constituents of Prakṛti[72] (*guṇa*-s). The qualities (*guṇa*-s) are *sattva, rajas* and *tamas*. They with the help of each other create a quiescence (*prakāśa*), action and inaction respectively.[73] The reason for pain, from the virtuous actions, is a repetition of enjoyment. Repetition does not cause pleasure, as attachment increases due to such repetition as well as dexterity of the power. This change in the state of pleasure produces contrary effect. These pains accrue due to an accumulated action (*karmāśaya*), the present and future actions (*anāgata*). Of these, pain from *anāgata* actions can be avoided.[74] The pleasures and pains are due to Avidyā. Due to Avidyā there is a conjunction of the knower (*draṣṭṛ*) and the knowable (*dṛśya*),[75] *i.e.* the power of knowing and power of being known respectively. This is brought about for the purpose of existence. This is the cause of avoidable pain.[76] This knowable is of the nature of illumination (*sattva*), activity (*rajas*) and inertia, inactivity (*tamas*). It consists of the elements and power of sensation, action, conscious (*thought*). According to Yoga philosophy its objects are emancipation and experience of the knower (Puruṣa)[77]. This experience of the knower consists in obtaining the knowledge of the nature of the desirable and undesirable phenomena of the *guṇa*-s. Emancipation is the ascertainment of the nature of the enjoyer (*Puruṣa*). As stated before, this conjunction of *daṣṭṛ* and *dṛśya* is due to Avidyā. This removal of Avidyā can be achieved by the discriminative knowledge. To know that the *citta* and Puruṣa are different, is the discriminative knowledge (*vivekakhyāti*).[78] It is the means of burning the seed of false knowledge (*Avidyā*) so that it would not sprout again. The philosophy of Yoga, describes the right accessories to remove these roots of Avidyā.[79] They are restraint (*yama*), observance (*niyama*), postures (*āsana-s*), regulation of breath (*prāṇāyāma*) obstruction of senses, *i.e.* (*pratyāhāra*), concentration (*dhāraṇā*), meditation (*dhyāna*) and trance (*samādhi*).[80] By dedicated practice of these, for a long period, the *yogin* achieves the steadiness of mind and body.[81]

The abstinence from injury (*ahiṁsā*), veracity (*satya*), abstinence from theft (*asteya*), chastity, continence (*brahmacarya*) and abstinence from avarice (*aparigraha*) are the restraints (*yama*).[82] The observances (*niyama-s*) are cleanliness, contentment, purificatory actions, study and the performance of all the actions with the motive of dedicating them to the Lord (*Īśvara*).[83] To avoid the germination of thoughts contrary to the observance of these *yama* and *niyama*, the mind should have good intentions.[84] By the observance of the *yama* and *niyama,* the mind is purified, then there comes high mindedness (*saumanasya*) as *rajas* and *tamas* are destroyed and *sattva* constituent becomes pure.[85] Postures are steady and easy states of body.[86] When the postures are mastered, there is a cessation of disturbances from the pairs of opposite.[87] The regulation of breath (*prāṇāyāma*) is the control over the inhaling and exhaling movements (of breath).[88] Obstruction (of senses) (*pratyāhāra*) is that by which the senses do not come into contact with their objects and follow the nature of the mind. Thus, control of senses (*indriya-s*) is *pratyāhāra*[89] and it is achieved by the aspirant by all these means of *yama, niyama, āsana-s* and *prāṇāyāma*. The mind then becomes fit for concentration.[90] These thoughts are reflected in the *Mbh.* at many places. Kṛṣṇa states that a person with uncontrolled and wavering mind does not have reasoning faculty. There is no peace for him and for the person without peace of mind, how can there be happiness? When the mind runs after the senses, it carries away the faculty of understanding, as a wind carries away a ship on the waters. Hence, one whose senses are withdrawn from their objects, has his intelligence firmly set.[91]

The state of a man who is stable in intelligence is described in the *Mbh.* as follows. He gives up all his desires. His soul is content in itself. His mind is controlled when he suffers from griefs. He does not entertain any desire when he is happy, his passions, fear, rage disappear. He is without affection. He neither rejoices nor loathes when he obtains good or evil.[92]

He, thus, withdraws the senses from the objects of senses from every side like a tortoise which withdraws its limbs into a shell. When the aspirant restrains, his *sattva* becomes pure and there appears a state of highmindedness, his mind is no more attracted towards the objects of senses, that is the state of *saumanasya.*[93] While explaining the nature of perfect *jñāna* to Arjuna, Kṛṣṇa beautifully described this state. He said, since the constituent of *sattva* is pure it illumines.[94] The *Mbh.* also presents a description of sense objects turning away from the soul who abstains from enjoying them. However, his interest still remains. He may strive to be discerning, his impetuous senses carry his mind forcibly.[95] This discretion of impetuous senses has appeared in *Y.S.*, when it states that when the thoughts contrary to such restraints appear in the mind, one should cultivate good ideas which would counter those thoughts.[96] The same thought appears again in the *Mbh.* which states that having brought all the senses under control, one should remain firm in Yoga. If the senses are under control, intellect would be firm. Hence, the aspirant should concentrate on the Highest Reality.[97] Here, the factor of Īśvara *praṇidhāna* appears.

Further, the aspirant who is satisfied with wisdom and knowledge, is firm and the master of his senses. The *Mbh.* again stresses that there is no doubt that the mind is difficult to curb and restless, but it can be controlled by a constant practice and non-attachment. Yoga is hard to attain by one who is not self-controlled, but for the self-controlled one,[98] it is attainable through proper means. The *Mbh.* also describes man as a hypocrite who restrains his organs of action but continues to brood over the objects of senses, whose nature is deluded. It praises one who controls the senses by the mind, without attachment, engages organs of action on the path of work, as superior. It states that when the mind of the aspirant is turned towards sense-objects, he becomes unhappy but when the sense organs are under control he experiences happiness. Hence, one should, through his intellect, control the mind which is running towards senses. One who follows the path of enjoyment which leads to sins, is reborn and acquires the fruit of actions (*karmāśaya*). He, therefore, should desist from the enjoyment of senses. Then he would get away from the objects of senses. However, the desire to have them still remains. But if one attains the Supreme Self, those desires would be uprooted.[99] According to the *Mbh.*, *manas* which goes after different objects of senses is very fickle. The *yogin*-s first control it, concentrate on it alongwith the sense organs and meditate.[100] Thereafter, the *manas* becomes steady for a while but again starts wandering after the objects of senses. The *yogin*, however, should not be disheartened by this. He should continue to concentrate even if afflictions continue to trouble him.[101]

Ultimately the *yogin* who steadies his mind and five sense-organs while treading the path of Yoga, achieves power and through constant practice attains deliverance thereafter.[102]

According to the *Mbh.* when the mind of an aspirant is attracted towards the objects of senses, he is not able to perceive the ultimate which is devoid of qualities. When he controls the senses and brings them within the fold of his heart, he can reach the Supreme Self. When his discriminative intellect (*vyavasāya-guṇopetā buddhi*) exists in his *manas*, it (*manas*) becomes pure. When *manas* discards all the *guṇa*-s and is steady, he attains the Ultimate Reality which is devoid of any attribute.[103]

Thus, control of senses according to *Y.S.* as well as the *Mbh.*, is the basis of meditation. Unless the aspirant controls them, his mind would not be calm and steady. With unsteady mind he cannot concentrate. Without concentration, meditation would not be possible. Without meditation, trance (*samādhi*) cannot be reached and the ultra meditative trance (*nirvikalpa samādhi*) which is the final stage, in which the aspirant realises that *jīva* is none other than Ātman himself, can be attained. Hence, just as the *Bh. G.* states that the reflection, in water which is calm, is clear, in the same way, the reflection of the Ātman would be clear in the calm and tranquil mind that has acquired the highest peace. He is one in whom the constituent of action (*rajas*) is subdued, he is free from sins and attains the Brahman. He alone attains the highest Bliss.[104]

The *Mbh.* has stressed importance of the control of senses, self restraint and truth to attain Brahman.[105] It states that the aspirant should abandon all his desires born of selfish will. Without thinking about anything else, he should control his intellect through steadfastness, fix his mind on the self and attain tranquility. When the mind wavers or wanders and is unsteady, he should restrain it and bring it under the control of the Self.[106]

Thus, the *Mbh.* expressly stated the importance of self-control to attain the final goal of absolute independence of the Self.

Means of Concentration according to Yoga Philosophy

For the control of senses (*pratyāhāra*) as described in the earlier topic, the means of postures (*āsana-s*) and control of breath (*prāṇāyāma-s*) are necessary. These two means would help the aspirant to be fit for concentration (*dhāraṇā*).

According to the Yoga philosophy, if there is no inhibition (*nirodha*), the Puruṣa, seer stands in his own nature.[107] However, due to three constituents of *sattva, rajas* and *tamas*, there are modifications in the *citta*. These modifications are real cognition (*pramāṇa*), unreal cognition (*viparyaya*), imagination (*vikalpa*), deep sleep (*nidrā*) and memory (*smṛti*).[108] These modifications inhibit the concentration of mind. Also, there are different stages of the mind. The state of inhibition is the highest among them. These five states of the mind are – distracted (*kṣipta*) stupefied (*mūḍha*), scattered (*vikṣipta*), concentrated (*ekāgra*) and restrained (*niruddha*). When the *citta* runs after the objects of sense, it is called as *kṣipta*. When *citta* is completely engrossed in the sense objects it is called *mūḍha*. The general state of the human being in everyday business is called *vikṣipta*. Here, there is a movement in his thoughts but they are not violent. When the Yogin is able to concentrate his mind pointedly it is called *ekāgra*. There are no inhibitions in this state of mind. When there is a preponderance of constituent of *tamas*, the mind is engrossed in the sense-objects (*mūḍha*), it instigates the being to perform sinful acts. When there is an influence of the constituent of *rajas*, the mind is constantly turned towards the sense-objects (*kṣipta*). But when there is a preponderance of the constituent of *sattva*, when *tamas* and *rajas* are weak, the state of mind is called *vikṣipta*. In this state, mind becomes placid, it experiences Bliss and the evil desires are uprooted, auspicious desires become strong with the practice of Yoga. Then the *yogin* has full concentration (*ekāgra*) and when all the inhibitions are completely controlled the *citta* becomes *niruḍha*. The *ekāgra* and *niruḍha* states are conducive to the Yogic practice. But these practices (*abhyāsa*-s) are to be followed diligently. *Āsana* and *prāṇāyāma*-s are such practices. Practice (*abhyāsa*) is the effort to steady the mind and body[109]. It is to be practised for a long time, without interruption and with devotion, only then would they be firmly rooted[110] to establish the *yogin* in indistinctive meditation (*nirvikalpa samādhi*) so that one can attain the state of *kaivalya*.

A posture (*āsana*) is one in which the mind and body are at ease and steady.[111] Voluntary movements of body are at rest and the mind can concentrate on the ultimate goal.[112] These postures help to remove the disturbances of the pairs of opposites.[113] Therefore, the aspirant has to practise regulation of breath (*prāṇāyāma*).The regulation of inhaling and exhaling activities of breath is called *prāṇāyāma*. Control while exhaling is called *recaka* and restraint while inhaling is called *pūraka*. When the breath inhaled or exhaled for a while is restrained fully either within or without is called *kumbhaka*. The *kumbhaka* which does not have external or internal spheres, is called *kevala kumbhaka*. Through this type of *prāṇāyāma*, the defects (*doṣa-s*) of *rajas* and *tamas*, enveloping the effulgence of the constituent of *sattva*, are destroyed and the mind of the *yogin* becomes calm and capable of further practice of *yoga*.[114]

The sixth means of *yoga* is concentration (*dhāraṇā*) that is steadfastness of the mind. Through this method (*dhāraṇā*), the mind is focused steadily on the navel, the lotus of the heart, the light of the brain, the fore parts of the nose, tongue etc. These plexuses (*cakra*-s) are seven, namely, *mūlādhāra cakra, svādhi ṣ ṭhāna cakra, maṇipūra cakra, anāhata cakra, viśuaddha cakra, ājñācakra* and *sahasrādhāra cakra*. These *cakra*-s are situated at the tail bone, between genitals and anus, at navel, heart, palate (*tālu*), forehead (*lalāṭa*) and brain (*mūrdhan*) respectively. [115] By concentrating on these plexuses, the sense organs, organs of action and the organs like heart, lungs, stomach etc. internal organs, on the functions of which, we do not have control, can function smoothly and they remain healthy.

The seventh means is *dhyāna*.[116] *Dhyāna* means continuation of the concentration. Through continuous effort, it culminates into meditation. In *dhyāna*, the mind has not only to concentrate on a particular sphere but has to reflect on particular thought (*bhāvanā*) for a longer time. This is meditation (*dhyāna*). In *dhyāna*, energy of the mind is saved, mind gathers strength and becomes strong. When the mind is strong, the body also becomes energetic.

By dedicated practice of *dhyāna*, a stage comes when no other thing is reflected in the mind except the object of concentration. Only that object shines before the mind, mind becomes one with that object. This state is called a trance or contemplation (*samādhi*).[117]

Dhāraṇā, *dhyāna*, and *samādhi* together are called *saṁyama* that is inner discipline.[118]

In the *Mbh.*, Kṛṣṇa, was sitting in the *yogic* posture. Yudhiṣṭhira graphically describes a *yogin*, in the fourth stage of *samādhi*. He states that Kṛṣṇa has attained the fourth stage of *samādhi*. He has gone beyond gross (*sthūla*), subtle (*sūkṣma*) and causal (*karaṇa*) body (*deha*). He has held completely his inhaling and exhaling breath, established his senses in his mind. All his sense-organs have merged into his intellect. He had placed, merged the *guṇa*-s and deities of different sense-organs in the embodied Soul. His body was horripilated, He was completely steady, unmoved. His mind and intellect also were stable. He became motionless like a wood, wall and stone. He appeared like a statue of stone and like an unwavering, steady flame of a burning lamp kept at an airtight place.[119] All the means, except *yama* and *niyama*, that is *āsana, prāṇāyāma, pratyāhāra, dhāraṇā, dhyāna* and *samādhi* are explained in this example. The *Mbh.* also narrates the state of a *yogin* who has conquered sleep, controlled his breath, senses and established himself in the constituent of *sattva* and who was constantly engrossed in the practice of Yoga.[120]

The *Mbh.* explains in detail, how a *yogin* should begin his practice of Yoga. It describes the place where he should sit and expects the seat, the place to be occupied by a *yogin* to be clean, pure, not very high, not very low, the mat made up of *darbha* grass, covered by deer-skin and cloth. Thereafter, he should practise Yoga to purify his mind. Holding his body (middle portion), head and neck straight, steadying himself and fixing his sight on the tip of his nose, without any distraction that is not looking anywhere else, he should abandon all the desires born of will and restrain his mind and senses.[121] Thereafter, he is expected to acquire the tranquility with the help of his intellect which is controlled and steadied. Uprooting all the thoughts, he then should fix his mind on the Self.[122]

The *Mbh.* again describes how a *yogin* should begin his meditation. It states that the aspirant should first free himself from the pairs of opposites such as cold and heat etc., destroy all his *doṣa*-s and observe *niyama*-s. He then should select a place which is free from desires and devoid of objects hampering the meditation. The place should also be calm and quiet. Thereafter, controlling his senses, he should steady himself like a wood and begin his meditation.[123] The *Mbh.* also discusses how a *yogin* should abstain his mind from all the objects, for perfect meditation. It states that he should control his senses and (the intellect interested in) the objects of senses along with *manas* and place them into the intellect. Withdrawing his mind from the things which are not to be thought of (*acintya*) (and thinking of the Highest Entity only) through meditation, he should control the mind from all the sides and attain the calmness of mind. He then frees himself from the sense of pride because of which he considered himself to be the doer and attains the eternal state.[124] Thus, he attains the Ultimate Truth through discriminative knowledge. Thus, here again, the necessity of meditation for attaining the Ultimate Principle is emphasized. The *Mbh.* presents a description of a meditating *yogin*, who concentrates on the navel, throat, brain, heart, chest, back (of the body), eyes, ears, nose etc. while meditating and merges himself into the Ātman which is subtle.[125] After the destruction of auspicious and inauspicious deeds he is released. This type of a *yogin*, with his Self merged into the Self remains unmoved.[126]

In one of the episodes of the *Mbh.*, there is a description of a Brāhmin who was a *jāpaka* and of a king, Ikṣvāku. The *jāpaka* desired to endow the fruit of *japa* to the king which the king was not ready to accept. Hence they decided to share the fruit of it together. They, therefore, resorted to the *yogic* meditation and entered the Brahmaloka. Both of them withdrew their minds from the senses, placed their different breaths, *viz. prāṇa, apāna, samāna, vyāna* in their hearts and merged their minds with the breaths *prāṇa* and *apāna*. Thereafter, fixing their sights in the middle of the eyebrows alongwith both the breaths merged them in the brains and attained *samādhi.*[127] The *Mbh.* then states that the Supreme Self abides in a person who has conquered his (lower) self and has attained tranquility. He is steadfast while experiencing different pairs of opposites such as cold and heat, pleasure and pain, honour and dishonour.[128] Through meditation, the *yogin*-s perceive the Self in the Self and by the Self.[129] The *Mbh.* describes a *yogin* who has subdued the constituents of *rajas* and *tamas* and is steadfast in the constituent of *sattva.*[130] Bhīṣma tells Yudhiṣṭ hira that a weak *yogin* is drawn towards sense objects, however, the *yogin* with the power of *yoga* becomes strong and effulgent power destroys all the defects like the sun drying up the entire world at the time of dissolution.[131]

A meditating *yogin* is sure to attain release.[132] Thus, here, Yoga is looked upon as a means to attain salvation.

The *Mbh.* presents a description of two types of yogic practices, *viz.* the gross (*sthūla*) and subtle (*sūkṣma*) as prescribed in the *Veda*-s. The gross type of *yoga* includes eight faculties which grant superhuman powers to the aspirant. These are *aṇimā, laghimā* etc. The subtle *yoga*, too prescribes eight means, *viz. yama*, *niyama* etc. The *yoga* has two different accessories, *viz.* qualitative (*saguṇa*) and devoid of qualities (*nirguṇa*) regulation of breath (*prāṇāyāma*) for concentration of the mind. *Saguṇa* type of *prāṇāyāma*, concentration of mind is on a certain object which functions as a support, whereas *nirguṇa* type of *prāṇāyāma* does not stand in need of any support for the concentration of mind.[133] *Y.S.* describes seeded[134] and unseeded trances. The unseeded trance suppresses all the potencies and roots out the vehicle of action and affliction and the mind has only one purpose to achieve, *i.e.* discriminative knowledge.[135] The mind then does not revert back to enjoyment. According to the Yoga philosophy, the aspirant attains seedless trance when all the potencies are suppressed.[136]

The *Mbh.* describes destruction of sins as sacrifice and states that those who are devoted to breath control, resort to *prāṇāyāma*, restrain inhaling breath (*prāṇa*) and outgoing breath *apāna*, pour the *prāṇa* into *apāna* and *apāna* into *prāṇa* as sacrifice, such people are called performers of *prāṇāyāma* (*i.e. prāṇāyāmin*-s).[137] Here, *prāṇāyāma* is considered as one of the instruments to perform sacrifice for the destruction of sins and removal of ignorance so that he can attain the Truth, Brahman, which is the ultimate goal of the human life. Thus, according to the *Mbh.,* the importance of *prāṇāyāma* is apparent for achieving the final beatitude.

Removal of Obstacles on the Path of Yoga Practice

While treading the path of Yoga, the aspirant has to overcome a number of obstacles.

They are disease (*vyādhi*), languor (*styāna*), indecision (*sanaśaya*), carelessness (*pramāda*), sloth (*ālasya*), sensuality (*avịtarati*), mistaken notion (*bhrānti darśana*), missing the point (*alabdhabhūmikatva*), instability (*anavasthitva*). They distract the mind of an aspirant. The pain, despair, shakiness, inspiration and expiration are the cọmpanions of these distractions.[138]

Vyādhi-s are caused by imbalance of three *dhātu*-s *viz.* wind (*vāta*), bile (*pitta*), phlegm (*kapha*). The attitude of non-action arising in the mind due to the preponderance of the constituent of *tamas* is *styāna*. Indecision *saṁśaya* is a doubt regarding the pursuit of *yogic* path. Carelessness, *pramāda* is carelessness towards the practice of Yoga. *Ālasya* is slothness which not only affects the mind but body too. The desire toward (enjoyment of) sensuality, though controlled apparently, is still alive in the mind, which shoots up with force is *avitarati*. When the aspirant reaches the stage of ultra meditative trance, but has not yet reached the essential cognition, *i.e. ṛtamabharā prajña*, but still thinks that he has reached it, this is called mistaken notion (*bhrānti darśana*). The eighth obstacle is missing the point, *alabdhabhūmikatva*. In this state, the aspirant has reached a certain stage, still he does not make progress inspite of his efforts, due to certain mental defects. The last obstacle is *anavasthitva*. The place at which the aspirant is unable to concentrate is called *anavasthitva*. Due to all these obstacles the aspirant's progress towards trance is hampered.

The *Mbh.* Describes various obstacles on the path of Yoga. It states that diseases, contacts with undesirables, exertion and trouble caused by uprooting of desires lead to displeasure. Hence, one should get rid of those diseases, discomforts by the means of Yoga (*kriyāyoga*). The wise, thereafter should subdue his passions and calm down the mind, since, if the *manas* is unhappy, the body too suffers.[139] There are thousands of reasons for sorrow and hundreds for fear, which stupefy the deluded person.[140] There are many defects too, which are contrary to knowledge, which lead to the destruction of welfare.[141] The person who has no faith, who is confused, indecisive perishes. For such a person there is neither this world nor the world beyond, nor is he entitled to get happiness.[142] Hence, one should have faith. The *yogin,* who controls his senses becomes free from passion (*rāga*) and repugnance (*dveṣa*). Such a *yogin* of disciplined mind, who moves among the sense objects, with the senses under control, free from attachment and aversion attains tranquility.[143] His intellect becomes firm. As his mind is complacent, the intellect of such a man of pure spirit is soon established (in the peace of the Self.)[144] He frees himself from self-sense and pride and attains peace.[145] It also states that the *yogin* who has uprooted the five defects, *viz.* passion, avarice, anger, desire and affection attains Brahman.[146]

These thoughts are in consonance with those of the Yogasūtra-s, which describe that the mind can become steadfast by freeing itself from passion and sorrow.[147]

The *Mbh.* states that a being who has discarded scepticism, is disinterested in action. He is not led away by the false notion that he is the doer.[148] A detailed description of the obstacles appears in the *Mbh.* The *yogin* has to transgress these obstacles such as desire, anger, pairs of opposite, rain, fear, sorrow, breath (*śvāsa*), objects of senses, insatiability, strong greed, touch, sleep etc. He then becomes desireless and capable of release and attains the Brahman.[149] The obstacles like sloth, sensuality, sorrow, inspiration and expiration (breath) are consistent with those mentioned in the *Y.S.*[150] Kolhatkar, K.K. explains that since the uncontrolled breathing disturbs concentration, breath is considered as an obstacle.[151]

The *Mbh.* describes mind as fickle, shaky, difficult to control. However, the *yogin* controls it by desirelessness. The *yogin* whose mind is steady in himself (Ātman) attains the ultimate delight of contact with the Brahman.[152]

Even, in a state of full concentration, at times, it is disturbed. The wise *yogin* does not get disheartened, by the distractions, he expels his sloth and hostility towards these distractions and continues his meditation. Doubts, indiscriminative thoughts about the *yogic* practice appear in his mind even at the commencement of meditation. Nevertheless, keeping aside these discomfitures, he should continue with his meditation removing these obstacles through concentration.[153]

These obstacles can be removed by various means. They can be removed by the knowledge of the God (Īśvara), that is, by concentrating one's own mind upon the God.[154] The *Y.S.* describes God as that distinct Puruṣa, untouched by the vehicle of afflictions like nescience (*avidyā*), egoism (*asmitā*), attachment (*rāga*), aversion (*dveṣa*) and love for life (*abhiniveśa*).[155] The sacred word (Oṁ) connotes Him.[156] This 'Oṁkāra' is named as '*praṇava*'. This nomenclature of *praṇava* is eternal. The syllable Oṁ is to be repeated, comprehending its meaning and habituating the mind with it, which would lead to the feeling of identity with Īśvara.[157] The mind would then be free from doubts and be fully focused. By constant repetition of *Praṇava*, the obstacles in the practice of Yoga are removed and the aspirant comprehends the nature of Īśvara.[158] Īśvara, then would manifest before the aspirant. These obstacles can also be removed and the mind can become steady by superphysical or 'higher sense activity' or by cultivation of desirelessness, *prāṇāyāma* or by meditation according to his predilection.[159]

Through meditation, the *yogin*'s power of cognition reaches the minutest stage or to the largest one.[160] On disappearance of modifications (*vṛtti-s*), the mind becomes transparent like a crystal and acquires the power of thought transformation (*samāpatti*).[161]

When the *yogin* attains 'Indistinct' (*savitarka*) thought transformation (*samāpatti*), the word, the meaning and the idea are mixed up. However, in indistinct (wordless) (*nirvikalpa*) thought transformation, mind shines out as the object alone since there is a cessation of memory (*smṛti*). Thereafter, the mind is as if devoid of its own nature.[162] This way, the support of meditation becomes minute and it becomes noumenal (*alinga*), unmanifest. In this trance (*samādhi*), where the seed of desire is not yet uprooted it is called a seeded trance (*sabīja samādhi*).[163] All the trances which need support of an object are *sabīja samādhi*-s. Thus, the repetition of *Praṇava* or concentration upon God (*Īśvara praṇidhāna*) etc. are qualitative ways of meditation.

The *Mbh.* describes that the *yogin* through his own *yogic* power, can enter any of the five gross elements, Brahmā, ṛṣi-s or deities. Even the deity of death (Yama) can not control the *yogin* who is extraordinarily effulgent. He can wander on the entire earth in any form.[164]. *Y.S.* also describes various achievements (*siddhi*-s) attained by the *yogin* by concentrating on different objects (supports). However, *Y.S.* also cautions that all such achievements are the obstacles on the path of the ultimate *samādhi*.[165] It also advises that a *yogin* should not get distracted by the enticement by the deities, they may turn to be harmful to him.[166] By rejecting these achievements, all the seeds of inauspiciousness would be destroyed and the *yogin* may attain complete independence.[167]

The *Mbh.* explains three ways of achieving salvation, *viz. vyakta, avyakta* and *anāśraya*. After preparatory arrangements such as place, seat etc., it advises the aspirant neither to look at the objects of sense, nor to think about them, as a matter of fact to completely forget about them. Let the mind merge into itself and be tranquil and balanced and undertake meditation either by concentrating on Brahman or repeating benefactory passages of the *Veda*-s or by chanting of *praṇava* or Gāyatrī *mantra*. By chanting the Vedic passages, his mind would become pure and he would obtain control over the senses. He would be free from desires, attachment, avarice and would cross the dualities of opposite conditions of heat and cold etc. He would never pride himself on being the doer. He then discards self-sense, is no more greedy. He neither censures anybody nor remains idle.[168] He is always eager to meditate.[169] It also cautions the aspirant against following just one of the *niyama*-s singly, against disrespecting the chanting and states that he should neither have affection not should he derive any pleasure through it. If he is proud due to chanting or if he insults others, if he performs actions only to secure the fruits or if he hankers after his achievements, such a chanter will go to the nether world.[170] The *Mbh.* also describes the stages reached by the chanter after his death. According to the *Mbh.*, such a chanter (*jāpaka*) enters Brahmā himself.[171] He can even become one with the Brahman.[172]

While explaining the methods of achieving salvation, the *Mbh.* states different defects to be avoided while observing the Yogic practice. A *yogin* is advised to expel delusion (*bhrama*), avarice (*moha*), indecision (*saṁśaya*), sloth (*ālasya*), intellect interested in different sense objects.[173] It advises people to be free from diseases (*vyādhi*-s) by eating limited, cooked food, to overcome avarice and delusion by contentment, to control mind and intellect through the ability to distinguish between right and wrong through the knowledge of the Self.[174] The obstacles mentioned by the *Y.S.*, on the path of the *yogic* practice such as disease, delusion, indecision, interest in different sense organs (*avitarati*), sloth etc.[175] are on the similar lines of the *Mbh.*

Kṛṣṇa describes the state of a *yogin* who has faith, is absorbed in wisdom and who has subdued senses. He secures the knowledge of the Highest Reality. Having gained wisdom, he quickly attains the Supreme peace. However, a man who is ignorant, who has no faith and who is indecisive perishes. For such a Soul there is neither this world nor the world beyond.[176] Hence, one has to lift himself by himself, since the Self alone is the friend of the Soul and Self alone is the enemy of the Self.[177] Kṛṣṇa, however, states that an utterance of syllable 'Oṁ' which is Brahman would lead the *yogin* to the highest goal.[178] *Y.S.*, however, states that the repetition of 'Oṁ' would lead to the feeling of identity with Īśvara.[179]

The *Mbh.* has also pointed out that the meditation is the main duty of a *yogin*. It is his highest strength. It also describes that there are two different ways of concentration (*i*) through *manas* and (*ii*) through *prāṇāyāma*. In *prāṇāyāma* when *manas* concentrates on a particular object or a symbol and is supported by that symbol, it is a qualitative *prāṇāyāma*. However, when the mind does not need any support of any symbol, but concentrates on *nirguṇa*, the entity which has no qualities,[180] obviously it is the Brahman, which is devoid of any qualities, it is *nirguṇa prāṇāyāma*. In the *Y.S.*, however, there is no description of qualitative and unqualitative *prāṇāyāma*. Instead, it describes the qualitative thought transformation (*samāpatti*). In this *samāpatti*, the seed, origin is in external object and these objects progressively become subtler. The province of this subtle element reaches up to noumenal (*aliṅga*). Thus, in all these *samādhi*-s, which have support of external objects, in which the seeds of earlier actions are not destroyed and by which a *yogin* cannot attain the release, are called seeded (*sabīja*) *samādhi*-s.[181]

Thus, the *Mbh.* describes the obstructions which hamper the Yogic practice and also the different means to attain qualitative meditation which are in consonance with those prescribed in the *Y.S.* However, the *Y.S.* advises concentration on Īśvara, whereas the *Mbh.* expects people to concentrate on Brahman.[182] The Brahman has been already described as eternal, unborn, omniscient, omnipresent, devoid of qualities. It is identical with the Ātman, whereas Īśvara of Yoga system is Puruṣa like others but a perfect one. The nature of Īśvara of Yoga system and its representation in the *Mbh.* are discussed in a separate section.

The Concept of Īśvara

The Yogic practice is hampered by different obstacles. In the earlier sections, all those obstacles and the means to overcome them have been discussed. *Īśvarapraṇidhāna* is one of those means. This section would discuss Īśvara according to the Yoga philosophy and how it is represented in the *Mbh.*

According to the Yoga philosophy, Īśvara has the constituent of *sattva* only. The constituents of *rajas* and *tamas* are absent in him. The constituent of *tamas* obscures knowledge due to its absence, Īśvara is omniscient.[183] Prior to the creation of the world, his omniscience is in the seed form. It is unlimited in relation to place, time and reality. He is said to be the teacher of the ancient,[184] since he taught them the *Veda*-s. The ancients like Brahmā etc. gods are *videhin*-s, who have freed from physical existence and enjoy a state something like absolute freedom.[185] The creation of the world takes place under the supervision of the God, Īśvara, but he is not the creator of the world.

This Īśvara according to the Yogic system is a distinct Puruṣ a, untouched by the vehicle of affection, action and fruition.[186] He is different from other Puruṣa-s. He has no bonds like them at present and he would never have them in future. He is ever free from equality or excess. The bondages are also not for the emancipated ones.

He helps the aspirants to remove the obstacles in the *yogic* practice. Contemplation on him would enable the *yogin* to attain seedless trance.[187] According to the Yoga philosophy, Prakṛti and Puruṣa are different from each other. The world is created by their union. This union is due to Avidyā. Though Īśvara does not create the world, it is implied in the *Y.S.* that the creation takes place under the supervision of Īśvara since he is omniscient.

Scholars have varied opinions about the Puruṣa or Īśvara of *Y.S.* Deussen P. opines that the conception of Īśvara is accepted by Yoga philosophy, purely on the external ground. They have preserved the theism of the later Upaniṣad-s in contrast to the chosen basis of the Sāṁkhya system as could be evident from the *Cūlikā Up.*, which starting from the twenty-five principles of the Sāṁkhya ranks Īśvara with them on purely external grounds, "as the twenty sixth" and recognizes Him to be different from the individual selves Puruṣa-s.[188] Ranade, R.D. too, is of the opinion that the deistic conception of God as advanced in the *Y.S.* is already present in the Upaniṣad-s as observed from the statement that the Universal Soul merely looks on while the individual Soul is engaged in the enjoyment of Prakṛti or the God described as being beyond the reach of the sorrow of the world, just as the Sun, who is the eye of the world, is beyond the reach of the defects of vision.[189] In the opinion of Hiriyanna M., according to Yoga, at the time of evolution, the stimulus for alteration comes from the God or Īśvara, as explained in *Bhoja Vṛtti.*[190] He is Puruṣa like others, but a perfect one. He is omniscient, omnipresent but unlike Īśvara of the Vedāntin, he is external to Matter (Prakṛti) as well as to the Souls. In other words, he is not Absolute. According to Patañjali, the existence in our experience of a graded scale of knowledge, wisdom etc. points to the infinite knowledge, wisdom etc. as their limit. The God is one to whom these latter belong.[191]

According to Kolhatkar, K.K., the Parabrahman of the Vedānta, Puruṣottama of the *Bh. G.* and the Puruṣaviśeṣa of the Yoga are one and the same. He also opines that the Yoga system does not believe in the duality of principles but in the monistic concept of the Vedānta, since after the seedless trance there is an experience of the Self by the Self and the realization that the body enveloped by gross elements is not the reality (*asat*). It is enveloped by sorrow and the Self has the *sat, cit, ānanda* forms of the Ātman. This release is on the lines of the Vedānta.[192]

Mitra, R. has stated that Īśvara is different from other selves (Puruṣa-s). His work is to liberate the whole world. This is due to the prevalence of *sattva guṇa* in him. This prevalence arises from His eminent knowledge. The knowledge and power are eternally abiding in the very substance of Īśvara. The union of

Prakṛti and Puruṣa, that is, the creation of the world, from the point of view of Yoga, would be impossible without the will of (such an) Īśvara.[193]

In the *Mbh.*, Kṛṣṇa describes himself as unconcerned, detached from the actions of Nature. However, creation takes place under his supervision.[194] Thus, this shows the supervising aspect of Īśvara as implied in the *Y.S.*[195] Kṛṣṇa also states that there is the third Puruṣa, who is the Highest Self, who is other than the two, namely destructible (*kṣara*) and indestructible (*akṣara*).[196] He is the highest Lord who pervades the three worlds and supports them. He denotes him as Uttama Puruṣa, Īśvara.[197] The destructible Puruṣa here is Prakṛti and the indestructible one is Puruṣa. Thus, Uttama Puruṣa who is different from these two appears like Īśvara of Yoga, who is different from the knower (*Dṛṣṭṛ*) and knowable the (*dṛśya*) which are equivalent to Puruṣa and Prakṛti. This Uttam Puruṣa, whom the wise worship,[198] appears like the Īśvara of Yogin. However, when Kṛṣṇa says I am that Uttama Puruṣa, who has occupied the hearts of all,[199] and the bodies of all, becoming Vaiśvānara,[200] that means he is the same as Parabrahman of the Vedānta.

Kṛṣṇa says that having steadied his senses, the Yogin should turn his mind to me and fix it on me alone. You are devoted to me, resorting to me, you continue your *yoga* practice.[201] One whose *citta* is stabilized by repeated recollection of me, who remembers Parama Puruṣa, who is the eternal controller of the word, the resort of all, minute like an atom, indestructible, would attain to Me.[202] This description of Kṛṣṇa as the support of worship, is similar to Īśvara Praṇidhāna of the *Y.S.*

There is a description of the Soul, as twenty sixth principle. When this Soul realizes that he is different from the twenty-five elements, he is the knower, knowledge which is indestructible[203] and the Supreme Self by the light of which, he understands what is Prakṛti and that his ignorance (*Avidyā*) is the reason of the bondage of Prakṛti, the Soul gets released.[204] This description of twenty-sixth element tallies with that of Īśvara of the *Y.S.* The *Mbh.* also describes Kṣetrajña to be self-illuminated, devoid of any mark and qualities. He has only knowledge as his sign. He knows the beginning, the middle and the end of all the creative actions of *guṇa*-s.[205] Treating the Kṣetrajña as the twenty-sixth element, describing knowledge as his sign and that he has the knowledge of all the creation, shows the similarity of this Kṣetrajña with that of Īśvara of the *Y.S.*

A comparative study of the Yoga, Vedānta and Sāṁkhya philosophies indicates that–

(*i*) Īśvara in the Yoga philosophy is similar to the Brahman in that of the Vedānta in respect of omniscience, eternity and the like.

(*ii*) According to the Vedānta philosophy, the Brahman is the creator of the world. According to Yoga system, Īśvara is not the creator of the world. He just supervises the act of the creation of the world.

However, he differs from Puruṣa of Sāṁkhya in respect of liberation of beings. Sāṁkhya philosophy believes that it is the Prakṛti that strives to liberate Puruṣa. The Yoga system believes that Īśvara is instrumental in liberation of beings since Īśvarapraṇidhāna is one of the means to attain Kaivalya. Moreover, as per the Yoga system, the concept of the final release or Kaivalya is that of self perception. It is on the line of the Vedānta. However, the Paramātman, Īśvara, the Self of the Vedānta is neither distinct from the Prakṛti nor from the individual Souls. It is the basic fundamental principle which creates the world. Nevertheless, Īśvara of the Yoga system is external to Prakṛti.

The Concept of Vairāgya according to Yoga Philosophy

Yoga system emphasises the importance of practice (*abhyāsa*) and desirelessness (*vairāgya*) which enable the being to restrain the mental modifications (*vṛtti*-s).[206] Due to these modifications, the mind flows either towards good or evil. The flow which leads the mind to perfect independence (*kaivalya*) down to the plane of discriminative knowledge, is named as the stream of happiness. That which leads to rebirth and flows to the plane of indiscriminative ignorance, is the stream of sin. The flow of desire, that of indiscriminative ignorance, is thinned by desirelessness. When the mind habituates with the experience of knowledge, the flow of discrimination is visible. This is *vairāgya.* The *vaśīkaraṇa vairāgya* means the supremacy of consciousness in the person who is free from thirst for the visible and spiritual enjoyments.[207] The empirical enjoyments (those that are experienced) are food, drinks, power etc. and those known from scriptures are the heaven, the attainment of state of a *videhin* etc. When there is an indifference towards the qualities (*guṇa*-s) due to knowledge of the Puruṣa, it is the higher desirelessness (*parama vairāgya*)[208]. The Yogin realizes the distinction between *sattva* and Puruṣa, acquires the power of omnipotence and omniscience. When the seed of the bondage is destroyed by desirelessness, through the twofold power, the Yogin attains absolute independence.

The *Mbh.* observes that one who has destroyed all the bondages and taken resort in desirelessness, is a *tyāgin*. Hence, one should with the aid of knowledge turn himself away from love of his relatives and friends and stop collecting wealth and rise above the body. Especially for the knowledgeable and the self possessed, there is no bondage of love.[209] The desire arises from the attachment and from it the thirst. This thirst adds to dejection and sin and binds man. Hence, one should keep himself away from this thirst (*tṛṣṇā*). Otherwise, it would destroy the being. Thus, in the *Mbh.* Manaki says to Kāma that I used to be worried about my wealth, but by sudden loss of wealth, I have become desireless and hence I am happy now. So now please do not entice me towards it. He then gives up the entire wealth, things of enjoyment and all desires and attains Brahman.[210] The *Mbh.* also states that one who is high souled, great intellectual, devoid of desire, attains the Self through meditation (*dhyāna*).[211] The *Mbh.* states that the life, youth, beauty, health, collection of wealth, the company of loved ones, in fact every thing is impermanent. It never binds those who are wise.[212] The wise call a person a man of learning whose all undertakings (*saṅkalpa*) are free from desire and whose works are burnt up by the fire of wisdom.[213] While explaining the term *jñāna,* Kṛṣṇa states that desirelessness towards the objects of senses is one of the facets of the knowledge. He also states that by engaging in meditation and taking refuge in dispassion (*vairāgya*), casting aside self-sense, force, arrogance, desire, anger, possession, becoming egoless and tranquil in mind, the *yogin* becomes worthy of becoming one with *Brahman.*[214]

Thus, the importance of *vairāgya* has been sufficiently brought about in the *Mbh.* It also states that *vairāgya* is one of the major means to attain Brahman. One whose intellect is always detached, who has subdued his Self and from whom desire has fled, reaches the Supreme state, transcending all the activities through renunciation, attains perfection which leads him to the Brahman.[215] There is also a description of a person who has attained the Supreme state by *vairāgya.* King Janaka says to Śuka that he does not discriminate between pleasure and sorrow, he does not have any avarice, he is not interested in song or dance etc. entertainment, he is not attracted to any objects of sence, does not have any affection towards his relatives. He treats the gold and clod of earth alike. He treads the path that is eternal and pure.[216] On these lines, Kṛṣṇa also describes a *yogin* who has attained desireless state. He states that the absence of attachment to one's own son, wife, home and like, and a constant equal mindedness towards all desirable and undesirable happenings, is the mark of such a *yogin.*[217]

Thus, according to the *Mbh.* desirelessness plays a major role in enabling the *yogin* to reach the ultimate stage.

The Concept of Absolute Independence (*Kaivalya*) according to Yoga Philosophy

When the mind of a *yogin* becomes steady and conducive

to meditation, he has the ultimate goal of absolute independence. This section would deal with the indistinct trance and *Kaivalya* doctrine of Yoga Philosophy.

In the indistinct trance (*savitarka samādhi*), the seed of desire is not destroyed. Hence, it is called seeded trance (*sabīja samādhi*)[218] or *saṁprajñāta samādhi*. The trance in which a *yogin* has no desire, since the *rajas* and *tamas* constituents are destroyed, it is called *nirvicāra samādhi* or *nirbīja samādhi.*[219] It is also called ultra meditative (*asaṁprajñāta samādhi*). In this state, potencies (*vṛtti*-s) are steady, however, the *yogin* still experiences distinctness between the knower and the knowledgeable, *i.e.* *draṣṭṛ* and *dṛśya*. There the subject illuminates due to the absence of constituents of *rajas* and *tamas*. Here, the aspirant acquires the faculty of essential cognition (*ṛtaṁbharā prajñā*).[220] This *prajñā* cognises the essence, the truth and there remains no trace of false knowledge. The subject of this cognition is different from verbal and inferential cognition, it has a particular cognition of the object.[221] In this *ṛtaṁbharā prajñā,* the residual potencies born from it, impede the other potencies (*saṁskāra*-s). However, in seedless trance (*nirbīja samādhi*), even these potencies are suppressed.

The residual potencies (*vāsanā*-s) are held together by cause, motive, substratum (the mind which has yet to perform duty) and object. When these four disappear, *vāsanā*-s too disappear. This is the trance where the *yogin* gets the cognition that the knower, the Ātman and the Prakṛti are separate and at this juncture the afflicting actions go away.[222] This is the *dharmamegha samādhi*. By attaining this stage, the afflictions caused by nescience etc. are uprooted and the *yogin* obtains freedom though still alive. There is very little that is yet to be known, as the knowledge has become infinite.[223] In this state the *yogin* becomes totally indifferent and dispassionate.

There is a preponderance of *sattva*, *prakāśa* and knowledge. Now that the *guṇa*-s have fulfilled their object, the succession of changes ends.[224] The *yogin* achieves absolute freedom, now that *guṇa*-s have achieved experience and emancipation of the Self, they are devoid of object, they become latent by inverse process. This is the absolute freedom (*kaivalya*).[225]

The *Mbh.* states that a *yogin* who strives with assiduity, cleanses himself of all the sins, perfects himself through many lives and attains the highest goal.[226] One who having given up attachment, resigning his actions to God, is not touched by sin like a lotus leaf untouched by water. Thus, one has to work by giving up attachment. It describes the *yogin* who has achieved the supreme happiness. One who is peaceful, whose passions are at rest, who is stainless and has become one with the God,[227] he having discarded his sins, ever harmonized experiences the infinite bliss by contact with the eternal. He perceives the Self abiding in all the beings and beings abiding in the Self. His mind liberated from all desires, established in the Self alone, he is to be cognized as harmonized.[228]

There is also a description of the *yogin* who controls his desires, goes beyond the pairs of opposite such as pleasure and pain. He is neither afraid of anybody nor is anybody afraid of him. He has no likes or dislikes, has discarded truth and untruth and has become placid. He keeps himself away from sinful behavior, he attains to the Brahman by his actions and words.[229]

Thus, he experiences such an existence so that he can perceive himself by his own Self. The state of such a person who has conquered his (lower) Self and has attained calmness of mind, his Supreme Self abiding in himself, he is at peace, in cold and heat, in pleasure and pain, honour and dishonour.[230]

The *yogin* obtains happiness by meditation and by engrossing in meditation attains that absolute freedom.[231] When his intellect is devoid of impressions of merits of action, the *yogin* becomes steady in his mind and through meditation he attains trance and cognizes Ātman.[232] The *yogin* discarding all the things, his sins, controlling his organs, by controlling senses, resorting to truth, attains the Supreme Self. He acquires the eternal, supreme and Absolute release by the power of meditation. One who meditates on the supreme Person by his thoughts attuned by constant practice, mind not wandering after anything, reaches the Supreme Divine Person.[233]

The intellect of such a *yogin* does not get impeded by activities. He does not transgress his nature through dispassion. Being devoid of *rajas*, he lives till his death.[234] He is *jīvanmukta*. Janaka describes his state in the *Mbh.* He has sharpened the sword of impassion on the stone of release and has broken the bondages of affluence, love etc. Hence, even though he is a householder, a king, following the other three goals of life namely *dharma*, *artha* and *kāma*, he is released.[235]

Such a *yogin* is always intent on meditation. Through his meditation he decides the object of his meditation and ultimately discarding that object, he attains trance. This is a *nirbīja samādhi*. He had discarded everything and has dissolved himself into Brāhamī state. With meditation as his means, he concentrates his attention on the Highest Reality. Later on he discontinues meditation, being free from desires, dissociates himself from life-breaths and unites with the Brahman.[236]

The knower becomes the same as that which is to be known, that is, the Soul within. The Self in union with the divine attains to the peace well founded by abandoning attachment for the fruit of works.[237] The *Mbh.* states that people who are bold, thinkers, knowers of the Brahman, the great Brāhmins are able to see that eternal, immortal principle. The *yogin*, whose thoughts are at rest, restrained by the practice of concentration, beholds the Self through the Self and rejoices.[238]

Though *Mbh.*, does not describe the various types of *samādhi* distinctively, the attainment of *samādhi*-s in which the *yogin* discards the object of meditation refers to *nirbīja samādhi*.[239] The state of release where the Self perceives the Self,[240] is similar to that described in the *Y.S.* The release of the *yogin* by dissolving himself in the Supreme Self, Brahman, shows the synthesis of the principles of Yoga with those of the Vedānta philosophy. Further, since the Brahman of the Vedānta is same as the Self, the difference between the Self of the Yoga system and the Vedānta thought is very thin. As regards Kaivalya of a *yogin*, Dixit, S.H. opines that it appears, that as if, the absolute independence does not mean an entanglement in the worldly affairs, keeping oneself away from them, or being disinterested in the day to day affairs of life. He, therefore, questions whether such absolute independence would be beneficial to the present day to day life. Is it not running away from life?[241] These questions can be answered with the help of *Yoga-sūtra*-s themselves. Y.S. II. 25 states that once the Avidyā, which is instrumental to the union of *draṣṭṛ* with *dṛśya*, is destroyed, these two get dissociated from each other. This is called *hāna*.[242] This *hāna* means the state of *Kaivalya*. In this state three *guṇa*-s are no more active, they no more affect the Self. In this state the *yogin* does not abandon his body, he is still alive and continues to perform his assigned duties. In fact now that *guṇa*-s no more rule over him, his actions are selfless. He works for the society selflessly. He attains *jīvanmukta* state like Janaka, Vyāsa, Kṛṣṇa and goes on performing actions which are beneficial to the society. The *Mbh.*, too, has accepted the *concept* of *jīvanmukta*. According to the *Mbh. videhamukti* that is the final and absolute release of a *yogin* takes place at the time of death. Till that time he enjoys the state of *jīvanmukta*.[243]

Moreover, according to Yoga philosophy, the *Kaivalya* is notional. Puruṣa is always independent. He enjoys the independence of the Self and is happy in the knowledge of the Self.

Thus, the *Mbh.* has stressed the importance of the principles of Yoga system several times. The eightfold Yoga system has explained the practical means of achieving salvation through the realization of the identity between the individual Self and the Self. Thus, it is closely related with that of the Vedānta, according to which the knowledge of the identity between the Soul and the Brahman leads to salvation. According to Yogayājñavalkya, the knowledge itself is Yoga which has eight subordinate parts.[244] In fact, Yoga is a practical aspect of the knowledge of the Supreme Reality (*Brahmavidyā*) and the Upaniṣadic knowledge or the Vedānta constitutes the theoretical aspect of Brahmavidyā. Through the monistic Vedānta, an aspirant can have an indirect verbal knowledge of Brahman. However, the Yoga system provides the practical means to realize it.[245]

According to Pātañjalayoga, *mokṣa* or *kaivalya* is the state, where the consciousness becomes established in its own nature (*svarūpa-pratiṣṭhā*) through distinct trance (*nirvikalpa samādhi*).[246] Yoga system aspires for the union (*saṁyoga*) of the individual Soul with the Supreme Soul.[247] The famous Upaniṣadic statement that "You are that"[248] connotes the same idea, *i.e.*, oneness of the Soul, non-duality of the individual Soul and the Supreme Soul. The Yoga and the Upaniṣad-s strive to establish the same truth. *Kaivalya* of the *yogin*-s is same as Brahmajñāna of the Vedāntins. Even the *Mbh.* considered the monistic doctrine of Brahman as the Ultimate Truth. It regarded Yoga, as a means to obtain that knowledge of the Supreme Self and incorporated the principles of Yoga. The *Bh. G.* also accepted the principles of Yoga, as a means to an end. According to it, *jñāna* leads to salvation and Yoga enables the aspirant to have knowledge (*jñāna*). The same thought has been propounded by Yājñavalkya in his *Y.Y.* The systematic description of eightfold Yoga, which includes *yama, niyama, āsana, prāṇāyāma* etc.[249] in the Y.Y. only shows that the principles of Yoga were popular for a ling time. Yoga-sūtra-s of Patañjali reflect an attempt at the systematization of the same.[250] The *Mbh.* being encyclopaedic in nature, incorporated such popular and practical principles of Yoga philosophy. Moreover, the restraints (*yama*-s) such as *ahiṁsā, satya, asteya, brahmacarya, aparigraha* and the observances (*niyama*-s) such as *śauca, santoṣa, tapas, svādhyāya* and *Īśvarapraṇidhāna* laid down by Patañjali in his Yoga-sūtra-s were not only beneficial to the upliftment of an individual but were also conducive to the social welfare in general and moral improvement of Indian society in particular. Knowing their importance, the *Mbh.* also incorporated the same. It led to the material as also the spiritual upliftment of society.

REFERENCES

1. Chakravarti S.C., *The Philosophy of Upanisads,* University of Calcutta, 1935, p. 60.
2. *Pātañjal Yogadarśansūtra* (*Y.S.*) I. 2.
   योगश्चित्तवृत्तिनिरोधः।
3. *Tattva Vaiśāradi* q. by Radhakrishnan, S., and Moore, C.A., *op. cit.*, p. 454 .
4. Kopardekar, S., *Pātañjala Yogadarśana* (Marathi), Indrayani Sahitya Prakashan, Pune, 1995, p. 3.
5. *Yogayājñavalkya* I. 49. q. by Kolhatkar, K.K., *op. cit.*, p. 100.
   संयोगो योग इत्युक्तो जीवात्मपरमात्मनोः।
6. Mitra, R. q. by Max Müller, F. *op. cit.*, p. 290.
7. *Ibid.*, pp. 250, 251.
8. *Mait., Up.* VI. 25.
9. Pandit, S.G., *The Purāṇas and the Philosophical Systems,* Bombay, 1964, p. 355.
10. *Mbh. Bh. P.* 24. 48[d].
11. *Ibid.*, 50 [d].
12. *Ibid.*, 28, 23[c].
13. Satavalekar, S.D., *Shrimadbhagavadgītā Purushārthabodhini Tīka* (Marathi), Pardi, Gujarat, 1959, pp. 54, 55.
14. Radhakrishnan, S., and Moore, C.A., *op. cit.*, p. 453. also Radhakrishnan, S., *Indian Philosophy,* Vol. II, London, 1927, p. 341.
15. Zimmer, H., *op. cit.*, p. 3.
16. Kane, P.V., *op. cit.*, p. 194.
17. Macdonell, A.A., *op. cit.*, p. 396.
18. *Encyclopedia of Indian Philosophy, op. cit.*, pp. 14-15.
19. Sutton, N., *op. cit.*, p. 24.

20. Hiriyanna, M., *op. cit.*, p. 270.
21. *The Encyclopedia of Philosophy*, Vol. 3 and 4, p. 159.
22. *Y.S.* ii. 18.

    प्रकाशक्रियास्थितिशीलं भूतेंद्रियात्मकं भोगापवर्गार्थं दृश्यम्।
23. *Ibid.*, 19.

    विशेषाविशेषलिंगमात्रालिंगानि गुणपर्वाणि।
24. *Ibid.*, 20.

    द्रष्टा दृशिमात्रः शुद्धोऽपि प्रत्ययानुपश्यः।
25. *Ibid.*, 21.

    तदर्थ एव दृश्यस्यात्मा॥
26. *Mbh. Śānti P.* 296. 9.

    अव्यक्तं न तु तद्ब्रह्म बुध्यते तात केवलम्।
    केवलं पञ्चविंशं च चतुर्विंशं नं पश्यति॥
27. *Ibid.*, 6-7.

    अनेनाप्रतिबुद्धेति वदन्त्यव्यक्तमच्युतम्।
    अव्यक्तबोधनाच्चैव बुध्यमानं वदन्त्युत॥
    पञ्चविंशं महात्मानं न चासावपि बुध्यते।
    षड्विंशं विमलं बुद्धमप्रमेयं सनातनम्॥
28. *Ibid.*, 8

    सततं पञ्चविंशं च चतुर्विंशं च बुध्यते।
    दृश्यादृश्ये ह्यनुगतमुभावेव महाद्युती॥
29. *Ibid.*, 16[ab]

    षड्विंशोऽहमिति प्राज्ञो गृह्यमाणोऽजरामरः।
30. *Ibid.*, 18.

    चेतनेन समेतस्य पञ्चविंशतिकस्य च।
    एकत्वं वै भवत्यस्य यदा बुद्ध्या न बुध्यते॥
31. *Ibid.*, *Bh P.* 30. 9[abc].

    कविं पुराणमनुशासितारमणोरणीयांसमनुस्मरेद्यः।
    सर्वस्य धातारम् ....॥
32. *Ibid.*, 8[c].

    परमं पुरुषं दिव्यं.........॥
33. *Ibid.*, 4[cd].

    अधियज्ञोऽहमेवात्र देहे देहभृतां वर॥

34. *Ibid.*, 10[cd].
तं परं पुरुषमुपैति दिव्यम्।।
35. *Ibid.*, 4[ab]
अधिभूतं क्षरो भावः पुरुषश्चाधिदैवतम्।।
36. *Ibid.*, 30. 13
ओमित्येकाक्षरं ब्रह्म व्याहरन्मामनुस्मरन्।
यः प्रयाति त्यजन्देहं स याति परमांगतिम्।
37. *Ibid.*, 14
अनन्यचेताः सततं यो मां स्मरति नित्यशः।
तस्याहं सुलभः पार्थ नित्ययुक्तस्य योगिनः।।
38. *Ibid.*, 31.10[ab] *op. cit.*
39. *Ibid.*, 30.11 *op. cit.*
40. *Y.S.* II. 3.
अविद्यास्मितारागद्वेषाभिनिवेशाःक्लेशाः।।
41. *Ibid.*, II 4
अविद्या क्षेत्रमुत्तरेषां प्रसुप्ततनुविछिन्नोदाराणाम्।।
42. *Ibid.*, 5
अनित्याशुचिदुःखानात्मसु नित्यशुचिसुखात्मख्यातिरविद्या।
43. *Ibid.*, 6.
दृग्दर्शनशक्त्योरेकात्मतेवास्मिता।।
44. *Ibid.*, 7.
सुखानुशयी रागः।
45. *Ibid.*, 8.
दुःखानुशयी द्वेषः।
46. *Ibid.*, 9.
स्वरसवाही विदुषोऽपि तन्वनुबंधोऽभिनिवेशः।।
47. *Ibid.*, 10.
ते प्रतिप्रसवहेयाः सूक्ष्माः।
48. *Ibid.*, 11.
ध्यानहेयास्तद्वृत्तयः।
49. *Ibid.*, 16-17.

हेयं दुःखमनागतम्। द्रष्ट्टदृश्ययोः संयोगो हेयहेतुः।

50. *Ibid.*, 23.

स्वस्वामिशक्त्योः स्वरूपोपलब्धिहेतुः संयोगः।

51. *Ibid.*, 21.

तदर्थ एव दृश्यस्यात्मा।

52. *Ibid.*, 18. *op. cit.*

53. *Ibid.*, 24.

तस्य हेतुरविद्या।

54. *Ibid.*, 25.

तदभावात्संयोगाभावो हानं तद्दृश्येः कैवल्यम्।

55. *Ibid.*, II. 26.

विवेकख्यातिरविप्लवा हानोपायः।

56. *Mbh Śānti P.* 295. 2.

अविद्यामाहुरव्यक्तं सर्गप्रलयधर्मि वै।
सर्गप्रलयनिर्मुक्तं विद्यां वै पञ्चविंशकम्।।

57. *Ibid.*, 7. 9.

बुद्धेः प्रकृतिरव्यक्तं तत्त्वानां परमेश्वरम्।
विद्या ज्ञेया नरश्रेष्ठ विधिश्च परमः स्मृतः।।

अव्यक्तस्य परं प्राहुर्विद्यां वै पञ्चविंशकम्।
सर्वस्य सर्वमित्युक्तं ज्ञेयं ज्ञानस्य पार्थिव।।

ज्ञानमव्यक्तमित्युक्तं ज्ञेयं वै पञ्चविंशकम्।
तथैव ज्ञानमव्यक्तं विज्ञाता पञ्चविंशकः।।

58. *Ibid.*, 294. 38-39.

अन्यदेव च क्षेत्रं स्यादन्यः क्षेत्रज्ञ उच्यते।
क्षेत्रमव्यक्तमित्युक्तं ज्ञाता वै पञ्चविंशकः।।

अन्यदेव च ज्ञानं स्यादन्यज्ज्ञेयं तदुच्यते।
ज्ञानमव्यक्तमित्युक्तं ज्ञेयो वै पञ्चविंशकः।।

59. *Ibid.*, 295. 16-17.

गुणा गुणेषु लीयन्ते तदैका प्रकृतिर्भवेत्।
क्षेत्रज्ञोऽपि यदा तात तत्क्षेत्रे संप्रलीयते।।

तदाक्षरत्वं प्रकृतिर्गच्छते गुणसंज्ञिता।
निर्गुणत्वं च वैदेह गुणेषु प्रतिवर्तनात्।।

60. *Ibid.*, 20.

    तदा विशुद्धो भवति प्रकृतेः परिवर्जनात्।
    अन्योऽहमन्येयमिति यदा बुध्यति बुद्धिमान्।।

61. *Ibid.*, *Bh. P.* 24. 62-63.

    ध्यायतो विषयान्पुंसः सङ्गस्तेषूपजायते।
    सङ्गात्संजायते कामः कामात्क्रोधोऽभिजायते।।

    क्रोधाद्भवति संमोहः संमोहात्स्मृतिविभ्रमः।
    स्मृतिभ्रंशाद्बुद्धिनाशो बुद्धिनाशात्प्रणश्यति।।

62. *Y.S.* II. 34

    वितर्का हिंसादयः कृतकारितानुमोदिता लोभक्रोध मोहपूर्वका मृदुमध्याधिमात्रा दुःखाज्ञानानन्तफला इति प्रतिपक्षभावनम्।

63. *Ibid.*, 3 *op. cit.*

64. *Mbh. Bh. P.* 40. 53.

    अहंकारं बलं दर्पं कामं क्रोधं परिग्रहम्।
    विमुच्य निर्ममः शान्तो ब्रह्मभूयाय कल्पते।।

65. *Ibid.*, *Bh. P.* 27. 16-17.

    ज्ञानेन तु तदज्ञानं येषां नाशितमात्मनः।
    तेषामादित्यवज्ज्ञानं प्रकाशयति तत्परम्।।

    तद्बुद्धयस्तदात्मानस्तन्निष्ठास्तत्परायणाः।
    गच्छन्त्यपुनरावृत्तिं ज्ञाननिर्धूतकल्मषाः।।

66. *Ibid.*, 26. 38.

    न हि ज्ञानेन सदृशं पवित्रमिह विद्यते।
    तत्स्वयं योगसंसिद्धः कालेनात्मनि विन्दति।।

67. *Ibid.*, 28. 8[abc].

    ज्ञानविज्ञानतृप्तात्मा कूटस्थो विजितेन्द्रियः।
    युक्त इत्युच्यते योगी ....।।

68. *Y.S.* II. 25-26 *op. cit.*

69. *Śānti P.* 295. 2 *op. cit.*

70. *Ibid.*, 16-17-20.

71. *Y.S.* II 14.

    ते ह्लादपरितापफलाः पुण्यापुण्यहेतुत्वात्।

72. *Ibid.*, 15.
    परिणामतापसंस्कारदुःखैर्गुणवृत्तिविरोधाच्च दुःखमेव सर्वं विवेकिनः।
73. *Ibid.*, 18. *op. cit.*
74. *Ibid.*, 16. *op. cit.*
75. *Ibid.*, 24. *op. cit.*
76. *Ibid.*, 17. *op. cit.*
77. *Ibid.*, 18. *op. cit.*
78. *Ibid.*, 26. *op. cit.*
79. *Ibid.*, I. 12.
    अभ्यासवैराग्याभ्यां तन्निरोधः।
80. *Ibid.*, II. 28-29.
    योगाङ्गानुष्ठानादशुद्धिक्षये ज्ञानदीप्तिराविवेकख्यातेः।
    यमनियमासनप्राणायामप्रत्याहारधारणाध्यानसमाधयोऽष्टावङ्गानि।।
81. *Ibid.*, I. 13-14.
    तत्र स्थितौ यत्नोऽभासः।
    स तु दीर्घकालनैरन्तर्यसत्कारासेवितो दृढभूमिः।
82. *Ibid.*, II. 30.
    अहिंसासत्यास्तेयब्रह्मचर्यापरिग्रहा यमाः।
83. *Ibid.*, 32.
    शौचसन्तोषतपःस्वाध्यायेश्वरप्रणिधानानि नियमाः।
84. *Ibid.*, 33.
    वितर्कबाधने प्रतिपक्षभावनम्।
85. *Ibid.*, 41.
    सत्त्वशुद्धिसौमनस्यैकाग्रयेंद्रियजयात्मदर्शनयोग्यत्वानि च।
86. *Ibid.*, 46.
    स्थिरसुखमासनम्।
87. *Ibid.*, 48.
    ततो द्वन्द्वानभिघातः।
88. *Ibid.*, 49.
    तस्मिन्सति श्वासप्रश्वासयोर्गतिविच्छेदः प्राणायामः।
89. *Ibid.*, 54.

स्वविषयासंप्रयोगे चित्तस्वरूपानुकार इवेन्द्रियाणां प्रत्याहारः।

90. *Ibid.*, 53.

    धारणासु च योग्यता मनसः।

91. *Mbh. Bh. P.* 24. 66-68

    नास्ति बुद्धिरयुक्तस्य न चायुक्तस्य भावना।
    न चाभावयतः शान्तिरशान्तस्य कुतः सुखम्।।

    इन्द्रियाणां हि चरतां यन्मनोऽनुविधीयते।
    तदस्य हरति प्रज्ञां वायुर्नावमिवाम्भसि।।

    तस्माद्यस्य महाबाहो निगृहीतानि सर्वशः।
    इन्द्रियाणीन्द्रियार्थेभ्यस्तस्य प्रज्ञा प्रतिष्ठिता।।

92. *Ibid.*, 55-57.

    प्रजहाति यदा कामान्सर्वान्पार्थ मनोगतान्।
    आत्मन्येवात्मना तुष्टः स्थितप्रज्ञस्तदोच्यते।।

    दुःखेष्वनुद्विग्नमनाः सुखेषु विगतस्पृहः।
    वीतरागभयक्रोधः स्थितधीर्मुनिरुच्यते।।

    यः सर्वत्रानभिस्नेहस्तत्तत्प्राप्य शुभाशुभम्।
    नाभिनन्दति न द्वेष्टि तस्य प्रज्ञा प्रतिष्ठिता।।

93. (*i*) *Ibid.*, 58.

    यदा संहरते चायं कूर्मोऽङ्गानीव सर्वशः।
    इन्द्रियाणीन्द्रियार्थेभ्यस्तस्य प्रज्ञा प्रतिष्ठिता।।

    (*ii*) *Ibid.*, *Śānti P* 313. 39.

    प्रसार्येह यथाङ्गानि कूर्म संहरते पुनः।
    तथेन्द्रियाणि मनसा संयन्तव्यानि भिक्षुणा।।

    (*iii*) *Ibid.*, 168. 39-40.

94. *Ibid.*, *Bh. P.* 36.6[ab]

    तत्र सत्त्वं निर्मलत्वात्प्रकाशकमनामयम्।।

95. *Ibid.*, 24. 59-61

96. *Y.S.* II 33.

97. *Mbh. Bh. P.* 24. 61

    तानि सर्वाणि संयम्य युक्त आसीत मत्परः।
    वशे हि यस्येन्द्रियाणि तस्य प्रज्ञा प्रतिष्ठिता।।

98. *Ibid.*, 28. 35-36.
असंशयं महाबाहो मनो दुर्निग्रहं चलम्।
अभ्यासेन तु कौन्तेय वैराग्येण च गृह्यते।।
असंयतात्मना योगो दुष्प्राप इति मे मतिः।
वश्यात्मना तु यतता शक्योऽवाप्तुमुपायतः।।

99. *Mbh. Śānti P* 197. 9. 15-16

100. *Ibid.*, 188. 9-10[ab]
विसंचारि निरालम्बं पञ्चद्वारं चलाचलम्।
पूर्वे ध्यानपथे धीरः समादध्यान्मनोऽन्तरम्।।
इन्द्रियाणि मनश्चैव यदा पिण्डीकरोत्ययम्।

101. *Ibid.*, 11-14

102. *Ibid.*, 20-22.

103. *Ibid.*, 198. 5-10.

104. *Ibid.*, *Bh. P.* 28. 27.
प्रशान्तमनसं ह्येनं योगिनं सुखमुत्तमम्।
उपैति शान्तरजसं ब्रह्मभूतकल्मषम्।।

105. *Ibid.*, *Āraṇ P.* 200. 52.

106. *Ibid.*, *Bh. P.* 28. 24-26
संकल्पप्रभावान्कामांस्त्यक्त्वा सर्वानशेषतः।
मनसैवेन्द्रियग्रामं विनियम्य समन्ततः।।
शनैः शनैरुपरमेद्बुद्ध्या धृतिगृहीतया।
आत्मसंस्थं मनः कृत्वा न किंचिदपि चिन्तयेत्।।
यतो यतो निश्चरति मनश्चञ्चलमस्थिरम्।
ततस्ततो नियम्यैतदात्मन्येव वशं नयेत्।।

107. *Y.S.* I. 3.
तदा द्रष्टुः स्वरूपेऽवस्थानम्।

108. *Y.S.* I. 6.
प्रमाणविपर्ययविकल्पनिद्रास्मृतयः।

109. *Ibid.*, I. 13.
तत्र स्थितौ यत्नोऽभ्यासः।

110. *Ibid.*, I. 14.
स तु दीर्घकालनैरन्तर्यसत्कारासेवितो दृढभूमिः।

111. *Ibid.*, II. 46.
स्थिरसुखमासनम्।

112. *Ibid.*, 47.
प्रयत्नशैथिल्यानन्तसमापत्तिभ्याम्।

113. *Ibid.*, 48.
ततो द्वन्द्वानभिघातः।

114. *Ibid.*, 49-53.
तस्मिन्सति श्वासप्रश्वासयोर्गतिविच्छेदः प्राणायामः।
स तु बाह्याभ्यन्तरस्तम्भवृत्तिर्देशकालसंख्याभिः परिदृष्टो दीर्घसूक्ष्मः।
बाह्याभ्यन्तरविषयाक्षेपी चतुर्थः।
ततः क्षीयते प्रकाशावरणम्।
धारणासु च योग्यता मनसः।

115. *Ibid.*, III 1.
देशबन्धश्चित्तस्य धारणा।

also refer for details Vaidya Shripad Mahadeo, *ṣaṭcakradarśana vā Bhedana*, (Marathi), Islampur, 1937. pp. 1-6.

116. *Ibid.*, 2.
तत्र प्रत्ययैकतानता ध्यानम्।

117. *Ibid.*, 3.
तदेवार्थमात्रनिर्भासं स्वरूपशून्यमिव समाधिः।

118. *Ibid.*, 4.
त्रयमेकत्र संयमः।

119. *Mbh. Śānti P* 46. 2-6.

120. *Ibid.*, 47. 35[ab]
यं विनिद्रा जितश्वासाः सत्त्वस्थाः संयतेन्द्रियाः।
ज्योतिः पश्यन्ति युञ्जानाः..............।।

121. *Ibid.*, *Bh. P.* 28. 10-14.

122. *Ibid.*, 24-26.

123. *Ibid.*, *Śānti P* 188. 4-5
निर्द्वंद्वा नित्यसत्त्वस्था विमुक्ता नित्यमाश्रिताः।
असङ्गीन्यविवादीनि मनःशान्तिकराणि च।।

तत्र स्वाध्यायसंश्लिष्टमेकाग्रं धारयेन्मनः।
पिण्डीकृत्येन्द्रियग्राममासीनः काष्ठवन्मुनि।।

124. *Ibid.*, 238. 6-7

अन्तरात्मनि संलीय मनःषष्ठानि मेधया।
इन्द्रियाणीन्द्रियार्थांश्च बहु चिन्त्यमचिन्तयन्।
ध्यानोपरमणं कृत्वा विद्यासंपादितं मनः।
अनीश्वरः प्रशान्तात्मा ततोऽर्छत्यमृतं पदम्।।

125. *Ibid.*, 289. 39-46

नाभ्यां कण्ठे च शीर्षे च हृदि वक्षसि पार्श्वयोः।
दर्शने स्पर्शने चापि घ्राणे चामितविक्रम।।

स्थानेष्वेतेषु यो योगी महाव्रतसमाहितः।
आत्मना सूक्ष्ममात्मानं युङ्क्ते सम्यग्विशां पते।।

126. *Ibid.*, 289. 41

स शीघ्रममलप्रज्ञः कर्म दग्ध्वा शुभाशुभम्।
उत्तमं योगमास्थाय यदीच्छति विमुच्यते।।

127. *Ibid.*, 193. 16-18

प्राणापानौ तथोदानं समानं व्यानमेव च।
एवं तान्मनसि स्थाप्य दधतुः प्राणयोर्मनः।।

उपस्थितकृतौ तत्र नासिकाग्रमधो भ्रुवौ।
कुङ्कुण्यां चैव मनसा शनैर्धारयतः स्म तौ।।

निश्चेष्टाभ्यां शरीराभ्यां स्थिरदृष्टी समाहितौ।
जितासनौ तथाधाय मूर्धन्यात्मानमेव च।।

128. *Ibid., Bh. p.* 28.7

जितात्मनः प्रशान्तस्य परमात्मा समाहितः।
शीतोष्णसुखदुःखेषु तथा मानावमानयोः।।

129. *Ibid.*, 35.24[ab]

ध्यानेनात्मनि पश्यन्ति केचिदात्मानमात्मना।

130. *Ibid., Śānti p. 315.*28

दिव्यं ते चक्षुरुत्पन्नं स्वस्थं ते निर्मलं मनः।
तमसा रजसा चापि त्यक्तः सत्त्वे व्यवस्थितः।।

131. *Ibid.*, 289.21-22

तद्वज्जातबलो योगी दीप्ततेजा महाबलः।
अन्तकाल इवादित्यः कृत्स्नं संशोषयेज्जगत्।।

दुर्बलश्च यथा राजन्स्रोतसा ह्रियते नरः।
बलहीनस्तथा योगो विषयैर्ह्रियतेऽवशः।।

132. *Ibid.*, 31[cd]

युक्तः सम्यक्तथा योगी मोक्षं प्राप्नोत्यसंशयम्।।

133. *Ibid.*, 304. 7-9

वेदेषु चाष्टगुणितं योगमाहुर्मनीषिणः।
सूक्ष्ममष्टगुणं प्राहुर्नेतरं नृपसत्तम।।

द्विगुणं योगकृत्यं तु योगानां प्राहुरुत्तमम्।
सगुणं निर्गुणं चैव यथाशास्त्रनिदर्शनम्।
धारणा चैव मनसः प्राणायामश्च पार्थिव।
प्राणायामो हि सगुणो निर्गुणं धारणं मनः।।

134. *Y.S.* I. 42-46.

तत्र शब्दार्थज्ञानविकल्पैः संकीर्णा सवितर्का समापत्तिः।
ता एव सबीजः समाधिः'

135. *Ibid.*, 50.

तज्जः संस्कारोऽन्यसंस्कारप्रतिबन्धी।

136. *Ibid.*, 51.

तस्यापि निरोधे सर्वनिरोधान्निर्बीजः समाधिः।

137. *Bh.* p. 26. 29-30

अपाने जुह्वति प्राणं प्राणेऽपानं तथापरे।
प्राणापानगती रुद्ध्वा प्राणायामपरायणाः।।

अपरे नियताहाराः प्राणान्प्राणेषु जुह्वति।
सर्वेऽप्येते यज्ञविदो यज्ञक्षपितकल्मषाः।।

138. *Y.S.* I 30-31

याधिस्त्यानसंशयप्रमादालस्यावितरतिभ्रान्तिदर्शनालब्धभूमिकत्वानव-स्थितत्वानि चित्तविक्षेपास्तेऽन्तरायाः।

दुःखदौर्मनस्याङ्गमेजयत्वश्वासप्रश्वासा विक्षेपसहभुवः।

139. *Mbh. Āraṇ P.* 2. 21-24.

140. *Ibid.*, 15.

शोकस्थानसहस्राणि भयस्थानशतानि च।
दिवसे दिवसे मूढमाविशन्ति न पण्डितम्।।

141. *Ibid.*, 27-28

142. *Ibid.*, *Bh.* p. 26.40

अज्ञश्चाश्रद्दधानश्च संशयात्मा विनश्यति।
नायं लोकोऽस्ति न परो न सुखं संशयात्मनः।।

143. *Ibid.*, 24. 56^{abc}-64.

144. *Ibid.*, 65.^{cd}
प्रसन्नचेतसो ह्याशु बुद्धिः पर्यवतिष्ठते।।

145. *Ibid.*, 71.
विहाय कामान्यः सर्वान्पुमांश्चरति निःस्पृहः।
निर्ममो निरहंकारः स शान्तिमधिगच्छति।।

146. *Ibid.*, *Śānti* p. 289.11.
रागं मोहं तथा स्नेहं कामं क्रोधं च केवलम्।
योगाच्छित्त्वादितो दोषान्पञ्चैतान्प्राप्नुवन्ति तत्।

147. *Y.S.* I. 35-37
विषयवती वा प्रवृत्तिरुत्पन्ना मनसः स्थितिनिबन्धिनी।।
विशोका वा ज्योतिष्मती।।
वीतरागविषयं वा चित्तम्।।

148. *Mbh. Bh.* p. 40.10.
न द्वेष्ट्यकुशलं कर्म कुशले नानुषज्जते।
त्यागी सत्त्वसमाविष्टो मेधावी छिन्नसंशयः।।

149. *Ibid.*, *Śānti* p. 289. 47-49

150. *Y.S.* I. 30-31 *op. cit.*

151. Kolhatkar, K.K., *Bhāratīya Manasasātra Athavā Sārth āṇi Savivaraṇa Pātañjala Yoga Darśana* (Marathi), 1951, (Shake 1873), Mumbai, p. 94.

152. *Mbh. Bh. P.* 28. 35-36.

153. *Ibid.*, *Śānti P.* 188. 13-16.

154. *Y.S.* I. 23.
ईश्वरप्रणिधानाद्वा।।

155. *Ibid.*, 24.
क्लेशकर्मविपाकाशयैरपरामृष्टः पुरुषविशेष ईश्वरः।।

156. *Ibid.*, 27.
तस्य वाचकः प्रणवः।।

157. *Ibid.*, 28.
तज्जपस्तदर्थभावनम्।।

158. *Ibid.*, 29.
ततः प्रत्यक्चेतनाधिगमोऽप्यन्तरायाभावश्च।।

159. *Ibid.*, 32, 36-39.
तत्प्रतिषेधार्थमेकतत्त्वाभ्यासः।
विशोका वा ज्योतिष्मती।
वीतरागविषयं वा चित्तम्।
स्वप्ननिद्राज्ञानालम्बनं वा।
यथाभिमतध्यानाद्वा।

160. *Ibid.*, 40.
परमाणुपरममहत्त्वान्तोऽस्य वशीकारः।।

161. *Ibid.*, 41.
क्षीणवृत्तेरभिजातस्येव मणेर्ग्रहीतृग्रहणग्राह्येषु।
तत्स्थतदञ्जनतासमापत्तिः।।

162. *Ibid.*, 44.
एतयैव सविचारा निर्विचारा च सूक्ष्मविषया व्याख्याता।

163. *Ibid.*, 45-46.
सूक्ष्मविषयत्वं चालिङ्गपर्यवसानम्।
ता एव सबीजः समाधिः।।

164. *Mbh. Śānti* P. 289. 58-61.

165. *Y.S.* III. 36-37.
ततः प्रातिभश्रावणवेदनादर्शास्वादवार्ता जायन्ते।
ते समाधावुपसर्गा व्युत्थाने सिद्धयः।

166. *Ibid.*, 51.
स्थान्युपनिमन्त्रणे संगस्मयाकरणं पुनरनिष्टप्रसङ्गात्।।

167. *Ibid.*, 50.
तद्वैराग्यादपि दोषबीजक्षये कैवल्यम्।।

168. *Mbh. Śānti P.* 189. 11-17.

169. *Ibid.*, 18.
ध्यानक्रियापरो युक्तो ध्यानवान्ध्याननिश्चयः।
ध्याने समाधिमुत्पाद्य तदपि त्यजति क्रमात्।।

170. *Ibid.*, 190. 2-11

171. *Ibid.*, 193. 24.

उष्यतां मयि चेत्युक्त्वाचेतयत्स ततः पुनः।
अथास्य प्रविवेशास्यं ब्राह्मणो विगतज्वरः॥

172. *Ibid.*, 192. 122.
अमृताच्चामृतं प्राप्तः शीतीभूतो निरात्मवान्।
ब्रह्मभूतः स निर्द्वंद्वः सुखी शान्तो निरामयः॥

173. *Ibid.*, 266. 7
भ्रमं प्रमोहमावर्तमभ्यासाद्विनिवर्तयेत्।
निद्रां च प्रतिभां चैव ज्ञानाभ्यासेन तत्त्ववित्॥

174. *Ibid.*, 269. 2
मोक्षधर्मेषु निरतो लघ्वाहारो जितेन्द्रियः।
प्राप्नोति परमं स्थानं यत्परं प्रकृतेर्ध्रुवम्॥

175. *Y.S.* I 30. *op. cit.*

176. *Bh. P.*26. 38-39. *op. cit.*

177. *Ibid.*, 28. 5
उद्धरेदात्मनात्मानं नात्मानमवसादयेत्।
आत्मैव ह्यात्मनो बन्धुरात्मैव रिपुरात्मनः॥

178. *Ibid.*, 30. 13
ओमित्येकाक्षरं ब्रह्म व्याहरन्मामनुस्मरन्।
यः प्रयाति त्यजन्देहं स याति परमां गतिम्॥

179. *Y.S.* I. 28. *op. cit.*

180. *Śānti* P. 294. 7-8
योगकृत्यं तु योगानां ध्यानमेव परं बलम्।
तच्चापि द्विविधं ध्यानमाहुर्वेदविदो जनाः॥
एकाग्रता च मनसः प्राणायामस्तथैव च।
प्राणायामस्तु सगुणो निर्गुणो मनसस्तथा॥

181. *Y.S.* I. 44 - 46.
एतयैव सविचारा निर्विचारा च सूक्ष्मविषया व्याख्याता।
सूक्ष्मविषयत्वं चालिङ्गपर्यवसानम्।
ता एव सबीजः समाधिः।

182. *Śānti P.* 289. 57[ab]-58[ab]
नानाशास्त्रेषु निष्पन्नं योगेष्विदमुदाहृतम्।
परं हि तद्ब्रह्म महन्महात्मन्ब्रह्माणमीशं वरदं च विष्णुम्।

183. *Y.S.* I. 25.
तत्र निरतिशयं सार्वज्ञबीजम्।
184. *Ibid.*, 26.
स एष पूर्वेषामपि गुरुः कालेनानवच्छेदात्।
185. *Ibid.*, 19.
भवप्रत्ययो विदेहप्रकृतिलयानाम्।
186. *Ibid.*, 24.
क्लेशकर्मविपाकाशयैरपरामृष्टः पुरुषविशेष ईश्वरः।
187. *Ibid.*, 23
ईश्वरप्रणिधानाद्वा।
188. Deussen, P., *op. cit.*, p. 384.
189. Ranade, R.D., *op. cit.*, p. 138.
190. Hiriyanna, M., *op. cit.*, p. 275.
191. *Ibid.*, pp. 282-83.
192. Kolhatkar, K.K., *op. cit.*, p. 76.
193. Mitra, R., *History of Indian Philosophy,* p. 300 q. by Max Müller F., *op. cit.*, p. 291 also Kolhatkar, K.K., *op. cit.*, pp. 78-79.
194. *Mbh. Bh. P.* 30. 9[cd]-10[ab]
195. *Y.S.* I. 25.
196. *Mbh. Bh. P.* 37-16.
द्वाविमौ पुरुषौ लोके क्षरश्चाक्षर एव च।
क्षरः सर्वाणि भूतानि कूटस्थोऽक्षर उच्यते।
197. *Ibid.*, 17.
उत्तमः पुरुषस्त्वन्यः परमात्मेत्युदाहृतः।
यो लोकत्रमाविश्य बिभर्त्यव्यय ईश्वरः।
198. *Ibid.*, 30. 7 [cd]-8-9
मय्यर्पितमनोबुद्धिर्मामेवैष्यस्यसंशयः॥
अभ्यासयोगयुक्तेन चेतसा नान्यगामिना।
परमं पुरुषं दिव्यं याति पार्थानुचिन्तयन्॥
कविं पुराणमनुशासितारमणोरणीयांसमनुस्मरेद्यः।
सर्वस्य धातारमचिन्त्यरूपमादित्यवर्णं तमसः परस्तात्।
199. *Ibid.*, 19.

यो मामेवमसंमूढो जानाति पुरुषोत्तमम्।
स सर्वविद्भजति मां सर्वभावेन भारत।।

200. *Ibid.*, 15[a]
सर्वस्य चाहं हृदि संनिविष्टो.........।

201. *Ibid.*, 14[ab]
अहं वैश्वानरो भूत्वा प्राणिनां देहमाश्रितः।

202. *Ibid.*, 28. 14.
प्रशान्तात्मा विगतभीर्ब्रह्मचारिव्रते स्थितः।
मनः संयम्य मच्चित्तो युक्त आसीत मत्परः।।

203. *Ibid., Śānti P.* 296. 16[ab]
षड्विंशोऽहमिति प्राज्ञो गृह्यमाणोऽजरामरः।
केवलेन बलेनैव समतां यात्यसंशयम्।।

204. *Ibid.*, 296. 17.
षड्विंशेन प्रबुद्धेन बुध्यमानोऽप्यबुद्धिमान्।
एतन्नानात्वमित्युक्तं सांख्यश्रुतिनिदर्शनात्।।

205. *Āśva.* P. 43. 36-40

206. *Y.S.* I. 12.
अभ्यासवैराग्याभ्यां तन्निरोधः।।

207. *Ibid.*, 15.
दृष्टानुश्रविकविषयवितृष्णस्य वशीकारसंज्ञा वैराग्यम्।।

208. *Ibid.*, 16.
तत्परं पुरुषख्यातेर्गुणवैतृष्ण्यम्।

209. *Mbh. Āraṇ. P.* 2. 31-32.
तस्मात्स्नेहं स्वपक्षेभ्यो मित्रेभ्यो धनसंचयात्।
स्वशरीरसमुत्थं तु ज्ञानेन विनिवर्तयेत्।।

ज्ञानान्वितेषु मुख्येषु शास्त्रज्ञेषु कृतात्मसु।
न तेषु सज्जते स्नेहः पद्मपत्रेष्विवोदकम्।।

210. *Ibid., Śānti P.* 171. 50-52
एष ब्रह्मप्रविष्टोऽहं ग्रीष्मे शीतमिव ह्रदम्।
शाम्यामि परिनिर्वामि सुखमासे च केवलम्।।

यच्च कामसुखं लोके यच्च दिव्यं महत्सुखम्।
तृष्णाक्षयसुखस्यैते नार्हतः षोडशीं कलाम्।।

आत्मना सप्तमं कामं हत्वा शत्रुमिवोत्तमम्।
प्राप्यावध्यं ब्रह्मपुरं राजेव स्यामहं सुखी॥

211. *Ibid.*, 289. 49

दीपयन्ति महात्मानः सूक्ष्ममात्मानमात्मना।
वीतरागा महाप्राज्ञा ध्यानाध्ययनसंपदा॥

212. *Ibid.*, *Āran.* P. 2. 45.

अनित्यं यौवनं रूपं जीवितं द्रव्यसंचयः।
ऐश्वर्यं प्रियसंवासो गृध्येदेषु न पण्डितः॥

213. *Ibid.*, *Bh. P.* 26. 19.

यस्य सर्वे समारम्भाः कामसंकल्पवर्जिताः।
ज्ञानाग्निदग्धकर्माणं तमाहुः पण्डितं बुधाः॥

214. *Ibid.*, 40. 52[cd]-53.

ध्यानयोगपरो नित्यं वैराग्यं समुपाश्रितः॥
अहंकारं बलं दर्पं कामं क्रोधं परिग्रहम्।
विमुच्य निर्ममः शान्तो ब्रह्मभूयाय कल्पते॥

215. *Ibid.*, 49-51.

असक्तबुद्धिः सर्वत्र जितात्मा विगतस्पृहः।
नैष्कर्म्यसिद्धिं परमां संन्यासेनाधिगच्छति॥

सिद्धिं प्राप्तो यथा ब्रह्म तथाप्नोति निबोध मे।
समासेनैव कौन्तेय निष्ठा ज्ञानस्य या परा॥

बुद्ध्या विशुद्ध्या युक्तो धृत्यात्मानं नियम्य च।
शब्दादीन्विषयांस्त्यक्त्वा रागद्वेषौ व्युदस्य च॥

216. *Śānti P.* 313. 48-50.

नास्ति ते सुखदुःखेषु विशेषो नास्ति लोलुपा।
नौत्सुक्यं नृत्तगीतेषु न राग उपजायते॥

न बन्धुषु निबन्धस्ते न भयेष्वस्ति ते भयम्।
पश्यामि त्वां महाभाग तुल्यलोष्टाश्मकाञ्चनम्॥

अहं च त्वानुपश्यामि ये चाप्यन्ये मनीषिणः।
आस्थितं परमं मार्गमक्षयं तमनामयम्॥

217. *Bh. P.* 35. 9

असक्तिरनभिष्वङ्गः पुत्रदारगृहादिषु।
नित्यं च समचित्तत्वमिष्टानिष्टोपपत्तिषु॥

218. *Y.S.* I. 46

ता एव सबीजः समाधिः।।

219. *Ibid.*, 47
निर्विचारवैशारद्येऽध्यात्मप्रसादः।

220. *Ibid.*, 48
ऋतम्भरा तत्र प्रज्ञा।

221. *Ibid.*, 49
श्रुतानुमानप्रज्ञाभ्यामन्यविषया विशेषार्थत्वात्।

222. *Ibid.*, IV 30
ततः क्लेशकर्मनिवृत्तिः।

223. *Ibid.*, 31
तदा सर्वावरणमलापेतस्य ज्ञानस्यानन्त्याज्ज्ञेयमल्पम्।

224. *Ibid.*, 32
ततः कृतार्थानां परिणामक्रमसमाप्तिर्गुणानाम्।

225. *Ibid.*, 34
पुरुषार्थशून्यानां गुणानां प्रतिप्रसवः कैवल्यं
स्वरूपप्रतिष्ठा वा चितिशक्तिरिति।

226. *Mbh. Bh. P.* 28. 45
प्रयत्नाद्यतमानस्तु योगी संशुद्धकिल्बिषः।
अनेकजन्मसंसिद्धस्ततो याति परां गतिम्।।

227. *Ibid.*, 27-29
प्रशान्तमनसं ह्येनं योगिनं सुखमुत्तमम्।
उपैति शान्तरजसं ब्रह्मभूतकल्मषम्।।
युञ्जन्नेवं सदात्मानं योगी विगतकल्मषः।
सुखेन ब्रह्मसंस्पर्शमत्यन्तं सुखमश्नुते।।

228. *Ibid.*, 18, 20, 21.
यदा विनियतं चित्तमात्मन्येवावतिष्ठते।
निःस्पृहः सर्वकामेभ्यो युक्त इत्युच्यते तदा।।
यत्रोपरमते चित्तं निरुद्धं योगसेवया।
यत्र चैवात्मनात्मानं पश्यन्नात्मनि तुष्यति।।
सुखमात्यन्तिकं यत्तद्बुद्धिग्राह्यमतीन्द्रियम्।
वेत्ति यत्र न चैवायं स्थितश्चलति तत्त्वतः।।

229. *Ibid.*, *Śānti P.* 168. 40-44.

230. *Ibid., Bh. P.* 28. 7.
जितात्मनः प्रशान्तस्य परमात्मा समाहितः।
शीतोष्णसुखदुःखेषु तथा मानावमानयोः।।

231. *Śānti P.* 188. 22.
सुखेन तेन संयुक्तो रंस्यन्ते ध्यानकर्मणि।
गच्छन्ति योगिनो ह्येवं निर्वाणं तन्निरामयम्।।

232. *Ibid.,* 198. 2.
यदा कर्मगुणोपेता बुद्धिर्मनसि वर्तते।
तदा प्रज्ञायते ब्रह्म ध्यानयोगसमाधिना।।

233. *Ibid., Bh. P.* 30. 8.
अभ्यासयोगयुक्तेन चेतसा नान्यगामिना।
परमं पुरुषं दिव्यं याति पार्थानुचिन्तयन्।।

234. *Ibid., Śānti P.* 21[cdef]-22.
कार्यैरव्याहतमतिर्वैराग्यात्प्रकृतौ स्थितः
आ देहादप्रमादाच्च देहान्ताद्विप्रमुच्यते।
हेतुयुक्तः सदोत्सर्गो भूतानां प्रलयस्तथा।
परप्रत्ययसर्गे तु नियतं नातिवर्तते।।

235. *Ibid.,* 308. 51-52
तस्माद्धर्मार्थकामेषु तथा राज्यपरिग्रहे।
बन्धनायतनेष्वेषु विद्ध्यबन्धे पदे स्थितम्।
राज्यैश्वर्यमयः पाशः स्नेहायतनबन्धनः।
मोक्षाश्मनिशितेनेह छिन्नस्त्यागासिना मया।।

236. *Ibid.,* 189. 18-19.
ध्यानक्रियापरो युक्तो ध्यानवान्ध्याननिश्चयः।
ध्याने समाधिमुत्पाद्य तदपि त्यजति क्रमात्।।
स वै तस्यामवस्थायाः सर्वत्यागकृतः सुखी।
निरीहस्त्यजति प्राणान्ब्राह्मीं संश्रयते तनुम्।।

237. *Ibid.,* 294. 19
तदा तमनुपश्येत यस्मिन्दृष्टे तु कथ्यते।
हृदयस्थोऽन्तरात्मेति ज्ञेयो ज्ञस्तात मद्विधैः।।

238. *Ibid.,* 21
यं पश्यन्ति महात्मानो धृतिमन्तो मनीषिणः।
ब्राह्मणा ब्रह्मयोनिस्था ह्ययोनिममृतात्मकम्।।

239. *Ibid.*, 189. 18-19. *op. cit.*

240. *Ibid.*, 294. 20, also 19. 21 *op. cit.*
विधूम इव सप्तार्चिरादित्य इव रश्मिमान्।
वैद्युतोऽग्निरिवाकाशे दृश्यतेऽऽत्मा तथात्मनि।

241. Dixit, S.H. *op. cit.*, p. 276.

242. *Y.S.* II. 25.
तदभावात्संयोगाभावो हानं तद्दृशेः कैवल्यम्।।

243. ***Mbh Śānti P*** 271. 54-55[abcd].
स यावदेवास्ति सशेषभुक्ते प्रजाश्च देव्यौ च तथैव शुक्ले।
तावत्तदा तेषु विशुद्धभावः संयम्य पञ्चेन्द्रियरूपमेतत्।
शुद्धां गतिं तां परमां परैति शुद्धेन नित्यं मनसा विचिन्वन्।
ततोऽव्ययं स्थानमुपैति ब्रह्म दुष्प्रापमभ्येति स शाश्वतं वै।।

244. *Yogayājñavaklya.* I. 49. For more details see Kolhatkar, K.K., *op. cit.*, pp. 88, 100.
ज्ञानं योगात्मकं विद्धि योगश्चाष्टांगसंयुतः।
संयोगो योग इत्युक्तो जीवात्मपरमात्मनोः।।

245. For more details see Kolhatkar, K.K., *op. cit.*, p. 88

246. *Y.S.* IV. 34. *op. cit.*

247. *Y.Y.* I. 49. *op. cit.*

248. *Chā. Up.*VI. 8. 7. *op. cit.*

249. *Y.Y.* I. 49 - II. 1. For more details see Kolhatkar, K.K., *op. cit.*, p. 101.
वक्ष्याम्यङ्गानि ते सम्यग् यथापूर्वं मया श्रुतम्।
समाहितमना गार्गि! ऋषिभिः सह संशृणु।।

यमश्च नियमश्चैव आसनं च तथैव च।
प्राणायामास्तथा गार्गि! प्रत्याहारश्च धारणा।
ध्यानं समाधिरेतानि योगाङ्गानि वरानने।
यमश्च नियमश्चैव दशधानुप्रकीर्तितौ।
अहिंसा सत्यमस्तेयं ब्रह्मचर्यं दयार्जवम्।।

क्षमा धृतिर्मिताहारः शौचं त्वेते यमा दश।
तपस्सन्तोषमास्तिक्यं दानमीश्वरपूजनम्।
सिद्धान्तश्रवणं चैव ह्रीर्मतिश्च जपो व्रतम्।।
एते तु नियमाः प्रोक्ताः।।

250. For more details see Max Müller, F., *op. cit.*, p. 297.

CHAPTER V

MISCELLANEOUS

The Principles of Vedānta, Sāṁkhya and Yoga philosophy incorporated in the *Mbh.* were discussed in the earlier chapters. Besides these important principles, the *Mbh.* contains a few scattered references to the orthodox views of Nyāya, Vaiśeṣika and even Pūrva-mīmāṁsā as also to the unorthodox principles of Buddhist, Jain and Cārvāka philosophy. In this chapter light will be thrown on them.

Chronology of Treatises

The period of these systems according to different scholars is as follows :

Jaimini's Mīmāṁsā Sūtra-s

Encyclopedia of Philosophy considers 200 B.C. to 200 A.D. as the period of the *M.S.* of Jaimini. Kane, P.V. states it as 500 to 200 B.C.,[2] whereas Radhakrishnan, S. and Benerji, S.C. regard it as 400 B.C.[3] Hiriyanna reckons it as 200 A.D.[4] and Bahadur, K.P. states it as 500 B.C.[5]

Vaiśeṣika Sūtra-s

The Vaiśeṣika system has roots as early as 600 B.C. However, it was systematised by 100 A.D.[6] Radhakrishnan, S. considers it as later than 300 B.C.[7] According to Hiriyanna, though the *Sūtra*-s existed long before, they were commented upon by Praśastapāda which probably belongs to the fifth century A.D.[8] Chakravarti, S.C. thinks that the period of the system is 500 A.D. However, germs of it were found in the earlier Upaniṣad-s.[9] Banerji, S.C. considers

Kaṇāda, who was traditionally regarded as the author of the Vaiśeṣ ika Sūtra, as the contemporary of Buddha (600-500 B.C.)[10] According to Bahadur, K.P., Vaiśeṣika-s date back to 300 B.C.[11]

Nyāya Sūtra-s

The Encyclopedia of Philosophy and Sinha, J. consider 200 A.D. as the period of these *Sūtra*-s.[12] Radhakrishnan, S. opines that the system belongs to the 3rd Century B.C.[13] Banerji, S.C. and Bahadur, K.P. have considered it as 600 B.C.[14] According to Hiriyanna, M., *Vātsyāyana Bhāṣya* on Gautam, *Sūtra*-s belongs to 400 A.D. Hence, the period of the *Sūtra*-s would be prior to 400 A.D.[15] Chakravarti, S.C. states it as 500 B.C.[16] and Dixit, S.H., reckons it as 550 B.C.[17]

Buddhism

According to Banerji, S.C., Gautama Buddha, propounder of Buddhism, attained Buddha-hood in 480 B.C.[18] Zimmer, H.[19] and Dixit, S.H.[20] considered the period of Buddha between 563 to 483 B.C. Hiriyanna, M. regarded the date of Buddha's death as 487 B.C.[21] Radhakrishnan and Moore, C.A. stated that Buddhism was systematised during the Epic period, *i.e.* approximately between 500-600 B.C. to 200 A.D.[22]

Jainism

Banerji, S.C. considered the period of Vardhamāna Mahāvīra as 600 B.C.[23] and Zimmer considered it as 526 B.C.[24] Hiriyanna, M. treated it as 540 B.C.[25] and Radhakrishnan and Moore, C.A. and Smith, V. A. opined that Gautam, Buddha and Mahāvīra were contemporaries.[26]

Cārvāka, Lokāyata System

No treatises expounding Cārvāka, Lokāyata doctrines are extant. However, there is *sūtra* on it, ascribed to Bṛhaspati, whom *Maitri Upaniṣad* describes as a heretical teacher.[27] Bṛhaspati is considered to be a founder of this system. It is, therefore, called

Bārhaspatya Darśana. Before 800 A.D., the system was referred to as Lokāyata or Bārhaspatya. From 800 A.D. it was generally called as Cārvāka.[28]

If we take into consideration the probable dates of these systems vis-a-vis that of the *Mbh.*, it is not at all surprising if the tenets of these systems got reflected in the *Mbh.* They will be examined in this chapter.

Nyāya Philosophy in the *Mbh.*

Etymologically, the word Nyāya is derived from the root '*nī*' to lead, carry etc. Nyāya means that with which one can arrive at a conclusion, an inference. The Nyāya and Vaiśeṣika systems believe that there cannot be any knowledge without a substance.[29] The Vaiśeṣika-s believed that the knowledge of material world is indispensible. Hence, their speculations were based on the analysis of the material. The Naiyāyika-s, on the other hand, believed that reasoning is necessary to secure knowledge. They, therefore, were of the opinion that by a thorough examination of modes and the sources of correct knowledge, the ends of life can be accomplished. For the same reasons, they laid emphasis on the study and application of logical method to interprete their thought in order to arrive at the truth. Bernard Theos opined that according to the Naiyāyika-s, a critical enquiry about the traditional teachings and evidence of the senses is necessary. They, therefore, enquired into the objects of perception, leaving the problem of the origin and manifestation for the other systems. Hence, they laid down the rules of syllogistic reasoning for the purpose of examining the objects of perception.[30]

The Naiyāyika-s consider sixteen categories and believe that the Supreme Bliss is attained through the knowledge of the true nature of these categories.[31] These are means of right knowledge (*pramāṇa*-s), objects of right knowledge (*prameya*-s), doubt (*saṁśaya*), purpose (*prayojana*), familiar example (*dṛṣṭānta*), an established tenet (*siddhānta*), members of a syllogism (*avyava*-s), confutation (*tarka*), ascertainment (*nirṇaya*), discussion (*vāda*), controversy (*jalpa*), cavil (*vitaṇḍa*), fallacy (*hetvābhāsa*), equivocation (*chala*), *jāti* and disagreement in principle (*nigrahasthāna*).

The means of right knowledge (*pramāṇa*-s) are perception (*pratyakṣa*), inference (*anumāna*)[32] comparison (*upamāna*) and verbal testimony (*śabda*). The sphere of perception is the present, that of inference is the past, present and future. Comparison is an instrument of perception to know the object by name.

The Nyāyasūtra-s also describe the objects of right knowledge (*prameya*-s) as soul, body, sense objects etc.,[33] different kinds of doubts and give meanings of *prayojana*,[34] *dṛṣṭānta*,[35] *siddhānta*[36] etc. categories.

Thus, they classified various things in the world. They found out the fundamental classes or things under which all the substances in the world can be classified as a result of the gradual evolution of things in the lower orders into things in the higher orders, their nature and qualities. According to them, there is no other root cause of the world except atoms.

The commencement (*ārambha*) of the mutual coalition or union of the original and permanent atoms results in all the perceptible things in the world coming into existence. This is the theory of commencement, *ārambha-vāda*. However, some followers of the Nyāya school believed that Īśvara brings about the fusion of atoms and thus the chain of creation of the world is complete. These Naiyayika-s are known as theistic Logicians.[37]

In the *Mbh.,* Bhīṣma explained the duties of the king (*rājadharma*) to Yudhiṣṭhira. He stated that while judging people, a king should always resort to the means of right knowledge *viz.* perception (*pratyakṣa*), inference (*anumāna*), comparison (*upamāna*) and verbal testimony (*upadeśa*).[38] The incorporation of four cannons of Nyāya system at a stretch shows that the system must have been in vogue at the time of the *Mbh.* However, besides this reference, there is only one reference to Nyāya philosophy and that too is of despicable nature.

There is an episode in the *Mbh.*, which despises logic, *anvikṣ ikī, tarkavidyā*. A learned *brāhmin* relates how he was enamoured by *tarka-vidyā* and debated on the basis of it, censuring the Veda-s and though was a fool, thought of himself to be knowledgeable. He was, therefore, punished and in the next birth became a jackal.[39] He, then asked the sage Kāśyapa, "Is it possible for me to be reborn as a human being again and be able to perform sacrifice, donate gifts and undertake penance etc. by concerted efforts?"[40]

In this connection, the observations made by various scholars regarding the Nyāya system getting a back seat, or its non-representation in the various literary and philosophical works are noteworthy. Bahadur, K.P. points out that the rational system founded by Gautama was pure logic and it was treated indifferently and even with animosity. The orthodox brāhmins were reluctant to recognise a creed in which ritual was altogether ignored. Manu disparaged those who relied on the *hetu-śāstra* or the science of logic. Vālmīki condemned, in his *Rāmāyaṇa*, people of perverse intellect who indulged in the frivolities of *ānvīkṣikī*. Vyāsa was even more censorious. He did not review the Nyāya system in his Brahma-sūtra-s. He warned the followers of the Vedānta against communicating their doctrines to a Naiyāyika-s. In the Naiṣ adhacarita, Kali dubbed Gautama as the "most bovine of sages."[41]

Mullick Bahadur states that Vyāsa was a pupil of Nyāya school. He founded a new school *viz.* the Vedic school, which began to discourse on metaphysics. He also compiled Brahma-sūtra-s. His preceptor, Gautama, was said to be offended by these developments and Vyāsa fell out with him. Mullick Bahadur also opines that the metaphysical speculations in the *Mbh.*, therefore, are centered around the performance of sacrifice sanctioned by the *Ṛv.*[42]

Radhakrishnan, S. also opines that Nyāya is undoubtedly a natural and necessary stage in the evolution of thought, but is by no means final. This philosophy repudiates mere subjectivism. However, no Hindu thought, not even that of Śaṅkara, accepts the view of mere mentalism. Further, a deeper analysis of experience on the logical side was undertaken by the Sāṁkhya and Vedānta.[43]

The absence of Nyāya doctrines and censorious representation of it in the *Mbh.* shows unfavourable outlook of the Mahābhāratakāra towards Nyāya tenets. The reasons for the same can be found in the above stated scholarly speculations.

Vaiśeṣika Philosophy in the *Mbh.*

The word Vaiśeṣika is to be derived from *Viśeṣa-vi+√śiṣ*-to differentiate, to distinguish. *Viśeṣa* means a distinguishing characteristic. The feeling of attraction or aversion is a source of all misery. When there is a knowledge of the distinguishing characteristic of the reality, the objects of perception do not awaken within us those feelings. The Vaiśeṣika philosophy reveals this type of knowledge. Hence, it is called by that name.

According to *Vaiśeṣika*-s, self-knowledge and self-realisation are the means of attaining liberation. It is, therefore, also called as *'Mokṣaśāstra'* and *'Adhyātmaśāstra'* that is, a treatise about the Supreme Spirit.

The Vaiśeṣika-s were of the opinion that a man is influenced by his environment and the things around him. He has a natural tendency to analyse them. Hence the knowledge of material world is indispensible. The truth is revealed when there is an agreement between the subjective world of thought and the objective world of forms. Thus, there has to be a co-ordination between the inner and outer worlds. Vaiśeṣika-s, therefore, strived to find out the basic realities of nature. They sought the practical means of philosophical insight to analyse and synthesize the world of experience and endeavoured to rationally explain the true nature of things. Thus, in this system there are no intellectual speculations about the origin of things. Their speculations are based on the analysis of the material.[44]

According to the Vaiśeṣikasūtra-s, the Supreme good results from the knowledge produced by a particular *dharma* of the essence of predicables (*padārtha*-s), substance (*dravya*), attributes (*guṇa*-s), action (*karman*), genus (*sāmānya*), species (*viśeṣa*) and combination (*samavāya*) by means of their resemblances and differences.[45] According to Kaṇāda, attributes, action, genus and species exist due to their combination with substance (*dravya*) in which they inhere. The eternal substances recognised are – 1. the atomic entities, namely, the earth (*pṛthvī*), the fire (*tejas*), water (*āpas*), air (*vāyu*) and the organ of thought or consciousness (*manas*), 2. all pervading entities, namely, the soul (*ātman*), ether (*ākāśa*), time (*kāla*) and space (*dik*). The perceptible substances are built up out of atoms, including *manas,* through which unconscious Soul is united to the complex psychosomatic entity.[46] The indivisible, partless and eternal particle of matter is called an atom (*paramāṇu*). All physical things are produced by the combinations of atoms. Creation, therefore, means the combination of atoms in different proportions and destruction means the dissolution of combinations. The material cause of the world is neither produced nor destroyed. The atomism of the Vaiśeṣika-s is not materialistic as they recognise the reality of the spiritual substances-Souls and God and admit the Law of Karman. Thus, according to them, atom is the material cause of the world and God, assisted by the Unseen Power, is the efficient cause. Evolution takes place due to the Unseen Power, which consists of merits and demerits of the individual Souls. Nyāya and Vaiśeṣika systems, however, did not accept the existence of God initially. Their theology was first developed in Udayanācārya's *Kusumāñjali* in 1200 A.D.[47]

The *Mbh.* describes only one of the categories *viz.* qualities (*guṇa*-s). It states various qualities possessed by the earth, water, fire, air and space. According to the *Mbh.,* the qualities of the earth are smell, taste and lubricity.[48] It also presents a detailed description of smell, which a being experiences from the earth. The smells are favourable, unfavourable, sweet, bitter, acrid, astringent, agreeable etc.[49] Water (*jala*) has four qualities *viz.* sound, touch, form and taste. These qualities of taste (*rasa*) are further described as sweet, salty, pungent, astringent, sour and bitter. Fire (*agni*) has three qualities of sound, touch and colour. The secondary qualities of colour have been mentioned as white, black, red, yellow, blue and orange. Air possesses two main qualities of sound and touch and secondary qualities as hot, cold, pure, pleasant, moist etc. Space has only one major quality of sound. The secondary qualities of sound total to seven which are *ṣaḍja, ṛṣabha, gāndhāra* etc.[50] The *Mbh.* also describes sense organs which comprehend these qualities.[51] It refers to the categories of position (*bhāva*), negation (*abhāva*) and time (*kāla*).[52] It states that *kāla* is eternal (*śāśvata*), steady (*acala*) and stable (*dhruva*). The *kāla* positions itself for the creation of the world.[53]

Kaṇāda has ascribed four qualities to the earth, three to water, two to light and one to air. These are principal characteristics. He also mentions some secondary qualities of the earth. The earth possesses fourteen such qualities, *i.e.* colour, taste, smell, touch, number, extension, individualities, gravity etc.[54] Water has colour, form (*rūpa*), taste and touch as its qualities. Fluidity, lubricity etc. are the secondary qualities of water.[55] Some of the qualities of the entities mentioned here are similar to those mentioned in the *Mbh.* However, some times they differ from those stated in the Vaiśeṣikasūtra-s.

The *Mbh.* also refers to Vaiśeṣika-s as *Sthūladarśin*-s, that is, those who perceive atom (grossness) as the cause of creation. Thus, it states the qualities of five atomic entities only. It also refers to the categories such as *kāla, bhāva* and *abhāva*. It must be noted that such references are very scanty, probably due to following reasons :

The Vaiśeṣika philosophy considers only some facts of experience regarding substances, qualities and actions. According to this philosophy, annihilation of *adṛṣṭa* destroys all contacts, puts an end to the cycle of births and deaths and culminates into salvation (*mokṣa*). *Adṛṣṭa* is formed due to adherence to the Vedic actions such as holy ablution (*snāna*), fasting, celebacy (*brahmacarya*), *vānaprastha*, *yajña,* and *dāna*. Thus, there are no philosophical speculations as such. Their explanation of the world in a naturalistic way was replaced by the purely naturalistic doctrine of the Sāṁkhya system. Sāṁkhya-s had propagated plurality of Souls alongwith unconscious Nature (*Prakṛti*) and stated that Prakṛti is the material cause of the objective world. The world had spontaneously evolved out of Prakṛti without any conscious guidance.

According to Tilak, B.G., since Sāṁkhya system attained great significance, it superseded the theory of Kaṇāda.[56] In the light of his opinion, it could further be stated that perhaps this was the reason why the references to the principles of Kaṇāda found in the *Mbh.* are few in number.

The Pūrva Mīmāṁsā

The rise of Buddhism compelled the followers of the Vedic *dharma* to review and recast the entire knowledge they possessed, prove its soundness and embody it in the form of the *sūtra*-s.[57] Jaimini attempted to establish the authority of the Veda-s and revive the Vedic rituals and doctrines. He systematised the rules of Mīmāṁsā and established their validity in his work.

Jaimini's philosophy is styled as Pūrvamīmāṁsā, 'an enquiry into the former portion of the Veda' or 'Karmamīmāmasā' an enquiry into the rituals of the Veda-s' and is concerned with the *mantra*-s and Brāhmaṇa-s. It focusses on the ceremonial questions such as sacrifice, doubts and discrepancies found in the Vedic texts. Monier William M. opines that in reality, the Mīmāṁsā is not a branch of any philosophical system, it is rather a system of the Vedic interpretation.[58] Jaimini considered only the Veda-s to be the authoritative texts. According to him, the Veda was practically the only God. The aim of his system was to know Dharma or duty, which consisted in the performance of the rites and sacrifices as prescribed by the Veda-s. Though the sacrifices were believed to be the means leading to certain kind of beatitude which could diminish the distress of men, this system did not strive to pursue the goal of the highest beatitude like other philosophies.[59] Jaimini developed a novel concept of the unforeseen (*adṛṣṭa*) which leads to a fruit, consequences of which are not visible. While commenting upon Jaimini (VI.1.1), Śabara stated that the injunctive passages (*vidhi*-s) of the Veda-s promise a reward. However, it cannot be secured immediately in the present life and *svarga* would lead to unsurpassable joy, which can be attained only in the next life.[60] Commenting on this concept of Adṛṣṭa, Dange, S.A. has stated that there is an expectation of fruit of action. However, as it is unseen (*adṛṣṭa*), there is no eagerness to achieve it.[61]

The path of action propagated by the Mīmāṁsaka-s implies *karman* without *jñāna*. It enables one to reach just the heaven. However, it does not lead to the final release called *Niṣṭhā*. The *Mbh.* has derogated the theory of the Mīmāṁsaka-s. It even criticized Mīmāṁsaka-s vehemently as undiscerning persons who always hanker after the fulfillment of their desires,[62] who are intent on reaching the heaven and who consider sacrifice to be the only thing existing in this world. Their intelligence is not well established in the Self.[63] Observance of rituals is of little value for the people who have spiritual insight. The action of the threefold constituents (*guṇa*-s) is the subject-matter of the Veda-s. However, one should accept only that portion of the Veda-s which would be suitable to oneself. One, therefore, should free oneself from the three-fold Nature, from the pairs of opposite and be firmly fixed in purity. Without caring for the acquisition (*yoga*) and preservation (*kṣema*), he should know the Self and perform actions without expecting the fruit thereof.[64] The above descriptions clearly indicate that the *Mbh.* is totally against the performance of action of securing carnal pleasures or for reaching the heaven. According to the *Mbh.*, the right of a man is limited just to action. It is not further to be extended to the fruit thereof. One should neither expect a fruit of any action nor should desist from performing it.[65] Thus, totally disregarding *Karmamīmāṁsā* of Jaimini, the *Mbh.* has ennobled the theory of Karman.

The *Mbh.* despised sacrifice performed by people who are self conceited, proud and arrogant due to wealth. Such sacrifices are only in name, ostentatious.[66] However, the *Mbh.* did not advocate relinquishment of acts of sacrifice, since sacrifice alongwith gifts and penance purifies the wise.[67] Nevertheless, sacrifice should be performed in accord with the scriptural rites, without attachment and without desire for reward.[68] The sacrifice performed with a sense of duty is said to be the best (*sāttvika*) sacrifice.[69] According to the *Mbh.*, a person who performs benevolent or inauspicious actions attains the fruit of those actions either in the form of heaven (*svarga*) or in the form of hell (*naraka*). Hence, one should perform sacrifices without violating scriptural dictates (*śāstra*) and give away gifts.[70] Thus, there is not outright opposition to sacrifice.

In fact, Arjuna advised Yudhiṣṭhira to obtain sacred knowledge of the three Veda-s, collect wealth by all the means and sacrifice.[71] The *Mbh.* reflects an attempt to glorify sacrifice stating that Brahmā created wealth for sacrifice, even Indra could reach the heaven through performance of sacrifice and the king Hariścandra was freed from grief. Śiva sacrificed himself and became the God of gods. His glory pervaded the entire world and he shined with his effulgence.[72] The perspective of the *Mbh.* of viewing sacrifice was very wide since it treated even restraint (*saṁyama*), penance (*tapas*) and control of breath (*prāṇāyāma*) as sacrifices.[73]

The *Mbh.* states that Brahmā created this world along with sacrifice and advised people to attain prosperity and fulfill desires by performing sacrifices. The gods, satisfied by the sacrifice would offer fruit desired by the sacrificer. However, one has to return it to them, it would otherwise amount to theft.[74] It is also stated that from food creatures originate, from rain food, from sacrifice rain and from action (*karman*)[75] sacrifice.

The *karman* originated from Brahman (the Veda-s) and Brahman created Veda-s. Hence, Brahman is stationed in sacrifice.[76] However, resorting to a broader view and widening the Mīmāṁsaka's narrow concept of sacrifice, the *Mbh.* ennobled sacrifice so as to lead to the general welfare of society. Śrīkṛṣṇa's statement, "I am the enjoyer of all sacrifices."[77] indicates how identification of sacrifice with Puruṣottama himself elevated the noble spirit of sacrifice.

The Buddhist Philosophy

Buddhism maintains that affliction (*kleśa*) and action (*karman*) are the root causes of all the miseries. These two causes should be destroyed in order to get rid of suffering. According to *Abhiddhammakośa*,[78] *kleśa*-s are of three types *viz.* ignorance (*avidyā*), desire (*tṛṣṇā*) and attachment (*upādāna*). Conformation (*saṁskāra*) and disposition for becoming (*bhāva*) represent *karman*. Consciousness, name and form, six organs of senses, contact, sensation, birth, old age and death are the substrata (*āśraya-vastu*) of *kleśa* and *karman*.

The Bauddha philosophy rejects eternal Soul. The Soul is supposed to be series of psychological entities. The theory of causation states that the emperical realities consist in events and all events are strictly momentary. One of the schools of the Buddhism, Sautrāntika-s, accepted the doctrine of momentariness and believed that Nirvāṇa is the result brought about by following the path (*magga*) which leads to Nirvāṇa. The Sabbastivādin-s believe that everything persistently exists. However, inspite of difference in views, the three fundamental principles are accepted by all the schools of Buddhism *viz.*, (*i*) Every thing is transitory, (*ii*) There is no such thing as Ātman and (*iii*) Nibbāna is peaceful. According to Buddhism, every object in the universe possesses characteristics of origination (*utpāda*), staying (*sthiti*), growth (*vṛddhi*), decay (*jarā*) and destruction (*nirodha*) and hold that all these happen simultaneously at the same *kṣaṇa* while Sautrāntika-s opine that they spread themselves successively over the limit of life period. This theory of momentariness leads to the theory of void (*śūnyatā*). It means conditionality or transitoriness of all phenomenal existence, *i.e.* it is *anitya*. It signifies negativity, the absence of particularity, it is an ever changing state of the phenomenal world. However, it is not absolute, nothingness or annihilation. Nāgārjuna in his commentary on *Prajñāpārimitasūtra* states that Buddha denies the existence of an eternal Ātman but asserts the existence of the empirical Self. When Tathāgata (Buddha) said, "There is no Ātman," it was in the sense of creator or perceiver or an absolute free agent.

There are allusions to the views of Buddhist schools of Kṣaṇikavādin-s, Sūnyavādins etc. in the *Mbh.* It is held that ignorance (*avidyā*) and *saṁskāra* (*karman*) refer to the life immediately preceding and activity of past life prompted by ignorance gives rise to the present.[79] This view of the Kṣaṇikavādin-s is refuted in the *Mbh.* It states that some people believe that Avidyā, *karman* and other afflictions like desire, avarice are the causes of rebirth, they consider *avidyā* to be *kṣetra*, seed of *karman* in the earlier birth and the desire to be the cause of attachment. They believe that body and soul are momentary (*kṣaṇika*).[80] The doctrine of Sūnyavādin-s, too, is refuted when Kṛṣṇa states that some people believe that this world is unreal. It is without any basis, without any Lord, not brought about in regular causal sequence that is caused by desire.[81] They are censured as ignorant, cruel etc. It must be noted that the *Mbh.* has incorporated the principles of Buddhism for the sake of refutation as Buddhism protested against the absolute authority of the Veda-s.

Cārvāka-s, Lokāyata-s and other Nāstika Systems

Cārvāka

The principles of Cārvāka philosophy are known from the refutation of their doctrines by their opponents. However, their presence in Indian philosophical scenario shows the all faceted nature of philosophical thinking in India. The main doctrine of the system is that perception (*pratyakṣa*) is the only means of valid knowledge. All the other means of knowledge including inference (*anumāna*) are rejected. The inference is nothing more than guess work. Cārvāka-s consider four elements (*bhūta-s*) *viz.* the earth, the fire, water and air. They do not recognise space (*ākāśa*) as an element as it can be known by inference. For the same reason, They do not recognize the Soul (Ātman). According to them the Soul is not independent. It belongs to the body and once the body disintegrates, the Soul disappears.

Lokāyata-s

Bhatta, Utpala in *Bṛhatsaṁhitā* states that Lokāyata-s hold that the creation of the universe, its diversity and its destruction are all due to nature (*svabhāva*).[82] This theory of spontaneous origination does not believe in any kind of causality.

The doctrines of Cārvāka-s, Lokāyata-s and Svabhāvavādin-s are refuted by the *Mbh.* They believe that there is nothing, *i.e.* Ātman in this world. The *Mbh.* called them *'hetumanaatḥ tarkavādinaḥ'* and stated that it is difficult to understand such people.[83] Some state that Ātman is different from body and once the *cetanā* in the body disappears, the being dies.[84] This view is refuted by the *Mbh.* The body still remains after the death. However, there is no more *cetanā* in it. It proves that body and *cetanā* are different and that body and Ātman are different from each other.[85] The view of Svabhāvavādin-s is again refuted by the *Mbh.* – "Some dullards (*alpacetasaḥ*) think that this world has originated by its own nature, there is no active substratum for the world. However, in the world, the activities like farming, building of houses, vehicles etc. are undertaken by the people. Had they been taken place on their own, nobody would have been inspired to undertake them."[86] The *Mbh.*, therefore, reiterates that all this world is created, pervaded controlled by the Supreme Soul.

Thus, the *Mbh.* does not accept the views contrary to the orthodox systems, *i.e.* the systems which do not recognise the Soul, Īśvara and the Supreme Soul who is the creator of the world.

Jain Philosophy

The *Mbh.* refutes the tenets of Baudha and Cārvāka philosophy (atheistic philosophy). However, there is no trace of Jain philosophy, not even in an indirect manner. There is a reference to Saṁvarta, the son of Aṅgiras who was "roaming around Benaras, clothed in air, astounding the people like a mad man."[87] According to Radhakrishnan, S., Saṁvarta is a Jain Śramaṇa.[88] However, it is not likely to be so, as the King Marutta had sought Saṁvarta's help for performing a sacrifice.[89] The absence of Jain doctrines in the *Mbh.* may be due to following reasons :

(*i*) The Jain Tīrthaṅkara-s were not vehementally preaching their doctrines.

(*ii*) Jain doctrines were being preached and followed long before the advent of Buddhism,

(*iii*) Moreover, Vardhamāna's method was to harmonize and assimilate many different contending sects as were consistent with his main ideal of Mokṣa.

(*iv*) Also, the tenets of Jainism were difficult to practice, hence very few people were attracted towards it. The practitioners of the Vedic religion, therefore, might not have felt threatened by them. Whereas, the Buddhist were aggressive in preaching their tenets. They vehementaly attacked the Veda-s and Vedic practices. Their religion was easy to practise and hence, large number of population was attracted towards it. The doctrines of Cārvāka, too, considered that one should enjoy till the life lasts. It seems that they discarded all the social norms prescribed by the society while enjoying the carnal pleasures. Hence, their tenets were refuted by the *Mbh.*

Dharma- in the *Mbh.*

The word *dharma* cannotes various meanings such as

religion, customary observances of a caste, sects etc., law, usage, ordinance, statute, religious or moral merits, virtue, righteousness, good works and many more. All the schools of Indian philosophy accept *dharma* as the moral law of the universe. Dharma also forms one of the goals of human existence (*puruṣārtha*-s) as considered by the Indian society. The other three goals are wealth (*artha*), delight (*kāma*) and salvation (*mokṣa*). Obtaining wealth through righteous means and observance of morals while enjoying the pleasures of life are precursors of the attainment of *Mokṣa*. Thus, *dharma* is the means to attain the ultimate aim of life.

The *Mbh.*, being encyclopaedic in nature could not ignore such an important and basic concept which deals with the moral fabric of society. The *Mbh.* considered *dharma* to be threefold, that followed by the respectable members of the society, that laid down by Dharmaśāstra and that prescribed in Veda-s. *Dharma* prescribed by Veda-s was considered to be the best.

The *Mbh.* considered the observance of moral standards, good manners and duties such as sacrifice, charity, penance, control over senses, truth, spirit of dedication, submission to the teacher, mercy for all beings, non-violence (as has been described in the Kalpasūtra-s),[90] absence of jealousy, forgiveness, peace, satisfaction, pleasing speech as principles of *śiṣṭācāra.*[91] The *Mbh.* praised virtues like straightforwardness, mercy, absence of pride, a sence of shame, patience etc.[92] It has praised truth (*satya*) to such an extent that it is equated to Brahman and *tapas.*[93] The world is sustained by *satya.* It enables the being to reach the heaven. *Satya* itself was looked upon as *dharma. Dharma* is identified with light and light with pleasure. *Satya* is also identified with *dharma* and *anṛta* with *adharma.*[94] *Satya* was considered everything. That was beneficial to men[95] and was treated as *dharma.*[96] Its opposite was *adharma.* According to the *Mbh.*, charity, absence of hatred and favour etc. are the norms of excellent conduct (*śīla*). *Śīla* and steadfastness leads to salvation.[97]

The last two *āśrama*-s *viz.* Vānaprasthāśrama and Saṁnyāsa pre-supposed detachment from sensual objects and they were stages to attain the ultimate goal *viz.* salvation. The *Mbh.* corroborates this view and states that detachment from sensual desires was instrumental in achieving salvation. Mere interest in enjoyment of pleasure was likely to have adverse effect on the intellect.[98]

The law of Karman is assumed by Vedāntins.[99] The *Mbh.* subscribes to this view and states that meritorious deeds, charity, non-violence enable one to attain the heaven.[100] The deeds of opposite nature lead to birth of human beings, whereas desire, violence, greed etc. lead one to the birth of animal (*tiryakyonitva*).[101]

As the *Br. Up.* says, "Therefore, one who thus knows, who has subdued his senses, who is calm, free from desire, enduring and composed in mind, beholds the Soul. The Soul alone beholds the whole soul, sin does not subdue him, he consumes sin. He is free from sin, free from doubt, he is pure. He is the true Brahman.[102]

The *Mbh.* accepted the age-old concept of *dharma*, as assumed by the *Śruti*-s, (Vedānta) and applied it to the present situation. It convinced people that by serving and worshipping their teacher, performing their day to day duties, attending to family responsibilities and social obligations such as helping poor, old, sick would uplift them to the status of Brahman. One can achieve salvation during his lifetime while in the world. Thus, the *Mbh.* paved the way for the masses to attain salvation through various practical means such as Yoga, Karmayoga, Bhaktiyoga and *dharma* in a wider sense.

Law of Karman and Transmigration

All the Indian philosophical systems with the exception of Cārvāka, believe that the principle, which regulates all the happenings in the world, the actions of all the beings and the fruit achieved according to those actions, has universal relation. This is the Law of Karman. In the life of a man, there are so many situations such as disease, accidents, short life etc., which apparently have no explicable cause. Physical sciences do have physiological reasoning for such occurences. However, some times they too do not have answers for such incidents. The Indian philosophers solved these questions from a different angle. They related such happenings to the actions of the beings. They considered that every incident has two aspects. They are governed by physiological as well as moral aspects. A good action performed by one may motivate the other to do a good deed. Thus, it provides a moral ground for action. The law of Karman establishes that there is nothing uncertain or capricious in the moral world. Every action has its own effect. This law is the other side of the physical law of uniformity.

The earliest trace of *Karman* theory can be found in the *Ṛv.* It is reflected in the *ṛta* as law and order. Varuṇa is the Lord of *ṛta*. Karman is unchanging action of the god. It is related to gods and is of the nature of reality. In a hymn uttered at the funeral occasion, a seer asks (the deity) to move the eye of the dead to the sun, which is its parallel, the breath to the wind and the soul to the heaven or earth according to their qualities or else to the water or the plants, if it suits its *dharma*. The word *dharma* implies the Karman as the Soul is asked to go to the heaven or the earth as per his qualities.[103]

The Upaniṣad-s stated that after the death, the Self becomes as per his works and behaviour. The person whose actions are good becomes good and the one whose actions are evil becomes evil. The man can become good by good actions and bad by bad actions.[104] The selfish actions bind man by the fetters of birth and death. The Upaniṣad-s described the actual manner in which the self departs after death. As the self moves out, life also goes after him, various vital airs depart after the life. His knowledge, his actions and earlier consciousness follow him.[105] The Upaniṣad-s believe that one can free himself from the bonds of Karman by selfless action. When one lives, thus, Karman does not cling to him.[106]

Thus, man has the freedom from the bonds of action. Every action has two consequences, the fruit of it in the world and the effect of it on the mind. The man has no control over the fruit of action but he can control his mental tendencies and destroy the effect of past actions and control the future actions by knowledge.

The doctrine of transmigration is a corollary to the theory of Karman. As stated before, many situations in the life of a man cannot be explained by his present actions. The Indian philosophers invented or might have borrowed from the aborigins the idea of transmigration and linked it with the doctrine of Karman.[107] As the time cannot blur and death cannot obliterate the effect of the action, the burden is carried over to the next birth. This thought is reflected in the *Ṛv*. When a dead man is advised, "To unite with the Fathers, Yama, with the reward of his sacrifice and good works in the highest heaven. Leaving blemish behind, go back to his home, unite with his body, full of vigour." In this connection, Macdonell's remark that the *Av.* often speaks of such being the state of things in the next life is noteworthy.[108] Thus, Vedic seers established a theory of an unbroken chain of existence and joined it with the moral principle of requittal.[109]

It is but natural if the same doctrine of transmigration appears in the Upaniṣad-s too.[110] It states, "And as a caterpillar, after reaching the end of a blade of grass, finds another place of support and then draws itself towards it, similarly this self, after reaching the end of this body, finds another place of support and then draws himself towards it. After throwing off this body and dispelling ignorance, takes on another newer and more beautiful form, whether it be of one of the manes, or demi-gods, or gods, or of Prajāpati, or Brahman, or of any other being. This Self, then, becomes as per his conduct and behaviour." Here, in one passage both the doctrines of transmigration and that of Karman are explicated.

The *Mbh.* accepts the Upaniṣadic theory of Karman that the beings are bound by Karman and are released by knowledge. The

Ṛgvedic thought that "the Karman is controlled by the god" also finds acceptance in the *Mbh.* The doctrine of transmigration too follows the doctrine of Karman. Draupadī states that what is obtained by chance, by providential dispensation, spontaneously or as a result of one's acts is, however, the consequence of the acts of former life. The God, the ordainer of the universe, judging the acts of the former lives, distributes among the men, their portion in this world according to the acts performed by a person, good or bad. Those are the results of God's arrangements, agreeable to the acts of a former life.[111] They attain the states according to their merits or sins.[112] A snake (*sarpa*) states that the person is born as a man or attains heaven (*svarga*) or birth as an animal according to his actions.[113] The *Mbh.* has presented a detailed description of a person who kills others, does not love anybody, goes to hell and if he is freed from hell, he is born as human being but his life is short. If his behaviour is of the opposite type, *i.e.* he loves others, does not cause harm to anybody, he goes to the heaven.[114] It is further stated that those who are established in goodness rise upward, the passionate remain in the middle (region) and the dull steeped in the lower tendencies sink downward. Here, the tendencies are related to actions of the man.[115] The *Mbh.* also states that the persons, who perform actions as per the prescribed rites which bear merits or sins, are entangled (reborn) in the cycle of the world and attain the states according to their merits or sins.[116]

The doctrine of Karman, however, does not imply that the man is helpless. There are three types of Karmans, *viz. prārabdha, sañcita* and *āgāmin. Prārabdha karman*-s are the *karman*-s of previous birth which have begun to bear fruit. The *samacita karman*-s are the actions of previous birth which are in a seed form. The actions of this life are *āgāmikarman*-s. The man has no control over the first type of *karman*-s, *i.e. prārabdha* ones, he has to endure the evil effects of these past actions. As regards *saṁcita karman*-s and the *āgāmikarman*-s, impressions of these two actions can be overcome by the real knowledge and expiatory rites. Thus, he can safeguard his future by controlling his present actions and wiping off the fruits of *sañcita* actions. Man is at liberty to carve out his future and hence, there is a possibility of release. If it would not have been in the hands of human beings to carve out their future, all the Indian philosophical systems would have lost their purpose and meaning. The fruit of his *sañcita*, present and future action, would be determined by him; it is not a chance. He has full freedom to chalk out his destiny. The same thought has been reflected in the *Mbh.* It states that it is not easy to obtain human life. Having obtained it, one should not allow himself to fall down. He should perform meritorious deeds and try to uplift himself.[117] If he had obtained sin in the past, due to ignorance, he should wipe off the effect of the same by practising penance.[118] Thus, the *Mbh.* has not only reiterated the views of Vedic and Upaniṣadic thoughts but has also provided the solution to wipe out the effects of bad actions performed unknowingly. This deep rooted ideology had shaped the belief system of people in ancient India. The *Mbh.* cherished the same.

Philosophy of the three Yoga-s

As stated in the introductory chapter, Indian philosophers believed that the philosophy is for life and it is to be lived with. The ultimate truth is just not to be known but to be realised. The man has to become one with it. The *Mbh.*, being the literature for the masses, tried to hand over this rich treasure of philosophical thought to them. It reflects an effort to take cognisance of different levels of aspirants, such as the seekers of spiritual knowledge through renunciation (*nivṛtti*), those who are interested in action (*pravṛtti*) and those who are interested in final deliverance but do not know the means to achieve it. To cater to the requirements of different aspirants, the *Mbh.* prescribed different means. Those who sought to know the ultimate truth through knowledge, were advised to follow the path of knowledge, Jñānayoga, which was based on the Vedānta. Others who were desirous to attain the Supreme Self through performance of action were prescribed the path of selfless action, action without the expectation of fruit *viz.* Karmayoga. The masses who were neither able to grasp the metaphysical aspects of Jñānamārga nor could understand the efficacy of the performance of desireless action were expected to follow an easier path of devotion, Bhaktiyoga.

The philosophy of these *Yoga*-s has its own pivotal importance. It will be discussed in this chapter.

Path of Knowledge–*Jñānayoga*

Man in his ignorance considers, this world as real and identifies himself with the body. He is oblivious of his identity with the ultimate principle, the pure consciousness, Brahman. Brahman underlies both the Self and the external world. Brahman, under the influence of *māyā* proliferates into many selves and hence, is considered to be divided into numerous objects and the Souls. The Vedānta philosophy shows the way to dispel this ignorance through right knowledge, *jñāna*.

Jñāna and *vijñāna* are the two kinds of knowledge that the *Bh.G.* recognises.[119] *Vijñāna* enables man to understand the phenomena of existence externally, through intellect. However, it is unable to realise the truth of the ultimate source of existence and the reality within. The Upaniṣad-s believe that it can be grasped only by intuitive knowledge,[120] which is called *jñāna*. The mind is to be turned inward for the development of the intuitive power. To attain this spiritual vision, man has to concentrate his mind on the Supreme Reality, by removing his spiritual blindness.

The Vedānta philosophy prescribes certain prerequisites for the attainment of identity with the Brahman.

1. Man has to cleanse his Soul of the defilement of the body, mind and senses, to develop spiritual vision and remove ignorance.

2. He has to suppress his desires, control his outward moving senses and steady his mind.

3. Having prepared the mind in the above way, he has to practise *śravaṇa, manana* and *nididhyāsana.*

Patañjali's Yogic practice prescribes the means to train the mind in the right direction. It lays down a psychic discipline to clear the intellect and free the mind of its illusions. It elevates the aspirant from the mortal level to the supernatural one and enables him to get direct perception of the Reality.[121]

The *Mbh.* adopts these means and prescribes the path of knowledge (*jñānamārga*). This yoga would empower the aspirant to acquire the right knowledge to reach the highest goal. The *Mbh.* states that there is nothing sacred like *jñāna* and the *yoga* would enable an aspirant to attain it in due course.[122] The first step towards acquiring *jñāna* is to approach an experienced and enlightened teacher to impart the knowledge of the Absolute. He should then begin to investigate (*pariprasna*).[123] Having obtained the Supreme knowledge, a *yogin* can perceive that all beings are stationed in the Supreme Self.[124] He then realises that the soul (*ātman*) is eternal, unborn and immortal.[125] It is different from the body, which is destructible.[126] One who thinks that he has killed and one who considers that he is killed, both these are ignorant.[127] The entire world is pervaded by that eternal principle, no one can destroy that immortal entity, the Soul.[128]

Thus, the wise man perceives effulgent entity once his ignorance is dispelled by the knowledge of the absolute principle.[129] He attains spiritual impartiality and experiences Brahman within himself, which is unblemished, equally present in all the beings.[130] He identifies himself with the Supreme Self.[131] Thus, a knower of Brahman, who with firm intellect and free from doubt has identified himself with Brahman, enjoys eternal bliss.[132] His defects are washed away, he is not reborn.[133]

The *Mbh.* also states that the self realized-one can live in this world in two ways. One way is, as the Veda-s have prescribed by adherence to total abandonment of action (*saṁnyāsa*) *i.e.* giving up all the actions after self realisation. This is the path of renunciation (*nivṛtti*). Here the path of knowledge, *jñānamārga,* is described as *sananyāsamārga*. The other way *viz.*, the path of action,[134] is the one that was followed by the Mīmāṁsaka-s. The actions performed by them had an expectation of fruits, which creates bondage. The *Mbh.* has synthesised both these paths and developed a novel idea of action (karmayoga), which advises people to renounce the fruit accrued from it. In this *Yoga,* the act is to be viewed as an end in itself and not as a means.

Path of Action–*Karmayoga*

The concept of action (Karman) is not new to Indian philosophy. The idea of action and its association with the idea of the world are reflected in the Upaniṣad-s. It is stated that some enter a womb (*yoni*) for rebirth, some others (those vile, *adharmin*-s) enter inanimate objects. The beings attain the states (*avasthā*-s) as per their knowledge and action.[135]

The word *karman* connotes various meanings. The actions performed with the help of sense organs and organs of action are called *karman.*[136] In that sense no one can remain without performing action even for a moment. However, the *Mbh.* does not refer to this *karman.* The ideal action according to the *Mbh.* is different from that stated by the Mīmāṁsaka-s. It also connotes action to be performed by oneself according to his nature. The actions performed for the sanctification of beings like sacrifice, charity, penance etc. are also treated as *karman*-s.[137] According to the *Mbh., karman* has originated from Brahman[138] and Brahmā created this world.[139] Hence, *karman* is the action within Brahman at the time of the manifestation of the world. Thus, the world comes into existence due to *karman.*

The word *yoga,* too, has many connotations as explained in the chapter on Yoga philosophy. The *Mbh.* defines *yoga* as a special skill, device, intelligent method or graceful way of performing action.[140] According to Tilak, B.G., *yoga* is a device of eliminating natural tendency of *karman*[141] to create a bondage. It also stands for the equanimity of mind.[142] The Yogasūtra-s have advised the aspirants to restrain mental modifications and achieve equanimity of mind.[143] Karmayoga expects one to have equanimity of mind by performing actions without expecting the fruits thereof.

The *Mbh.* advises people to act as per one's own nature.[144] The activity (*karman*) is natural not only to mankind. It is so even to the creator of the world. However, the activity has to be directed appropriately. Otherwise it may lead to the achievement of selfish and material gains. The *Mbh.* indicates this direction *viz.* performance of duties according to one's own nature (*svabhāva*) This is the *svadharma* of man.

A man whose undertakings are free from desire, whose actions are burnt up in the fire of wisdom, is a man of learning.[145] The man who has abandoned attachment for the fruit of action, who is ever content, who does not depend on any one, though appears to be performing action, in reality, does not function. The person, who sees action in inaction and inaction in action, is a *yogin* in the real sense of the term. He accomplishes all his works.[146] In this state, which is *naiṣkarmya,* the *yogin* realises that he is not the doer since he is not different from the Supreme Self, which is the motivating force behind the action.

Even though, the *yogin* does not have any fruit in view, the fruit accrues. It leads to the spiritual betterment of the *yogin* and the welfare of the entire society. Yogin's *karman* yields neither sins nor merits. Such a person is ever satisfied with whatever comes by, he is beyond the dualities of opposites, free from jealousy and equanimous in all the situations. He is not bound by his actions. His actions are sacrifices in true nature, with attachments sundered, steady in mind, he is released.[147]

Action without expectation of fruit implies non pre-supposition of the fruit. In the case of Arjuna, before performing his action *viz.* to fight the war, he was thinking about the consequences of his action, which diverted his thought from the task before him. Moreover, his dejection too was not justifiable.

He was not supposed to think about the consequence when the decision to fight was taken considering all the pros and cons of the same. It is inappropriate to abandon action at the crucial period. Such an abandonment is a *tāmasika* one.[148] If one abandons action since it is troublesome or due to fear of bodily affliction, such renouncement (*tyāga*) would be of *rājasa* type, it would not yield fruit.[149] The action, which is performed without desire or without the expectation of fruit is the *sāttvika* type of action.[150]

According to the *Mbh.,* fruits are bad, good or of mixed nature. Persons who do not practise charity obtain these fruits after death. The *Saṁnyāsin*-s are not bound by such fruits.[151] He who treats *karman* as the Brahman and sacrifices it to the Brahman is the Brahman himself.[152] Thus, *Karmayoga* is a means to know the Supreme Brahman and attain the final release. King Janaka was the example of a man enlightened, who enjoyed the state of release in life. He was a true *karmayogin* who, inspite of performance of royal and household duties, continued to practise selfless action without yearning for fruits. He attained the state of liberation in life, *jīvanmukta*.

Knowing very well that the vast majority of people cannot perform actions with the spirit of dedication, without the desire to have the fruit, the *Mbh.* propounded *bhaktiyoga,* which was the easiest path following which one can achieve salvation.

Path of Devotion–*Bhaktiyoga*

The word 'Bhakti' is derived from the root √*bhaj* to worship, to wait upon, to serve etc. Hence, *bhakti* means service to someone who is superior to the worshipper. This service is to be rendered with love and affection. It is an intense love of God, not motivated by any desire. This concept of *bhakti* indicates the doctrine of the right activity of the emotional aspect of man which is distinct from knowledge or action.

The meaning of *yoga* in the *Mbh., Bh.G.* in particular, is construed as getting to God, relating oneself to the power that rules the universe. It is yoking of all the forces of heart, mind and will to God.[153]

In the Upaniṣadic period, an era of reflective speculation, the fourth goal of life *viz.* release (*mokṣa*) gained importance. It was believed that mere sacrifice would not enable an aspirant to attain the final goal, *i.e.* the state of being one with the Soul. *Kaṭh. Up.* states that Ātman can neither be reached by discourse nor by keen intellect.[154] It can be attained by the people who are selected by Him (Supreme Soul). The concept of *bhakti* was developed by the *Mbh.* on similar lines.

During the age of the *Mbh.,* there were various sects and pantheons worshipping different deities. There was a need to bring about unity among them. The path of knowledge (*jñānamārga*) was pursued by the intelligentsia and by those who could not perform rigid sacrifices and pay sacrificial fee and spend a lot for the performance of sacrifice. Animal sacrifice was rampant. Gautama Buddha's teachings of mercy for all creatures, opposition for ceremonials, the idea of human brotherhood which undermined the growing rigours of caste, the institution of the *saṅgha* and its spirit of discipline attracted the masses. The Brāhmanic religion had to undergo a transformation to attract the masses toward it. There was dire necessity to simplify the religious practices. This task of simplification was undertaken by the *Mbh.* It laid down a path which was within the reach of all, *i.e.* devotion to God, *bhakti.*[155]

Kṛṣṇa simplified the means of worship to such an extent that an offering of fruits, flowers, leaves or even water was sufficient.[156] Kṛṣṇa further stated that devotion to any deity would ultimately enable the devotee to reach him.[157] He assured that whosoever worshipped him would attain complete salvation (*mokṣa*). In this salvation, there was no fear for the devotee of being left to himself. Kṛṣṇa was certain about the merging of the devotee into the God.[158] The devotee, by an unswerving devotion for Him, can know Him, see Him and enter into Him.[159] He promised them that He would look after them.[160] The fruitful consequence of this assurance is evident in the case of the Pāṇḍva-s who were helped by him every now and then. He was aware of the devotion of Bhīṣma and hence he imparted divine knowledge of the three times to him when he was lying on the deathbed of arrows.[161]

According to Śrīkṛṣṇa, even a man of bad conduct, who worshipped him, and had resorted to him, was to be deemed good. He would obtain tranquility. He would never be ruined. Even those who are of sinful birth, women, Vaiśyas and Śūdras, who resort to Him would attain the Supreme goal. Then what to speak of holy Brāhmin-s and royal saints who are his devotees?[162] The *yogin*, who resorts to him with his mind and intellect set on Him, is dear to Him. One who is friendly and liked by all, who is indifferent to pleasure, fear, aversion etc., one who is desireless, pure, clever, impartial, free from fear, has renounced all undertakings and worships Him is dear to Him.[163] A person who carries out His work, who has delivered himself to Him, devoid of attachment and enmity reaches Him.[164] Thus, whosoever is united with the God is liberated. He attains a state similar to that of the God. He enjoys the company of the God. He assured his worshippers that He will free those who resort to Him from the ocean of worldly affairs.[165] All sorts of devotees, the followers of *Jñānayoga, Karmayoga* have access to Him. Śrīkṛṣṇa stated that the aspirants, who had the capacity to merge into the Supreme Soul (Brahmabhāva) through the knowledge of the Self, would attain the fourth state of Bhakti (*parābhakti*).[166] He also stated that the wise (*jñānin*), who knows Him to be the Supreme Self (Parama Puruṣa), becomes omniscient and worships Him.[167] Śrīkṛṣ ṇa further stated that through one's own action (*karman*), one attains the state of detachment by worshipping the God.[168] He, therefore, advised Arjuna to consign unto Him all his *karman*-s and assured that the devotee who has faith in him would attain release through his actions.[169] He has not left even the *yogins* outside the ambit of *bhakti*, when he stated that the one who worships Him is a Yogin.[170] Thus, according to the *Mbh.*, devotion (*bhakti*) is a means which would lead to the attainment of the ultimate truth. Thus, there is an attempt to bring these three paths in harmony with one another. Śrīkṛṣṇa not only simplified the means of worship but made the God approachable by all. He emphasized that God lives in each individual.

The teaching of the three *yoga*-s propounded in the *Bh. G.* lays down distinct ways of realisation of the ultimate truth. However, each path complements the other two. Moreover, the practice of Pātañjala Yoga would enable the aspirant to turn his mind inward by controlling his senses. The *Jñānayoga* which involves study of the truth, practice of penance, celibacy would reveal to him the Self within. These means would toughen him to face the rigours of spirituality. There is a need to realise the futility of life to attain the equanimity of mind. The *Karmayoga* would provide the means to develop aversion toward the worldly things. To attract the masses towards any of these practices, their fear of unknown, *i.e.* the state after death is to be allayed. They would need an assurance that they would not be all alone to face it. The device to attain it is *Bhaktiyoga*. Thus, the *Mbh.* had made a fool proof arrangement to encourage the aspirants to practise any one or more of these *yoga*-s to attain the self-realisation in the present life and final beatitude thereafter.

Kṛṣṇa's tolerance towards different pantheistic, theistic and transcendental views shows his belief in the thought that there is one substratum underlying them all. There is only one entity in the world, whether one calls it as Brahman, Īśvara, God or any other deity preferred by him. It shows the comprehensive outlook of the Mahābhāratakāra and the belief in the principle of unity. The *Mbh.* leaves a scope for the Upaniṣdic vision to the new conditions prevailing at the time of the *Mbh.* Kṛṣṇa demonstrated that the speculative, spiritual idealism of the Upaniṣad-s had the scope for fulfillment of personal, emotional requirements of human nature.[171] The shift from the reflective philosophy to the practical one revealed the humane aspect of metaphysical speculation. The field of knowledge of the Supreme Self was no more the domain of the intellectuals, *yogin*-s etc. The masses too had an access to that knowledge. It opened the new vistas of knowledge for the general population. It provided for them an opportunity to attain the fourth goal of life (*mokṣa*) prescribed by the scriptures. This was the leap forward towards the assimilation of the masses to the religious stream and was instrumental in halting the exodus of intelligentsia and masses alike to the Buddhist faith.

Cosmogony in the *Mbh.*

Human beings ponder over the happenings in the nature. They are interested in the search for the ultimate cause of cosmos, that is the search for the genesis of the universe. Such speculations are reflected in Indian philosophical literature right from the Ṛgvedic age. It states "In the beginning there was only that one (*tad ekam*). It was hidden in the dark shell (*apraketam salilam*). Out of this it was born. It was desire (*kāma*), the first seed of mind. The sages found in their hearts, through wisdom, the bond of the existent in the non-existent."[172] Also it was *vāc,* which in the beginning actuated the father of the universe and was again born in the water, distributed herself over living beings.[173] The *Ṛv.* also states, "There was one and only one *Sat* perceptible. However, wise people say they are many."[174] The *Tait. Up.* echoes this thought when it says, "At first there was no (phenomenal) world, there was only (Brahman) unmanifested (*asat*), the world was then in that (Brahman). The world with all its names and forms then manifested itself. It was as if that (Brahman) created it this way."

The Brahman created it, it came to be called as *sukṛta* (*i.e.* "well created" or "self created").[175]

The *Mbh.* expresses this creation process when it says that the Brahman is the unmanifest, it is the cause of order (*ṛtam*); it is existence (*satyam*) known (*veditam*), knowable (*veditavyam*). It is the Ātman of every being, moving, unmoving, it is excellent, benevolent.[176] All the moveable and immovable things have emanated from *satya.*[177] It also states that the world was enveloped with darkness. It alone existed there. It is the first cause of the cosmos, it is *Satyam,* Truth, Existence. It is the light (*jyotiḥ*) and the eternal (*sanātana*). It is imperceptible, it pervades the entire world, it is unimaginable, it is being (*sat*) and it is non-being (*asat*)."[178]

It was also speculated that it was water, that was the source of the entire cosmos. The *Br. Up.* states "In the beginning truly, the water alone existed, from the waters was born Satya or Truth; Satya created Brahman, Brahman gave birth to Prajāpati and from Prajāpati were born the gods; these gods worship Satya alone."[179] Ranade, R.D. states that no personal being or Ātman existed originally. It was water alone that existed and from water everything came into existence later. Here, it is Satya that created Brahman. Hence, Ranade, R.D. opines that the word 'Brahman' is not to be understood as Primal Reality and Satya, too, being born from water is to be considered as the ultimate 'concrete' existence.[180]

The *Mbh.* equates Satyam with the Brahman and vice-a-versa probably due to the Upaniṣadic statements such as, "He (Brahman) wished to be born as many. He then thought and decided and created all that exists. Having created, He entered into it all and also became formless, empirically true or its opposite, that Truth manifested itself. Whatever there is, (the knowers of Brahman) refer to it (Brahman) as Truth."[181]

The *Mbh.* also states that there was only water everywhere, there was no space (*ākāśa*) nor the earth. Everywhere there was darkness. This ocean of water was very deep and boundless. In this water, Pitāmaha was born. Thereafter, he created air, fire, water, the sun, the space above and the earth below etc.[182]

The *Ch. Up.* states that fire was the first to evolve from the primeval Being. From fire, water evolved and from water, the earth.[183] Thus, according to this Upaniṣad, the fire is not considered as the very origin of all the things. However, in the *Mbh.,*

Bṛhaspati, while praising *Agni,* eulogizes fire as the creator of all the three worlds. It has also depicted fire as the absorbent of all the worlds.[184] Fire as the creator, sustainer and the destroyer has also appeared in the *Ādi P.*[185]

The *Ch. Up.* states, "All the beings emerge from space and finally absorb into it. Space is greater than all the things. It is the final habitat."[186] The *Mbh.* states that in the beginning there was only space, no moon, sun or air. From this space, water emanated, from it air.[187]

The *Ch. Up.* describes Brahman as '*Tajjalan*'.[188] Here, *tat* is 'Brahman', *jan* means 'arisen', *li* means 'to disappear' and *an* means 'breath' as per Śaṅkara's commentary.[189] Thus, Brahman is the principle which creates and sustains the universe and into which it (universe) gets absorbed. The *Tait. Up.* strengthens this view when it says "All these beings are created from Him. Having born they live and proceed towards Him, and ultimately they resolve in Him."[190] This *Up.* further professes that "He desired I will become many, will propagate myself. Accordingly, he practised self mortification. Then he created the entire universe, whatever exists. Having created it he entered into it."[191] The originator, the sustainer and absorbent nature of the Brahman is brought out by Lord Kṛṣṇa in the *Mbh.* He says, "I have, in my manifest form pervaded all the universe; all beings dwell in me, but I dwell not in them. Nor yet in me do all beings dwell. Behold my power as the Lord! As the Sustainer of all beings, yet not dwelling in beings, it is my Self that brings beings to existence. All beings come to my Nature when their Period comes to an end. When the Period begins, I send them forth again."[192] Here by *bhūtā*-s the material side of beings developed by Prakṛti and Puruṣa is stressed. It implies the creation of lower nature whereas Kṛṣṇa who is Brahman incarnate is of higher nature. Thus, the *bhūtā*-s are equivalent to body on the individual level where embodied soul (*kṣetrajña*) is seperate from the body (*kṣetra*). Kṣetrajña is related to the Supreme Soul. Thus, the *bhūtā*-s which are equivalent to *kṣetra* cannot said to be the part of the Supreme

Self. But the Supreme Self like the embodied Self can dwell in the *bhūtā*-s. In the same section, the Lord declares himself to be the father, the mother, the supporter, the grandsire, an object of knowledge, the purifier, the syllable Oṁ, the *Ṛk, Sāman,* the origin and dissolutin, the witness, the ground, the resting place, imperishable seed, that is, everything in the world being him.[193] The same features of the Lord are reflected in the *Śānti P.* too.[194]

In the *Taitt. Up.* there is a progressive order of origination of inorganic bodies from the Ātman. From the Ātman, there issues forth (*sambhūti*) the space, from the space, air, from air fire emanates, from fire waters and from waters the earth.[195] Here, there is not a creation but emanation of inorganic bodies from the Ātman, the emanation of all the five elements one after the other. Thus, it is not the creation but emanation from the Ātman which is the only entity according to Upaniṣadic thought. For the creation there is a necessity of other element which is not necessary for the emanation (*saṁbhūti*). Thus, absoluteness of the Brahman is maintained here. There is one more example of emanation theory which appears in the *Muṇḍ. Up.* which draws an excellent picture of the origination of the world from the Brahman, it describes "just as a spider creates and retracts its threads, as the herbs and trees grow upon the surface of the earth, just as from living person the hair of the head and body grow, similarly, from this immutable Brahman does the entire universe spring."[196]

This emanation theory of the world from the immutable principle is reflected in the *Śānti P.* When Manu says, from this immutable, the space emanates. Here the word *jāyate* implies emanation. From space air, from air fire, from fire waters and from the waters this earth originates. It further explains that after the death these beings merge in water, from water to fire, from fire to air and from air to the space.[197] Thus, the world merges into the elements in the same manner in which it originated, however, in the reverse order.

The emanation of the world through imperceptible, immutable, eternal principle is again illustrated in the *Śānti P.*, which states from this immutable principle all beings emanate.[198] However, there is an intermediator which is called *Mahat,* and then this Mahat element, *i.e.* intelligence in the form of a god created space, then from space waters, from waters fire and air, from the combined element of fire and air there is a creation of the earth.[199] Thus, here there is a change in the order of elements and there is a combination of elements, as compared to the Upaniṣadic concept. Also, here there is a combination of two theories of creation of the cosmos. One that is of personalised creation by Mahat god but from him there is a creation of inorganic elements before the creation of organic world.

This feature connects the cosmic theory propounded in the *Ait. Up.* which narrates that in the beginning Ātman alone existed and that there was no other Self illuminated then whatsoever. Ātman thought to himself, let me create the world. Then he created the worlds of super celestial region of water, heaven with their celestial lights, the mortal earth and the subterranean region of water. Then he created a first world person.[200] Thus, the theory goes on to narrate the creation of the entire world progressively. Due to the characteristics (of Brahman) of manifestation,[201] Brahman was equated with the Prajāpati, the creator in the Brāhmaṇa literature. The *Śatapath Brāhmaṇa* ascribed the job of creation to Brahman which was hitherto ascribed to Prajāpati.[202]

The concept of Prajāpati as the first element of creation and subsequent creation through him has appeared in the *Ch. Up.* There is a myth of creation from the universal egg. It is said that the Parabrahman, Supreme Self created food (*oṣadhi*-s) for sustenance of the beings. Then he created the sun, who had come out of the golden egg. The creative agency, created within the two parts of that egg shell, space. The two parts of the egg shell were the heaven (*dyau*) and the earth (*pṛthvī*).[203] Thus, the myth explains the details of creation. The reflection of this myth appears in *Harivaṁśa* where Vaiśampāyana describes the creation by the Lord Kṛṣṇa who is the creator of the world.[204] He created *Brahmā* who has come out of golden egg and Brahmā created space between the two parts of the egg.[205] *Harivaṁśa* again narrates the creation theory by Prajāpati. It says Prajāpati created this world by dividing himself into two parts, the half of his body became a male and the other half being female. Then he created beings with her help.[206] This is similar to the Upaniṣadic concept of creation through duality of sex. It is propagated that "Brahman alone was in existence. He was afraid that He was alone and hence wished for a second and divided the self into two, he becoming man as well as woman and then there was creation."[207] Thus, here theory of creation by sex division is reflected. This feature is also reflected in the *Mbh.* when the Lord Kṛṣṇa as the creator of the world declares that, "The greater Brahman is my womb (*yoniḥ*), the generative principle, in which I cast my seed and from it *jīva*-s, beings take birth."[208]

In Sāṁkhya philosophy, Prakṛti alone creates in the presence of Puruṣa where Puruṣa is a passive element. Whereas, in the *Mbh.*, the Lord being a creator, places his seed in the great Brahman which is his womb. Though the great Brahman is the same as Prakṛti of Sāṁkhya-s, the concept of the Lord being a male and Mahadbrahma as the female counterpart is similar to the Upaniṣadic concept of duel sex. The Sāṁkhya concept of Mahadbrahma has been applied to clarify the Upaniṣadic idea of duel sex. This shows deep influence of the Upaniṣadic philosophy on the *Mbh.*

In *Kauṣi. Up.*, Brahman speaks to the soul, "The primeval waters are my universe (as *hiraṇyagarbha*) and it is thine."[209] *Ait. Up.* states that he deliberated "I will create the world, the ocean, the realms of light, death, the waters (*ambhas, marīcin, maram, āpas*)."[210] Thus, all these are theories of personalised creation. In the *Mbh.* Kṛṣṇa says, "I am the first cause of this world and all this world is my creation."[211]

The *Muṇḍ. Up.* propagates a personal impersonal theory of the origin of the universe. It states that at the beginning of the creation, there existed a heavenly 'Formless Person' who was unborn, without mind, lustrous. He transcended even the highest immutable. From him were born life, mind and the senses, ether, air, fire, water and the all-supporting earth.[212] The *Mbh.* describes a somewhat similar theory when it states that there appeared Puruṣa, Hari, resorting to the qualities of Nārāyaṇa. That Puruṣ a was undecaying, immortal, without limit, ungraspable, unborn, truth, non violent, beautiful, consisting of different manifestations, without spite, without form, all pervading, doer of all the actions and eternal. From this Puruṣa, Brahmā was born and all the other creations came into existence.[213]

The *Ādi. P.* describes that this entire universe is created by Puruṣa. He has occupied all the things in the world. All the trees, four leggeds, bipeds; In fact, all the living things were conceived by him.[214]

There are also theistic theories of creation in the *Śveta. Up.*, which are reflected in the *Mbh.* The *Śveta. Up.* considers Rudra as the Supreme Godhead who creates this world, is the Supreme Cause, the lord of all souls, he has neither any generator nor the protector. He is self-subsisting, the mover of the unmoving, primal seed etc.[215] Ranade, R.D. opines that the *Śveta. Up.* has at many places equated the god Śiva with the Supreme Godhead. The *Mbh.*, too, states that Śaṅkara has created moveable and immovable, *i.e.* animate and inanimate things. However, it is Prajāpati who has created Śaṅkara. Here, Kṛṣṇa eulogizes that there is no deity greater than Śaṅkara since he has created all the beings.[216] However, elsewhere the *Mbh.* considers Nārāyaṇa as the godhead and the creator of the world.[217] *Āśva. P.* also considers Visṇu as the creator of the world.[218]

The *Tait. Up.* says that, "In reality, it is the Brahman out of which these beings arise."[219] This function of Brahman, Ātman appears at many places in the *Mbh.* Kṛṣṇa states, "My spirit is the source of all the beings."[220] and "Entering the earth, I support all the beings."[221] The *Āraṇ. P.* too describes the creative role of Ātman. It states, "Having created gods and human beings, semi divine beings (*gandharva-s*), serpents and demons, movable and immovable things he destroys them by his *māyā*."[222] The *Śānti. P.* too states that it is Brahman alone who created all the moveable and immovable things in the world.[223]

In the same Parvan, it is also stated that Kāla, time which is beginningless, eternal creates all the beings and it is *Kāla* which positions itself for the creation of the beings.[224]

Finally the *Śve. Up.* sums up the different theories of creation when it questions "some people say that it is Time, others say nature, some say necessity, others chance, some others as element or the Person. Still others the combination of those and yet a few others say the Ātman, which is the cause of all things whatsoever."[225]

The *Mbh.* has covered the speculations regarding the origin of the universe from *Ṛv.* to not only those appearing in the Upaniṣad-s but those in the Sāṁkhya, Yoga, theistic theories like Vaiṣṇavism, Śaivism as well as creation by sex division etc., which indicate the process of synthesizing. This was done, apparently with a view to bring together different theistic cults, philosophical systems and finally to establish the thought that the entities considered to be the creators of the world, by them are not different from one another but are the different forms of one entity. There is only one creator of this universe.

The cosmological accounts in the Upaniṣad-s and the *Mbh.* exhibit the impetus of the ultimate principle to unfold itself in the world. This creative impulse is present in the beings too, which surfaces as Kāma in them. Thus, the topic of creation is the substratum of life, cosmic as well as individual.

It forms a vital part of any philosophy. In fact, as stated by Jacobi, H., cosmological speculations are the first manifestations of philosophical thought throughout the world.[226] The Mahābhāratakāra incorporated the cosmological speculations regarding the Vedānta, Sāṁkhya, Yoga and the like in order to appeal to masses. This transitional stage might have further led to similar attempts undertaken by the composers of the Purāṇa-s.

It can be concluded that the *Mbh.,* on the lines of Upaniṣad-s, considers that there is only one entity which creates,[227] sustains and governs this world *viz.* Brahman.[228] The Uttama Puruṣa of the *Bh. G.* is equivalent to Brahman who is over and above the mutable and immutable principles.[229] It also refers to the Ultimate Principle as the twenty-fifth and twenty-sixth element and states that the Unmanifest Supreme Self and the individual self are not different from each other.[230] The *Mbh.* has thus synthesized the Sāmakhya and the Yoga principles. However, they are utilized to establish the Upaniṣadic concept of the Supreme Self, Brahman. Thus, there is a great influence of Upaniṣadic philosophy on the *Mbh.*

Characters in the *Mbh.* and their Philosophy

Philosophy is a wider concept. It can cover even temperaments, mental inclinations of human beings towards life. Hence, it will be interesting to explore and take note of the philosophies of life, the different perspectives of some prominent characters in the *Mbh.,* with which they viewed their lives. They might have moulded their personalities and shaped their attitudes, temperaments and behavioural patterns. Their brief examination would indicate the same.

Dhṛtarāṣṭra : is a prime character who was mainly responsible for the Mahābhārata war. His intellect was blinded by his love for his son.[231] Being under the sway of Duryodhana his perspective to view the life was obscured. Consequently, he was unable to follow the right counsel of Bhīṣma and Droṇa.[232] His demerits such as delusion, egoistic attitude (*ahaṁkāra*) unsatiated desire, hatred etc. can be compared to the details enlisted in the Yogasūtra-s.[233] His jealousy, crafty nature, covetousness, selfishness, hypocracy and the like can be said to be the outcomes of the predominence of *tamas* element of his Prakṛti as per the principles of Sāṁkhya philosophy.

Duryodhana : too was jealous and revengeful.[234]

These traits of his character alongwith the utmost importance which he attached to the fulfillment of his desires and his feeling of hatred were due to the lack of self control as explained in the Yogasūtra-s.[235] However, he was a true warrior (*kṣatriya*)[236] and had full confidence in his valour.[237] He was a good administrator and a benevolent king.[238] This shows that at times *tamas* element predominated his nature, at the same time he also has *rājas* and *sāttvika* characteristics.

Duḥśāsana : His stupidity and inability to think independently before obeying the orders of Duryodhana, his senseless action leading to Draupadi's miserable plight[239] show the preponderance of *tamas* element as the main trait of his nature.

Śakuni : His cunningness, keenness for not missing even a single opportunity to harass Pāṇḍava-s with the help of Duryodhana and his attempt to instigate Duryodhana to insult them[240] are indicative of *tamas* element predominating his Prakṛti.

Karṇa : He was brought up by a Sūta. The status of Sūta was inferior to that of Kṣatriya-s. For the same reason people humiliated him. Due to the inferiority complex and jealousy towards Arjuna's skill, he was antagonistic towards the Pāṇḍava-s.[241] Karṇa was a man of split personality. On the one hand, he was a donor par excellence who prized the values of generosity and cherishment of his own reputation[242] but on the other hand his revengeful nature overshadowed his virtues. His vow of bestowing gifts was a *kāmya* one, as he was motivated to observe it with a view to attain glory.[243] Hence, it was not an ideal or *sāttvika* type of donation, but of a *rājasa* type. However, he was the most faithful friend of Duryodhana. He always felt obliged by Duryodhana's favour. He refused to desert Duryodhana even after knowing his relation with the Pāṇḍava-s.[244] His outlook towards life was narrow. He strived for the attainment of desirable (*preyas*) rather than for beneficial (*śreyas*). He, thus, had a combination of *sattva, rajas* and *tamas* elements in his Prakṛti.

Droṇācārya : A Brāhmaṇa by birth, possessed the spirit of magnanimity (*brāhmatejas*), he could have utilized it to prevent Duryodhana from committing sins. However, he preferred to be a mute spectator, when Draupadi was being insulted in the assembly. Draupadi, therefore, rightly remarked that *sattva* element was lacking in Droṇa.[245] He too, was revengeful, a quality unbecoming of a Brāhmaṇa. He took revenge by defeating Drupada through his discriples.[246] Having once accepted the occupation of a warrior (*kṣātravṛtti*), abandonment of weapons in the Mahābhārata war,[247] was not an appropriate deed on his part. Thus, inspite of having an advantageous position of being a Brāhmaṇa and possessing the prowess of Kṣatriya, he failed to utilised them at appropriate time. His utterance that a man is a slave of wealth[248] followed by his undertaking thereafter reflects his outlook towards life.

Bhīṣma : A man of principles and a towering personality of the epic, is seem to have followed the Upaniṣadic instructions as, "Never deviate from truth and stick to your duties."[249] He was a self restrained man who has renounced his right to kingdom and the right of marriage for the happiness of his father and had spent his entire life for serving Kuru dynasty. As per the definition of the knower of *dharma* in the *Mbh.* as "One who by his action, mind and speech is continuously engrossed in the welfare of other,[250] he can be regarded as the knower of *dharma*" in the true sense of the term. He highly valued the discrimination between just and unjust. He did not hesitate to fight even with Paraśurāma, his own preceptor.[251] He was a Karmayogin as described in the *Bh. G.*[252]

His detachment towards life was so great that he even revealed the secret of his death to Pāṇḍava-s who were fighting with him.[253] He imparted instruction to Yudhiṣṭhira regarding the duties of a king, statecraft, philosophy etc. even when he was on deathbed.[254] This reminds us of a detached man (*virakta*) described in the Yogasūtra-s.[255] He was a *jīvanmukta*, who was characterised by ideal traits of a Jñānayogin and Karmayogin. He not only preached philosophy, but lived it. Hence one can conclude that his outlook towards life was unique, in fact difficult to emulate. He was a royal sage (*rājarṣi*) in the true sense of the term with the element of *sattva* predominating in him.

Vidura : Born of a Śūdra mother and believing in the *varṇāśrama dharma,*[256] he was loyal to his master and duties.[257] He accompanied Dṛtarāṣṭra till the end of his life. Like Bhīṣma, he was righteous, truthful[258] and just. He never hesitated to be outspoken while interacting with Dṛtarāṣṭra[259] and Duryodhana.[260] He was a great Yogin, a philosopher and was an incarnation of *dharma.*[261] Sacrificing personal benefits he always strived to help others.[262] He, thus, was a staunch follower of Karmayoga, whose Prakṛti was characterized by the preponderance of *sattva* element.

Gāndhārī : was a magnanimous, virtuous lady, who was loyal and devoted to her husband. She was never blind towards the wrongs done by her sons. She had a keen sense of justice and truth.[263] She always emphasized that the Pāṇḍava-s who were the real heirs to the throne should rule over the entire kingdom.[264] She even reminded Dṛtarāstra, that he should have abandoned Duryodhana who was the cause of destruction of Kuru-s.[265] She could not tolerate the unjust act of Bhīma of hitting Duryodhana's thigh[266] and cursed Śrīkṛṣṇa of being a mute spectator of the destruction of all her sons.[267] Thus, devotion to her husband, truthfulness and justice were the principles she firmly believed in. Her philosophy of life was magnanimous.

Kunti : was a dutiful daughter-in-law, a devoted wife[268] and a caring mother.[269] The only aim of her life was to see to it that her sons become strong and valorous warriors who would fight the wrongdoers (Kaurava-s) and regain their kingdom.[270] She did not induce Pāṇḍava-s to fight Kaurava-s to enjoy royal pleasures.[271] She was an ideal Kṣatriya mother, who practiced *Karmayoga* throughout her life.

Draupadī : was a dutiful and loyal wife (*pativratā*). Her advice to Satyabhāmā corroborated this fact.[272] She was characterized by the lustre of fire. Being a woman from a warrior clan (*kṣatriyāṇi*), she expected her husbands to fight against injustice.[273] Having known that Yudhiṣṭhira was defeated in the game of dice, she thought that every creature is a victim of the will of the God.[274] This reflects her belief in super natural power. At the same time she was a woman of self-respect and resolution. She advised Śrīkṛṣṇa to be irascible with Kaurava-s and expected him not to indulge in a treaty of peace.[275] Thus, at times *rajas* element was dominant in her whereas on other occasion *sattva* element predominated her Prakṛti.

Yudhiṣṭhira : He was an incarnation of *dharma* and a man of virtue. He valued righteousness (*dharma*) more than anything else. He considered truth to be superior to prosperity, kingdom, sons, fame and wealth.[276] He was an epitome of selflessness,[277] virtuosity and moral uprightness.[278] He was patient and believed that well planned and thoughtful action bear fruit only if the destiny is favourable.[279] Thus, there was a preponderance of *sattva* element in his Prakṛti. However, his utter loss in the game of dice indicates the trait of *tamas* element present in him.

Bhīma : Believing in the policy of "Tit for tat", he could never tolerate injustice. To protect the weak and destroy the wicked people was the motto of his life. According to him strength was more important than virtuosity.[280] He believed that hurting ones own near ones was not righteous deed.[281] He firmly believed that a *kṣatriya* who secures victory on the battlefield rules over the earth and one dying on the battlefield would reach the heaven.[282] He truly believed in the Kṣātradharma. According to him, wedging war, sustainance of subjects were the different kinds of austerity to be practised by a Kṣatriya.[283] Thus, there was a preponderance of *rajas* element in him. However, the brutal treatment meted out by him to Kīcaka, Duḥśāsana and Duryodhana indicates the trait of even *tamas* element present in him.

Arjuna : was a self controlled and self-disciplined man, who has conquered his self by subduing his desires and passions.[284]

He was a dedicated student.[285] He was an ideal friend, to be praised for devotion and love. Even Śrikṛṣṇa thought that Arjuna was his friend, disciple and relative.[286] All the qualities that the follower of Yoga is supposed to possess were present in him.[287]

Being an integral part of Mūla Prakṛti, Prakṛti of every individual is exactly similar to it. It is determined on the basis of the predominance of one of these three elements in ones own nature (*svabhāva*). The above observation regarding the various characters in the *Mbh.* show the universal applicability of the principles of Sāṁkha philosophy with the psyche of any person under the sun. For the same reason, the characters on the *Mbh.* also epitomized a combination of these three elements with the preponderance of one of them.

REFERENCES

1. *Encyclopedia of Philosophy,* Vol. 3-4, *op. cit.,* p. 157.
2. Kane, P.V., *op. cit.,* p. XI.
3. Radhakrishnan, S., *Indian Philosophy.* Vol. II. p. 376. also Banerji, S.C., *A Companion to Indian Philosophy,* Delhi, 1996, pp. 60, 177.
4. Hiriyanna, M. *op. cit.,* p. 301.
5. Bahadur, K.P., *The Wisdom of Nyāya,* Delhi, 1988, p. 10.
6. *Encyclopedia of Philosophy, op. cit.,* p. 157.
7. Radhakrishnan, S., *op. cit.,* p. 179.
8. Hiriyanna, M., *op. cit.,* p. 225.
9. Chakravarti, S.C., *op. cit.,* p. 52.
10. Banerji S.C., *op. cit.,* p. 181.
11. Bahadur, K.P., *op. cit.,* p. 10.
12. *Encyclopedia. of Philosophy, op. cit.,* p. 157. also Sinha, J.A., *History of Indian Philosophy,* Pilani, Rajasthan, 1956, p. 451.
13. Radhakrishnan, S., *op. cit.,* p.36.
14. Banerji, S.C., *op. cit.,* p.50; also Bhadur K.P. *op. cit.* p. 10.
15. Hiriyanna, M., *op. cit.,* p. 226.

16. Chakravarti, S.C., *op. cit.*, p. 52.
17. Dixit, S.H., *op. cit.*, p. 184.
18. Banerji, S.C., p. V.
19. Zimmer, H., *op. cit.*, p. 3.
20. Dixit, S.H., *op. cit.*, p. 131.
21. Hiriyanna, M., *op. cit.*, p. 13.
22. Radhakrishnan, S., Moore C.A., *op. cit.*, pp. XVI-XVII.
23. Banerji, S.C., *op. cit.*, p. V.
24. Zimmer, H., *op. cit.*, p. 157.
25. Hiriyanna, M., *op. cit.*, p.155.
26. Radhakrishnan, S., Moore C.A., *op. cit.*, pp. XVI-XVII, also Smith, Vincent A., *The Early History of India*, London, Edinburgh, Glasgow, New York, Toronto, Melbourne, Bombay. 1914., p. 29.
27. *Mait.Up.* VII. 9 also Hiriyanna, M., *op. cit.*, p.187.
28. Dixit, S.H., *op. cit.*, p. 98.
29. *Vātsyāyana – Nyāyasūtra Bhāṣya* 4. 1-32.
    न च अविषया काचित् उपलब्धिः।
30. Bernard Theos, *op. cit.*, p. 23.
31. *Vātsyāyana – Nyāyasūtra Bhāṣya* 1.1.1.
    तत्त्वज्ञानात् निःश्रेयसाधिगमः।
32. *Ibid.*, 3
    प्रत्यक्षानुमानोपमान शब्दाः प्रमाणानि।
33. *Ibid.*, 9
    आत्मा शरीरैन्द्रियार्थ मन प्रवृत्ति दोष प्रेत्यभाव दुःखापवर्गास्तु प्रमेयम्।
34. *Ibid.*, 24
    यमार्थमधिकृत्य प्रवर्तते तत्प्रयोजनः।
35. *Ibid.*, 25
    लौकिके परोक्षकारणं यस्मिनार्थे बुद्धिसामान्यं सः दृष्टान्तः।
36. *Ibid.*, 26
    तन्त्राधिकरणाभ्युपगमसंस्थितिः सिद्धान्तः।।
37. B.G. Tilak, *op. cit.*, pp. 204-205.

38. *Mbh. Śānti P.* 56.41
प्रत्यक्षेणानुमानेन तथौपम्योपदेशतः।
परीक्ष्यास्ते महाराज स्वे परे चैव सर्वदा।

39. *Mbh. Śānti P.* 173.45-47.
अहमासं पण्डितको हैतुको वेदनिन्दकः।
आन्वीक्षिकीं तर्कविद्यामनुरक्तो निरर्थिकाम्।
हेतुवादान्प्रवदिता वक्ता संसत्सु हेतुमत्।
आक्रोष्टा चाभिवक्ता च ब्रह्मयज्ञेषु वै द्विजान्।
नास्तिकः सर्वशङ्की च मूर्खः पण्डितमानिकः।
तस्येयं फलनिर्वृत्ति सृगालत्वं मम द्विज।

40. *Ibid.,* 48-49
अपि जातु तथा तत्स्यादहोरात्रशतैरपि।
यदहं मानुषीं योनिं सृगालः प्राप्नुयां पुनः।
संतुष्टश्चाप्रमत्तश्च यज्ञदानतपोरतिः।
ज्ञेयज्ञाता भवेयं वै वर्ज्यवर्जयिता तथा।

41. Bahadur, K.P., *op. cit.*, 1988, p. 32.
42. Mullick, Bahadur R.P.N., *op. cit.,* p. 22.
43. Radhakrishnan, S., *op. cit.,* pp.174-175.
44. For more details, see Bernard Theos, *op. cit.,* p. 46.
45. Vaiśeṣikasūtra I.1- 4.
धर्मविशेषप्रसूताद्द्रव्यगुणकर्मसामान्यविशेषसमवायानां।
पदार्थानां साधर्म्यवैधर्म्याभ्यां तत्त्वज्ञानान्निःश्रेयसम्।
पृथिव्यापस्तेजो वायुराकाशं कालो दिगात्मा मन इति द्रव्याणि।
46. *Ibid.,* I. 1. 5.
47. For more details see Macdonell, A.A., *op. cit.,* p. 405, also Sharma Chandradhara, *Indian Philosophy,* Banaras, 1952.
48. *Mbh. Śānti P.* 176.17.
रसनां सर्वगन्धानां स्नेहानां प्राणिनां तथा।
भूमिर्योनिरिह ज्ञेया यस्यां सर्वं प्रसूयते।।
49. *Ibid.,* 177.27-28
तस्य गन्धस्य वक्ष्यामि विस्तराभिहितान्गुणान्।
इष्टश्चानिष्टगन्धश्च मधुरः कटुरेव च।।
निर्हारी संहतः स्निग्धो रूक्षो विशद एव च।
एवं नवविधो ज्ञेयः पार्थिवो गन्धविस्तरः।।

50. *Ibid.*, 29-37.
51. *Ibid.*, 244.3-9, 247.1-8.
52. *Ibid.*, 244. 2.
    आकाशं मारुतो ज्योतिरापः पृथ्वी च पञ्चमी।
    भावाभावौ च कालश्च सर्वभूतेषु पञ्चसु॥
53. *Ibid.*, 224.71[ab]
    विहितं कालनानात्वमनादिनिधनं तथा।
54. *Vai. Su.* II 1-4.
    रूपरसगन्धस्पर्शवती पृथिवी।
    रूपरसस्पर्शवत्य आपो द्रवाः स्निग्धाः॥
    तेजो रूपस्पर्शवत्।
    स्पर्शवान् वायुः॥
    also *Ibid.*, II. 2. 2-5.
55. *Ibid.*, VII 1. 2-6.
56. Tilak, B.G., *op. cit.*, p. 203.
57. Radhakrishnan, S., *Indian Philosophy*, Vol. II, *op. cit.*, p. 375.
58. Monier Williams M., *Hinduism*, Calcutta. 1877, p. 140.
59. For more details see *Ibid.*, p. 140.
60. Śabara's commentary on *Jaimini-Sūtra*-s, VI. 1.1.
61. Dange, S.A., *op. cit.*, p. 276.
62. *Mbh. Bh. P.* 24. 43.
    कामात्मानः स्वर्गपरा जन्मकर्मफलप्रदाम्।
    क्रियाविशेषबहुलां भोगैश्वर्यगतिं प्रति॥
63. *Ibid.*, 44.
    भोगैश्वर्यप्रसक्तानां तयापहृतचेतसाम्।
    व्यवसायात्मिका बुद्धिः समाधौ न विधीयते॥
64. *Mbh. Bh. P.* 24. 45-46.
65. *Ibid.*, 47.
    कर्मण्येवाधिकारस्ते मा फलेषु कदाचन।
    मा कर्मफलहेतुर्भूर्मा ते सङ्गोऽस्त्वकर्मणि॥
66. *Ibid.*, 38.17

आत्मसंभाविताः स्तब्धा धनमानमदान्विताः।
यजन्ते नामयज्ञैस्ते दम्भेनाविधिपूर्वकम्॥

67. *Ibid.*, 40.5

    यज्ञदानतपःकर्म न त्याज्यं कार्यमेवतत्।
    यज्ञो दानं तपश्चैव पावनानि मनीषिणाम्॥

68. *Ibid.*, 6

    एतान्यपि तु कर्माणि सङ्गं त्यक्त्वा फलानि च।
    कर्तव्यानीति मे पार्थ निश्चितं मतमुत्तमम्॥

69. *Ibid.*, 9

    कार्यमित्येव यत्कर्म नियतं क्रियतेऽर्जुन।
    सङ्गं त्यक्त्वा फलं चैव स त्यागः सात्त्विको मतः॥

70. *Mbh. Śānti P.* 307-14

    द्रष्टा स्वर्गस्य न ह्यस्ति तथैव नरकस्य च।
    आगमांस्त्वनतिक्रम्य दद्याच्चैव यजेत च॥

71. *Ibid.*, 8.27

    अध्येतव्या त्रयी विद्या भवितव्यं विपश्चिता।
    सर्वथा धनमाहार्यं यष्टव्यं चापि यत्नतः॥

72. *Ibid.*, 20.10-14.
73. *Ibid., Bh. P.* 26.23-28.
74. *Ibid.*, 25.10-12.
75. *Ibid.*, 14.
76. *Ibid.*, 15.
77. *Ibid.*, 31.24[ab]

    अहं हि सर्वयज्ञानां भोक्ता च प्रभुरेव च।

78. *Abhidhammakośa* III. 26. q. by Umesh Mishra, *History of India Philosophy,* Allahabad, 1957, p. 328.
79. *Mbh. Śānti P.* 211.31

    अविद्याकर्मचेष्टानां केचिदाहुः पुनर्भवम्।
    कारणं लोभमोहौ तु दोषाणां च निषेवणम्॥

80. *Ibid.*, 32-35.
81. *Ibid., Bh. P.* 38.8.

असत्यमप्रतिष्ठं ते जगदाहुरनीश्वरम्।
अपरस्परसंभूतं किमन्यत्कामहैतुकम्।।

82. For more details see Umesh Mishra, *History of Indian Philosophy,* pp. 197-198.
83. *Mbh. Śānti P.* 19.23-24.
84. *Ibid.,* 211. 22-26.
85. *Ibid.,* 27-28.
86. *Ibid.,* 229.3-6.
87. *Ibid., Āśva P.* 6.18.

राजन्नङ्गिरसः पुत्रः संवर्तो नाम धार्मिकः।
चङ्क्रमीति दिशः सर्वा दिग्वासा मोहयन्प्रजाः।।

88. Radhakrishnn, S., *op. cit.,* Vol. I p. 484.
89. *Mbh. Āśva P.* 6-19. 23. also *Ibid.,* 7. 17.
90. *Gautama's Kalpa Sūtras.* II. 19-23, IX. 70.
91. *Ibid., Āraṇ. P.* 198.91

अनसूया क्षमा शान्तिः संतोष प्रियवादिता।
कामक्रोधपरित्यागः शिष्टाचारनिषेवणम्।।

92. *Ibid.,* 57-62.
93. *Ibid., Śānti P.* 156-5[ab]

सत्यं धर्मस्तपो योगः सत्यं ब्रह्म सनातनम्।

94. *Ibid., Śānti P.* 183.1-5.
95. *Ibid., Āraṇ. P.* 200.2.

श्रुतिप्रमाणो धर्मो हि वृद्धानामिति भाषितम्।
सूक्ष्मा गतिर्हि धर्मस्य बहुशाखा ह्यनन्तिका।।

96. *Ibid., Śānti* P. 156.4, 5[ab]

सत्यं सत्सु सदा धर्मः सत्यं धर्मः सनातनः।
सत्यमेव नमस्येत सत्यं हि परमा गतिः।

97. *Ibid., Bh. P.* 27. 20 also *Ibid., Āraṇ. P.* 178. 9-10, 12.
98. *Ibid., Śānti* P. 123.5-14.
99. *Br. Up.* III.2.13

पुण्यौ वै पुण्येन कर्मणा भवति पापः पापेन।

100. *Ibid., Anu P.*6.6-7

यादृशं वपते बीजं क्षेत्रमासाद्य कर्षकः।
सुकृते दुष्कृते वापि तादृशं लभते फलम्।।
यथा बीजं विना क्षेत्रमुप्तं भवति निष्फलम्।
तथा पुरुषकारेण विना दैवं न सिध्यति।।

101. *Ibid., Āraṇ. P.* 178.9-12.

102. *Br. Up.* IV. 4.23.

तस्मादेवंविच्छांतो दान्त उपरतस्तितिक्षुः समाहितो।
भूत्वा आत्मन्यात्मानं पश्यति। सर्वमात्मानं पश्यति।
नैनं पाप्मा तरति, सर्वं पाप्मानं तरति,
नैनं पाप्मा तपति, सर्वं पाप्मानं तपति,
विपापो विरजोऽविचिकित्सो ब्राह्मणो भवति।।

103. *Ṛv.* X. 16.3

सूर्यं चक्षुर्गच्छतु वातमात्मा द्यां च गच्छ पृथिवीं च धर्मणा।
अपो वा गच्छ यदि तत्र ते हितं ओषधीषु प्रतितिष्ठा शरीरेः।।

104. *Br. Up.* IV. 4.5

स वा अयमात्मा यथाकारी यथाचारी तथा भवति साधुकारी साधुर्भवति पापकारी पापो भवति पुण्यः पुण्येन कर्मणा भवति पापः पापेन।

105. *Br. Up.* IV. 4. 1-2.

आत्मा निष्क्रामति चक्षुष्टो वा मूर्ध्नो वाऽन्येभ्यो वा शरीरदेशेभ्यः, तमुत्क्रामंतं प्राणोऽनूत्क्रामति प्राणमनूक्रामन्तं सर्वे प्राणा अनूत्क्रामन्ति.... तं विद्याकर्मणी समन्वारेभेते पूर्वप्रज्ञा च।

106. *Īśā. Up.* 2

कुर्वन्नेवेह कर्माणि जिजीविषेच्छतं समाः।
एवं त्वयि नान्यथेतोऽस्ति न कर्म लिप्यते नरे।।

107. Macdonell, A.A., *History of Sanskrit Literature, op. cit.,* p. 387.

108. Macdonell, A.A., *A Vedic Reader for Students,* Delhi, First Published in English, 1917, p. 170.

109. For more details please refer Macdonell, A.A., *History of Sanskrit Literature, op. cit.,* p. 387.

110. *Br. Up.* IV. 4. 3-5

तद्यथा तृणजलायुका तृणस्यांतं गत्वाऽन्यमाक्रममाक्रम्यात्मानमुपसंहरत्येवमेवायमात्मा इदं शरीरं निहत्य....अन्यमाक्रममाक्रम्या-त्मानमुपसंहरति।.... कल्याणतर रूपं तनुत एवमेवायमात्मा इदं शरीरं निहत्य अविद्यां

गमयित्वाऽन्यन्नवतरं कल्याणतरं रूपं कुरुते, पित्र्यं वा गांधर्वं वा दैवं वा प्रजापत्यं वा ब्राह्मं वाऽन्येषां वा भूतानाम्।

111. *Mbh. Āraṇ. P.* 33. 18-19

एवं हठाच्च दैवाच्च स्वभावात्कर्मणस्तथा।
यानि प्राप्नोति पुरुषस्तत्फलं पूर्वकर्मणः।।
धातापि हि स्वकर्मैव तैस्तैर्हेतुभिरीश्वरः।
विदधाति विभज्येह फलं पूर्वकृतं नृणाम्।।

112. *Ibid. Śānti P.* 279. 9

सुकृतासुकृतं कर्म निषेव्य विविधैः क्रमैः।
दशार्धप्रविभक्तानां भूतानां बहुधा गतिः।

113. *Ibid., Āraṇ. P.* 178. 9

तिस्रो वै गतयो राजन्परिदृष्टाः स्वकर्मभिः।
मानुष्यं स्वर्गवासश्च तिर्यग्योनिश्च तत्त्रिधा।।

114. *Ibid., Anu.* P. 132.47-51

115. *Ibid., Bh. P.* 36.18

ऊर्ध्वं गच्छन्ति सत्त्वस्था मध्ये तिष्ठन्ति राजसाः।
जघन्यगुणवृत्तस्था अधो गच्छन्ति तामसाः।।

116. *Ibid., Śānti* P. 197-15

प्रणीतं कर्मणा मार्गं नीयमानः पुनः पुनः।
प्राप्नोत्ययं कर्मफलं प्रवृद्धं धर्ममात्मवान्।

117. *Ibid.,* 280.3

आयुर्नसुलभं लब्ध्वा नावकर्षेद्विशां पते।
उत्कर्षार्थं प्रयतते नरः पुण्येन कर्मणा।।

118. *Ibid.,* 6[ab]

अज्ञानाद्धि कृतं पापं तपसैवाभिनिर्णुदेत्।

119. *Mbh. Bh. P.* 25.41[cd]

पाप्मानं प्रजहि ह्येनं ज्ञानविज्ञाननाशनम्।

120. *Kaṭh. Up.* I. 3.12

एष सर्वेषु भूतेषु गूढोऽऽत्मा न प्रकाशते।
दृश्यते त्वग्र्यया बुद्धया सूक्ष्मया सूक्ष्मदर्शिभिः।।

121. For more details see Radhakrishnan, S., *op. cit.*, p. 532.

122. *Mbh. Bh. P.* 26.38.

न हि ज्ञानेन सदृश्यं पवित्रमिह विद्यते।
तत्स्वयं योगसंसिद्धः कालेनात्मनि विन्दति।।

123. *Ibid.*, 34

तद्विद्धि प्रणिपातेन परिप्रश्नेन सेवया।
उपदेक्ष्यन्ति ते ज्ञानं ज्ञानिनस्तत्त्वदर्शिनः।।

124. *Ibid.*, 35[cd]

येन भूतान्यशेषेण द्रक्ष्मस्यात्मन्यथो मयि।।

125. *Ibid.*, 24.20[c]

अजो नित्यः शाश्वतोऽयं पुराणो....।।

126. *Ibid.*, 18[abc]

अन्तवन्त इमे देहा नित्यस्योक्ताः शरीरिणः।
अनाशिनोऽप्रमेयस्य.....।।

127. *Ibid.*, 19

य एनं वेत्ति हन्तारं यश्चैनं मन्यते हतम्।
उभौ तौ न विजानीतो नायं हन्ति न हन्यते।।

128. *Ibid.*, 17

अविनाशि तु तद्विद्धि येन सर्वमिदं ततम्।
विनाशमव्ययस्यास्य न कश्चित्कर्तुमर्हति।।

129. *Ibid.*, 27.16

ज्ञानेन तु तदज्ञानं येषां नाशितमात्मनः।
तेषामादित्यवज्ज्ञानं प्रकाशयति तत्परम्।।

130. *Ibid.*, 19

इहैव तैर्जितः सर्गो येषां साम्ये स्थितं मनः।
निर्दोषं हि समं ब्रह्म तस्माद्ब्रह्मणि ते स्थिताः।।

131. *Ibid.*, 28.15[cd]

शान्तिं निर्वाणपरमां मत्संस्थामधिगच्छति।।

132. *Ibid.*, 27.20[cd]-21[cd]

स्थिरबुद्धिरसंमूढो ब्रह्मविद्ब्रह्मणि स्थितः।
स ब्रह्मयोगयुक्तात्मा सुखमक्षयमश्नुते।।

133. *Ibid.*, 17[cd]

गच्छन्त्यपुनरावृत्तिं ज्ञाननिर्धूतकल्मषाः।।

134. *Ibid.*, *Śānti P.* 233.6.7[ab]

द्वाविमावथ पन्थानौ यत्र वेदाः प्रतिष्ठिताः।
प्रवृत्तिलक्षणो धर्मो निवृत्तौ च सुभाषितः।।
कर्मणा बध्यते जन्तुर्विद्यया तु प्रमुच्यते।

135. *Kaṭh. Up.* II. ii. 7
योनिमन्ये प्रपद्यन्ते शरीरत्वाय देहिनः।
स्थाणुमन्येऽनुसंयन्ति यथाकर्म यथाश्रुतम्।।

136. *Mbh. Bh. P.* 40.48[ab]
सहजं कर्म कौन्तेय सदोषमपि न त्यजेत्।

137. *Ibid.*, 5 *op. cit.*

138. *Ibid.*, 25.15.
कर्म ब्रह्मोद्भवं विद्धि ब्रह्माक्षरसमुद्भवम्।
तस्मात्सर्वगतं ब्रह्म नित्यं यज्ञे प्रतिष्ठितम्।।

139. *Ibid.*, 10[ab]

140. *Ibid.*, 24.50[d]
....योगः कर्मसु कौशलम्।।

141. Tilak, B.G., *op. cit.*, p. 77.

142. *Mbh. Bh. P.* 24.48[cd].
सिद्ध्यसिद्ध्योः समो भूत्वा समत्वं योग उच्यते।

143. *Y.S.* I. 2. *op. cit.*

144. *Ibid.*; *Bh. P.* 26.1-3.

145. *Ibid.*, 40.47[cd]
स्वभावनियतं कर्म कुर्वन्नाप्नोति किल्बिषम्।।

146. *Mbh. Bh. P.* 26.18-20
कर्मण्यकर्म यः पश्येदकर्मणि च कर्म यः।
स बुद्धिमान्मनुष्येसु स युक्तः कामसंकल्पवर्जिताः।।
यस्य सर्वे समारम्भाः कामसंकल्पवर्जिताः।
ज्ञानाग्निदग्धकर्माणं तमाहुः पण्डितं बुधाः।।
त्यक्त्वा कर्मफलासङ्गं नित्यतृप्तो निराश्रयः।
कर्मण्यभिप्रवृत्तोऽपि नैव किंचित्करोति सः।।

147. *Ibid.*, 23
गतसङ्गस्य मुक्तस्य ज्ञानावस्थितचेतसः।
यज्ञायाचरतः कर्म समग्रं प्रविलीयते।।

148. *Mbh. Bh. P.* 40.7.
नियतस्य तु संन्यासः कर्मणो नोपपद्यते।
मोहात्तस्य परित्यागस्तामसः परिकीर्तितः।।

149. *Ibid.*, 8
दुःखमित्येव यत्कर्म कायक्लेशभयात्त्यजेत्।
स कृत्वा राजसं त्यागं नैव त्यागफलं लभेत्।।

150. *Ibid.*, 9
कार्यमित्येव यत्कर्म नियतं क्रियतेऽर्जुन।
सङ्गं त्यक्त्वा फलं चैव स त्यागः सात्त्विको मतः।।

151. *Ibid.*, 12
अनिष्टमिष्टं मिश्रं च त्रिविधं कर्मणः फलम्।
भवत्यत्यागिनां प्रेत्य न तु संन्यासिनां क्वचित्।।

152. *Ibid.*, 26.24
ब्रह्मार्पणं ब्रह्म हविर्ब्रह्माग्नौ ब्रह्मणा हुतम्।
ब्रह्मैव तेन गन्तव्यं ब्रह्मकर्मसमाधिना।।

153. Radhakrishnan, S., *op. cit.*, Vol. I, p. 532.

154. *Kaṭh. Up.* I. 2. 23.
नायमात्मा प्रवचनेन लभ्यो न मेधया न बहुना श्रुतेन।

155. *Mbh. Bh. P.* 34.6[cd]-7[ab]

156. *Ibid.*, 31.26.
पत्रं पुष्पं फलं तोयं यो मे भक्त्या प्रयच्छति।
तदहं भक्त्युपहृतमश्नामि प्रयतात्मनः।।

157. *Ibid.*, 29.20-22

158. *Ibid.*, 34.2
मय्यावेश्य मनो ये मां नित्ययुक्ता उपासते।
श्रद्धया परयोपेतास्ते मे युक्ततमा मताः।।

159. *Mbh. Bh. P.* 33.54
भक्त्या त्वनन्यया शक्य अहमेवंविधोऽर्जुन।
ज्ञातुं द्रष्टुं च तत्त्वेन प्रवेष्टुं च परंतप।।

160. *Ibid.*, 31.22
अनन्याश्चिन्तयन्तो मां ये जनाः पर्युपासते।
तेषां नित्याभियुक्ताना योगक्षेमं वहाम्यहम्।।

161. *Ibid., Sānti P.* 47.65

अभिगम्य तु योगेन भक्तिं भीष्मस्य माधवः।
त्रैकाल्यदर्शनं ज्ञानं दिव्यं दातुं ययौ हरिः।।

162. *Ibid., Bh. P.* 31.30-33.

163. *Ibid.*, 34.12-16.

164. *Ibid.*, 33.55.

मत्कर्मकृन्मत्परमों मद्भक्तः सङ्गवर्जितः।
निर्वैरः सर्वभूतेषु यः स मामेति पाण्डव।।

165. *Ibid.*, 34.6[cd]-7[ab]

अनन्येनैव योगेन मां ध्यायन्त उपासते।
तेषामहं समुद्धर्ता मृत्युसंसारसागरात्।।

166. *Ibid.*, 40.54

ब्रह्मभूतः प्रसन्नात्मा न शोचति न काङ्क्षति।
समः सर्वेषु भूतेषु मद्भक्तिं लभते पराम्।।

167. *Ibid.*, 37.19

यो मामेवमसंमूढो जानाति पुरुषोत्तमम्।
स सर्वविद्भजति मां सर्वभावेन भारत।।

168. *Ibid.*, 40-46[cd]

स्वकर्मणा तमभ्यर्च्य सिद्धिं विन्दति मानवः।।

169. *Ibid.*, 25.30

मयि सर्वाणि कर्माणि संन्यस्याध्यात्मचेतसा।
निराशीर्निर्ममो भूत्वा युध्यस्व विगतज्वरः।।

170. *Ibid.*, 28.47

योगिनामपि सर्वेषां मत्तेनान्तरात्मना।
श्रद्धावान्भजते यो मां स मे युक्ततमो मतः।।

171. For more details see Radhakrishnan, S., *op. cit.*, pp. 530-31.

172. *Ṛv.* X. 129. 3-4.

तम आसीत्तमसा गूळ्हमग्रेऽप्रकेतं सलिलं सर्वमा इदम्।
तुच्छ्येनाभ्वपिहितं यदासीत् तपसस्तन्महिनाजायतैकम्।।
कामस्तदग्रे समवर्तताधि मनसो रेतः प्रथमं यदासीत्।
सतो बन्धुमसति निरविन्दन् हृदि प्रतीष्या कवयो मनीषा।।

173. *Ṛv.* X. 125.

174. *Ṛv.* I. 164. 46.
एकं सद् विप्रा बहुधा वदन्ति।

175. *Tait. Up.*, II. 7. 1.
असद्वा इदमग्र आसीत्।। ततो वै सदजायत।। तदात्मानँ
स्वयमकुरुत।। तस्मात्तत्सुकृतमुच्यत इति।। यद्वै तत्सुकृतम्।।

176. *Mbh. Śānti P.*, 262. 44.
ऋतं सत्यं विदितं वेदितव्यं सर्वस्यात्मा जङ्गमं स्थावरं च।
सर्वं सुखं यच्छिवमुत्तमं च ब्रह्माव्यक्तं प्रभवश्चाव्ययश्च।।

177. *Ibid., Āsva P.*, 35. 22[ab].
सत्याद्भूतानि जातानि स्थावराणि चराणि च।

178. *Ibid., Adi. P.*, 1. 27-29.
निष्प्रभेऽस्मिन्निरालोके सर्वतस्तमसावृते।
बृहदण्डमभूदेकं प्रजानां बीजमक्षयम्।।
युगस्यादौ निमित्तं तन्महद्दिव्यं प्रचक्षते।
यस्मिंस्तच्छ्रूयते सत्यं ज्योतिर्ब्रह्म सनातनम्।।
अद्भूतं चाप्यचिन्त्यं च सर्वत्र समतां गतम्।
अव्यक्तं कारणं सूक्ष्मं यत्तत्सदसदात्मकम्।।

179. *Br. Up.* V. 5. 1.
आप एवेदमग्र आसुस्ता आपः सत्यमसृजन्त सत्यं ब्रह्म ब्रह्म प्रजापतिं प्रजापतिर्देवाँस्ते देवाः सत्यमेवोपासते।

180. Ranade, R.D., *op. cit.*, pp. 55-56.

181. *Tait. Up.* II. 6. 1.
सोऽकामयता बहु स्यां प्रजायेयेति। य तपोऽतप्यत। स तपस्तप्वा। इदं सर्वमसृजत। यदिदं किंच। तत्सृष्ट्वा तदेवानुप्राविशत्। तदनुप्रविश्यासच्च त्यच्चाभवत्। .....। यदिदं किंच। तत्सत्यमित्याचक्षते....।

182. *Mbh. Śānti P.* 160. 11-13.
सलिलैकार्णवं तात पुरा सर्वमभूदिदम्।
निष्प्रकम्पमनाकाशमनिर्देश्यमहीतलम्।।
तमःसंवृतमस्पर्शमतिगम्भीरदर्शनम्।
निःशब्दं चाप्रमेयं च तत्र जज्ञे पितामहः।।
सोऽसृजद्वायुमग्निं च भास्करं चापि वीर्यवान्।
आकाशमसृजच्चोर्ध्वमधो भूमिं च नैर्ऋतिम्।।

183. *Ch. Up.* VI. 8. 4.

एवमेव खलु सोम्य अन्नेन शुंगेनापोमूलमन्विच्छ, अद्भिः सोम्य शुंगेन तेजोमूलमन्विच्छ तेजसा सोम्य शुंगेन सन्मूलमन्विच्छा सन्मूलाः सोम्येमाः सर्वाः प्रजाः सदायतनाः सत्प्रतिष्ठाः।

184. *Mbh. Udyo. P.* 16 . 5-6.

सृष्ट्वा लोकांस्त्रीनिमान्हव्यवाह प्राप्ते काले पचसि पुनः समिद्धः।
सर्वस्यास्य भुवनस्य प्रसूतिस्त्वमेवाग्ने भवसि पुनः प्रतिष्ठा।।

त्वामग्ने जलदानाहुर्विद्युतश्च त्वमेव हि।
दहन्ति सर्वभूतानि त्वत्तो निष्क्रम्य हायनाः।।

185. *Ibid., Ādi. P.* 223. 12-15.

186. *Ch. Up.* I. 9. 1.

अस्य लोकस्य का गतिरित्याकाश इति होवाच।
सर्वाणि ह वा इमानि भूतान्याकाशादेव समुत्पद्यन्ते आकाशं प्रत्यस्तं यन्ति।
आकाशो हि एव एभ्यो ज्यायान् आकाशः परायणम्।

187. *Mbh. Śānti P.* 176. 9-10.

पुरा स्तिमितनिःशब्दमाकाशमचलोपमम्।
नष्टचन्द्रार्कपवनं प्रसुप्तमिव संबभौ।।

ततः सलिलमुत्पन्नं तमसीवापरं तमः।
तस्माच्च सलिलोत्पीडादुदतिष्ठत मारुतः।।

188. *Ch. Up.* III. 14. 1.

तज्ज्लानिति शान्त उपासीत।

189. Śaṅkara, q. Deussen, P., *op. cit.*, pp. 180-181.

190. *Tait. Up.* III. 1.

यतो वा इमानि भूतानि जायन्ते, येन जातनि जीवन्ति, यत्प्रयन्त्यभिसंविशन्ति तद्विजिज्ञासस्व तद्ब्रह्मेति।

191. *Tait. Up.* II. 6.

सोऽकामयत। बहु स्यां प्रजायेयेति।
स तपोऽतप्यत। स तपस्तत्वा। इदँ सर्वमसृजत।
यदिदं किंच। तत्सृष्ट्वा तदेवानुप्राविशत्।।

192. *Mbh. Bh. P.* 31. 4-7.

193. *Ibid.*, 31. 17-18.

पिताहमस्य जगतो माता धाता पितामहः।
वेद्यं पवित्रमोंकार ऋक्साम यजुरेव च।।

गतिर्भर्ता प्रभुः साक्षी निवासः शरणं सुहृत्।
प्रभवः प्रलयः स्थानं निधानं बीजमव्ययम्।।

194. *Ibid., Śānti P.* 47. 53-55.

पञ्चभूतात्मभूताय भूतादिनिधनात्मने।
अक्रोधद्रोहमोहाय तस्मै शान्तात्मने नमः।।

यस्मिन्सर्वं यतः सर्वं यः सर्वं सर्वतश्च यः।
यश्च सर्वमयो नित्यं तस्मै सर्वात्मने नमः।।

विश्वकर्मन्नमस्तेऽस्तु विश्वात्मन्विश्वसंभव।
अपवर्गोऽसि भूतानां पञ्चानां परतः स्थितः।।

195. *Tait. Up.*, II. 1.

तस्माद्वा एतस्मादात्मन आकाशः संभूतः। आकाशाद्वायुः।
वायोरग्निः। अग्नेरापः। अद्भ्यः पृथिवा।।

196. *Muṇḍ. Up.* I. 1. 7.

यथोर्णनाभिः सृजते गृह्णते च यथा पृथिव्यामोषधयः संभवन्ति।
यथा सतः पुरुषात्केशलोमानि तथाऽक्षरात्संभवतीह विश्वम्।।

197. *Mbh. Śānti P.* 195. 1-2.

अक्षरात्खं ततो वायुर्वायोर्ज्योतिस्ततो जलम्।
जलात्प्रसूता जगती जगत्यां जायते जगत्।।

इमे शरीरैर्जलमेव गत्वा जलाच्च तेजः पवनोऽन्तरिक्षम्।
खाद्वै निवर्तन्ति नभाविनस्ते ये भाविनस्ते परमाप्नुवन्ति।

198. *Ibid.*, 175. 12-14.

अव्यक्त इति विख्यातः शाश्वतोऽथाक्षरोऽव्ययः।
यतः सृष्टानि भूतानि जायन्ते च म्रियन्ति च।।

सोऽसृजत्प्रथमं देवो महान्तं नाम नामतः।
आकाशमिति विख्यातं सर्वभूतधरः प्रभुः।।

आकाशादभवद्वारी सलिलादग्निमारुतौ।
अग्निमारुतसंयोगात्ततः समभवन्मही।।

199. *Ibid.*, 175. 13-14.

200. *Ait. Up.* I. 1.1-3.

आत्मा वा इदमेक एवाग्र आसीन्नान्यत्किंचन मिषत्।
स ईक्षत लोकान्नुसृजा इति। स इमांल्लोकानसृजत।।
अम्भो मरीचीर्मरमापोऽदोऽम्भः परेण दिवं द्यौः प्रतिष्ठाऽन्तरिक्षं मरीचयः।
पृथिवी मरो या अधस्तात्ता आपः।।

स ईक्षतेमे नु लोका लोकपालान्नु सृजा इति।।
सोऽद्भ्य एव पुरुषं समुद्धृत्यामूर्च्छयत्।।

201. *Tait. Up.* II . 6. *op. cit.*

202. *Śat. Br.* 3. 6. 2. 8.

203. *Ch. Up.* III. 19. 1 -3.

204. *Mbh. Hari P.* 1. 23, 25.

विष्णुः स्वयंभूर्भगवान्सिसृक्षुर्विविधाः प्रजाः।
अप एव ससर्जादौ तासु वीर्यमवासृजत्।।

हिरण्यवर्णमभवत्तदण्डमुदकेशयम्।
तत्र जज्ञे स्वयं ब्रह्मा स्वयंभूरिति नः श्रुतम्।।

205. *Ibid., P.* 1. 26-27.

हिरण्यगर्भो भगवानुषित्वा परिवत्सरम्।
तदण्डमकरोद्द्वैधं दिवं भुवमथापि च।।

तयोः शकलयोर्मध्यमाकाशमकरोत्प्रभुः
अप्सु पारिप्लवां पृथ्वीं दिशश्च दशधा दधे।।

206. *Ibid., P.* 1. 37.

द्विधा कृत्वात्मनो देहमर्धेन पुरुषोऽभवत्।
अर्धेन नारी तस्यां स ससृजे विविधाः प्रजाः।
दिवं च पृथिवीं चैव महिम्ना व्याप्य तिष्ठति।।

207. *Br. Up.* I. 4. 1-4.

..... स द्वितीयमैच्छत्....। स इममेवात्मानं द्वेधाऽपातयत्ततः पतिश्च पत्नी चाभवताम्....। ..... अजायन्त एवमेव यदिदं किंच मिथुनमापिपीलिकाभ्यः, तत्सर्वमसृजत।

208. *Mbh. Bh. P.* 36. 3.

मम योनिर्महद्ब्रह्म तस्मिन्गर्भं दधाम्यहम्।
संभवः सर्वभूतानां ततो भवति भारत।।

209. *Kauṣi Up.* I. 6.

आपो वै खलु मे ह्यसावयं ते लोक इति सा या ब्रह्मणो जितिर्या व्यष्टिस्तां जितिं जयति तां व्यष्टिं व्यश्नुते य एवं वेद य एवं वेद।।

210. *Ait. Up.* I . 1-3. *op. cit.*

211. *Mbh. Bh. P.* 32. 8 [ab].

अहं सर्वस्य प्रभवो मत्तः सर्वं प्रवर्तते।

212. *Muṇḍ. Up.* II. 1. 2-3.

दिव्यो ह्यमूर्तः पुरुषः सबाह्याभ्यन्तरो ह्यजः।
अप्राणो ह्यमनाः शुभ्रो ह्यक्षरात् परतः परः।।

एतस्माज्जायते प्राणो मनः सर्वेन्द्रियाणि च।
खं वायुर्ज्योतिरापः पृथिवी विश्वस्य धारिणी।।

213. *Mbh. Śānti P.* 329. 3 (4, 6) – 5 (12).

तम इत्येवाभिभूतेऽसंज्ञकेऽद्वितीये प्रतिष्ठिते। एतस्यामवस्थायां नारायणगुणाश्रयादक्षयादजरादनिन्द्रियादग्राह्यादसंभवात्सत्यादहिंस्राल्ल्लामाद्विविधप्रवृत्तिविशेषात्। तस्येदानीं तमःसंभवस्य पुरुषस्य पद्मयोनेर्ब्रह्मणः प्रादुर्भावे स पुरुषः प्रजाः सिसृक्षमाणो नेत्राभ्यामग्नीषोमौ ससर्ज। ततो भूतसर्गे प्रवृत्ते प्रजाक्रमवशाद्ब्रह्मक्षत्रमुपातिष्ठत्।

214. *Ibid., Ādi. P.* 85-10-11.

अस्रं रेतः पुष्पफलानुपृक्तमन्वेति तद्वै पुरुषेण सृष्टम्।
स वै तस्या रज आपद्यते वै स गर्भभूतः समुपैति तत्र।।

वनस्पतींश्चौषधीश्चाविशन्ति अपो वायुं पृथिवीं चान्तरिक्षम्।
चतुष्पदं, द्विपदं चापि सर्वमेवंभूता गर्भभूता भवन्ति।।

215. *Śveta. UP.* III . 2.

एको हि रुद्रो न द्वितीयाय तस्थुः य इमांल्लोकान् ईशत ईशानीभिः।
प्रत्यङ्जनास्तिष्ठति संचुकोचान्तकाले संसृज्य विश्वा भुवनानि गोपाः।।

Also Ranade, R.D., *op. cit.*, pp. 71-72.

216. *Mbh. Anu. P.* 145. 5-6.

प्रजापतिस्तत्ससृजे तपसोऽन्ते महातपाः।
शंकरस्त्वसृजत्तात प्रजाः स्थावरजङ्गमाः।।

नास्ति किंचित्परं भूतं महादेवाद्विशां पते।
इह त्रिष्वपि लोकेषु भूतानां प्रभवो हि सः।।

217. *Ibid. Śānti P.* 335.11[ab]

ईश्वरो हि जगत्स्रष्टा प्रभुर्नारायणो विराट्।

218. *Ibid. Āśva P.* 40.8[ef]

विष्णुरेवादिसर्गेषु स्वयंभूर्भवति प्रभुः।।

219. *Tait. Up.*, III . 1. *op. cit.*

220. *Mbh. Bh. P.* 31. 4[ab]

मया ततमिदं सर्वं जगदव्यक्तमूर्तिना।

221. *Ibid.*, 37. 13[ab].

गामाविश्य च भूतानि धारयाम्यहमोजसा।

222. *Ibid., Āraṇ. P.* 187 . 28[cd], 29.
प्रविष्टो मानुषं देहं सर्वं प्रशमयाम्यहम्।।
सृष्ट्वा देवमनुष्यांश्च गन्धर्वोरगराक्षसान्
स्थावराणि च भूतानि संहराम्यात्ममायया।।

223. *Ibid., Śānti P.* 224. 32.
ब्रह्म तेजोमयं शुक्रं यस्य सर्वमिदं जगत्।।
एकस्य भूतं भूतस्य द्वयं स्थावरजङ्गमम्।।

224. *Ibid.*, 71, 72[ab]
विहितं कालनानात्वमनादिनिधनं तथा।
कीर्तितं यत्पुरस्तात्ते तत्सूते चात्ति च प्रजाः।।
दधाति प्रभवे स्थानं भूतानां संयमो यमः।

225. *Śve. Up.* I . 2.
कालः स्वभावो नियतिर्यदृच्छा भूतानि योनिः पुरुष इति चिंत्यम्।
संयोग एषां न त्वात्मभावादात्माप्यनीशः सुख-दुःखहेतोः।।

226. Article by Jacobi H. *Encyclopedia of Religion and Ethics.* Vol. IV, Edit. Hastings James, *op. cit.*, p. 155.

227. *Mbh, Śānti P.*, 194. 22[a]
यतो जगत्सर्वमिदं प्रसूतं।

228. *Ibid., Bh. P.* 35. 22. *op. cit.*

229. *Ibid.*, 37. 16-18.

230. *Ibid., Śānti.P.* 306-53-55.

231. *Ibid., Sabhā P.* 66.27; Also *Ibid. Āran* P. 5. 18.
अकामानां च सर्वेषां सुहृदामर्थदर्शिनाम्।
अकरोत्पाण्डवाह्वानं धृतराष्ट्रः सुतप्रियः।।
असंशयं तेऽपि ममैव पुत्रा दुर्योधनस्तु मम देहात्प्रसूतः।
स्वं वै देहं परहेतोस्त्यजेति को न ब्रूयात्समतामन्ववेक्षन्।।

232. *Ibid. Udyog P.* 48. 45[cd]-47.
न ह्यस्य त्रिषु लोकेषु सदृशोऽस्ति धनुर्धरः।
अनादृत्य तु तद्वाक्यमर्थवद्द्रोणभीष्मयोः।
ततः स संजयं राजा पर्यपृच्छत पाण्डवान्।।
तदैव कुरवः सर्वे निराशा जीवितेऽभवन्।
भीष्मद्रोणौ यदा राजा न सम्यगनुभाषते।।

233. *Y.S.* II. 3. *Op. cit.*
अविस्मतारागद्वेभिनिवेशाल्केः।

234. *Mbh. Sabhā P.* 46. 27-28[ab].
वस्त्रमुत्कर्षति मयि प्राहसत्स वृकोदरः।
शत्रोर्ऋद्धिविशेषेण विमूढं रत्नवर्जितम्॥
तत्र स्म यदि शक्तः स्यां पातयेयं वृकोदरम्।

235. *Y.S.* II. 3. *op. cit.*

236. *Mbh. Udyog. P.*125. 16.
मुख्यश्चैवैष नो धर्मः क्षत्रियाणां जनार्दन।
यच्छयीमहि संग्रामे शरतल्पगता वयम्॥

237. *Ibid.*, 54. 30-31.
समर्थं मन्यसे यच्च कुन्तीपुत्रं वृकोदरम्।
तन्मिथ्या न हि मे कृत्स्नं प्रभावं वेत्सि भारत॥
मत्समो हि गदायुद्धे पृथिव्यां नास्ति कश्चन।
नासीत्कश्चिदतिक्रान्तो भविता न च कश्चन॥

238. *Ibid., Āśram. P.* 15. 20-21[abcd].
तथा दुर्योधनेनापि राजा सुपरिपालिताः॥
न स्वल्पमपि पुत्रस्ते व्यलीकं कृतवान्नृप।
पितरीव सुविश्वस्तास्तस्मिन्नपि नराधिपे।

239. *Ibid., Sabhā P.* 60. 18, 19, 20[ab].
दुःशासनैष मम सूतपुत्रो वृकोदरादुद्विजतेऽल्पचेताः।
स्वयं प्रगृह्यानय याज्ञसेनीं किं ते करिष्यन्त्यवशाः सपत्नाः॥
ततः समुत्थाय स राजपुत्रः श्रुत्वा भ्रातुः कोपविरक्तदृष्टिः॥
प्रविश्य तद्वेश्म महारथानामित्यब्रवीद् दौपदीं राजपुत्रीम्॥
एह्येहि पाञ्चालि जितासि कृष्णे दुर्योधनं पश्य विमुक्तलज्जा।

240. *Ibid., Āraṇ. P.* 226. 11[cd]-14[cd]. 21.
पश्यामसतान् श्रिया हीनान् पाण्डवान् वनवासिनः॥
असमृद्धान् समृद्धार्थः पश्य पाण्डुसुतान् नृप॥
न तथा हि सभामध्ये तस्या भवितुमर्हति।
वैमनस्यं यथा दृष्ट्वा तव भार्याः स्वलङ्कृताः॥

241. *Ibid., Ādī. P.* 122. 47.
सूतपुत्रश्च राधेयो गुरुं द्रोणामियात्तदा॥
स्पर्धमानस्तु पार्थेन सूतपुत्रोऽत्यमर्षणः।

दुर्योधनं उपाश्रित्य पाण्डवानत्यमन्यत।।

242. *Ibid., Āraṇ. P.* 284. 27[ab]. 28[ab].

दास्यामि विबुधश्रेष्ठ कुण्डले वर्म चोत्तमम्।
मद्विधस्यायशस्यं हि न युक्तं प्राणरक्षणम्।

243. *Ibid., Āraṇ. P.* 284. 25.

व्रतं वै मम लोकोऽयं वेत्ति कृत्स्नो विभावसो।
यथाहं द्विजमुख्येभ्यो दद्यां प्राणानपि ध्रुवम्।।

244. *Ibid., Udyō. P.* 144. 15. 16.

अयं हि कालः संप्राप्तो धार्तराष्ट्रोपजीविनाम्।
निर्वेष्टव्यं मया तत्र प्राणानपरिरक्षता।।

कृतार्थाः सुभृता ये हि कृत्यकाल उपस्थिते।
अनवेक्ष्य कृतं पापा विकुर्वन्त्यनवस्थिताः।।

245. *Ibid., Sabhā P.* 60. 34.

द्रोणस्य भीष्मस्य च नास्ति सत्त्वम्।

246. *Ibid., Ādī. P.* 128. 6. 7[ab].

भग्नदर्पंहृतधनं तथा च वशमागतम्।।
स वैरं मनसा ध्यात्वा द्रोणो द्रुपदमब्रवीत्।
प्रमृद्य तरसा राष्ट्रं पुरं ते मृदितं मया।।

247. *Ibid., Droṇā. P.* 165. 35.

उत्सृज्य च रणे शस्त्रं रथोपस्थे निवेश्य च।
अभयं सर्वभूतानां प्रददौ योगयुक्तवान्।।

248. *Ibid., Bh. P.* 41. 51.

अर्थस्य पुरुषो दासो दासस्त्वर्थो न कस्यचित्।
इति सत्यं महाराज बद्धोऽस्म्यर्थेन कौरवैः।।

249. *Tait.* I. 11. 1.

सत्यान्न प्रमदितव्यम्। धर्मान्न प्रमदितव्यम्।

250. *Mbh, Śānti P.,* 254. 9.

सर्वेषां यः सुहृन्नित्यं सर्वेषां च हिते रतः।
कर्मणा मनसा वाचा स धर्मं वेद जाजले।।

251. *Ibid., Udyog P.* 178. 25.

स त्वं गुरुरिति प्रेम्णा मया संमानितो भृशम्।
गुरुवृत्तं न जानीषे तस्माद्योत्स्यामि अहं त्वया।।

252. *Ibid., Bh. P.* 27. 7.

योगयुक्तो विशुद्धात्मा विजितात्मा जितेन्द्रियः।
सर्वभूतात्मभूतात्मा कुर्वन्नपि न लिप्यते॥

253. *Ibid., Bh. P.* 103. 78, 81.

अमङ्गल्यध्वजे तस्मिन् स्त्रीपूर्वे च विशेषतः।
न प्रहर्तुमभीप्सामि गृहीतेषुं कथञ्चन।
एष तस्मात् पुरोधाय कञ्चिदन्यं ममाग्रतः।
मां पातयतु बीभत्सुरेवं तव विजयो भवेत्॥

254. *Ibid., Anu. P.* 152. 7-8-10.

क्षत्रधर्मरतः पार्थ पितृन्देवांश्च तर्पय।
श्रेयसा योक्ष्यसे चैव व्येतु ते मानसो ज्वरः॥

रञ्जयस्व प्रजाः सर्वाः प्रकृतीः परिसान्त्वय।
आगन्तव्यं च भवता समये मम पार्थिव।
विनिवृत्ते दिनकरे प्रवृत्ते चोत्तरायणे॥

255. Y.S. I. 37.

वीतरागविषयं वा चित्तम्।

256. *Mbh. Udyog* P. 41. 5.

शूद्रयोनावहं जातो नातोऽन्यद् वक्तुमुत्सहे।
कुमारस्य तु या बुद्धिर्वेद तां शाश्वतीमहम्।

257. *Ibid.,* 146.6[ab].

नीचैः स्थित्वा तु विदुर उपास्ते स्म विनीतवान्।

258. *Ibid.,* 9[d].

विदुरः सत्यसङ्गरः।

259. *Ibid., Sabhā P.* 55. I

महाराज विजानीहि यत्त्वां वक्ष्यामि तच्छृणु।
मुमूर्षोरौषधमिव न रोचेतापि ते श्रुतम्।

260. *Ibid.,* 57. 18.

यस्तु धर्मे पराश्वस्य हित्वा भर्तुः प्रियाप्रिये।
अप्रियाण्याह पथ्यानि तेन राजा सहायवान्॥

261. *Ibid., Ādī. P.* 100.28, 101.28[bc].

धर्मो विदुररूपेण शापात्तस्य महात्मनः।
मांडव्यस्यार्थतत्त्वज्ञः कामक्रोधविवर्जितः॥
दीर्घदर्शी शमपरः कुरुणां च हिते रतः॥

262. *Ibid.*, 133.28.

विषादग्नेश्च बोधव्यं इति मां विदुरोऽब्रवीत्।
पन्थाश्च वो नाविदितः कश्चित्स्यादिति चाब्रवीत्।।

263. *Ibid.*, *Udyog P.* 127. 49.

अमर्षवशमापन्नो मा कुरूंस्तात जीघनः।
सर्वा हि पृथिवी स्पृष्टा त्वत्पाण्डवकृते वधम्।।

264. *Ibid.*, 146.32.

राज्यं तु पाण्डोरिदमप्रधृष्यं तस्याद्य पुत्राः प्रभवन्ति नान्ये।
राज्यं तदेतन्निखिलं पाण्डवानां पैतामहं पुत्रपौत्रानुगामी।।

265. *Ibid.*, *Sabhā P.* 66.29[cd], 30[cd].

नीयतां परलोकाय साध्वयं कुलपांसनः।।
अन्तो नूनं कुलस्यास्य कुरवस्तन्निबोधत।।

266. *Ibid.*, *Stri P.* 13.18[cd].

अधो नाभ्यां प्रहृतवांस्तन्मे कोपवर्धयत्।

267. *Ibid.*, 25.38[ab]-39.

इच्छतोपेक्षितो नाशः कुरुणां मधुसूदन।
पतिशुश्रूषया यन्मे तपः किञ्चिदुपार्जितम्।
तेन त्वां दुरवापात्मञ्शप्स्ये चक्रगदाधर।।

268. *Ibid.*, *Āśra. P.* 23. 19[cd], 20[ab].

पतिलोकानहं पुण्यान्कामये तपसा विभो।
श्वश्रूश्वशुरयोः कृत्वा शुश्रूषां वनवासिनोः।।

269. *Ibid.*, *Sabhā P.* 70. 12[ab], 16.

तदवस्थान्सुतान्सर्वानुपसृत्यानिवत्सला।
कथं वत्स्यथ दुर्गेषु वनेष्वृद्धिविनाकृताः।
वीर्यसत्त्वबलोत्साहतेजोभिरकृशाः कृशाः।।

270. *Ibid.*, *Āśra.* 23. 1-2.

एवमेतन्महाबाहो यथा वदसि पाण्डव।
कृतमुद्धर्षणं पूर्वं मया वः सीदतां नृपाः।
द्यूतापहृतराज्यानां पतितानां सुखादपि।
ज्ञातिभिः परिभूतानां कृतमुद्धर्षणं मया।।

271. *Ibid.*, 19[ab].

नाहं राज्यफलं पुत्र कामये पुत्रनिर्जितम्।

272. *Ibid.*, *Āraṇ. P.* 222. 11-57.

273. *Ibid.*, 28. 35, 29. 34.

यो न दर्शयते तेजः क्षत्रियः काल आगते।
सर्वभूतानि तं पार्थ सदा परिभवन्त्युत।
नहि कश्चित्क्षमाकालो विद्यतेऽद्य कुरून्प्रति।
तेजसश्चागते काले तेज उत्स्रष्टुमर्हसि।।

274. *Ibid.*, 31. 20[cd]-21.

ईश्वरस्य वशे लोकस्तिष्ठते नात्मनो यथा।
धातैव खलु भूतानां सुखदुःखे प्रियाप्रिये।
दधाति सर्वमीशानः पुरस्ताच्छुक्रमुच्चरन्।

275. *Ibid.*, *Udyog. P.* 80. 32[cd], 36.

धार्तराष्ट्रेषु वै कोपः सर्वः कृष्ण विधीयताम्।
अयं ते पुण्डरीकाक्ष दुःशासनकरोद्धृतः।
स्मर्तव्यः सर्वकालेषु परेषां संधिमिच्छता।।

276. *Ibid.*, *Āraṇ. P.* 35. 21.

मम प्रतिज्ञां च निबोध सत्यां वृणे धर्ममममृताज्जीविताच्च।
राज्यं च पुत्राश्च यशो धनं च सर्वं न सत्यस्य कलामुपैति।।

277. *Ibid.*, 297. 72[cd], 73.

स्वधर्मान्न चलिष्यामि नकुलो यक्ष जीवतु।
यथा कुन्ती तथा माद्री विशेषो नास्ति मे तयोः।
मातृभ्यां सममिक्ष्छामि नकुलो यक्ष जीवतु।।

278. *Ibid.*, *Mahāprā. P.* 3. 20.

अयं श्वा भक्त इत्येव त्यक्तो देवरथस्त्वया।
तस्मात्स्वर्गे न ते तुल्यः कश्चिदस्ति नराधिप।।

279. *Ibid.*, *Āraṇ. P.* 37. 5.

सुमन्त्रिते सुविक्रान्ते सुकृते सुविचारिते।
सिध्यन्त्यर्था महाबाहो दैवं चात्र प्रदक्षिणम्।।

280. *Ibid.*, *Āraṇ. P.* 34. 56[ab], 50[cd].

न हि केवलधर्मात्मा पृथिवीं जातु कश्चन।
क्षत्रियस्य विशेषेण धर्मस्तु बलमौरसम्।।

281. *Ibid.*, 21.

कर्शनार्थो हि यो धर्मो मित्राणामात्मनस्तथा।
व्यसनं नाम तद्राजन्न स धर्मः कुधर्म तत्।।

282. *Ibid.*, 17.

तत्र चेद्युध्यमानानामजिह्ममनिवर्तिनाम्।
सर्वशो हि वधः श्रेयान्प्रेत्य लोकाल्लँभेमहि।।

283. *Ibid.*, *P.* 69-70[ab].

यथा राजन्प्रजाः सर्वाः सूर्यः पाति गभस्तिभिः।
अत्ति चैव तथैव त्वं सवितुः सद्दशो भव।।

एतद्ध्यपि तपो राजन्पुराणमिति नः श्रुतम्।

284. *Ibid.*, *Virāṭ*. *P.* 67. 5[cd]-6.

शुद्धो जितेन्द्रियो दान्तस्तस्याः शुद्धिः कृता मया।।
स्नुषाया दुहितुर्वापि पुत्रे चात्मनि वा पुनः।
अत्र शङ्कां न पश्यामि तेन शुद्धिर्भविष्यति।।

285. *Ibid.*, *Ādī*. *P.* 122. 41[ab], 42[cd], 43.

प्रतिगृह्य च तान्सर्वान्द्रोणो वचनमब्रवीत्।
कृतास्त्रैस्तत्प्रदेयं मे तद्यतं वदतानघाः।।

तत्छद्दत्वा कौरवेयास्ते तूष्णीमासन्विशां पते।
अर्जुनस्तु ततः सर्वं प्रतिजज्ञे परंतपः।।

286. *Ibid.*, *Bh. P.* 103. 33-34.

तव भ्राता मम सखा संबन्धी शिष्य एव च।
मांसान्युत्कृत्य वै दद्यामर्जुनार्थे महीपते।।

एष चापि नरव्याघ्रो मत्कृते जीवितं त्यजेत्।
एष नः समयस्तात तारयेम परस्परम्।।

287. *Y.S.* I. 33.

मैत्रीकरुणामुदितोपेक्षाणां सुखदुःखपुण्यापुण्यविषयाणां भावनातश्चित्तप्रसादनम्।

CHAPTER VI

CONCLUSION

The present study aimed at finding out the course of various Indian philosophical thoughts, conceptions as propagated in different philosophical systems, especially in the six philosophical systems and search whether they have been represented in the *Mbh.* as fully developed systems or whether the systems appear in the process of development. It also aimed at scrutinizing the factors that might have led to the appearance of these philosophical portions in the epic, whether these philosophical portions formed the vital constituent part of the main nucleus or whether the propounders of different systems incorporated their thoughts to propagate their own theories.

Moreover, philosophy is a wider concept. It can even cover attitude, temperaments, mental inclinations of human beings towards life. Hence, an attempt was undertaken to explore the philosophies of life of some important characters in the *Mbh.* towards their lives.

The philosophical portions in the *Mbh.* indicate that the trends of Vedānta, Sāṁkhya and Yoga philosophy have been profusely incorporated. Among the three, the trends of the Vedānta philosophy seems to be the prominent ones.

The fundamental doctrines of the Upaniṣad-s revolve around Brahman which was looked upon as the Supreme Reality. The *Mbh.* described the Brahman as the unmanifest, creative, first cause supporting the universe and the Soul of every being. The thought that the individual Soul, the Ātman is the same as the omnipresent Supreme Reality *viz.* the Brahman is emphasized throughout the *Mbh.*[1] The Upaniṣadic search for the self from a gross to subtle level,[2] the knowledge of the inner world (*vidyā*) and that of the outer would (*avidyā*) which veils *vidyā*, finds expression in the *Mbh.*[3] It also discusses the process of realisation of the Ultimate truth on the lines of the Vedānta philosophy.[4] The monistic concept of the Upaniṣad-s according to which Brahman is the only cause of the world seems to be having a strong impact on the philosophy of the *Mbh.*

The *Mbh.* explained the nature of the constituents of Prakṛti, that of Puruṣa and other twenty three elements of Sāṁkhya philosophy and expounded the concept of release. However, while doing so, the Sāṁkhya concept of release is synthesized with that of the Upaniṣadic concept. Thus, although it incorporated all the terms of Sāṁkhya philosophy, it did not accept the dualism. The Prakṛti of Sāṁkhya is insentient and Puruṣa is indifferent. Hence, their union cannot create the world. The *Mbh.*, therefore, considered Uttama Puruṣa, who is equivalent to the Brahman of the Vedānta, to be the presiding one, leading to creation through Prakṛti.[5]

The *Mbh.* has dealt with in detail, the main concepts of Yoga philosophy namely *vidyā-avidyā,*[6] eight accessories of *yama, niyama* etc.[7] obstacles in the path of Yoga practice,[8] concepts of *vairāgya*[9] and *kaivalya.*[10]

However, it has accepted the eightfold Yoga system mainly to facilitate the aspirant to concentrate his mind and his senses and attain the final release by obtaining the right knowledge of the identity between the individual Soul and the Self. This Self is the same as the Brahman of the Vedānta philosophy.

The philosophy of Nyāya and Pūrvamīmāṁsā do not find much representation in the *Mbh.* As regards the philosophical trends of Pūrvamīmāṁsā, there is no outright opposition to sacrifice in the *Mbh.* Nevertheless, sacrifice has been ennobled so as to lead to the general welfare of the society. The various categories of substances considered by Vaiśeṣika philosophy have been mentioned in the *Mbh.* However, they are of subordinate importance.

The *Mbh.* contains references to the views of different Buddhist schools. They have been incorporated mainly in order to refute them.[11] The principles of Cārvāka or Lokāyata philosophy too have been refuted in the *Mbh.*[12] The trends of Jain philosophy, however, are not reflected at all. The *Mbh.* has also incorporated the concepts of Dharma, Law of Transmigration, the cosmogonic accounts from the Ṛgveda, those of Sāṁkhya-s and even theistic cults like Vaiṣṇavism.

The Bhārata composed by Vyāsa was enlarged by him in order to assimilate different didactic, philosophical, mythological contents. Taking into account the views of different scholars it can be conclusively stated that the philosophical portions of the *Mbh.* were added to the original heroic story at a later stage, when it was being transformed into a Brahmanical work.[13]

Before considering the question as to whether the philosophical systems presented in the *Mbh.* were fully developed or whether they were in the process of development, it is pertinent to examine the nature of a system.

The Oxford English Dictionary has explained the term system as–

(*i*) a set of correlated principles, ideas or statements belonging to some department of knowledge or a belief considered as an original whole, a connected and regularly arranged scheme of the whole of some subject, a comprehensive body of doctrines, conclusions, speculat-ions or thesis.

(*ii*) A work or writing containing a comprehensive and regularly arranged exposition of some subject, a systematic treatise.[14]

An American Dictionary of the English Language (*Webster's Larger Dictionary*) has defined the term system as–

An assemblage of things adjusted into a regular whole; or a whole plan or scheme consisting of many parts connected in such a manner as to create a chain of mutual dependencies; or a regular union of principles or parts forming one entire thing. Thus, it can be a system of logic, a system of philosophy, a system of government etc.[15]

According to Deussen P., a system means an association of thoughts which collectively belong to and are dependent on a single centre. A system has, therefore, always an individual author, whether he himself originated the thoughts brought together in the scheme, or has only adjusted to one another and welded into a consistent whole, imperfect thoughts derived from without.[16]

In India six systems of philosophy are called Darśana-s. *Bharatiya Sanskṛti Kosha* has explained the term *darśana* as

(*i*) *'Dṛśyate yathārthatattvam anena iti.'* The science by which the true knowledge of the principle is perceived (*Sa. K.*).

(*ii*) *'Tattvajñānasādhanam śāstram'* (*Nyāya Kośa*) *i.e.* the science which enables one to obtain the knowledge of principles.[17]

Keith, A.B. has stated that after the period of the Upaniṣad-s, the ideas of the earlier thinkers were gradually taken up and turned into definite systems, *darśana*-s; taught in philosophical schools in the sense of series of teachers who developed or at least expounded one definite body of doctrine and after this development had been in existence for some time, there ultimately came the desire to fix in definitive form the doctrines of the school and this led to the compositions of the Sūtra-s.[18]

Hence, the term system can be applied to the doctrines of any science only when they are systematically arranged in a set of correlated principles, ideas or statements belonging to that particular department of knowledge or when they form a comprehensive and regularly arranged exposition of a systematic treatise.

In this connection, the opinions of Deussen and Radhakrishnan are worth taking note of. Deussen has remarked that strictly speaking, the system of Upaniṣad-s does not exist. However, there is a gradual development of a system which in the post-Vedic times developed into a general system of theological and philosophical nature at the hands of Bādarāyaṇa.[19] Radhakrishnan has opined that the Upaniṣad-s are but a series of glances at truth from various points of view, and not an attempt to think out the great questions consecutively. However, those who believed them as revealed truth wanted to show that their teachings formed a consistent whole. Bādarāyaṇa attempted this work of systematization. The date of Bādarāyaṇa as assigned by Hopkins is 200 A.D. Keith treats it not later than 200 A.D. According to Indian scholars, however, the period of the composition of Sūtra-s was between 500 and 200 B.C. Frazer assigned it to 400 B.C. According to Max Müller, the age of the *Vedāntasūtra*-s and that of Bādarāyaṇa was earlier than the date of the *Bhagavadgītā*.[20]

Radhakrishnan has further stated that though there were reconstructing movements of thought in the early epic period, they did not attain their full strength till the end of the epic era. During this period, the teaching of Vedic seers as also of the Upaniṣad-s were condensed into *Sūtra*-s. Logical and highly devotional systems of thought were promulgated. The Cārvāka philosophy, the Buddhism and the Jainism appeared first and immediately thereafter, as a sort of reaction, attempts were made to emphasize the theistic Upaniṣadic teachings. However, neither the ethical teachings of Buddhism and Jainism fulfilled the deeper spiritual desires of people nor could the abstraction of the Upaniṣad-s quench the thirst of the masses for metaphysical knowledge. Hence people indulging in speculative ideas tried to develop new philosophical concepts. The system of Sāṁkhya, Yoga, Nyāya, Vaiśeṣika and those of earlier and later Mīmāṁsā-s were definitely propounded at the end of epic period.[21]

The philosophical portions of the *Mbh.* reveal that the views of different seers have been incorporated in it at different places. At times Brahman is considered as the seventeenth,[22] sometimes as the twenty fifth principle,[23] whereas on other occasions it is considered to be the twenty sixth element.[24] The *Mbh.* tries to explain the Upaniṣadic principles with the help of the Sāṁkhya concepts. This synthesis of Vedānta and Sāṁkhya is evident in the *Bhagavadgītā,* portion of the *Bhīṣma P.* and also in the *Śānti Parva.* However, the later parts of the *Mbh.* reflect a systematic presentation of the Sāṁkhya philosophy namely in the *Āśvamedhika P.* The *Mbh.* has also presented a detailed description of the three *guṇa*-s of Prakṛti. There are systematic descriptions of the manifestation of *Mahat* from unevolved Prakṛti, of *ahaṁkāra* from *Mahat* and thereafter of five great elements, *manas,* five sense organs, organs of action, sense objects from *ahaṁkāra*.[25] However, the *Mbh.* does not deal with the Sāṁkhya concept of the manifestation of Prakṛti in the presence of Puruṣa. The creation of the world here is through Satya[26] which is considered to be identical with Brahman, *tapas* or Prajāpati.[27] Thus, the Sāṁkhya concept of creation is never hinted at in the *Mbh.*

It must also be noted that according to the *Mbh., Mokṣa* is secured through the attainment of the Highest Principle, *i.e.* the Brahman[28] and not through the realization by Puruṣa, that he is different from Prakṛti as stated in the *Sā. K.*[29] The *Bh. G.* refers to the creation of the world by Prakṛti and Puruṣa. However, taking note of the fact that the insentient Prakṛti and passive Puruṣa cannot create the universe on their own accord, the Mahābhāratakāra considered Puruṣottam, (Uttama Puruṣa) to be the presiding entity under whose supervision the creation takes place.[30]

Radhakrisnan, S., stated that the Sāṁkhya system was fully developed towards the concluding period of the *Mbh.*[31] The contents of the *Bh.G.* also hint at the same point that the Sāṁkhya system was fully developed during the period of the *Mbh.*

However, it must be noted that due to a strong impact of the monistic philosophy of Upaniṣad-s accoding to which Brahman is the only cause of the universe, the concept of the creation by Prakṛti in the presence of Puruṣa was not accepted by the *Mbh.*

The Anugītā portion of the *Mbh.* reflects different beliefs. Thus, it has stated that according to some, the eternal principle is impermanent, which according to some others it exists. Still some others have stated that it exists, at the same time, it does not exist. It is single, say some, whereas it is twofold according to others. Some hold that it is both single as also twofold. Some who know Brahman and perceive the truth believe that it is just one. According to some, it is distinct, whereas others say that it is manifold.[32] While commenting on this portion of the Anugītā, Radhakrishnan, S., has stated that this reflects the existence of a large number of philosophical schools, a collection of different beliefs, a syncretism but not a system.[33]

As regards the philosophical trends reflected in the epic, the views expressed by various scholars are conflicting in nature–

According to Radhakrishnan, S., the present version of the *Mbh.* is an enlarged version of earlier tradition called the Bhārata. In the Bhārata, the old ballad story of tribal heroes was modified with a view to reconcile it with the Āryan culture. He has further stated that the ballad stage, where the local bards were singing the heroic deeds of tribal heroes, was the first stage. It did not contain didactic or philosophical matter. At the second stage *i.e.,* Bhārata stage an attempt was made to reconcile the culture of the Āryan and the mass of facts and fiction, history and mythology. However, soon new material accumulated and the attempt to assimilate it resulted into the composition of the *Mahābhārata.* The next stage of thought represents the period when the Greeks, the Parthians and the Scythians entered the country. The heroic poem was transformed into a Brahmanical work, in a theistic treatise, Visṇu or Śiva was elevated to the rank of the Supreme. The *Bh. G.* perhaps belongs to this stage. The philosophical portions of the *Mbh.* were incorporated at this, *i.e.* the last stage.[34]

Macdonell, A.A. too held that the *Mbh.* is an extension of the original story of war between the descendants of Bhārata. To this epic kernel of the "Great Battle", a vast number of old legends, accounts of cosmogony, theogony, expositions on philosophy, law etc. were added. Thus, while the two armies were standing in opposition with each other the *Bhagavadgītā* containing valuable advice for Arjuna is inserted.[35]

However, Sukthankar, V.S. has opined that the *Bh. G.* constitutes the inseparable part of the epic, from the metaphysical angle. It is the real kernel of the Great Epic.[36] Radhakrisahnan, S. considered that though a philosophical discourse at the beginning of the battle appears "incongruous and irrelevant, such stimulation of thought about the ultimate values occurs at such crucial moments and the spiritually disposed minds acquire the tension necessary to break the barricades of sense and touch the inner Reality. Śrīkṛṣṇa might have imparted a pointed advice to Arjuna which might have been worked up into a long poem by the *Mahābhārata* poet later on. The Mahābhāratakāra always grabbed the opportunity to elaborate the principles of *dharma.*[37] Also there are internal references to the *Bh. G.* in the *Mbh.*"[38]

According to Tilak, B.G. the stylistic resemblances between the *Bh. G.* and other portions of the *Mbh.* show that and they constitute a single whole.[39] Thus, there is a sufficient proof to show that the *Bh. G.,* containing a philosophical discourse, forms an integral part of the *Mbh.*

However, the philosophical portions appearing in the *Śānti P.* present diverse views about the origin of the universe and the number of elements that constitute this world. The universe is said to have originated from *satyam* or from Brahman,[40] or from water[41] or from space[42] or from an immutable principle[43] or from Mahat element,[44] or from Puruṣa[45] or from Nārāyaṇa[46] etc. Also the world is considered to be consisting of seventeen,[47] twenty five[48] or twenty six[49] elements. These contents have been presented as the views of different sages, who considered Brahman to be the Ultimate Principle. This indicates that these deliberations have been incorporated by the propounders of different systems to propagate their own theories.

REFERENCES

1. *Mbh. Śānti P.* 180. 27. Also *Ibid., Bh. P.* 37. 15[a]-19[ab].
एवं सर्वेषु भूतेषु गूढश्चरति संवृतः।
दृश्यते त्वग्रयया बुद्ध्या सूक्ष्मया तत्त्वदर्शिभिः।
सर्वस्य चाहं हृदि संनिवेष्टो।
यो मामेवमसंमूढो जानाति पुरुषोत्तमम्।

2. *Ibid., Bh. P.* 29. 4-5.
भूमिरापोऽनलो वायुः खं मनो बुद्धिरेव च।
अहंकार इतीयं मे भिन्ना प्रकृतिरष्टधा।।
अपरेयमितस्त्वन्यां प्रकृतिं विद्धि मे पराम्।
जीवभूतां महाबाहो ययेदं धार्यते जगत्।।

3. *Ibid., Śānti P.* 295. 2.
अविद्यामाहुरव्यक्तं सर्गप्रलयधर्मि वै।
सर्गप्रलयनिर्मुक्तं विद्यां वै पञ्चविंशकम्।

4. *Ibid.*, 21. 3, 5.
यदा संहरते कामान्कूर्मोऽङ्गानीव सर्वशः।
तदात्मज्योतिरात्मैव स्वात्मनैव प्रसीदति।।
यदासौ सर्वभूतानां न क्रुध्यति न दुष्यति।
कर्मणा मनसा वाचा ब्रह्म संपद्यते तदा।।

5. *Ibid., Bh. P.* 37. 17.
उत्तमः पुरुषस्त्वन्यः परमात्मेत्युदाहृतः।
यो लोकत्रयमाविश्य बिभर्त्यव्यय ईश्वरः।।

6. *Ibid., Śānti P.* 295. 2.

7. *Ibid.*, 289. 31-48.

8. *Ibid., Āraṇ. P.* 2. 15[ab], also *Bh. P.* 26. 40[ab].
शोकस्थानसहस्राणि भयस्थानशतानि च।
अज्ञश्चाश्रद्दधानश्च संशयात्मा विनश्यति।

9. *Ibid., Śānti P.* 289. 49.
दीपयन्ति महात्मानः सूक्ष्ममात्मानमात्मना।
वीतरागा महाप्राज्ञा ध्यानाध्ययनसम्पदा।

10. *Ibid., Bh. P.* 28. 20.
यत्रोपरमते चित्तं निरुद्धं योगसेवया।
यत्र चैवात्मनात्मानं पश्यन्नात्मनि तुष्यति।

11. *Mbh. Bh. P.* 38. 8.
असत्यमप्रतिष्ठं ते जगदाहुरनीश्वरम्।
अपरस्परसंभूतं किमन्यत्कामहैतुकम्।

12. *Ibid., Śānti P.* 19. 23-24.
भवन्ति सुदुरावर्ता हेतुमन्तोऽपि पण्डिताः।
दृढपूर्वश्रुता मूढा नैतदस्तीति वादिनः॥
अमृतस्यावमन्तारो वक्तारो जनसंसदि।
चरन्ति वसुधां कृत्स्नां वावदूका बहुश्रुताः।

13. Radhakrishnan, S. *op. cit.,* Vol. I p. 481.

14. *Oxford English Dictionary,* Vol. XII, second Edition, Oxford University Press, New York 1989, p. 497.

15. *An American Dicitonary of the Engligh Language* (*Webster's Larger Dictionary*), L. George and Charles Merriam, U.S.A., 1848, p. 1123.

16. Deussen, P., *op. cit.,* p. 51.

17. *Bhāratīya Sanskriti Kosha,* Vol. 4 यंत्रशास्त्र to नाणी p. 299.

18. Keith, A.B., *A History of Sanskrit Literature,* London, 1928, p. 471.

19. Deussen, P., *op. cit.,* pp. 51-52.

20. Hopkins, Keith, Frazer and Max Müller q. by Radhakrishnan, S., *op. cit.,* pp. 431, 433.

21. Radharishnan, S., *op. cit.,* pp. 275-276.

22. *Mbh. Śānti P.* 231. 15-16.
एवं सप्तदशं देहे वृतं षोडशभिर्गुणैः।
मनीषी मनसा विप्रः पश्यत्यात्मानमात्मनि॥
न ह्ययं चक्षुषा दृश्यो न च सर्वैरपीन्द्रियैः।
मनसा संप्रदीप्तेन महानात्मा प्रकाशते।

23. *Ibid.,* 293. 38.
एवमप्यनुमानेन ह्यलिङ्गमुपलभ्यते।
पञ्चविंशतिमस्तात लिङ्गेष्वनियतात्मकः॥

24. *Ibid.*, 296. 17.

षड्विंशेन प्रबुद्धेन बुध्यमानोऽप्यबुद्धिमान्।
एतन्नानात्वमित्युक्तं सांख्यश्रुतिनिदर्शनात्।।

25. *Ibid., Āśva. P.* 40. 1-3, 41. 1, 42. 1-27.

26. *Ibid., Āśva. P.* 35. 22.

सत्याद्भूतानि जातानि स्थावराणि चराणि च।
तपसा तानि जीवन्ति इति तद्वित्त सुव्रताः।।

27. *Ibid.*, 24.

ब्रह्म सत्यं तपः सत्यं सत्यं चैव प्रजापतिः।
सत्याद्भूतानि जातानि भूतं सत्यमयं महत्।।

28. *Ibid.*, 47. 2-4..

अविदूरात्परं ब्रह्म वेदविद्याव्यपाश्रयम्।
निर्द्वंद्वं निर्गुणं नित्यमचिन्त्यं गुह्यमुत्तमम्।।

ज्ञानेन तपसा चैव धीराः पश्यन्ति तत्पदम्।
निर्णिक्ततमसः पूता व्युत्क्रान्तरजसोऽमलाः।।

तपसा क्षेममध्वानं गच्छन्ति परमैषिणः।
संन्यासनिरता नित्यं ये ब्रह्मविदुषो जनाः।।

29. *Sā. K..* 63-64.

रूपैः सप्तभिरेव तु बध्नात्यात्मानमात्मना प्रकृतिः।
सैव च पुरुषार्थं प्रति विमोचयत्येकरूपेण।।

एवं तत्त्वाऽभ्यासान्नास्मि न मे नाहमित्यपरिशेषम्।
अविपर्ययाद्विशुद्धं केवलमुत्पद्यते ज्ञानम्।।

30. *Mbh. Bh.. P.* 37. 16-17.

द्वाविमौ पुरुषौ लोके क्षरश्चाक्षर एव च।
क्षरः सर्वाणि भूतानि कूटस्थोऽक्षर उच्यते।।

उत्तमः पुरुषस्त्वन्यः परमात्मेत्युदाहृतः।
यो लोकत्रयमाविश्य बिभर्त्यव्यय ईश्वरः।।

31. Radhakrishnan, S., *op. cit.*, p. 483.

32. *Ibid., Āśva. P.* 48. 16. 17[ab].

अनित्यं नित्यमित्येके नास्त्यस्तीत्यपि चापरे।
एकरूपं द्विधेत्येके व्यामिश्रमिति चापरे।।

एकमेके पृथक्चान्ये बहुत्वमिति चापरे।
मन्यन्ते ब्राह्मणा एवं प्राज्ञास्तत्त्वार्थदर्शिनः।।

33. Radhakrishnan, S., *op. cit.,* p. 483.
34. Radhakrishnan, S., *op. cit.,* pp. 478-81.
35. Macdonell, A.A., *A History of Sanskrit Literature,* p. 283.
36. Sukthankar, V.S., *op. cit.,* pp. 115-119.
37. Radhakrishnan, S., *op. cit.,* p. 523.
38. *Mbh. Ādi. P.* 1. 124, 2. 56[ab]. 156.
    यदाश्रौषं कश्मलेनाभिपन्ने रथोपस्थे सीदमानेऽर्जुने वै।
    कृष्णं लोकान्दर्शयानं शरीरे तदा नाशंसे विजयाय संजय।।
    पर्वोक्तं भगवत्तीता पर्व भीष्मवधस्ततः।
    कश्मलं यत्र पार्थस्य वासुदेवो महामतिः।
    मोहजं नाशयामास हेतुभिर्मोक्षदर्शनैः।।
39. Tilak, B.G., *op. cit.,* p. 720.
40. *Mbh. Śānti P.* 262. 44.
41. *Ibid.*, 160. 11-13.
42. *Ibid.*, 176. 9-10.
43. *Ibid.*, 195. 1-2.
44. *Ibid.*, 175. 13-14.
45. *Ibid.*, 329. 3-5.
46. *Ibid.*, 335. 11.
47. *Ibid.*, 231. 15. 16.
48. *Ibid.*, 293. 38.
49. *Ibid.*, 296. 17.

BIBLIOGRAPHY

(A) SANSKRIT TEXTS

Aitareya Upaniṣad : Ed. by Advaita Ashrama, Culcutta, Swami Ananyananda President Advaita Ashram, Pithoragarh. Year (not printed).

Bṛhadāraṇyaka Upaniṣad : Shri Ramakrishna Matha, Madras.

Caraka Saṁhitā (Śrīmadagniveçen Praṇītā Carakadṛḍhabalābhyām pratisankṛtā) : Ed. by Chaukhambha Bharati Academy, Varanasi, 1991.(Hindi commentary by Kashinātha Śāstri and Gorakhanātha Chaturvedi).

Gauḍapāda-Kārikā : Ed. by Karmarkar Raghunath Damodar, Bhandarkar Oriental Research Institute Poona, 1973.

Īśvarakṛṣṇa's Sāṁkhya Kārikā : Ed. Kunhan Raja C., V.V. Research Institute, Hoshiarpur, 1963.

Īśāvāsya Upaniṣad : Ed. by Vivekanand Kendra, Marathi Prakashan Vibhaga, Pune, 1993.

Kaṭha Upaniṣad : Ed. by Advaita Ashrama, Calcutta, Pub. Swami Ananyananda, President, Advaita Ashrama, Mayavati, Pithoragarh, 1987.

Kauṣītaki Upaniṣad : Ed. Jagdish Shastri, Upaniṣad Saṅgraha, Motilal Banarsidass, Delhi, 1998.

Kena Upaniṣad : Ed. by Vivekananda Kendra Marathi Prakashan, Pune, 1995.

Mahābhārata : Bhandarkar Oriental Research Institute (BORI) Pune Vol-I 1971, Vol-II 1972, Vol-III 1974, Vol-IV 1975, Vol. V 1976.

Maitrī Upaniṣad : Ed. by Vivekananda Kendra Marathi Prakashan, Pune.

Muṇḍaka Upaniṣad : Ed. by Sri Ramakrishna Math, Mylapore, Madras.

Māṇḍūkya Upaniṣad : Ed. by Jagdish Shastri, Upaniṣad Saṅgraha, Motilal Banarsidass, Delhi, 1998.

***Nyāyadarśana* The Śāstra-s of Gautama and Bhāṣyā of Vātsyāyana** : Ed. by Jha, Gangānāth and Nyāyopadhyāya Shastri Dhundirāja, Chowkhamba Sanskrit Series, Benaras, 1925.

***Nyāyaśāstra* Gautama's Nyāya Śāstra with Vātsyāyana's Commentary** : Ed. and translation by Mrinalkanti Gangopadhyaya Pub-D. Chattopadhyaya, Indian Studies, Calcutta, 1982

Praśna Upaniṣad : Ed. by Vivekananda Kendra Marathi Prakashana Vibhaga, Pune, 1995.

Pātañjala Yogadarśana : Ed. by Kolhatkar Krishnaji Keshav, Dhawale D.B. and Dhawale K.B. Mumbai, (Shake 1873), 1951.

Ṛgveda : Ed. by Vaidika Samshodhan Mandal, Pune, 1933-51.

Śatapatha Brāhmaṇa : Ed. Śāstri, Chinnaswami, Kashi Sanskrit Series, The Chowkhamba Sanskrit Series Office, Varanasi, 1937.

Śivādityacaryasutritā Saptapadārthī (Srijinavardhana-Śurīkṛtavyākhyayā Sahitā) : Ed. by Jetly Jitendra S., Lalbhai Dalapatbhai Bharatiya Sanskriti Vidyamandir, Ahmedabad, 1963.

Śvetāśvatara Upaniṣad : Ed. by Sri Ramakrishna Math, Madras.

Śāṅkarabhāṣya on Śrīmadbhagavadgītā Śāṅkarabhāṣyādisaptatīkopetā : Ed. by Vittal Dhundiraj, Gujarati Mudranalaya, Mumbai, 1908.

***Taittirīya Upaniṣad* :** Ed. by Ramkrishna Mission Instritute of Culture, Calcutta, 1996.

***Vaiśeṣika Darśana (Śrīkaṇaadamunipraṇītam) with Upaskara Vivṛtti and Bhāṣya* :** Ed. by Bakre Mahadeo Gangadhara Gujarathi Mudranalaya, Mumbai, 1913.

***Yogayājñavalkya* :** Ed. by Kolhatkar K.K., Dhawale B.D. and Dhawale K.B., Mumbai, (shake 1873) 1951.

(B) ENGLISH BOOKS

Banerji, Suresh Chandra : *A Companion to Indian Philosophy,* B.R. Publishing Corporation, (A Division of BRPC [India] Ltd.), Delhi, 1996.

Barth, A. : *Religions of India,* Kegan Paul, Trench, Trhbner and Co. Ltd., London, 1891 (Trans. Rv. J. Wood.)

Belvalkar, S.K., Ranade, R.D. *History of Indian Philosophy*, Bilvakunj Publishing House, Poona (Under the patronage of University of Bombay), 1927.

Bernard Theos : *Hindu Philosophy,* Motilal Banarsidass Publishers Pvt. Ltd., Delhi, 1981.

Bhahadur, K.P. : *The Wisdom of Nyaya*, Sterling Publishers Pvt. Ltd., New Delhi, 1988.

Bhandarkar, R.G. : *Vaiṣṇavism, Śaivism and Minor Religious Systems,* Karl J. Trhbner (for Oxford University Press), Bombay, 1913.

Buitenen, J.A.B. van (Trans. and Edited.) : *The Mahābhārata,* Book I, The University of Chicago Press, Chicago and London, 1973.

Chaitanya Krishna : *The Mahabharata – A Literary Study,* Clarion Books, New Delhi, 1985.

Chakravarti, Sureshchandra : *The Philosophy of the Upanishads,* University of Calcutta, Calcutta, 1935.

Dasgupta, S.N. : *A History of Sanskrit Literature,* Sri Sibendranath Kanjilal, Calcutta, 1962.

Dasgupta, S.N. : *Philosophical Essays,* University of Calcutta, Calcutta, 1941.

Dasgupta, Surendranath : *The History of Indian Philosophy,* Cambridge University Press, London, 1922.

Datta, Dhirendra Mohan : *Philosophical Perspective,* Bharati Bhavan, Patna, 1972.

Davis John : *The Samkhyakarika of Isvara Krisna,* An exposition of the system of Kapila (Reprinted of Oxford University Press, London), Sushil Gupta (India) Ltd., Calcutta, 1928.

Desai, S.G. : *A Critical Study of the Later Upaniṣads,* Bharatiya Vidya Bhavan, Mumbai, 1996.

Deussen Paul : *The Philosophy of Upanishads* – (tran. Rev A.S. Geden), (Reprinted of 1919), Dover Publication Inc., New York, 1966.

Devaraj, N.K. : *Indian Philosophy Today,* The Macmillan Carpn. of India Ltd., Delhi, 1975.

Divatia Shuchita C. : *Idealistic Thought in Indian Philosophy,* D.K. Printworld (P) Ltd., New Delhi, 1993.

Durant Will : *The Pleasure of Philosophy,* A Survey of Human Life and Destiny, Simon and Schuster, New York, 1953.

Frauwllner Erich (trans. Bedekar V.M.) : *History of Indian Philosophy,* Vol. I, Motilal Banarsidass Publishers Pvt. Ltd., Delhi, 1973.

Ganguli, Kishori Mohan : *The Mahabharata of Krishna Dwaipayana Vyasa* – Trans. Into English Vol-I, Munshiram Manoharlal Publishers Pvt. Ltd., New Delhi, 1993.

Garg, R.K. : *Upaniṣadic Challenge to Science,* Sandeep Prakashan, Delhi, 1978.

Held, G.J. : *The Mahābhārata An Ethnological Study,* Kegan Paul, Trench, Trhbner and Co. Ltd., Holland, 1935.

Hill W. Douglas P. : *The Bhagavadgītā,* trans. and commented, Oxford University Press London, 1928.

Hiriyanna, M. : *Outlines of Indian Philosophy,* Motilal Banarsidass Publishers Pvt. Ltd., Delhi, 1993.

Hopkins, E.W. : *Epic Mythology* Motilal Banarasidass, Delhi, (First published in Strassburg 1915), Reprinted in Delhi, 1974.

Hume Robert E. : *Thirteen Principal Upanisads,* Oxford University Press, Delhi, 1992.

Kane, P.V. : *History of Dharmaśāstra,* Bhandarkar Oriental Research Institute, Poona, 1968.

Keith, A., Berriedale : *History of Sanskrit Literature,* Oxford University Press, Great Britain, 1928.

Kunhan Raja C. : *Sāmakhya Kārikā of Īśvarakṛṣṇa* – A Philosophical Exposition, Dev Dutt Shastri, V.V. Research Institute, Hoshiarpur, 1963.

Macdonell, Arthur A. : *A History of Sanskrit Literature,* Munsi Ram Manohar Lal, Delhi, 1900.

Max Müller, Friedrich : *The Six Systems of Indian Philosophy* Associated Publishing House, New Delhi, 1897.

Mishra, Umesh : *History of Indian Philosophy* – Vol. I, Tirabhukti Publication, Allahabad, 1957.

Monier Willians M. : *Hinduism,* Sushil Gupta for Sushil Gupta (India) Ltd., Calcutta, 1878.

Mullick Bahadur R.P.N. : *The Mahabharata as it was, is and ever shall be,* The Pioneer Press, Allahabad, Calcutta, 1934.

Murthy, Satchidanand K. : *Philosophy in India,* Motilal Banarasidass, New Delhi, 1985.

Nozick Robert : *Introduction of Philosophical Explanation,* Oxford University Press, London, Glasgo, New York, Toranto, Delhi, Bombay, Calcutta, 1981.

Puligandla, Ramkrihna : *Fundamentals of Indian Philosophy,* D.K. Printworld (P) Ltd., New Delhi, New York, 1975.

Radhakrishnan, S. : *Indian Philosophy* – Vol. I, George Allen and Unwin Ltd., London, 1923., Indian Edition 1940.

Radhakrishnan, S. : *Indian Philosophy* – Vol. II, Gearge Allen and University, London, 1927. Indian Edition 1940.

Radhakrishnan S. and Moore Charles A. : *A Source Book in Indian Philosophy,* Princeton University Press, Princeton, New Jersey, 1957.

Raju, P.T. : *The Philosophical Tradition of India,* George Allen and Union Ltd., London, 1971.

Ranade, R.D. : *A Constructive Survey of Upanishadic Philosophy,* Bharatiya Vidya Bhavan, Bombay, 1986.

Ranade, R.D. : *Philosophical and Other Essays* Part I, W.T. Apte, Chairman of Shri Gurudeo Ranade Satkar Samiti, Jamkhandi, Puna, 1956.

Roychaudhary, Hemchandra : *Materials for the Study of the Early History of Vaiṣṇava Sect.,* University of Calcutta, Calcutta, 1920.

Sandal, Mohan Lal : *Philosophical Teaching in the Upanisads,* B.D. Basu, The Panini Office, Allahabad, 1945.

Sharma, Chandradhar : *Indian Philosophy,* Nand Kishor and Brothers, Banaras, 1952.

Sharma, Har Dutt (Edited and Translated) : *The Sāṁkhyakārikā-Śrimadīśvarakṛṣṇapraṇitāḥ Sagauḍapādabhāṣyaḥ.,* Oriental Book Agency, Poona, 1933.

Sinha, Jadunath : *A History of Indian Philosophy,* Vol. II, (Reprint of Jatindranath Sen, Central Book Agency, Calcutta, 1952.)

Smith Vincent : *Early History of India,* 3rd Edi. Revised and Enlarged, Humphrey Milford., 1914, Oxford University Press, London, Edinburgh, Glasgow New York, Toronto, Melbourne, Bombay.

Sukthankar, V.S. : *On the Meaning of the Mahābhārata,* Motilal Banarsidass Publishers Pvt. Ltd., Delhi and Asiatic Society of Bombay, Bombay, 1957.

Sullivan, Bruce M. : *Seer of the Fifth Veda* (Kṛṣṇa Dvaipāyana Vyāsa in the Mahābhārata), Motilal Banarsidass, Delhi, 1990.

Sutton, Nicholas : *Religious Doctrines in the Mahābhārata,* Motilal Banarasidass Publishers Pvt. Ltd., Delhi, 2000.

Telang, K.T. : *Bhagavadgītā with Sanatsugatīya and Anugītā* (reprint of Motilal Banarsidass, Delhi, 1882, Sacred Books of the East translated by Various Oriental Scholars, Henry Frowde Publisher to the University of Oxford, London, Edinburg, New York, Toranto and Melbourn.)

Tilak, Bal Gangadhar : *Śrimad Bhagavadgītā Rahasya or Karma Yoga-Śāstra-* Vol. II., (trans. Sukthankar B.S.), For Tilak Bros by R.B. Tilak, Poona City, (Sake 1857), 1935.

Tomlin, E.W.F. : *Philosophies of East and West,* Ajanta Publications (India), Delhi, 1988.

Upadhyay, Veermani Prasad : *Lights of Vedant,* Chowkhamba Sanskrit Series Office, Varanasi, 1959.

Vaidya, C.V. : *The Mahābhārata – A Criticism,* Bombay Book Depot, Bombay, 1929.

Winternitz M. : *History of Indian Literature,* Vol. I, Part-II, Epics and Puranas (trans S. Ketkar), Sibendranath Kanjilal, Calcutta, 1963.

Winternitz, M. : *History of Indian Literature* Vol. I, Part II, Revised Introduction, Veda, Epics, Puranas and Trantras. (trans. V. Srinivas Sarma), Motilal Banarsidass, Delhi, 1981.

Zimmer Heinrich : *Pilosophies of India,* (Ed. by Campbell Joseph) Princeton University Press, New Jersey, U.S.A., 1969.

(C) MARATHI BOOKS

Athavle, A.D. : *Mahābhāratāche Vāstavā Darshan,* Sushila Patankar, Continental Book Service, Pune, 1970.

Dandekar, S.V. : *Sārth Jñāyaneshvarī,* Svanand Prakashan, Pune, 1989.

Dange, Sadhashiv A. : *Hindu Dharma āṇi Tattvajñāna,* Shri Lekhan Vachan Bhandar, Pune, 1973.

Dixit, Hari Shrinivas : *Bhāratīya Tattvajñāna,* Suvichar Prakashan Mandal, S.S. Banahatti, Pune, 1963.

Kolhatkar Krishnaji Keshav : *Bhāratiyā Mānasa Śāstra athavā Sārtha āṇi Savivaraṇa Pātañjala Yogadarsana,* Dhanan-jaya Balkrishna Dhavale, Keshav Bhikaji Dhavale, Mumbai, (Shake 1873.) 1951.

Kopardekar, Sharadchandra : *Pātañjal, Yoga Darshan,* Indrayani Sahitya Prakashan, Pune, 1995.

Panashikar Daji : *Mahābhārata Ek Sādachā Pravāsa,* Jyotna Behre, Raviraj Prakashan, Pune, 1977.

Satavalekar Shripad Damodar : *Śrīmadbhagavadgītā Puruṣartha-bodhinī Tīkā,* V.S. Satavalekar, Svadhyaya Mandal, Pardi, Gujrat, 1952.

Vaidya Shripad Mahadeo : *Ṣatcakradarśana vā Bhedana,* Islampur, 1937.

(D) HINDI BOOKS

Bhargav, Dayanand : *Annambhattpranitah-Tark-Sangraha-Svopagya Vyākhyātarkadīpikasahitah,* Motilal Banarsidass Publisher Pvt. Ltd., Delhi, 1971.

Shastri, Kashinath and Chaturvedi, Gorakhnath : *Caraka Samahitā of Agniveśa Savimarśa-Vidyotinī (Hindī*

Vyakhyopeta – Hindī commentary on Carakasaṁhitā), Chaukhambha Bharati Academy, Varanasi, Patna, 1991.

(E) RESEARCH PAPERS AND THESIS

Pandit Shriram G. : *Purāṇas and the Philosophical Systems*, Thesis – Bombay University, Bombay, 1964.

(F) ENCYCLOPAEDIA

Chambers's Encyclopaedia **New Revised Edition Vol. II** : International Learning Systems Corpn. Ltd., London, 1973.

Encyclopaedia of Religion and Ethics : Edit. James Hastings with assistance of James A. Selbie and Louis H. Gary, T. and T. Clerk, Edinburg, 1915.

Encyclopedia of Indian Philosophies **Vol. IV** : Ed. by Gerald James Larson and Ram Shankar Bhattacharya, Motilal Banarsidass, Delhi, Varanasi, Patna, Madras, 1987.

Routledge Encyclopedia of Philosophy **Vol. 4** : Ed. by Edward Craig Routledge, London, Routledge, New York, U.S.A., and Canada, 1998.

The Encyclopedia of Philosophy : Vols. 5 and 6. Edit. Paul Edwards, Macmillan Publishing Co. In and Free Press New York, Collier Macmillan Publishers, London, 1967.

The New Book of Knowledge : Grolier Incorporated New York, 1972.

The Encyclopedia of Philosophy : Vols. 5 and 6. Edit. Paul Edwards, Macmillan Publishing Co. In and Free Press New York., Collier Macmillan Publishers, London, 1967.

The New Book of Knowledge : Grolier Incorporated, New York, 1972.

The New Encyclopedia of Britanica : William Benton, The University of Chicago, Vol. 14, Chicago, London, Manila, Seoul, Johannesburg, Toranto, Geneva, Sydney, Tokyo, 1973.

(G) DICTIONARIES AND KOSHA-S

An American Dictionary of the English Language **(Webster's Larger Dictionary) :** Ed. by Noah Webster, New Haven, U.S.A., 1847.

Little Oxford Dictionary : Ed. George Ostler. Oxford University Press, Delhi, 1998.

The Oxford English Dictionary **Vol. XVII :** Ed. J.A. Simpson and E.S.C. Weiner, Clarendon Press, New York, 1989.

Roget's Thesaurus of Synonyms and Antonyms **in Dictionary Form :** Ed. Peter Mark Roget Ashwini Goyal for Goyal Sāāb Publishers and Distributors, Delhi, 1988.

Bhāratīya Sanskriti Kośa : Ed. Joshi Mahadeo and Hodarkar Padmaja, Bharatiya Sanskriti Kosh Mandal, Pune, (Shake 1889) 1967.

Marathi Vishvakosha : Maharastra Rajya Sahitya Sanskraiti Mandal, Mumbai, 1976.

The Student's Sanskrit-English Dictonary : Ed. Apte Vaman Shivaram Motilal Banarsidass Publishers Pvt. Ltd., Delhi, 1970.

INDEX

P